On
Tugboats

On Tugboats

Stories of Work and Life Aboard

Virginia L. Thorndike

Down East Books

In memory of deckhand Chris Cordeau,
good friend of a friend of mine,
who was accidentally killed on the tugboat *Pete*
in Portland, Maine, on December 4, 2003

Design by Janet L. Patterson
Printed at Versa Press, E. Peoria, Ill.
5 4 3 2 1

Down East Books
A division of Down East Enterprise, Inc.
www.downeastbooks.com
Book orders: 1-800-766-1670

Cover photograph: *Captain Sweet,* now *Susan McAllister*. © Jeffrey Stevensen

Contents

Author's Note

There are tugboats all over the planet, doing all manner of jobs, and I make no pretense to covering or understanding each of them or all their jobs. I live in Maine, and I admit there is perhaps a disproportionate degree of Maine connection in this book. I defend myself on a number of levels, the most obvious being that Maine is convenient to me. But also, Maine has an important and continuing maritime tradition, no small part of which relates to tugboating. In Castine, Maine has an excellent maritime academy—for a long time, the only one in the United States to offer hands-on tug-and-barge classes—and many Maine Maritime alumni are in tugboating today, all over the country. Many hawsepipers come from Maine, too—men and women who started working on deck and made their way up to captaincy; some live in Maine today, and some don't. And finally, while Maine has no monopoly on fun projects, it perhaps does have more than its share. The Maine stories included here undoubtedly exemplify those which can be found on the water wherever tugs are active.

The matter of nomenclature always comes into any maritime book, and tugboat folks can be just as concerned about it as any other group. Take the term *captain*, for example. Merchant vessels are commanded by a master—*Captain* is a courtesy title. One tugboat master asked that I not refer to him as Captain, as he had only a 1600-ton Near Coastal license and was just running what he called a "little" 120-foot boat. Some of the other people I interviewed were no doubt licensed as Unlimited Masters of All Oceans but were working in another capacity and I therefore do not refer to them as captains. "I wear a lot of hats," the above master said. "Today I'm a captain—tomorrow I'll be a painter." He has a Coast Guard master's license, albeit a relatively limited one, and the honorific that goes with that is "Captain," but he didn't want to make anyone unhappy. I asked the same fellow whether protocol would suggest that I refer to a young licensed master as Captain, even if he has not yet worked in that position. His response was that the man had earned the license, and deserved the respectful appellation. Some people take this stuff very seriously, and not always with consistency. Certainly the licenses themselves are serious, and I hope I've offended no one by the way I've used the word *captain*.

I understand that there's a big deal about licenses, endorsements and documents, too. The world of tugboating—of all maritime endeavor, for that matter—is full of credentials. I can only apologize up front for using *license* when in fact the particular piece of paper that defines a person's position or legal capability is a *document* or an *endorsement*. In common English, *document* doesn't carry the same strength of meaning as does *license*, and *endorsement* means something else entirely. To be honest, I'm not always clear myself which credentials are which.

A relatively simple nomenclature issue is the use of the terms *tugboat* and *towboat*. On the rivers, the large boats invariably push barges and are called towboats. The term *tug* is reserved on the rivers for smaller boats that assist in moving barges in and out of docks and through particularly tricky passages. On both oceans and in the Gulf of Mexico, the two terms are often used interchangeably, and a person who works on one of those vessels might be called either a tugboater or a towboater.

I've learned a great deal about tugboating during the time I've spent researching this book, but undoubtedly I have gotten some facts and details wrong. If I've attributed an erroneous concept to someone else, I'm sure it's my error, not his.

Often I shall use "he" when what I mean is "he or she." The fact is, far more men are involved in tugboats than women, and it is simply convenient to refer to unnamed people in the masculine, but this in no way is meant to ignore or disparage the members of my own gender who are in this world. The convention also makes it easier to distinguish between people and boats, which are almost always feminine. I admit I'm amused by the confusion in gender that can appear in talking about boats and their people. Vessels are apparently anthropomorphized and sometimes called "he" when what's meant is the captain or personnel, as in "The *Queen Elizabeth II* is coming, but he'll stay to the north side of the channel." I am not the only maritime writer to use these irregular conventions, however, and they're commonplace in the spoken language.

Some of the tales I pass along come from people with decades and decades in the business; others were told me by people whose stay with tugboats was short but nonetheless memorable. Perhaps one or two stories need to be taken with a grain of salt, but on the whole, these people told things as they remembered them, and the situations they recount really were that difficult, or funny, or dangerous. And it is my hope all of them, taken together, give an accurate picture of the world of tugboats.

Acknowledgments

This book has been great fun to work on. The subject is interesting, and the people in tugboating almost without exception talked freely and enthusiastically about their world. I was made to feel welcome by an amazing variety of folks in the industry in all roles. I just wish I had been able to accept all the invitations to ride that I received!

Thanks must go to Andy Chase, of Maine Maritime Academy, who has snuck into other pieces I've written, but for this one, his role has been primarily as a connection to people—and wonderful people too. (It has been interesting just finding the people sometimes, as the active sailors are away from home half the time or more, and phone numbers don't always work. For instance, one number became inoperative when its owner dropped his cell phone overboard. Hazards of the trade.) Andy says he'll take a million bucks for his help. I have told him he can have the second million that any one of my books makes me, and here is my promise in print. I admit I don't expect to have to give him any money, but I suspect and hope it will be the schooner *Bowdoin* who benefits if it ever should happen.

And to John O'Reilly, one of many folks that Andy hooked me up with, I have to give particular thanks. Right up to the end, John went far out of his way to answer my questions, read chapters, and write descriptions and explanations. He did all this during the two weeks he was home each month, when I know he had plenty of better things to do. I have to thank his wife, Moe, too.

Jim Sharp, too, read through much of the draft and worked hard with me on bits of it. He also made some important connections for me. And my old friend Roland Aldridge, who didn't think he had any interest in tugboating and knew nothing whatever about it, leapt in to give a few chapters a read when I needed a read made. I'm hoping maybe he looks at tugs differently now. Or at least looks at them.

Dave Boone, Arthur Fournier, Bob Hill, Steve Lang, Bob Mattsson, Don Sutherland, Franz VonRiedel, and all the rest of the photographers and collectors of images certainly contributed tremendously to the book. The folks at K-Sea Transportation Partners, and in particular the guys on the *Adriatic Sea* in May of 2002, I must thank for their generosity and friendliness.

Then there's Hugh Ware. At the last minute, he volunteered to help with pulling together the mess of disconnected pieces I had amassed, and he has done an amazing job. If this book has any cohesion, it is he who must be given credit. Thank you, Hugh. And it was always a pleasure working with you.

As always, I have to thank my husband, Phil Roberts, who didn't always want to spend a day as I wanted or felt I needed to for this book, and who kept things going at home while I went off riding tugboats. (To be sure, sometimes he got in on the fun, too.)

I hesitate to name anyone else as there are so many people who have been extremely helpful; I couldn't begin to mention all and wouldn't want to imply a ranking. But I sincerely thank you, every one! Most of you appear in the book by name; those few who don't will undoubtedly know why, as you spoke of sensitive matters that are best presented without attribution. I most certainly appreciate your candor.

The people I write of and the tales they tell are not unique. Rather, they are typical of tugboaters, and my goal in writing this was to show, by their example, what their world is like. While I can't express fully enough my gratitude to each of these people, the fact is that it's happenstance that I spoke with them and not with others in the industry who have their own interesting and exciting stories to tell. To those with whom I didn't have the fortune to cross paths, I can only say, I wish I had!

1
Tugboats 101

Everyone loves tugboats. I'm not sure we all know why we feel that way but, if nothing else, there's an appealing element of David and Goliath about a tugboat with its charge, whether a passenger ship in New York Harbor or a flotilla of nine (or perhaps forty-five) multicolored barges on the Mississippi. The myriad children's books about tugs encourage that thinking, and, in fact, the image of the little tugboat who faces this challenge or that and wins out with his sheer determination isn't too far off the mark.

Simply put, tugs are powerful, heavy boats used to move things on water. They have huge power plants for their size and often have only boat enough to float their engines, fuel, and equipment and house the people who work on them—which is actually quite a lot of boat. Tugs can be 50 feet in length or less (even as small as 15 feet), and some surpass 250 feet (there are two 324-foot Russian salvage tugs), but most are in the 80- to 140-foot range. They are unusually deep for their visible size. Fifty years ago, they were typically powered with a single 400-horsepower engine—that was large, then. The average new harbor tug has a pair of 2,000-horse propulsion engines, and some deep-sea tugs have engines with more than 20,000 horsepower. Fuel capacity is scaled accordingly.

There are still a few boats around that, like the first tugs, were built to run on steam, but they're all converted now to diesel or diesel-electric. In 1975, the *Clyde B. Holmes*, said to be the last steam-powered coastwise tug in North America, was retired in Belfast, Maine. Many single-screw boats are still out there, particularly on the Great Lakes, but most working tugs nowadays have traditional twin-screws, and more and more are being powered with advanced propulsive units that permit movement in any direction. The new boats all have diesel engines.

The jobs they do haven't changed all that much except in scale.

Tugs move ships, barges and miscellaneous objects. "If it floats, we can tow it," was the motto of the old Russell Brothers company in New York Harbor. Other companies today have similar slogans. There are all manner of operations, from one-tug businesses to huge companies with representation in harbors all along a seaboard or even internationally. Many tug companies do some of everything, while others specialize in what they push or pull around.

As an example, a string of companies along the north shore of Staten Island demonstrate the range of specialties that tug companies can hold. K-Sea Transportation Partners transports petroleum products: gasoline, jet fuel, diesel fuel, heating oil, bunker oil. McAllister Towing is one of the biggest companies in the U.S., with offices in ten Atlantic ports from Portland, Maine, to San Juan, Puerto Rico. They do just about every kind of towboating, but in New York Harbor, the greatest share of their work is ship docking—assisting large vessels entering and leaving busy channels and piers. Brown Towing is a small company; they just bought their third boat and specialize in small shifting work, moving gravel scows and little construction barges from one place to another within the harbor. Moran Towing Corporation is another of the big East Coast players, and their tugs work in nearly every imaginable job, from ship docking to long-distance towing to barge work and the occasional salvage job. Like K-Sea, Penn Maritime handles petroleum products but their real niche

The tug *A.G. Prentiss* towing a schooner on the Saco River, 1911.
FROM THE MAINE HISTORICAL PHOTOGRAPH COLLECTION.

is in asphalt—for moving asphalt, the Penn company is the big guy. Kosnac Floating Derrick Corp. specializes in just what its name implies, crane work.

There are more tug companies along that stretch of water, and all around New York harbor there are any number of others, large and small, with their own particular niches. Great Lakes Dredge & Dock is the largest dredging company in the U.S.— they clear and deepen harbors and channels and remove the dredged materials, both in this country and overseas. Donjon Marine, of Hillside, New Jersey, is the major salvage company in the harbor—perhaps on the East Coast—but also does deep-sea towing, heavy lifting, dredging, icebreaking, and construction work.

Like the companies, the tugs themselves can be either jacks of all trades—towing or pushing or docking as asked—or specialized. Probably the most extremely specialized are the Ship Docking Modules of Seabulk International and Marine Towing of Tampa, which do their job better than any other design ever has but perhaps can't do much else. Other tugs are connected, in effect permanently, to their barges, making them essentially the power for a two-part tanker.

New tugs are being launched frequently, but there are also a few nineteenth-century tugs still working, and a couple from the early twentieth century can be found in nearly every harbor. The Great Lakes are full of such tugs.

The 22,000 horsepower Dutch tug *Smitwijs London* towed the new 750-foot-long drydock from China to Bath Iron Works, arriving in February 2001. Another six tugs from Moran and Winslow assisted on the final run up the Kennebec. AUTHOR PHOTO.

Identification can get confusing because new owners often change the name of a boat. A former *Mary L. McAllister* is working for the Zenith Tugboat Company on the Great Lakes as the *Seneca*, for example. But there's still a *Mary L. McAllister* out there earning her keep. Many owners, including McAllister itself, often reuse a name. McAllister has a tug in New York today that has been called the *Marjorie McAllister,* the *Tracy Ann Witte,* the *Thor,* and finally, when bought back by the McAllister company, the *Mary L. McAllister.*

The crews of tugs are smaller than they once were. Some harbor tugs are "lunch bucket boats," often manned only by a captain and deckhand who live at home and come onto the boat simply to do specific jobs, perhaps bringing their lunches (or suppers or breakfasts) with them. In smaller ports, many docking tugs with few jobs are crewed this way.

Most tugs outside the harbor and many in larger ports are manned around the clock and have accommodations for their people. Like any ship, these boats run on watches—specified periods when specified crewmembers are on duty. The master is always responsible for the boat, however, whether on watch or off. A typical tug that is manned full-time may have captain, deckhand, and engineer on one watch, and mate, deckhand, and assistant engineer on the other. When pushing or towing a barge of petroleum products, as many tugs do these days, there may be another person or two aboard who are certified to load and unload the cargo—or, increasingly often, one of the officers may have that certification. Offshore, boats keep three watches, often led by mates, with the master not on a specific watch but always on call.

There are two complete crews for each fully manned boat. Each crew is aboard for a certain number of days and then off for a particular number. In the Northeast and on the West Coast, it's often "two-and-two"—two weeks on and two weeks off— or three-and-three. In the Gulf of Mexico, where the pay scale is lower, it's more apt to be "two for one"—two periods worked for one period off. Sometimes people on their odd week fill in on a tug other than their regular one.

Crews making long-distance hauls commonly are aboard for two or even three months at a time, and then are home for a similar period. Certainly, one of the appeals of working on tugboats is that there is so much uninterrupted time at home. Whether pay is good or not is a matter of discussion, but most people recognize that, for 180 days at work per year, it's not too bad.

Many of the people who run tugboats have boat-handling skills that no other element of the merchant marine can surpass. Tugs must be handy, wriggling in and out of small spaces while docking barges or picking them up, or handling ships that are large and, sometimes, fragile. Tugs aren't fast, but they are strong and maneuverable, and they depend on every person on board doing his job. In years past, many tugboat masters were hawsepipers, men who came up through the ranks, men who had learned how to run their boats by instinct. Their abilities far surpassed their formal education. Many of them were rough-and-ready "cowboys." Tugboat engineers are an inventive lot, forced by circumstance to create ingenious fixes to problems that arise while far from the shop. A deckhand who knows his job and his captain can make life simpler for both of them.

While much of tugboating is monotonous, things can get tense every time a tug comes near something, intentionally or otherwise. The engines had better run correctly; the helmsman had better get the boat where she is supposed to be; the deckhand had better get his lines to a ship where they need to go or hook or unhook the connecting wires or lines to a tow. And it is appreciated if the person making supper does a good job, too. (These days, that task falls into the deckhand's job description more often than not.)

On the *Adriatic Sea,* Trevor Campbell aligns the shackles to hook up the wires to the barge. AUTHOR PHOTO.

In the U.S. and Canada today, crews are highly regulated, and specific credentials are required for each position under each set of conditions. Most American sailors must have STCW-95 certification, for example, which demonstrates that they have undergone training in basic safety, including particular technologies and firefighting. Engineers, people handling petroleum products, and deck officers each have additional and particular licensing programs, including documented experience at sea. Nonetheless, in today's merchant marine, it's the tugboaters who come closest to living and working like the independent cowboys who once dominated the tug industry.

There has been increasing concern about the safety of working on tugboats. Intrinsically and historically, tugboats have been anything but safe. The cable or

It's essential that a deckhand pay attention to details. Captain Bob Glover tells of an incident where it was only by luck that someone wasn't maimed. They were servicing mooring buoys in Alaska from the *Arctic Salvor*. When they first lifted the buoy shown here— two hours before this picture was taken—the shackle wasn't attached properly. It had slipped so that the wires were pulling on the sides of the shackle instead of on the pin and the bow. There were ten men on deck when "the shackle exploded like a shotgun. Pieces went in every direction and flew into the water like bullets" and the eight- or nine-ton buoy fell back into the water. "It's amazing nobody got hit. It was a dumb thing on our part."
COURTESY OF CAPT. ROBERT C. GLOVER III.

hawser connecting a tug to her tow can be under tremendous tension, and should it snap, any person in the wrong place could easily be killed as the end whips across the deck. Everyone in the industry knows of someone who lost his life in that manner. The shackles that connect wires to one another are very heavy, often forty pounds apiece or more. It doesn't take much of an unexpected movement of a fitting like that to break a crewperson's arm or leg, and the sea is seldom still. Electrical equipment is always dangerous, as are winches. The towed objects themselves are hazardous, too. Moving about on barges under way is inherently dangerous, and the cargoes of petroleum and chemical barges offer obvious physical hazards. And barges are a serious threat in themselves; under some circumstances, a barge may go faster than its tug and pass and capsize it, or even ride onto or over the tug itself. Tugs and towboats, as the push-tugs used on the inland rivers paradoxically are always called, have been said to account for the greatest fatality rates of any occupation in the United States, including fishing.

Ever-increasing regulation bears on the transportation of petroleum products—one of tugboats' major jobs. The rules are reviewed and tightened each time there's a significant incident. There is no doubt that the movement of petroleum products has become far safer since the days of *Exxon Valdez,* or even the more recent spill from the tank barge *North Cape,* attended by the tug *Scandia* in Rhode Island waters. But spills still happen, and undoubtedly there is more yet that can be done to prevent them. Environmental issues are on everyone's minds these days.

Although discouraged by the increased role of the Coast Guard in their profession, many of the older men in tugboats remain proud of their boats and their crews and what they have accomplished over the years. The younger people, many of them maritime academy graduates, may come to their jobs from a different point of view, but they too take pride in their boat-handling abilities and their engineering and deck skills. And all tugboaters take seriously the responsibilities that they face every day they're aboard. Serious those responsibilities are, with the dangers to humans and the environment that are always so close at hand.

Design of Tugs

Designing tugs is just like designing any other vessel, if you believe Bruce Washburn, of Washburn & Doughty in East Boothbay, Maine. It's all a matter of analyzing how the boat's going to be used, calculating the weights going into her, and balancing up the hull.

A spectator checks out the Bruce Washburn–designed tug *Gramma Lee T. Moran* just before launching.
AUTHOR PHOTO.

To illustrate this principle, Bruce compares two types of fishing boats, offshore lobsterboats and draggers. The design process and considerations are the same, only the criteria are different. A lobsterboat has to have a platform that can handle weight, and you don't want it rolling when you've got traps stacked five high. When it does roll, it's got a snappy motion that would destroy a fisherman's back and knees on a dragger as he's working the gear. A dragger should have a deeper, more gentle roll—perhaps to a higher angle, but softer. "There are different challenges, just understanding the nature of how a boat operates."

Of course, some of the performance standards with tugboats, and therefore the specifics of construction, are different from those of other vessels Bruce has designed. "For a casino boat or a ferry, you're concerned with speed. You want lightweight plates, and you design them so they're going to stay fair." But with a tugboat, the concern is strength. A tug's hull may be constructed of rugged half-inch plate, and the fairness of the hull isn't usually a concern. On the other hand, bending that plate is difficult. That's one reason Washburn & Doughty—and almost every other builder these days—build their tugs with hard chines (sharp edges where the sides of the boat meet the bottom) instead of with smooth, rounded underbody shapes.

"Tugs are interesting," Bruce says. "They're raw power." An engine for a big yacht might be 450 horsepower and have a three-inch-diameter drive shaft, while the biggest dragger they have built at Washburn & Doughty had 2,000 horsepower, half of which was used for the generator running off the shaft. The tugs they're building now might be the same length as a dragger or yacht, but they have 5,000 horses or more and a ten-inch drive shaft. By comparison, these are huge power plants.

Still, the design issues are the same.

"You look at what's been done before, and you know what a tug's supposed to look like," says Bruce. "And I have my own ideas about what makes a good hull form, balancing sea-keeping abilities with stability."

Propulsion Systems

Let's take a break here to talk about the means of making a tug move through the water. Nowadays, just about all the engines are diesels but there are two means of propulsion: propellers and a patented system called the Voith-Schneider cycloidal system. Propellers can be affixed to the ends of nearly horizontal drive shafts extending from the boat. Such tugs, whether having one, two, or more propellers, are known as conventional-drive tugs. Propellers can also be used in what are called azimuthing drives. These are somewhat like giant outboard motors sticking down from the tug's hull. Each drive can be turned, or azimuthed, 360 degrees and acts as a rudder in the same way an outboard motor does, allowing the boat to move in any direction. They are often referred to generically as Z-drives, even though that is a copyrighted name,

Rolls-Royce azimuthing drives and bow thruster. Courtesy of Rolls-Royce.

because the flow of power is from the engine through a shaft to the top of the azimuthing-drive unit, where it takes a right-angled bend down its leg and then bends another ninety degrees to the propeller. The units are usually mounted aft, like traditional propellers, and the tugs work facing the ship in the traditional North American manner, with lines run from the bow.

Kort nozzles appear on many propeller-driven tugs, whether conventional or azimuthing. A nozzle is a circular shroud, airfoil-shaped in cross-section, that surrounds a propeller. They were originally invented to reduce erosion of German canal banks. When it was discovered that, compared to an open propeller, nozzles could increase the power of a tug by 30 to 40 percent (particularly at lower speeds), they were soon adopted on tugs around the world.

The cycloidal Voith-Schneider propellers, usually installed in pairs and forward in the tug, have a number of vertical blades that turn in a circle beneath the boat. Each blade also rotates on its own vertical axis, thus allowing the helmsman to direct the amount and direction of thrust. The engine itself keeps a steady speed. Very precise maneuvering of the tug is possible with the Voith system, and the controls facing the captain are surprisingly simple: a steering wheel and a pitch lever for each unit. In simple terms, the pitch lever controls whether the unit pushes forward or astern and with how much force, and the wheel determines how much sideways thrust there will be. With the wheel turned all the way to one side, the thrust is also entirely to the side. The two Voith units may be operated in the same direction or opposing ("twin-screwing"), so the boat can go in virtually any direction. "You can dock a ship without breaking any eggshells," says one operator. Possibly because they developed in Europe, where most tug work is done over the stern, the assist lines on a Voith boat are run over the stern rather than over the bow. The width of the stern makes a very wide and stable working platform, and by working with the stern toward a ship, the tug can get in underneath the flare of the ship's hull.

In common parlance, both azimuth and Voith-driven tugs are called tractor tugs. The Voiths are the original tractors, and some people, notably Voith-Schneider salesmen, argue that only their configuration is the true tractor tug, meaning a vessel that pulls herself through the water. And some people insist on using "reverse tractor" for the stern-driven azimuthing tugs, while others don't approve of that term either. With apologies to anyone who cares, I, like most people out there on the water, shall use the term "tractor" to refer to both types. The key factor in what is now called a tractor tug is that its propulsion system allows it to use its full power in any direction, which traditional boats never can do. The various forms of tractor tugs have totally changed everything. "Now maneuvering has completely turned topsy turvy," says Bruce.

Kort nozzle on the tug *Yankee,* which has 3,600 horsepower per engine and 144-inch diameter propellers with a 138-inch pitch.

PHOTO BY ROBERT MAGAS, COURTESY OF K-SEA TRANSPORTATION PARTNERS.

The cycloidal propellers of a Voith-Schneider boat are well forward, and look totally unlike any traditional arrangement.

COURTESY OF CROWLEY MARINE SERVICES.

Within conventional power systems, the decision whether the boat is to be single-screw or twin-screw brings other factors with it. A single-screw boat will probably be deep, narrow, and relatively low-powered for its size. Bruce Washburn says that tug-boat operators prefer them in some circumstances: "In strong currents, they prefer single-screw boats. They can control them better, apparently." Nevertheless, for its operations on the Piscataqua River between Maine and New Hampshire, Moran has recently decided to trade in a couple of single-screw boats for a twin-screw boat with significantly more horsepower. They liked how the single-screw boats handled the difficult river currents but felt they needed additional horsepower to handle the big-ger ships they're seeing of late.

When towing offshore, a tug has to move through the water easily. When the sea causes the hawser to tighten up, the tug's momentum has to pull the barge forward instead of the barge pulling the tug backward. A heavy, narrow hull is good in this situation, so an offshore tug is built longer and deeper than a harbor tug. She also carries more fuel. But that configuration tends to roll.

On a harbor tug, which doesn't need as much weight and can take advantage of having less draft, the hull will be wider and consequently more stable. It's handy if they don't roll too much and smash into the ships they're docking, but there *will* be contact, no matter what. "The visor on any old docking tug looks as though some-body took a baseball bat to it," says Bruce. (Most older tugs have a visor over the pilothouse windows to help keep the sun out of the helmsman's eyes.)

A harbor tug, particularly in smaller harbors, has to be versatile enough to do any job that comes her way—docking, towing locally from harbor to harbor, and even, occasionally, towing offshore.

In the larger ports, tugs are specialized to a greater degree. Bigger companies have a wide range of vessels available, from small run-around boats to large salvage tugs, and a number of multipurpose middle-sized boats for docking and barge work. The tractor-type Ship Docking Modules are the most specialized ship-assist tugs in the world.

Trained in naval architecture at the University of Michigan, Bruce had been de-signing boats for twenty years in 1991 when the Winslows asked him to design his first tug. Captain David Winslow was then running Winslow Marine, the company his father, Eliot, had started. He invited Bruce to ride along as they worked, to show him what they liked and wanted in a tug to be used primarily for docking but also for pushing barges around and doing coastal towing.

David wanted a relatively small, conventional twin-screw tug of about 3,000 horsepower—one able to work well in the close quarters he finds himself in from time to time. The resulting boat, the *Alice Winslow*, is ninety feet long and thirty feet wide. (She is the second tug in the Winslow fleet named the *Alice Winslow*, after Eliot's mother.) David wanted wide deck spaces, with the superstructure recessed in so it wouldn't hit the flare on ships during docking. He wanted the bow table—the bow bitts—to go athwartships, as they were on the old railroad tugs, to more easily handle two head lines. And he wanted the propellers to be open—no nozzles—and to turn outboard. (Looking from the stern, the starboard wheel (propeller) turns clockwise, the port counter-clockwise.) "If you back the starboard engine, she'll back to port, and if you back the port engine, she'll back to starboard." David explains. "They say you don't get as much power that way, but you gain maneuverability.

"She's a simple boat. That's why everyone likes her," he continues. "She's about as handy as they come—you can't outmaneuver her. With my knowledge of ship-docking, and Bruce's knowledge of design, we got a pretty good boat."

A few years later, Bruce was hired to design the 4,400-horsepower *Fort Bragg* for Cape Fear Towing of Wilmington, North Carolina. Being a practical man, he asked David Winslow what worked well on the *Alice* and what could be improved. David said he would change one thing. On the *Alice*, the maximum beam is carried right back to the stern. "When you're trying to peel away from a ship after leaving a pilot on board or picking one up, she won't round away." If her sides curved more, she would have less suction alongside a moving ship and it would be easier to break loose.

Bruce started with the lines of the *Alice Winslow* and widened the new model a bit amidships. But the *Fort Bragg* was to be a twin Z-drive tug, so bigger changes had to be made to accommodate that propulsion system. The weight distribution on an azimuth thruster system is entirely different, with much of the weight considerably further aft than on a conventional tug. Just the two drives hanging on the back end of the boat weigh 40,000 pounds each.

The other issue facing Bruce was that azimuthing propellers need more room than do the wheels and rudders on a conventional tug. A conventional twin-screw tug like the *Alice* has a pair of 100- to 110-inch propellers. With Kort nozzles to intensify the power, the propellers could be somewhat smaller but the configuration beneath the hull would be the same, with rudders aft of the props. Z-drives, on the other hand, act as rudders as well as propulsion units and must be able to spin all the way around, at any time, in any direction, without running into each other. They must therefore be placed further outboard than the wheels on a conventional twin-screw.

Cape Fear's new tug had to be wider to make these accommodations. Bruce also added more buoyancy by deepening the after end of the tug, so the stern on the *Fort Bragg* is eighteen inches deeper than the *Alice*'s. When the tug made the delivery trip to North Carolina in January 1996, her owner reported to Bruce that she must be a pretty good sea boat because, although the crew aboard was reporting that every third wave was going over the top of the pilothouse, they weren't complaining.

In 1998, Moran ordered six similar tugs from Washburn & Doughty to fulfill a contract to handle navy ships in Norfolk. Navy criteria included length, minimum and maximum horsepower, and bollard pull (a gauge of a tug's ability to pull, which relates to both horsepower and design). The tugs would be required to go as much as fifty miles offshore for a disabled ship, so they needed to be seaworthy for that job. They are two feet longer than the *Alice Winslow* to improve their performance moving astern, as well as two feet wider. (Washburn & Doughty have built several more tugs for Moran since the original six.)

Two of these Moran tugs—known in the industry as the Marci class because the first one was named the *Marci Moran*—had to be designed to handle submarines. "Lots of rubber on the bottom," says Bruce. They spaced rubber along the chines three-quarters of the way aft so the tug could come alongside a submarine without making metal contact. The specs called for rubber all the way down the stempiece and well around the curve onto the keel. To accommodate all that, they inserted a ten-inch pipe into the stem to ease the angle on the bow. The bulwarks at the bow are vertical, unlike on the *Fort Bragg* (which, with her raked bulwarks, can go underneath a flared ship bow more easily). These Moran tugs are called on to move barges more often than ships—the additional rubber contact from the vertical bulwarks make for less wear and tear on the rubber itself, and the helmsman can see the point of contact better than he can with raked bulwarks. "Everyone's got their own ideas as to what works best within any type," Bruce says.

In a Z-drive tug, if you're going 13 knots astern, you can come to a stop in less than a boat length, but when the tug pushes forward again, "she digs the water out from underneath herself, and then she climbs out of the hole." A lot of water can come aboard: "On the *Marci,* they had the pin on the towing bitt under water." Bruce builds a stepped-up poop deck in his Z-drive tugs. This gives headroom over the drives, which eases maintenance, but it also keeps water off the deck.

The same phenomenon happens going from forward to reverse, too. Bruce was on the receiving end when they were doing sea trials on the *Marci*. He was running a photo boat, looping around the new tug as she went through her paces. She was running along at some speed, and as he was crossing her bow, she suddenly pushed astern. "I looked up and saw her bow drop eight feet, but the wave she was dragging along didn't stop—it kept coming at me. I turned tail and ran!"

The Z-drive tugs are relatively fast (for tugs.) When he was designing the *Fort Bragg*, Bruce was asked what speed he expected her to make. His calculations showed she ought to make well over the speed he guessed out loud, 12 knots, but he didn't want to get anyone's expectations up too high. "It is a displacement hull, and you are digging a big hole," Bruce explains. In sea trials, however, she actually made 14½ knots.

In some locations, it is required that tugs accompany loaded tankers in confined waters, and specially designed tugs are preferred. Speed is important for ship-escort work—to get a line on, the tug will have to stay with the entering ship before she's fully slowed down.

Escort tugs have other design requirements in addition to the need for speed. A tug astern may have to steer a ship by driving off to one side, pulling the ship's stern to the desired direction. The tug needs cross-sectional area to balance herself against the line, and she can turn the ship faster with the center of area forward, so azimuthing tractor escort tugs are being built with big box keels—skegs—forward. Yet the

With protective fendering already in place on her bow, the *Gramma Lee T. Moran* is ready to launch. Author photo.

escort tug needs enough stability to keep herself upright and manageable, and with a skeg too far forward, the boat gets squirrelly and hard to steer. "It's like a fat man in the bow of a canoe," says Bruce.

The eighth Z-drive tug that Washburn & Doughty built, the *Captain Harry*, was designed by Robert Allen. Since then, the yard has turned out several more tugs of Bruce's design for Moran, Boston Towing & Transportation, and other companies from along the East Coast.

Z-drives have become competitive in price with conventional propulsion systems of equivalent horsepower, Bruce says. This is because the price of transmissions for traditional tugs has been going up along with the prices of most equipment, while the price of Z-drives has benefited from economies of scale as more are being built. And the Z system is actually easier for the shipyard to install than a conventional system. There is less alignment to be done, and since the propulsion unit is also the steering system, there are no struts and no propeller shaft or rudder stock tubes to build into the hull. "They said I'd save a lot of time installing it, but I didn't believe it until I saw it," Bruce acknowledges. "And after you've done one or two, it's definitely less time-consuming."

A Launching

Just after sundown on May 22, 2002, the eighth tug Washburn & Doughty built for Moran, the *Gramma Lee T. Moran*, slid down rails well-greased with orange gook and into the water. David Winslow and his small tug *Charles Winslow* caught the new boat—actually, they encouraged her to come along with a good pull on the hawser. (It's bad luck when a boat stops on her way into the water on launch, David says. He gives as an example the *Irene's Way*, which got stuck on the ways a few years back at Goudy and Stevens, also in East Boothbay. A year later, to the day, the owner died aboard her.) But the *Gramma* didn't hesitate. "She's comin'," said the voice on the radio to David. A horn blatted. "There she goes, David!" and David put the wood to the *Charles* to get out of her way. With a big splash, the new tug hit the water and slowed.

"Beautiful," said David's father, Eliot, who had come for the ride. Then ninety-three, he said he wanted to make one more trip before he met the undertaker. There was a lot of joking about whether the undertaker had a boat with which to come get Eliot; if he didn't, maybe they could lease him one.

David had swung the *Charles* off to starboard to pull the new tug around. At first the *Gramma* didn't want to turn, but in a few minutes she came. The men on the new tug dropped the hawser, and the deckhands on the *Charles* pulled the big line in as fast as they could, hand over hand, so it wouldn't tangle in the wheel. Meanwhile, the *Gramma* quietly drifted toward the *Charles* as if asking to be caught. The *Charles* made up to her. Eliot looked at the new Z-drive tug covetously. He'd love to have a tractor tug, but it's just not justified for their business. "When the dollar bills that go into building the tug equal the weight of the boat itself," he said, "the tug is completed."

Quietly David took the new boat to the barge Washburn & Doughty use as a pier. "That's a half a railroad car carrier," Eliot told us. The Winslows had sold it to the yard fifteen years ago or better. "See how it's raked just on one end?" Eliot asked. "The square end is where it was cut off." The old barge looks rough. It has leaked for years, probably decades. A year or two back, Eliot said, Bruce Washburn asked if the warranty was still on it. But it works as a float for the boat builders, and *Gramma* slid easily into place alongside. "Gonna come all stop and see how she does. OK?" David asked the man on the barge.

"Perfect," he said.

"OK, we'll shut her down." The *Charles* would stay tied to the new boat overnight.

"Very nice, Dave," said Eliot. "That's the fastest you've ever done it."

"Well, she just came over to me," said David.

"When things go well, it looks very easy," Eliot remarked.

The *Gramma Lee T. Moran* splashes. AUTHOR PHOTO.

Pleasing the Navy Brass

That the U.S. Navy started requiring tractor tugs for their contract work in the late 1990s may be attributed in some part to a demonstration of that technology a decade and a half earlier with young Adam Wronowski at the helm. Adam had been on the water all his life—he doesn't remember a time he wasn't riding tugs or working in the shipyard. When the navy brass came aboard to see the *Paul A. Wronowski,* Thames Towboat Company's Z-drive tug, he had been running it for a couple of years. He was twelve or thirteen years old. The tug was one of the first tractors in North America. Almost all the other early ones were Canadian.

Adam's grandfather, John H. Wronowski, had developed his innate talent for understanding things mechanical into assuming part and eventually full ownership of a ferry company, and later Thames Towboat and the related Thames Shipyard. The *Paul A. Wronowski,* named after one of John H.'s sons, Adam's uncle, was developed from his own engineering experience and instinct combined with the expertise of naval architect Bob Hill, well known as the designer of tugboats and then working with John Gilbert's marine architecture firm in Boston.

In 1983, the navy was considering replacing all its YTBs, as they call their large harbor tugs. (The acronym stands for Yard Tug, Big.) Bob was working on a design for one of the bidders on that program and arranged the demonstration of Wronowski's Z-drive at the submarine base in Groton, Connecticut. He was aboard, along with John H. Wronowski, then seventy-four years old, and Adam, who today has no idea who the other visitors on the boat were beyond that they were important navy people, in uniform and pretty intimidating to a youngster. "Admirals or captains or commanders—I don't know."

Bob tells the story: "The tug is tucked in the slip, and getting out isn't easy. Everyone is in the pilothouse ready to go, and old John comes up the steps, drops a milk crate in front of the steering stand, and then steps back."

"There you go, son," Adam remembers his grandfather saying. "Let's get under way." And the youngster got on the crate and gave the deckhands the OK to let the lines go.

Continues Bob: "He starts working the controls for the Z-drives and gets us off the pier and out into the channel in no time, never hitting the dock once. He gets on the radio, calls the railroad bridge for an open."

The navy people were standing in silence, Bob reports. They didn't know what to say. "Here is this little kid working the tug like a pro. We get through the bridge. So we go upstream, with the kid at the controls." Meanwhile, John H. explained the workings of the boat to the navy folks. As they approached the base, the navy's harbor pilot hailed the tug. Adam answered him. "Chinese," said the pilot, meaning that the tug would be oriented in the opposite direction from the submarine, head-to-tail. "Head-in on the port side. OK with you, Cap?"

Adam responded, "OK. Chinese on the port side, bow-in." But before the demonstration could start, the *Paul* had to go into another pier to take aboard more navy personnel. John H. was continuing his technical explanations when one of the bigwigs interrupted to ask when they'd be alongside to dock—but Adam had already brought the tug into the dock and had gotten a couple of lines out. "You didn't realize it," John said. "Adam laid her in there so soft you didn't even feel it."

Adam still at the wheel, they backed back away from the pier to approach the submarine they were going to move around to demonstrate the capabilities of the tug. At this point, Bob recounts, the navy faces showed sheer panic. One of the brass looked at old John H. "OK, it's great the tug is so easy to work that a kid can do it, but we can't have a kid operating a tugboat near a nuclear sub!"

"No one else on this boat who knows how to run it," John H. replied. "Do you?" He was exaggerating just a bit—of course he knew how to run it himself. Then he

Liberty, a Washburn & Doughty Z-drive tug launched in 2003 for Boston Towing & Transportation. Her mast is down for ship handling. AUTHOR PHOTO.

reassured them. "Adam works the boat all the time. Don't worry about it." Bob reports that the man's face turned ashen gray.

With Adam still at the controls, they made up to the sub with a single line, brought her out into the stream, and spun her around. This job normally would require two tugs, but Adam and the *Paul* could handle it themselves with just a bowline out. Says Bob: "The navy people were, in a word, dumbfounded. You could see they were all assuming they were going to be unemployed or court-martialed. But Adam never put a scratch on the sub."

John H. finally did take the controls, because he wanted to show off just how quickly the tug could switch from one side of the sub to the other, moving the lines. "Of course, *I* took it pretty easy, but *he* wanted to put the coal to it," Adam remembers.

Although the navy brass were then impressed enough that they planned for their new YTBs to have Z-drives, that project folded. But in the late 1990s, when the navy decided to charter private tugs for their yard work rather than replacing their own aging fleet, they required that contractors use tractors. And that's when Moran commissioned its first six tugs from Washburn & Doughty, to fulfill one of those navy contracts.

Today the *Paul A. Wronowski* is on charter to the submarine base in Groton, Connecticut. Adam is proud to say that, although the tug was nearly twenty years old when she was classed by Lloyd's Register in order to get that contract, she required no significant modification. Bob Hill, Jack Gilbert, and John H. Wronowski had done their job well indeed.

Deckhands

A good deckhand is essential on a tug. Again and again I've been told that no one should run a tug until he's worked the deck and understands what the deckhand faces. A tug can't do much without connecting up with barges or ships, and the connections are all made by the deckhand handling lines, chains, and wires—throwing them and quickly making them fast with the correct placements and tensions. A captain certainly appreciates a skilled deckie, and a bad one can get him in trouble.

A green mate coming out of a maritime school doesn't automatically understand how important the deck is, but the wheelhouse certainly knows. A deckhand who can throw the line well is a tremendous asset in the kills (channels with often-tricky currents), with the tug maneuvering around to catch a second, third, or fourth barge, particularly in a breeze. "If the wind's blowing, you're a big sail," explains Captain

Matt Luba pulls in the ladder that serves as the *Adriatic Sea*'s gangway from wherever she happens to be tied.
AUTHOR PHOTO.

Chris Holt, who worked in New York Harbor and is now a pilot on the Piscataquis River between New Hampshire and Maine. "You save a lot of jams by getting the line on in time. Deckhand is the lowest position, but his job is just as important as any other on the boat. An experienced man is worth his weight in gold."

Even though the Able Bodied Seaman used to be a career position—ABs made good money with a lot of overtime and weekend pay—those days are over. It's an unusual AB these days who is satisfied to keep that rating. "Most people don't last," says Lenny Greiner, mate on the K-Sea tug *Adriatic Sea*. "Either they move up to tankerman—so they can load and discharge barges—the pay's up—or they go for mate or engineer." Or they leave the business altogether—most do that. But there are a few exceptions. Matt Luba, deckhand on the *Adriatic Sea,* is one.

Matt is in his mid-thirties. He started on a harbor tanker with Lenny fourteen years ago. "We were on some pretty bad boats," he says, but working on the *Adriatic Sea* under Captain Vernon Elburn is a top-notch assignment. Matt's brother is the director of human resources for K-Sea. His two other brothers worked on tugs and then left for jobs ashore, but Matt likes his work.

Lenny says Matt's a lifelong bachelor and doesn't want the commotion or responsibility of being an officer. "He's a happy-go-lucky, nice guy. He doesn't drive, he takes public transportation. He has a boat and hunts and fishes. He just doesn't want

In the upper wheelhouse on the *Adriatic Sea*, mate Lenny Greiner keeps up with the ever-required paperwork. AUTHOR PHOTO.

the stress of the wheelhouse. He's happy where he is." His house on Long Island is three blocks from the one he grew up in, where his father still lives, but he doesn't spend much time there. "I don't like to be home," he says. He was on the boat a total of eight months last year.

In the past fourteen years, Lenny has obtained his 1600-ton Master of Oceans and Second Mate Unlimited Tonnage Oceans licenses. By comparison, Matt says, "I'm not confident enough to be in the wheelhouse. I'd rather guide someone into the dock than be steering. It's more of an accomplishment for me."

He's a very good cook, too. "It's not required that a deckhand cook well," says Captain Elburn. "But most of them, if they want to stay on, learn how." Rarely is a full-time cook found on a tugboat anymore. Usually just one full meal is served each day, and the men fend for themselves the rest of the time.

Trevor Campbell is from Tobago. He's a rugged man with a big grin always waiting to break out, gold-backed teeth flashing against his very dark face. He came to the States nine years ago to be with his family, but now the kids are grown and gone, and he and his wife have split up. He's been on K-Sea boats for five years and says he likes decking. "It's physical work. Keeps you active." Trevor is in his fifties, but by appearance, he could be any age at all. He has amazing strength. "He only uses the capstan so's not to show up the crew," Lenny likes to say of him. But Trevor would like to get his tankerman's license.

Russell Cleary is now on the *Adriatic Sea*'s other crew; he used to work under Vernon and Lenny. He came to tugboats when he was in his mid-forties after working in various other fields, including house painting, finance (at Merrill Lynch and then in his own company) and offshore fishing. Like most tugboaters, at least once on every trip he wonders if he couldn't come up with something better than this work. "But if we thought there was something better, we'd be out doing it," he says. "Painting houses, at the end of the day you could see you've improved things. But it was the same place and the same job every day. Managing a mutual fund, you don't know when you go home at night if you've made the right move or the wrong one. And if you stop exerting yourself for a moment, you stop making money."

Tugboating is different. "It's the variety. You don't go to work the same place every day. You look out the portlight or step out on deck, and the scenery changes." The work itself varies a lot, too. "As a deckhand, for awhile you might get down and dirty, chipping and sanding, getting rid of rust. And then you'll prepare a meal, or handle lines, or you might be on lookout, or clean the heads or the pilothouse—or pilothouses, if you have two, the way we do."

He likes the feeling of accomplishment he gets every time they've completed a trip, docking a barge after running it from point A to point B safely and efficiently. But he also says that one of the appeals of working on tugs is that you can cram 2,200 hours of work into 180 days each year, leaving 180 days free to do other things. In fact, even though they're away from their families half the time, tugboat people may actually be able to spend more time with their kids than many people with land-based jobs, he says, because when they're home, they're home.

Pay isn't what it used to be before the strikes in the 1980s. Many tugboaters, whatever their job on the boat, work at something else at least part of the time they're home. Russell knows a tankerman who does accounting during his two weeks at home each month. In the merchant marine, he has the advantages that come from working for a big corporation, such as health insurance, yet he has his own business too. Russell and Lenny both run commercial sportfishing boats.

Russell would like to move into the pilothouse. He has run as second mate occasionally when his boat went offshore and the vessel had to have three watch officers. "I got higher pay then, and experience in the pilothouse. But I've yet to get the experience Lenny has, making up to barges and docking. It requires a different category of skill, and you have to have aptitude for it to begin with."

Lenny concurs with this. "It takes more than the ticket. You have to have God-given talent to do it without hurting someone or causing damage. To get in the saddle and handle situations in the harbor, that's tough. It's difficult to get where you can do it. You can get your license, but actual handling is an art as much as a science." Some deckhands have what it takes, and some don't—or, at least, it comes easier to some.

Even as deckhands, crewmen have serious responsibility. And always, team-work is important. Says Captain Elburn, "Most everything you're doing, you depend on somebody. Guys on deck depend on the guys running the boat or operating the machinery. In the wheelhouse, we depend on the guys on deck, tying up barges and all. If you're expecting them to catch a line, you only get one chance or you'll have to back out and start over. Some places you go, once you miss, the second try is ten times harder than the first. Not necessarily more dangerous, but a lot more trouble." In backing up and remaneuvering, the wheelwash (turbulence off the propellers) cre-ates a whole new system of currents. "And it doesn't run in one direction; it goes in whirls. It takes a half an hour before the river current gets control again."

Getting on and off the wire—moving the barge into position to tow or to push— are dangerous operations, and their success depends on the deckhands. Each maneu-ver may take an hour, and the men have to handle the shackle, which weighs forty pounds or better and at any moment could jerk. "You've got to have your fingers in there to take the nut off and the pin out of the shackle and physically put it on the wire," Lenny describes. And it's that much trickier with weather.

Like many captains, Captain Pamela Hepburn admires a good deckhand. She speaks of bringing a trio of barges out of the dock, jackknifing them. "Leaving, you make up the three—let one go until the line's all flaked out, and then you let the next go quickly, and they all play out. It's poetic, beautiful."

Engineer Gary Matthews has spent a lot of towing time on the Hudson and knows about jackknifing. He works for Empire Harbor Marine, of Albany, moving dirt, stone, salt, scrap, and bulk products. "We tow big messes of junk. The company doesn't seem to let us tow one type of barge. As you go by this place, pick up these—maybe one stone, two scrap, and so on."

He explains the process of jackknifing barges off a pier. The end goal is that you're under way with two lines between the tug and the first barge and two lines between each barge and the one behind it. The barges are pulled out by one line apiece, unfolding out of their dock one by one, and the guy on the last barge works his way back to the tug tying the second lines. "If he screws up one thing, he's stuck on that last barge."

It's highly complicated, jackknifing a number of barges, Gary admits. "Jack-knifing uses the wind, tide, and the tug to move the weight of the barge." If it doesn't go right, you have a big crash. "Scrap barges and stone barges don't complain. They're so beat up, you can't really damage them too much. But there are fewer and fewer people who totally get into it," he says. "A lot of the work can't happen that way anymore." It is ten times as much work to pull the barges out one at a time, and takes ten times as long, but for some people it's as well to take the sure route. Gary knows one wheelman who has no interest in learning the trickier stuff. He takes the conservative approach. "Balancing productivity and efficiency against the sure thing, safety. I can't knock the guy. Another captain isn't unsafe doing that stuff, but it would be unsafe for *him* to."

But, he says, "I have a crew that's totally into it. My deckhand knows how to jackknife ten barges with one line, three tiers of three, one on the end, set up all the ropes so you pull one rope and they'd all string themselves out in one line in the right order." As Captain Pamela Hepburn says, poetic. "This is why I'm still in the indus-try," Gary says. "These scenarios can still exist."

A while back, briefly, there was a new guy on the *Adriatic Sea*. "If gunpowder was ambition, he wouldn't have enough for a spark," Vernon says about the kid, who just didn't learn how to do things. "I won't have him back. I had to get Matt up to do anything."

Vernon knows what makes a good deckhand. "He's interested in doing a good job. He likes his job. He can handle lines good. He knows how to work with cable. He knows his job without direction. If I had to stick my head out the window all the time to direct him, then I'd be neglecting my own job. If I tell him we have to make up alongside, or go into push gear, or hook up the wires to tow, he can carry out those things. We work together a little while, and we know what each other's gonna do without speaking to each other."

In the Engine Room

"Nobody rides for free," says the sign on the door to the engine room on the *Bouchard Boys*. The boat, launched in 1969, is just a little older than her senior chief engineer, Dennis Danforth, and he certainly doesn't ride for free. "She tells me what to do a lit-tle bit," he says of the boat. He actually enjoys that she is showing her age more than he is. "We've had a lot of breakdowns—that's the advantage of an old boat. That's how you learn," he says. "I'm still hungry for it, but I'm tired of the same thing break-ing down all the time."

Dennis has had a wide range of repairs to make, fixing overheating or totally broken-down main and generator engines, adjusting and re-creating water pumps and steering pumps, stopping leaks in systems and in the rudder room. Most of the serious problems happen in bad weather, too. "I'm going back across the back deck, and the water's pouring over it, the cable's moving around—that's the stuff you don't tell your wife about." A storm leaves the engineer particularly alert. "Please, God, don't let anything bad happen to the engines tonight," Dennis prays when seas are rough. He particularly dreads pulling a piston. "I don't want to have to change the pack out when I'm walking on walls." (Changing a piston and its cylinder is referred to as "changing the power pack." On some engines, the piston works in a removable sleeve, simplifying the change.)

On a two-watch boat like the *Bouchard Boys,* the chief has one assistant engineer (AE), who works the mate's watch, twelve to six. That doesn't mean the chief is asleep twelve hours a day. "In the afternoon, I'm usually up. I keep the AE busy. At midnight, I don't care what he does," says Dennis. His assistant has three or four years' experience and knows the engine room, so when Dennis goes to bed he can sleep. "He might not be able to fix it, but he's a good gauge-watcher, eyes and ears. Better than a guy who thinks he can fix something—he can get you in more trouble."

And the bottom line is, "If there's a problem, I'm up twenty-four hours." Or forty. Whatever it takes. The responsibility for the functioning of the boat and all its equipment falls on the chief engineer. This means that engineers don't get to enjoy the time the boat's in port the way the rest of the crew might. That's the only down time for repairs that can't can be made under way, and they're overseeing supplies and fuel being taken on, too. Fueling a tug isn't a quick job; even the relatively small *Bouchard Boys* holds 63,000 gallons. It's hard to get good bunk time in port. When nothing else is going on, Dennis turns the alarm panel to sound in his room and goes to bed.

The 226-foot *Powhatan* carries 206,000 gallons of fuel, enough to cross the Atlantic and the Mediterranean with a tow. Tom Balzano, *Powhatan*'s engineer for two years, has gone more than sixty days without ever getting off the ship. "We work harder when we're at the dock than at sea," he says. Still, it must be easier to make repairs on the dock than in the conditions they're apt to encounter at sea.

"You gotta be an expert in everything," says Tom. "You're out there on the North Atlantic—you can't just pull over and call the Triple A. It takes a couple of years for deck guys to learn the boat, how it responds, how it works—you're the guy they're calling. You're second only to the captain, in charge of the material condition of the ship, the status of the machinery."

About forty days after Hurricane Floyd, the *Powhatan* was in the Aegean Sea for a small salvage job for the U.S. Navy, going along full ahead at 14 knots in the middle of the night when the mechanical device that turned the controllable-pitch propeller blades broke. The controls appeared to work, but the blades went into the position of minimal resistance—full reverse. "It scared the bejeezus out of a bunch of people," recalls Tom.

Using two pieces of strong wire and a little pulley, Tom built a hand-operated control. Al, an assistant engineer, sat on a five-gallon pail watching Tom flip flashcard commands to him from the control station: Slow, Half Ahead, Full Ahead, and the same for reverse. Al had a dial in front of him that let him know what the propeller's pitch should be for each command, and he adjusted it by pulling a cord.

Meanwhile, the *Powhatan* was sent off to get a bulk carrier that had burned up her engine room halfway between the Azores and Bermuda. Four days later, they pulled up alongside the carrier, still with no control on that engine. "The captain is hollering down to me like on an old bell boat. That's how we maneuvered alongside, with Al sitting there pulling the cord."

When the *Bouchard Boys* is steaming, the engine room temperature is 116 degrees. "When you paint the engines, it dries pretty quick," says Dennis. "Bakes on." But even major discomforts don't matter when you're working on something. Dennis crushed a finger on his right hand and then drove a wire straight down through one on his left while trying to get an engine back on line one time. His assistant suggested taking a twenty-minute break. "You're gonna tell the captain we're going to take a twenty-minute break when he's down to one engine? What if he lost the other one?"

The scale of an engineer's efforts varies widely, perhaps even more on a salvage vessel than some others. The guided missile frigate USS *Underwood* was denied permission to enter Alexandria, Egypt, and managed to get herself involved with an uncharted wreck, holing herself. Among the support equipment called was the *Powhatan*. Her crew patched the hole, deballasted the *Underwood* and floated her off, and—at two knots—dragged her out to open ocean and across to drydock at Haifa, Israel.

The law of the sea being that if anyone's in trouble, whoever's around goes to help, the engineer's abilities sometimes are used on another vessel. Tom tells of hearing a distress call from a shrimp boat off Louisiana, where they'd picked up a couple of dredge-barges to go to New York. "We rigged him some gauges and built him a mechanical starter. That's jury-rigged Yankee ingenuity. He gave us a hundred pounds of shrimp in appreciation."

Ingenuity is essential. "We can't do Albany in winter," Dennis says. "They know better than to send us up there. You're gonna bust the engines. Slush clogs the strainers, water pumps start surging, losing suction." Cooling is compromised, at the least. But fuel oil has to get upstate, and the tugs and barges get sent. Normally, when the barge is light they'd be towing it, but not in winter, because if the tug were to get caught in ice, the barge would keep coming and run them down. So they push, and it's hard work.

Dennis remembers one trip. The on-line generator's temperature was rising. They pulled back on the main engines, stopping the cavitation, but they wanted to keep pressure on the circulation system so that warmer water would come back from the engine and melt the slush in the sea chest, the raw-water intake.

"We blew the pipe, and got a lot of water in the engine room. For twelve hours, I'm switching generators—you lose your generators, you lose your steering. Every time one heats up, I shut it down and bring the other one up. Every ten minutes. No one's getting any sleep. Finally we rigged a system from the fire pump's sea chest. There's plenty of pressure there. It draws more water than the generator's, and made everything run cooler." Tugboats carry tools and equipment and plenty of spare stuff,

The *Adriatic Sea* pushing the *DBL101* on the Hudson River, February 2004. The photo was taken from the *Irish Sea,* running ahead of them as icebreaker. COURTESY OF CAPT. GREG SEVERINO.

but they certainly don't have everything that a shoreside shop would have. "I keep the boat running with what I've got," says Dennis. "If that screwdriver's holding the door shut, that's the way it is. Nobody likes to hear 'I can't do it because I don't have this or that.'" (Other remarks better left unsaid on a tug are "I'm tired" or "It's not my job.")

Of course there are times that they can't fix a problem while underway. Dennis tells another story: "We lost a wheel [propeller] off Canada in six- to eight-foot seas, 120 miles off St. John, 160 miles from Portland—out in the Gulf of Maine. I was in the engine room switching a fuel valve, and there was a serious vibration. The stern was bouncing up and down. Captain pulled back on one throttle. I thought it was fishing gear, but it felt like we had a Volkswagen tied to the bottom of the boat. I went down in the rudder room, and when I set my flashlight down it started bouncing a foot off the deck. You couldn't touch anything." He secured the propeller shaft with two straps overhead so it couldn't move either way, shifted the air lines, and locked the clutches.

The cell phone wouldn't work, but they got through to Canada on single-sideband radio. Canada wouldn't allow the *Bouchard Boys* to bring the barge in under only one engine. They went back to Portland, where Fournier grabbed the barge from them, and they sent a diver down. He found that a weld had let go on the inch-thick cavitation plate that protects the hull from the propeller wash. The plate was hitting the wheel. Dennis got the plate off, but there was still a big vibration. Another tug came up from New York to take the barge where it was going, while they returned to New York with the *Bouchard Boys* on one engine. Back in the yard, they changed the wheels and found there were stress cracks in the hull under the cavitation plate. Dennis changed out the Cutless bearing and repacked the shafts and air-tested, and they ground the stress cracks and welded it all back in, and they were ready to go again.

There are times when engineers are so wrapped up in the engine room that they're not aware of much else, let alone why that engine room and the tug around it are where they are. "I'm outa touch down there," admits Dennis. "Engineers are the last ones to know what's going on, where you're going, what you're doing. They tell you you're going to California, and then the orders change. A typical engineer's question, just like a little kid's, is 'How much farther is it?'"

Captain Jim Sharp describes the time an engineer nearly caused a megamillion-dollar disaster after a guided-missile frigate was launched at Bath Iron Works. It was winter, ice cakes crashing down the river and into the single-screw tug—*bang bang bang*. They were working against the tide, almost under the abutment of the bridge, and had to stop their momentum over the bottom and work the tug in alongside the ship to dock it. "We had to parallel-park the ship alongside the dock, and as we got closer to the dock, there was less current, so we had to keep bleeding off headway." He was 150 feet off the dock and moving sideways when the engineer called up to him. The engine was overheating, and he had to shut it down immediately.

"Like the devil you will!" said Jim. He said a few other things, too. "You won't touch that engine as long as she's turning!"

The engineer said he wouldn't be responsible for what happened.

"I'll take responsibility for the whole thing," Jim told him, "but I've got a sixty-million dollar frigate alongside here, and we're leaving that engine till I get docked." (Everyone made it safely home.)

The advantage to becoming an engineer is that the skills translate well ashore. Engine room people find the same machinery in manufacturing plants, hospitals—anyplace. This means not only that there are other options for a fellow who's tired of being at sea but that, for the guys who want them, there are always boat jobs available. It also means that sometimes the relief guy doesn't show up—and sometimes an engineer may get shanghaied. When Dennis was on another Bouchard boat approaching New York, the captain told him to get some rest—he'd wake him up when they got into their berth, and he could go home. "I wake up, and we're under the Verrazano Bridge on our way to Freeport, Bahamas."

It's not in the list of official duties for an engineer to work on deck, but most do from time to time. A single deckhand has a tough time making up to a barge, and the engineer pitches in, just as anyone off-watch may if he happens to be around. And sometimes the skills he uses picking up the pieces after someone else's blunder have nothing to do with his technical training. One engineer tells of being on the stern as they were rounding up on their barge. The mate was in the wheelhouse for this maneuver. "He had already almost killed us several times." The retrieval line was off the barge, and the engineer saw it was likely to wind up in the wheel. The mate shrugged him off, everything's fine. The engineer got the captain, but sure enough, the line got caught. And it was the engineer who ended up leaning way out over the stern to cut them free. "I had my knife, the captain's holding me by my belt, and I'm cutting the line—and the son of a gun engages the engines. And he doesn't even have the concept that if you backed the engines, it might undo the tangle. But you gotta do what you gotta do. I got it cut out."

Captain John O'Reilly speaks clearly about engineers. "These guys most often are miracle workers," he says. "Most shoreside engineers would just read the failed object its last rites and order new parts. There are no hardware stores out in the middle of the Atlantic. It's at times like this that these people show a quality that surpasses sheer genius."

"You got engineers, and the rest of the people on the boat are passengers," says Dennis.

Lines

Without the various lines that a tugboat carries, she would be nearly useless. Using her hawser or hawsers—wire or soft synthetic rope—she tows. With her bow line (head line) and her other lines, she assists and moves other vessels about. And like any other vessel, she has docklines sized in proportion to her weight. To get the heavier lines where they need to go there are heaving lines and messengers. There are chains of various sorts, and to hook all this gear up to the boat there are bitts and towing machines (winches).

Towing machine configurations vary. The *Atlantic Salvor*'s (shown here) has a nylon hawser on one side and a wire on the other. Hanging over the railing are a braided line and a laid one. The petroleum-handling tug *Adriatic Sea* has two wires, one for the tow wire, and the other to hook up to the barge. Author photo.

When the landlubber thinks of rope, he may think of the traditional manila, but nobody in the tugboat world uses manila for anything anymore. For a given size, manila breaks at less than half the load that today's "ordinary" synthetics can bear. It weighs as much or more than the synthetics, and it rots easily. There's a wide variety of synthetics available, each with specialized characteristics and uses, and many can be found on tugs.

Typical of ship-assist tugs, at least in the smaller harbors, is Maineport Towboats' venerable multipurpose 1,800-horse harbor tug *Verona*, built in 1913 and still working into the twenty-first century. Because most of her work is shipdocking, the most important lines are her head line and a couple of quarter lines. For towing, she carries a nine-inch circumference, 1,200-foot hawser, which, like most East Coast hawsers, is made of nylon. It is kept on the boat deck (the deck where the lifeboat is stored) on a drying rack and under a tarp, out of the sun. Also stashed aboard are a set of wire bridles (for use when she tows a barge) and an assortment of other lines, many of them leftover sections of retired quarterlines. *Verona* doesn't do much towing, and what she does is usually local, perhaps moving a contractor's barge.

The material used for each line is specifically selected for its purpose. As a tug surges against a barge, under its own power or in a sea, the towline must act as a

Because there happen to be extra people aboard *Verona*, Melissa Terry gets help with the hawser this time. AUTHOR PHOTO.

spring so it doesn't snap. In contrast, towing on the West Coast is usually done with a rig that has virtually no stretch, explains Jim Conway, West Coast tug supervisor for SeaRiver Maritime. The continental shelf is just offshore, and the depth of the water often drops to seven thousand feet just outside the sea buoy. This fact, along with the bigger ocean swell on the Pacific Ocean, changes all the rules for tow rigs, because a long towing wire may sag several hundred feet deep. In winter conditions, with big seas, the typical West Coast barge has a bridle of two ninety-foot shots of three-inch chain, each link of which weighs some 110 pounds. The two legs of the bridle are attached on the front corners of the barge and lead to what's called a fish plate, a triangle made of inch-and-a-half or two-inch steel plate. Connected to the point of the fish plate is another shot—or possibly two—of three-inch chain, to which is shackled the tow wire itself. In summer conditions, with less swell, there might only be forty-five feet of additional chain between the fish plate and the wire.

The wire towing cable is allowed to run out far enough behind the tug so that the catenary created by the weight of the chain and wire acts as a shock absorber. For a big 7,200-horsepower tug, the towing cable may be a mile long and will have several hundred feet of catenary sag.

"You want enough wire out so it'll not pull out of the water in the heaviest surge," explains Jim. "The captain looks at the angle the wire makes at the stern of the tug to judge how long the wire needs to be." Most often he'll want it to be underwater from a point 100 to 200 feet aft of the boat. "The worst thing is to have too short a wire and eliminate the catenary—the wire will snap." It's not usually dramatic when a tow wire snaps—the cable just drops straight down from both ends—but it's cumbersome to repair it and to capture the tow again. "And conditions are never ideal when you have to go chase a tow."

By contrast, on the East Coast the water beneath a coastwise tow is often less than a hundred feet in depth. "You can only let a wire hang down sixty or seventy feet, or you'll haul it back up again as shiny as a nickel, and worn," says Jim. The average tow wire, two-and-a-half or two-and-three-quarters inches in diameter and five thousand feet long, costs about $40,000 and lasts a year and a half in steady use, he says. "You don't want to wear it out prematurely."

A nylon hawser is often used instead of wire for coastwise towing on the East Coast because it doesn't depend on a catenary for shock absorption. Under a load, nylon stretches up to 35 percent, or even more, allowing the necessary give. Three-inch diameter nylon is nearly equivalent to inch-and-five-eighths steel wire with six strands, each containing thirty-six smaller strands (called 6x36 in the business).

Nylon is considerably less expensive than wire and requires less deck machinery. It is easier to set than wire; picking up a tow with a wire requires shackling and bridle adjustments not needed with a line. But the towing machine customary with wire hawsers makes the job far less labor-intensive once the tow is in place. To shorten up, slow the boat and winch in the wire, and to lengthen it, spool it out. There are towing machines with dynamic load meters that can automatically pay out a little wire when the load gets too high, and then retrieve wire when tension slackens. A nylon hawser the size of *Verona*'s weighs close to two-hundred pounds per hundred feet, and if there is no towing machine, any adjustment to it has to be made by hand. Not only is this hard work, but the back deck is an intrinsically dangerous place to be whenever there's a tow out.

Nylon lines store up tremendous energy when they stretch, which makes them potentially lethal when they part. Says Captain John O'Reilly, "When they snap, all hell breaks loose. I remember one report from over thirty years ago where a crew on a ship was attempting to move a spare anchor using a nylon line. The line snapped, and amongst the dozen or so injured and killed, several were cut completely in half."

Wire is sometimes used on the East Coast too, particularly for the big petroleum barges, but much less chain is used on the bridle. The size of the cable depends not on the weight you tow—the *Adriatic Sea,* for example, usually towed 130,000 barrels, though she had in the past taken half again as much—but on the horsepower of the tug. The 3,900-horsepower *Adriatic Sea,* before her conversion to an articulated coupling, ran a 7x16 cable two inches in diameter. "If you had the cable to hold the horsepower, you could tow Manhattan if you wanted to," says Captain Vernon Elburn.

Chafe is always an issue, even with wire. On the *Adriatic Sea,* rollers on the stern give with the cable as the boat moves. Once a day or up to four times a day, depending on the weather, the crew moves the wear point on the wire. "The contact point is twelve inches—so you move it two to ten feet at a time and try to stagger it out." They keep an eye on the cable and record the mileage, and every fourteen months or 25,000 miles, they swap it end-for-end and inspect it before recertifying it. They open it up and look at it internally, check the grease in it, look for any broken strands, and caliper the outside for wear. A cable is condemned if it has lost a certain amount of its diameter.

There is such a thing as wire rope, too, which is differentiated from cable-lay (twisted) wire by its braided construction. (In common usage, however, "wire rope" often refers to any wire.) Wire rope is pliable, like polyester or other synthetic rope, and is useful for handling the heavy chains. Like cable, it has negligible stretch, but it's flexible enough to wrap around the capstan and haul in the immensely heavy chain bridles used on the West Coast.

Chain is measured by the diameter of the stock of which it is formed. A single link of the three-and-a-half-inch chain Crowley Marine Services uses for ocean tows is twenty-one inches long and more than a foot wide. A shot of that chain (ninety feet) weighs 10,500 pounds. For their bridles they use Dialock chain, known as stud link chain on the East Coast. Each link of this chain has an internal crosspiece to add strength, preventing the link from stretching.

Verona's bow line, the line she uses for ship docking day in and day out, is two hundred feet of eight-strand braided rope eight and a half inches in circumference. (For some reason, larger fiber lines are usually measured by circumference, while wire is measured by diameter.) It is made of a blend of polypropylene and polyester. Polypropylene is the strongest single material for its weight, and it has little stretch. It floats. It's not well-suited for abrasive situations, however, so a polyester sheathing is added on each strand of polypropylene rope.

Chains on tugboats can be serious stuff. This chain is made of 3-inch diameter steel; a 90-foot shot weighs a ton and a half. On the rail, aft, three Norman pins have been raised hydraulically to keep the chain and cable in place. Courtesy of Capt. Robert C. Glover III.

The eight-strand blend braid is more resistant to abrasion than the same blend in laid line because it spreads the pressure over a wider surface and offers fewer proud edges. But equally important in *Verona*'s case, says John Worth, former co-owner of Maineport Towboats, is that the braided line is easier to splice once it's had a load on it. "It's like a Chinese finger puzzle," John says. As soon as the pressure's off, it loosens up. By contrast, the twist of three-strand laid rope gets tighter and tighter with use and more and more difficult to splice.

Splicing is important. "As a head line gets tired, first we end-for-end it," John says, "and then as it gets more tired, we shorten it." Each of these changes requires more splicing. "Finally we retire it. It lasts us a year or maybe longer, depending on traffic." Other factors affect the lifespan, too, such as the maintenance of the ships they handle. If the ships' fittings are kept rust-free, John says, they can dock ten ships without seeing a change in the line. "But dock a single ship with rusty chocks or fairleads, and you can see wear."

The combination line wears considerably better than straight polypropylene, but still it weighs considerably less than all-polyester rope. "It takes a good load," says John, "and if it does part, it doesn't tend to recoil. It goes straight toward wherever it's made fast."

It is for head lines, however, that some tugs use the most exotic materials available today. One of these is Spectra (called Dyneema outside the U.S.), a high-performance polyethylene fiber that is ten times stronger for its weight than steel. It is also very expensive, at something like $32 a foot at the time of this writing. But the new tractor tugs have so much pulling power, it would take a huge line, sixteen inches in circumference, to be as strong as the eight-and-a-half-inch Spectra line Sea-River's tractors are fitted with. Even if sixteen-inch line were manageable for crews, there wouldn't be a tugboat winch big enough to handle it.

The shortcoming of Spectra, aside from its price, is that it is very susceptible to the heat from friction. In a static pull situation, the stuff would last forever, Jim Conway explains, but the end where it passes through ships' chocks wears relatively quickly. For that reason, SeaRiver splices in a twenty-eight-foot sacrificial piece of Spectra that gets changed-out regularly. (On-the-spot chafe protection can be provided by a woven nylon jacket or sleeve placed over the wear point.)

Joel Altus is the rigging supervisor at Foss Maritime in Seattle, and in that position has the responsibility to know as much as any person can about ropes and cables, their makeup, and their use. He explains that modern tugs with Voith-Schneider or azimuthing propulsion systems and huge skegs to create lateral resistance under the water can exert a pull two or almost three times the theoretical bollard pull of the vessel. "Therefore," he says, "the lines required have to be three, four, even five times stronger than the simple towing forces."

Foss has developed a line even stronger than Spectra by modifying the chemical makeup of Spectra and creating a product half again as strong for its weight. And to accommodate these extraordinarily strong lines, says Joel, "all deck fixtures, winches, and the towing staple and deck appointments on the ship being assisted have to be at the requisite strength." Ship design is changing in response. "Chocks and towing points have to be made specifically for high-performance lines with appropriate radii, and chocks that will carry the loads whether dressed directly or sideloaded. All this is governed by rigging."

Unfortunately, ship fittings *aren't* keeping up with the tugs' pulling powers. This problem was the major complaint at an International Tug and Salvage conference in Spain in 2002. Shipping companies had been given the increased-horsepower tugs they wanted—and now too many chocks were breaking and too much shrapnel was flying around.

On the *Verona*, the 300-foot quarter lines are made of the same mixture of poly-ester and polypropylene as her head line, but in a three-strand laid rope of inch-and-a-half or two-inch diameter. "Braid tends not to have a good memory," says John Worth, "which makes it harder to handle. Three-strand lay is easy to coil, easy to get in." As a particular line gets worn or develops a weak spot, shorter sections of it are used to tie up the tug or to tie the *Verona* to other tugs. "The lines travel around to different places, downgrading to lower levels of importance."

Like the head line, quarter lines are sometimes used while docking ships, for instance as a lazy line to hold the tug at right angles to the ship. They—or the shorter pieces remaining from old quarter lines—are also used to make up alongside a tow, or to push. When a tug is made up behind a tow, the lines cannot have much stretch or else the tug will not be able to steer the unit. When the sea's too rough to allow the tug to take the barge on the hip, quarter lines might be used as gate lines for short tows through tight passages. These run from the quarter bitt on each side of the tug straight back to the corners of a barge behind. This configuration gives the tug a lot of control. Having two hawsers to deal with and less shock absorption isn't good for long distances, however.

John notes that a quarter line should be a little less rugged than the head line. If the bow line parts when a tug is moving along at a good clip with a barge alongside, the barge suddenly takes over, dragging the tug by her stern or the quarter bitt. It would be easy for water to come over the stern or for the tug to get rolled under. "This doesn't happen very often," John assures. "You make sure you're well-tied, with the towing strap going ahead good and rugged. But if that bow line parts, you want the stern line to give up too."

The smallest line on a tug is the heaving line, which a deckhand attaches to a heavier line and throws to a pier or another vessel so someone there can then haul in the heavy line. *Verona* has at least three heaving lines at any given time, each made of three-eighths-inch Dacron with a monkey's fist on one end to give some weight as it's thrown. "We do creative things for the weight of the monkey's fist," says John. "Right now, I think, we've got a zinc off an outboard motor in there. You want it heavy enough to throw but not so heavy as to hurt anyone. If it's too heavy, it scares people when it comes flying over the rail. Sometimes we splice the old monkey's fist in—

Deckhand Trevor Campbell throws the heaving line from the *Adriatic Sea* to the barge mate, Dan Bruton.
AUTHOR PHOTO.

it just saves time." The heaving lines are replaced when they get worn at all. Sometimes they are put onto a capstan to haul the heavy line across, and they are critical for the ship docking *Verona* does. You don't want one letting go.

Throwing a heaving line is the mark of a good deckhand. "You can embarrass yourself pretty heavily if you're not practiced at it," says John. It's difficult on a docking tug sometimes, as a light ship may be thirty feet up, nearly vertically over the deckhand's head, and a good breeze only adds to the challenge. It's an indicator of a good, seasoned deckhand to get a heaving line where it needs to go, and John enjoys seeing how creative they can be. The supreme challenge is to get the line through the ship's hawsepipe—when a deckhand manages that, he's pretty pleased with himself.

Unlike some tugs, the *Verona* doesn't carry messengers, which are simply lines of a size in between that of a heaving line and the line that ultimately will be taken across. The heaving line may simply take across a messenger, which, in turn, is used to pull in the big line. On rare occasions, the *Verona* might ask a ship to drop a messenger down. A messenger doesn't have a monkey's fist on it because it is too heavy to throw.

No matter of what kind of rope is used for a particular purpose, no knots are used except onto a messenger or heaving line. With all the force applied to lines on tugs, no one would ever be able to untie a knot. On most of the modern tractor tugs, huge hydraulic or electric winches hold and store the entire length of their working lines. On traditional older boats, a line may be pulled in by a capstan and is always belayed on bitts on the tug, while the loop on the other end is simply dropped around a cleat, bitt, or bollard on a ship, barge, or pier. In either case, the tug is in charge of adjustment.

The H-bitt is the most-used fitting on a tug. Its vertical posts are crossed by a horizontal piece, the cavel, leaving four horns on which lines may be secured, chosen according to the direction of pull. Many turns are taken around one or more horns, often figure-eighted. Each complete turn decreases the pressure more than twice, but the rule is simple: When in doubt, take another turn. The deckhand must be careful that the load-bearing line is not atop a successive wrap or it could all jam up. Turns of a laid line are made in a clockwise direction in order to prevent it from unlaying.

Says Joel Altus, "One of the most interesting things about tugboats is that the variety of work they do is enormous." And, he says, that variety of work requires very specific types of rigging, chain, wire ropes, cables, and lines of particular characteristics. Even on a small, traditional tug like the *Verona*, very different types of line are in use. And the new technology in tugboats has required new technology in lines and rigging.

Fendering

The image we all have of tugboats is that their exteriors are covered in black rubber, with tires and mats and blocks of the stuff strewn all over them. As a tugboat's job is to run into things, albeit gently (usually), fendering makes sense both for tug and for the object being bumped into. Fendering has another purpose as well. It must provide a "sticky" surface to hold the tug in place alongside a moving ship.

Traditionally, protection came from wooden lumber dangling over a tug's sides, but wood was rigid and splintered. Next used were manila lines no longer useful for holding anything. They were matted by seamen in their free hours, working for so-much a foot. They braided and ratted the old rope into puddings (for the bow), puddenings (on the side or transom) and fenders that hung from the rail. These worked well to protect both tug and barge or ship but wore out and had to be replaced from time to time.

When a tug spent time laid up in the shop berth, pier rats often would take up residence in the pudding. The first fender-contact after the boat went back to work sent rats scurrying every which way.

Along came rubber tires, which, once they were no longer good for their original purpose, proved ideal as tug fenders, either in their entirety or cut up and layered. Not all wheelhouse guys liked the change. Sodden old manila puddings stuck to the sides of ships better than rubber, which had a little bounce to it. Captains had to re-learn how to land alongside a ship but, whenever another guy figured it out, there'd be a lot of radio banter in the harbor about relative prowess with the new fenders.

Of late, as disposal of used tires ashore becomes more of a problem, foundling tires sometimes appear at tug yards by themselves, like kittens at a farm. Tugboat operators can afford to be a little fussy about the tires they accept—many aren't stiff enough to give the deflection and energy absorption needed. The big, tough tires used on excavators and large tractors work best on the bow. The very largest tires can be purchased for around $150 apiece, used. Large airplane tires are good further aft, where they are used simply to prevent steel-on-steel contact. These sell for up to $75, used. Tires rarely need replacement. If one should rip off its attachments, it's simply a matter of drilling new holes and re-chaining it. To be sure, drilling holes in old tires is no small feat. It takes a hole saw, kept well-lubricated with soap so the rubber doesn't melt and twist itself in a knot.

Various manufactured fenders are available commercially, many of them created from bits and pieces of waste tires, either simply piled together into a solid block or looped to deflect and absorb energy of contact. Other fenders, far more expensive, are

Manila pudding and fenders on the old canaler *Russell 16.* Canalers' low pilot-houses allowed them to sneak under bridges. FROM THE COLLECTION OF FRED REEP.

Cape Rosier displays an assortment of rubber fenders. AUTHOR PHOTO.

made of extruded rubber, formed to a particular shape for a specific application. As a typical example of a ship-handling tug, the *Capt. Harry,* launched at the Washburn & Doughty yard in 2001, has fourteen heavy aircraft tires on each side, and rows and rows of soft-loop rubber fendering. It adds up to well over twenty tons of rubber with a value not too far from $50,000. She's well protected, as is anything she touches. Aside from the little bit of grab that rubber gives for ship-assist work, fendering is all about a softer landing. That it happens also to put back into use some old tires is entirely a coincidental side benefit to the planet.

Lights and Signals

Navigation lights are required of any vessel under way at night, though the actual requirements vary with her size, type and occupation. A mariner seeing a vessel's configuration of lights in the darkness can at least tell which direction she's going, and perhaps what she's up to, and certainly he can determine whose responsibility it is to keep clear. The regulations about lights vary somewhat between U.S. inland and international waters but, by way of example, we'll look here at only the U.S. inland rules, which cover rivers, bays, lakes and sounds.

Between sunset and sunrise, even the smallest outboard must show a red side-light on the port side and a green one on starboard, along with a white light visible from all around the boat. A vessel more than twelve meters in length must show two masthead lights, one forward and the second aft of and higher than the first. On vessels of various sizes, the distance from which the lights can be seen is prescribed, too. The colored lights are only visible from the side or ahead of the vessel, the stern light only shows from the side and aft, and masthead lights can be seen all the way around the boat.

The lights allow a viewer to determine in what direction another vessel is moving. For example, if only a red light and one or more white ones are visible, then the vessel has the forward part of her port side to the viewer. If there is no red or green light visible, she's going safely away. The placement of the white lights further helps recognition. The scariest pattern, of course, is when both red and green lights show and two white masthead lights line up perfectly one atop the other. Then the vessel is relatively large and is aimed directly at the viewer.

In the daytime, vessels hoist various black shapes so viewers can identify their mission. For example, a big fishing vessel at work displays two cones, pointed ends together. A ship at anchor raises a ball, and a tow more than 200 meters long shows a diamond shape where it can easily be seen.

Stone barges under tow in New York Harbor at dusk. The tug has her towing lights lit. The deck of a tug is usually well lit, also. AUTHOR PHOTO.

At night, a vessel with a tow shows additional lights, which describe the towing configuration. A tug (or any other vessel) has the stern and sidelights of a vessel her size and, in addition, regardless of size when towing, shows a second masthead light vertically above the first. These are visible from dead ahead to 22.5 degrees aft of the beam on each side. She also shows a yellow towing light, mounted directly above the stern light and, like the stern light, visible from the stern and 67.5 degrees forward on each side. If the total length of the towline and whatever's being towed is more than two hundred meters from the stern of the towboat, a third masthead light is lit. Any towed vessel shows sidelights and stern light.

When a tug has barges or other vessels or objects ahead or alongside, making a single block, the tug shows two yellow towing lights aft, one above the other, but she and her charge may be lit as if the group were one vessel. The vessel alongside also shows a yellow flashing light on its forward end. A rigidly connected tug and barge (an integrated or articulated tug-and-barge) are considered one vessel and show the lights of a single ship of the same length.

Often a tug will shine a searchlight back onto the tow to make the tow more obvious.

The Crews

Unless things go terribly wrong, or someone just feels like helping, usually members of only one watch will be working at a time. When watch-change time comes, even right in the middle of some maneuver, each person on the new watch takes his position, and the relieved crewmembers often head directly to their bunks and may not reappear till the next watch-change, making time only to eat. Or they may hang out in the galley, playing cribbage or joking around with their shipmates or watching videos. "The engineer's in charge of the TV remote," says Chief Engineer Dennis Danforth. On many boats, the off-watch deckhand prepares the single formal meal of the day at 5:30 p.m., just before watch-change. The other deckie will clean up after dinner. (Everyone agrees: If you don't have good food, you don't have a happy crew.)

When a crew gets back to the boat after time ashore, they're pretty civilized, says Captain Bob Peterson. "You say hello to everybody and shake their hands, talk about all the sewing-circle shit you been doing at home." But it's not very long before the communication gets rougher. "Just catch the fucking line, willya?" Bob gives by way of example. "It gets worse and worse. The last day of the trip, the only word you use is *fuck*. It means everything." (I have to say here that my own experience on the last days of a rotation aboard the *Adriatic Sea* was nothing like what Bob describes. Only once did I hear that or any other word that might be offensive. Whether this is typical of the boat or only was that way for my benefit I cannot say, but in either case, it speaks well of the sensitivities of the people aboard.)

Cary Brown has a mate's license but hadn't been able to find a mate's job when I met him; he was filling in on deck on Donjon Marine's *Atlantic Salvor*. He usually works on the *Powhatan*, thirty-five days on, thirty-five off. He says he never actually gets thirty-five off, however—always he seems to get asked to fill in for at least part of someone else's scheduled time aboard. He obviously likes to cook—during a slack morning when the port engineer was making repairs to the *Salvor,* Cary was in the galley, grilling sausages and later a spicy rice dish. (Didn't that smell good!) "You gotta do something, keep busy." said Cary. "If you lay around, you get heavy. Set around and think about home, you get crazy. But look at that—it's ten-thirty, and my watch is almost over."

In general, I've been told that things are more laid-back on the East Coast than in the Gulf. The friction isn't racial so much as regional. There are bad feelings between northeast crews and southern crews, particularly in the wheelhouse. The expression "coon ass" is often used in the world of tugboating, with different meanings according to who's using it. "Where I work," says one captain based in New York, "it's anyone with a Southern accent that probably didn't work in New York Harbor before the strike. It's not meant to be a complimentary term." (Eastern captains still feel resentment because Gulf people were brought in to New York to run the boats during the labor dispute of 1988.)

"Coon ass captains come up here but can't do anything in New York," says a

Maine-raised towboater who works from New York Harbor. "They can sail up and down the coast, but can't sail from the pier to the Statue of Liberty. They're in there holding the dock up, and we're the only boat moving barges, the only one that can."

On the East Coast there's a strong belief that there are grandfathered captains in the South who shouldn't be running boats at all. Certainly, working in New York Harbor is not the same as in a quieter port elsewhere, but I've been told more than once that there are captains in the oil patch—the Gulf of Mexico—who can't read or write and who haven't kept up with the times in many respects. (The Coast Guard is increasing its endorsement requirements and weeding out some of the less educated towboaters, a fact that is received with varying amounts of enthusiasm.) And I've been told that many of the southerners don't like northerners, seeing them as an arrogant lot.

But to a "real" coon ass, the term means something else. Living in the bayou area of Louisiana, Engineer Sid Hebert is proud to be a coon ass, and gives the definitive description: "We'll eat anything that don't eat us first, be mean if we want, but most times we just like to party." He adds, "They used to think that was a bad name, but now everyone wants to be a coon ass." But he's very clear that you can't be one unless you come from South Louisiana: "Anything above I-10, we call that Yankees."

Regardless of the meaning of the phrase, its use often demonstrates the fact that there is bad feeling between southerners and northerners, bad feeling that is seen more on boats in the Gulf than in the Northeast. At the time I was on board, members of the *Atlantic Salvor*'s crew hailed from Louisiana, Idaho via Louisiana, North Carolina via Georgia, Maine via Michigan, Pennsylvania, Florida—pretty well everywhere. "On the East Coast, everyone gets along," says the African-American Cary Brown. "We kinda help each other out. This is our family, out here. We watch each other's backs."

Obviously, there are times when people *don't* get along. "If you don't like somebody, that's your personal business," says Cary, stirring his rice. "You depend on him, and he depends on you. Take it up with him here [in the galley], not on deck."

Captain Richie Bates likes to say that nobody rides for free, but he and his engineer, Dennis Danforth, both say that it's not so, that half the crew is holding up less than their share of the load. The business is no longer filled with career folk, the way it was when many of today's captains were starting.

But among the career people, there's a loyalty, a feeling of "us against the company," as described by one tugboat officer. "What happens on the boat stays on the boat." He told his assistant, "If you get hurt, I'm gonna give you a couple more kicks to be sure you're hurt." But, he says, he'll go to bat for you with the company. Just the same, you don't sue unless it's absolutely necessary, he says. None of this "I didn't know rain would make the deck slippery" stuff. And if two guys have a fistfight, they have to work it out, no one's going to expect the office to take care of it.

This is an aspect of the job that surprised one captain as he made the step up from mate. If he's able, the mate does all the same boat handling that the skipper does, but the ultimate responsibility for the vessel is the captain's, and that includes personnel issues. He has to maintain respect from his crew. If he has two guys, both good at their jobs, who are at odds, he tries to smooth it over between them. With a small crew, you know who's slacking off or who's making life miserable. That person's got to go, if it's possible. Sometimes, because the company is having trouble finding replacements, it isn't possible, and it falls on the captain to motivate him.

There are always people who work at sea to get away from home, and some of them bring their discomfort with them. But there's a lot of camaraderie aboard the boats, card-playing and other wagering, joking and prank-playing. Dennis Danforth tells with a little glee about how as an assistant engineer he sprayed water around the head so that it would flow out across the galley floor. "What the hell is this?" asked his chief engineer. He looked for leaks, pressure problems, any explanation he could find, without success. He'd camp out in the head. "He'd be waiting to see it happen, and the minute he'd leave, I do it again." Dennis kept the game going for a week straight through, and then once in a while for six or eight months more. "The day he left and I got promoted to chief, I told him."

The same kind of prank has been played on him, too. He worked on an ailing ice-maker all one evening, finally got it going, and went to bed. But there was no ice in the morning. Why not? Something too hot? Condenser failing? He took it all apart again, put it back together, and it was working fine—but again, there was no ice in the morning. His shipmates were throwing all the ice overboard while he slept.

Life is not always easy. Captain Melissa Terry worked for a few months as a deckhand on a towboat in New York. "I left the company. It wasn't for me, anyway. The grind of New York—heavy, heavy gear, constantly shifting barges from one part of the harbor to another, ship docking—an endless grind. From a deckhand's perspective, it's tough. I like what I do here in Maine better, and I like the people a lot better. Maybe it wasn't New York, maybe it was just that crew. They went through a lot of deckhands before me, and a lot after. People know jobs are a dime a dozen there. Nobody cares. There's no desire to stay. Every company pays the same, does the same thing, same schedule. People shift around till they find a boat where they get along with the other people."

Tugboat crews honor some traditions one might not think of. One is that a new guy coming on a boat always brings a newspaper and donuts. If another tug comes by, the one with a newspaper asks if the other has today's news and passes over the paper if not. There's a sense of "we're all in this together" that certainly makes the job safer, but also more pleasant. On one boat a couple of days before crew-change time, the oncoming captain and engineer, both new to the boat, came aboard to ride the last leg of a trip to get used to the boat. Arriving in New York Harbor when the time came for the shift, the off-going captain got on the radio, hailing any passing tug. "Crew change. Anyone give us a ride?" and the two got picked off and taken ashore by a tug from another company.

Sure, the box everyone's living in may be small, particularly on the smaller tugs. But there are advantages. Says Captain Jack Colomara, who's been in the business forty-five years, "It suits my lifestyle. You don't have to get dressed every morning, you don't have to shave. If you don't shower, it's not the end of the world. (I do, but that's just my choice.) You don't have to put up a facade. I have a beard—have for twenty years—but if you want to shave, you shave. If you want to change your pants, you change your pants."

Says engineer Tom Balzano, "You all get very friendly and get to know the most intimate details of a guy's life—you eat together, work together, watch TV together. In a thirty- or sixty-day period, if people get along, they know just about everything about each other. And that's good—trust has to develop. When the shit hits the fan, you gotta know they're going to get you out, and they have to know you'll come for them and not be upstairs launching the life raft."

Weather

What's a boat story without bad weather? Plenty of storms will come into this book as part of more complete stories, but I've heard other little tales that are worth sharing, for their images or for showing some of the issues facing tugs in weather.

Fatigue is perhaps the most significant issue in a storm, assuming that the tug and whatever she's moving out there are all right. "Any sleep you do get is not very restful—even when you're sleeping, you're holding on," says Captain Dave Riddick. He describes being in the pilothouse during a particularly nasty storm. His eyes were twenty-eight feet above the water, and there were times when he didn't see anything but water. "Green water, not that foamy stuff. If there'd been a fish in there, you'd have seen it," he says. "Every time a wave come over, you're hopin' and prayin' that

The *Eugene F. Moran* in tough conditions. FROM THE COLLECTION OF BOB MATTSSON.

the windows wouldn't wash in and flood the boat. One six-hour period, we went backward a mile and a half."

In the forty-five years Captain Jack Colomara has been on tugs, he has seen some
weather. For Moran, he towed sludge barges out to the dumping grounds two hundred
miles offshore. On one trip they ran into tremendous seas. He doesn't give an estimate
of the wave heights—he says that most people, including himself, overestimate the
size of seas. On this particular sunny December day, the wind blew like crazy, but it
wasn't so cold that they were making ice. The boat would drop down into a trough and
"the water would swell up in front of the boat and on both sides, and it would get like
dusk. Then she'd pop to the top, and it would be a beautiful sunny day again."

Some years back, Lenny Greiner was on what he calls a tiny tug, only eighty-
five feet long, 2,000 horsepower. (Of course there was a time when that would have
been a big, powerful tug.) This little tug, the *Falcon,* works in New York Harbor now,
"where it belongs." The rumor is that she was built of all the scraps left over when
they built another, bigger tug. When Lenny was aboard her, she was running a dry
cargo barge on quadrilateral trade runs from New York to Puerto Rico to New Orleans
to Suriname carrying a variety of cargoes: steel reinforcing rods, sugar, whatever.
"Every trip, we had some kind of problem, engineering or something." This particular trip, they had a "freak load" of used machinery, old mill equipment, and a couple
of containers headed north to New York.

Six hundred miles offshore, they were caught in a tropical storm that turned into a hurricane, with twenty-five-foot seas. "I had to get on one knee and look up into the sky to look past the visor to see the tops of the waves." To this day, Lenny is amazed that the cargo on the barge didn't break loose and punch a hole in the sides.

"Hurricanes and tropical storms travel pretty fast," he explains. This one was north of them and was forecast to go west. "That evening the sky was looking ugly, the wind was blowing the tops of the waves off, and the barometer was falling. 'Man, this doesn't look right,' I said to the captain. We talked to a forecaster on the single sideband, and he read off the position of the low, and it was the same exact numbers as on our GPS." They were right in the center of the hurricane. "I don't know how the National Weather Service blew that one so bad."

The worst of the storm lasted twenty-four hours, starting as it began to get dark. "That night we would look behind us and see no lights on the barge—it would be behind a sea—and then see one running light, and then both running lights and the stern light, as the barge surfed down a wave." The barge was eight hundred feet behind them, as much wire as they could put out.

Lenny says the captain, Chris Berg, who graduated from King's Point just before World War II, is still working. "Son," Captain Berg said to Lenny during the storm, "they tell me you could drown in a teacup if you wanted to, so what are you worried about being out here for?" According to Lenny, any time there were no submarines, Captain Berg was happy. "He was the best guy to be out there with—he had no fear whatever."

Tugs typically have between two and eight huge fuel tanks and a day tank from which the engines actually run. They draw fuel into the day tank from one of the

The sea washes over the back deck of the *Christian Reinauer.* COURTESY OF BOB HILL.

storage tanks as needed. The sea was so rough that it stirred up the junk in the bottom of the day tank, and the fuel line was getting blocked. "The engineer had to beat on the pipe all night to keep the generator on line—it would completely clog up and go off line, and he'd have the other one ready to fire up. Without the generator, you don't have air, and air controls the throttles. Craig Thibodeau, from Louisiana. He saved our lives that night."

When the storm was finally over, Lenny walked by the engineer's room and saw the door was open. Craig was lying in bed with all his clothes on, reading the Bible. Lenny knew Craig wasn't a Bible-reading type. "What you doing?" he asked him.

"I'm catching up," said Craig.

After that trip, Lenny told the personnel guy the only way he'd set foot on that tug again would be to walk across her to get to the dock. "Every time I look at her, I can't believe we did that stuff on her. Did it for eight months, into the summer and after. Only three or four trips, thirty-five- to forty-five-day trips. That was the hairiest weather situation I've ever seen.

"I never thought much of engineers before—a lot of times they just walk around with a rag in their pocket or spend hours looking at TV in the galley—but after that, I had a whole new feeling."

Seasickness

I spent a few days on the K-Sea tug *Adriatic Sea,* much of the time in hurry-up-and-wait mode. There was a lot of chatting about tugboat life during that time, and the subject of seasickness came up. All the guys enjoyed telling a story about one pilot from Searsport. The *Adriatic* was outbound, light barge in tow, on a windy day. The forecast was for fifteen to twenty knots southwest, but, says Captain Vernon Elburn, "the weather people didn't hit it too good." They had thirty to thirty-five. Vernon came on watch as they were passing through Two Bush Channel, just as the bay started to get sloppy. The pilot was steering and had slowed down a little because of the chop.

At the end of the channel, it was time to lengthen out the tow wire. They had to come head-to-wind to hook up the hobble, a shackle around the cable that attaches to a pad-eye in the stern and keeps the cable on the roller. In a head sea, the tug lurches when the water comes back and hits the blisters—the fendering blocks that protect the tug when she's pushing the barge, her nose in the barge's notch. "It's like trying to drive a taxicab through a snow bank with the doors open," Vernon says. Not the ideal conditions to work on deck, and not perfectly comfortable in the wheelhouse, either.

"We came into the wind to hook up the hobble, and the pilot got a little fidgety. I took over and eased the wire out and put her on course. I didn't put full throttle on, but he made a beeline for the door and we knew he was sick." Deckhand Matt Luba was sitting by the open window. They hit a sea slightly on the starboard bow, water came in the window, and Matt got soaked. Some of the indicator lights on the dash shorted out for a time. Matt had to mop up the floor and go change his shirt. The further they went, the worse the sea got. The pilot ended up crawling across the pilot-house on all fours, the window half-open to let in some fresh air.

Sometimes it's too rough for the pilot to get off a ship and he ends up riding to the Cape Cod Canal or wherever the ship's going, but this guy was determined he was not staying on the *Adriatic*. They called for the pilot boat, which at Monhegan was a lobsterboat. "Most pilot boats are logy and heavy, but this one is pretty lively," Vernon notes. Matt retrieved the pilot's GPS antenna off the roof and carried the rest of his stuff down for him. The pilot refused to go down through the interior of the tug, instead climbing down the steep ladders on the outside to the back deck. As the pilot boat approached, Vernon tried to place the tug to give as much protection from the wind as he could. In another three or four minutes, the boat would have been closer alongside the tug, but the pilot was not staying on the *Adriatic* a second longer than he had to. He threw his bags over into the boat and took a running start, jumped, and dove headfirst into the pilot boat, hollering, "Go!"

The guys on the tug laughed about that all the way back to New York. "That's the first time I ever saw a pilot leave us like that. Highlight of that tour, anyway," says Vernon.

It was rough, no question. The tide and the wind were working against each other, making the seas shorter and sharper. The barge carried two men too, and it wasn't long before they radioed and asked the tug to slow down. When even a light sea hits the barge's bow, it causes vibration that comes back through with a ripple effect, magnifying as it goes. That day, the refrigerator on the barge was walking across the floor. (There are a couple of reasons that companies don't like manned barges. One is that they aren't permitted to load them as heavily, and the other is that sometimes the people aboard call for the tug to slow down. The companies don't like anything that slows things down.)

The weather wasn't enough that it really bothered the *Adriatic* or the barge itself, which wasn't taking solid water over the bow, just a lot of spray. "If you get in a real storm, you can mess up the framing in the bow of the barge, but this wasn't anything out of the ordinary for us," Vernon says. "We were on schedule."

A day or two later, the pilot called the company and said he wasn't going to pilot any more of their tugs.

But Captain Elburn has been seasick too. "When I was younger, I used to get sick a lot. I used to have to take seasick pills. I've always paid a lot of attention to the weather, and I've tried to avoid the bad stuff whenever possible. The last fifteen years or so, I've been pretty much OK. Sometimes, if I haven't been out in a while, I get a little queasy.

"When I first started using reading glasses, I'd take my glasses off and look around and I was fairly good, but then I'd put my glasses on to read the chart, and my stomach would just come apart."

Seasickness hits most everyone at one time or another, but that Searsport pilot has become famous on the *Adriatic Sea*.

Home and Work

Captain Jack Colomara says that the biggest problem a tugboater faces is his family life. (For convenience, I'm assuming the towboater is male, and the person left home is his wife. Most tugboaters are male, although today there are more women working in the field than there once were.) The life of a tugboater's spouse isn't much different from that of any other mariner's, unless the job is a harbor job by the day, which few are. The traditional maritime system has been one day off for every day worked. In many tug companies this continues, but sometimes it's a day off for every two worked, particularly in the Gulf of Mexico. The period on the boat may be a week, or it may be two weeks or a month. For offshore tugs, it might be three months, and then the mariner is home for an extended, if not equal, length of time.

That leaves their wives picking up a lot of slack. The divorce rate among mariners is high. "It's tough on a family," says Captain Jim Cheatham, who was usually on the river for forty-five days at a time throughout his long marriage. "One heck of a strain on your wife. She has to be mother and father and everything, all at once." Although at this writing they are separated, he speaks with great appreciation of his wife, Rose. "It takes a very special lady to put up with a riverman, I'll tell you. She was a very special one, one of a kind." He respects how she took care of everything, particularly the financial aspects of their life. "I worked with some poor guys out there whose wives spent everything. When they got home, they didn't have nothing. I was lucky that way."

It's a lonely life for the wife, Rose Cheatham says. "You raise your children alone. You do everything alone. I'm ready to retire from it—it's long enough—but he's still working. It's not an easy life being married to a riverman," she says. "If they're going to work out there, they'd better stay single."

I heard this same thought from Cary Brown, the deckhand on the *Atlantic Salvor*. He too has a wife and children, and they live in New Orleans. It bothers many mariners that they miss so many of their kids' special events: games, recitals, holidays, and personal milestones. Cary tells of leaving for work when his daughter was riding her bike with training wheels and coming home to find her fluent on two wheels. He's sad to miss these changes. It's hard to break away from the boat, though. The money's good, and better on the East Coast than nearer home in the Gulf. He couldn't afford a shorter rotation, with all the travel expenses.

Captain John O'Reilly says he's noticed one thing: "Nothing ever happens while you are home to take care of it."

The particular schedule certainly makes a difference. Lenny Greiner is mate on the *Adriatic Sea*. His wife, Debbie, likes two weeks on and two weeks off. "We have done the week on and off, and that was really hard because whenever we were just getting used to him being home, it was time to leave again." Worst of all was being on call. "Len would drive home the six hours and get the call that he had to be back the next day." That happened three times during the single summer Lenny tried being on call. But just as bad was a three-month rotation. Debbie was left with a six-year old, a four-and-a-half-year old, and a six-month old baby. "I thought I would have a breakdown."

It can be hard on the towboater himself, too. Captain Colomara says that he's known a dozen or more men who have almost gone crazy. "They had it in their head that their women aren't being true to them. Probably it wasn't true, but they had it in their head. I've seen good men go really bad."

The schedule has its advantages, too, though. Some men feel that they have better time with their kids than many people. Says engineer Tom Balzano, "When I'm home, that's what I do—play with them. A land job, you're on the treadmill and you never have quality time with your kids. Maybe I'm deluding myself, but I think they get a lot more out of me with my 182½ days off. We travel more, too—Florida, New York—my schedule allows me to do that stuff."

Captain Bob Peterson fished for many years, a life he's glad to have left behind him. "I blinked, and my daughter was born. I blinked again, and she's graduated high school. And that sucks." He and his first wife split up long ago. But he's married again. "She's a sane, intelligent person," he says of his second wife, adding that her taste in men is not what it should be, "but that's good for me." She doesn't come from a maritime background, and the life is a struggle for her. "She supports me, but I know she doesn't like it when I get up and go." Still, he's been at sea nearly all his adult life, and he knows he'd be miserable if he were ashore all the time. He thinks she wouldn't want him around very long either. As it is, the first day home is an adjustment. "I'll get calmed down in a little bit. My wife scolds me when the language gets bad. I'll know it's coming, but I can't stop it. On the boat it gets worse and worse, and I have to get it slapped outa me when I get home."

Being home isn't altogether simple. "We come home just long enough to upset their routine," says Chief Engineer Dennis Danforth, who has a three week on, three off schedule with Bouchard. "I don't sleep the first week. At three in the morning, I'm out checking rounds." The first week home is for his family. The second is for himself—he goes snowmobiling, hunting, or four-wheeling. Then, in the third week, "I get bored and start ripping the house apart. Even the kids say, 'All right, Dad, you can go.'"

But those same children wonder why he can't get a "regular job." A guy who works regular hours running a crewboat for a towing company tells how he ran tugs for twenty years, until one day his son plaintively asked him, "Daddy, when are you coming home?"

"Next day, I got off tugboats. At least I stopped being away."

For some towboaters, such as Lenny Greiner, the last thing they want is contact with the guys from the crew in their off time, but others have to stay in touch with their boat. The cell phone, so much a part of all the family men's lives when they're at work, keeps Dennis connected to the captain and the boat during his home time, too. "It's good to keep in touch," he says, but he thinks his wife sometimes feels jealous of the boat and the life that takes her husband so far from their East Millinocket, Maine, home. On his left arm, he has thirteen anchors tattooed, one for each year he worked on deck, and on his right he's started a series of anchors for his time in the engine room. He had her name tattooed on the left arm to finish the circle. "That helped a little bit," he says. "I appreciate what she's done for me. When I get compliments on how good my kids are, I know things are going well at home."

A number of men say that the last day at home is the hardest. Naturally, the wife wants some special time with her husband, but all he can think about is whether he's got this or that to take with him, or are the batteries charged for his cell phone, and does he have the right travel schedule. And the boat's calling all day with changes of plan, and often the wife drives her husband somewhere to catch a bus or the boat itself, and then the boat isn't where it was supposed to be until twelve hours later. "And I got up at three in the morning to get you there?"

Captain Steve Rhodes notices a change during the last three days he's home. "I kind of get in a zone." His wife knows it's not a time for controversial subjects. "Even though I've been doing it thirty years, I still get nervous," he says, speaking of a heightened state of awareness that reawakens even before he gets back to the boat. "It's how you can deal with an emergency."

Captain Doug O'Leary has been married forty years and was at sea for most of that time. He says that after he came ashore it took about four years before he got used to having someone in his bunk all the time. "At sea, if I felt like farting, I farted. Who gives a shit?"

Many couples actually like the on-again, off-again lifestyle and either do or think they would find it difficult to be together full-time. Steve, married twenty-five years, likes three weeks on, three off. "Two weeks is too short. Four weeks, it's hard to make your money last. She misses me after three weeks and she's sick of me after three."

After ten years of half on, half off, when Captain John O'Reilly took a teaching job, he and his wife, Maureen, weren't sure they could live together full-time. "Now we don't want to be separated," she says. He's back at sea, but they're looking forward to a time when he can come ashore for good. She harasses him, though. "Moe always says that I'm the only person who remembers all the courses up and down the coast but can't remember to pick up a loaf of bread and a bottle of milk at the store!" He adds that he knows a lot of other people with the same problem. All their first names are "Captain" too.

John also says that when he's home, he's right out straight doing all the things he would have been taking care of at a more reasonable pace if he hadn't been away. "Sometimes I think my blood pressure is higher at home than at work." And then there's always the chance that things will change at the last moment. John was recently called back to the boat almost as soon as he'd gotten home because his counterpart's mother had passed away. "It goes with the territory—and Bill, my relief, would do anything to return the favor when it's my turn."

Betty Elburn, Captain Vernon Elburn's wife of seventeen years, says it has been amusing for her having her husband home half the time and gone half the time. "A lot of women envy us," she says. "But I always miss him when he's gone. Thank goodness for the cell phone—he calls home most every day." Betty is Vernon's third wife. She says the life is hard on the wives. Everything always breaks down when he's gone. "The vacuum cleaner's broken now, and last time the heat went off. And we're raising a granddaughter. It sure is hard, but we're older now, so we've adjusted." And she recognizes what is the bottom-line truth for many mariners: "That is his life. It's the love of his life."

Learning the Job

Some tug officers learn on deck or in the engine room and then get promoted. But an increasing number come from one of the maritime academies and schools. One is Maine Maritime Academy.

"We try to put the students into serious skids," says Captain Tim Leach, "and then help them get out." Tim teaches Maine Maritime's Tug and Barge Operations course, held every fall for a fortunate thirty-two seniors. He compares learning to run a tug and barge to learning to handle a car on ice. If all you've ever experienced is well-sanded roads, it doesn't matter how many lectures you've heard about handling a skid. Same deal with tugboats. MMA is the first maritime college to offer practical hands-on experience with a full-size tug and barge.

In their junior year, the MMA students took either the ship handling or work-boat classes that included day-long labs on the Academy's 76-foot twin-screw tug, *Pentagoet*. There, they learned about the physics of boathandling, the effects of the wind and currents, the workings of a twin-screw system, and the impact of the boat's own manners and momentum. They've learned to hold the tug on station using the natural forces to assist, not hinder. The nearly 200-ton tug doesn't simply sit and stay when she's taken out of gear, and there's a delay time caused by the automation between pilothouse and engine. "It's all hand-eye coordination, and a lot of ranges and bearings," explains Tim.

The Tug and Barge elective is a time-hungry course, one that not all students can fit into their schedule but, even so, it's perhaps the most popular. On the spring day on which juniors can sign up for their next fall's classes, students desirous of the course camp out in front of the registrar's office, taking the demerits for skipping mandatory morning colors.

There are two seminars a week, in which the theory of towing methods and procedures and maneuvers are discussed, and then there are the labs. Every other week, eight at a time, the students spend twelve hours aboard the *Pentagoet*, practicing what they've been talking about in class. That's one of the appeals of the course. Even though perhaps few are intending to enter the tugboating world, after three years at the Academy, the students all want to get their hands on the *Pentagoet* and be in control of everything themselves. "The tug is a little small," says MMA graduate Jeff Haines, who went through the class in 1997, "but she's just complicated enough to be interesting. She has air controls, with a three-second delay on the clutch—you have to plan ahead at least a little bit. The power's not a whole lot, but it's enough to do real damage." He adds, "Tugs are just a lot of fun to drive anyway."

In 1999 K-Sea Transportation donated the 21,000-barrel barge *Cleanwater 21* to the academy, giving would-be tugboat operators the opportunity to handle a good-sized barge, heavy or light. With only eight students aboard, there's plenty of time for everyone to try everything, often more than once. "At the end of the day," says Tim, "we want them saying, 'Gee, I'm glad we're going home,' instead of feeling that they didn't have enough time."

Tim explains that it's not just handling they're learning about. "It's also life on board a small vessel." The students bring the food, prepare it, and clean up, just as they would on a working vessel.

The course starts in September, when they take advantage of the nice weather to work in Penobscot Bay towing the barge behind the tug, learning how to stream it out to the right length, how to slow it down, how to recover it and get alongside. They practice putting up a line and making up in a three-line system with a strap acting like a spring line, a bow line, and finally pulling the hawser in as a stern line to tighten it all up.

They learn about putting the boat in the notch and setting up different push-gear arrangements. They put their experience to work with piloting drills, paying attention to the tides and the set of the wind and current. "It's new to many of them to have to think about two vessels. They're concentrating on getting the tug by a buoy, and forget about the barge." Then they put the barge on the hip and turn it around—"that's a project in itself, turning," says Tim—and push it back in, in various configurations, using the radar and piloting techniques. They learn about getting on ranges to tell their course over the bottom. Particularly on the hip, they're often going in a different direction than the tug is pointing, and each setup is very different from the others.

An old unused pipeline dock in protected Stockton Springs Harbor offers a site for barge-docking practice when the weather has really gone to pieces.

The whole program is small scale, Tim says, "but real life, and dangerous." If the force of the barge is pulling 90 degrees to the centerline of the tug, it can roll the boat. They have to learn how to get out of tripping situations. "We're trying to let them get close to the edge without falling over, to experience that horror, the death grip on the throttle.

"It's hard on the poor instructor's nerves, but we get through it." It's Tim's job to show them the importance of patience, and of always looking ahead, predicting, drawing a plan of how to handle what you expect—and how to execute a different plan when things change. Captains of tugs have to be loose enough to depart from the plan when they see what's actually happening. "If you're not always trying to predict, you're not in the game." explains Tim. "We teach a lot of What Ifs, thinking ahead, and, if you get into trouble, how you're going to get out of it." A pilot, too, needs to always be thinking about the tide, the wind, the help available ashore, what other tugs are available—and then if one tug breaks down in the middle of a maneuver, you have to adjust the plan.

"We're trying to send serious professionals into the industry," Tim emphasizes, and MMA's program has been well-accepted by that industry. Tug companies are looking for graduates and are happy to take on students in co-op jobs during the summer. The trainees work on deck, which everyone agrees is an important thing for a tugboat captain to have done. "It's a dangerous place to be," says Tim. "There's a lot going on there. You don't belong in the wheelhouse if you don't understand what goes on on the deck."

Working with Pilots

Harbor tugs and pilots are inextricably entwined, regardless of the relationship between the tug company and the pilots, which varies from port to port. In fact, the whole piloting system is convoluted, with two types of pilots, state and federal, each with their own jurisdiction and set of rules. In all cases, the pilot has the local knowledge to lead a ship through a tricky passage or into port or the dock there.

Simplified, the rules state that no commercial vessel of over 1,600 gross tons may be operated in United States waters without a pilot, although the master or another crewmember on a U.S. vessel may act as pilot if he's properly licensed. Any foreign vessel, or U.S.-flagged ship headed or coming back from overseas, must have a pilot.

Vessels under 1,600 gross tons are in a peculiar limbo, with inconsistent rules. With experience on four round trips into a particular port or river, a master or mate of a coastwise vessel under 1,600 tons may take the ship in or out of that port. (If the cargo is petroleum, a dozen trips are required.) But if that same vessel in the same hands is headed overseas, then she needs a licensed pilot.

And perhaps the largest inconsistency involves tugboats sailing coastwise, which—even if they have a significant barge fully laden with cargo, even petroleum—

The tanker *World Texas* approaches Bucksport, Maine, in March 1982, with the tugs *Cape Fear* and *Patrick McAllister* to help. From the collection of Capt. Arthur Fournier.

are pretty nearly free to come and go at will. This simple fact is one reason why tugs with barges so commonly run from coastal port to coastal port in this country and tankers are so rare.

The specific systems for hiring pilots vary from one harbor to the next. For example, in Virginia's Hampton Roads, a state pilot brings a ship into Chesapeake Bay and then the ship will hire a tug company and its docking pilot for docking the ship. Historically in that area, the senior captain on the tugboats on a job was the docking pilot; he would go onto a ship's bridge and direct the tugs from there. However, it has developed over time that the pilots in that area are independent contractors, associated with one or the other of the two major ship-assist companies in the area, McAllister and Moran.

Separating the tugs and the pilots clarified liability, which is always an issue. "By tradition of pilotage, a pilot is legally hired by the ship, putting liability of any error of judgment on his part onto the shipping company, not the tugboat," explains Captain Kevin Eley, docking pilot in Hampton Roads. On the other hand, if a tug breaks down or doesn't follow the pilot's direction, then the liability is on the tug company.

In any case, the pilot is legally an advisor to the captain of the ship, who is still nominally in command. "Usually, a captain turns the conn over to the pilot and does what he's told," says Kevin, "but in a precarious situation, he's damned if he acts and damned if he doesn't. If he thinks they're getting in trouble and takes over and there's an accident, the bad situation looks like it's his fault, but if he stands by and the pilot gets in trouble, then that's just as bad." The obvious bottom line is that it's best if no one gets in trouble, and all efforts are made by all concerned to prevent that from happening. Indeed, that's why pilots are required.

"It comes down to whose insurance company pays," says Kevin. "As the old timers tell it, it used to be that if there was an accident, everyone would write an explanation of what happened, the insurance company would pay, and nothing ever went to court. Now, even a minor incident is full of lawyers."

There are seven pilots in Kevin's group, which works with McAllister and their five docking tugs. Four pilots are on call at any given time. Their on-call time might be twelve or twenty-four hours, and they're always juggling schedules. "There's no rhyme nor reason to when ships come—there'll be spurts and slow spells," Kevin observes. Sometimes one pilot can handle it all, going from job to job, sometimes it takes two or three of them, and occasionally all four. "There's no predicting how much work there'll be. The information isn't very good much more than twenty-four hours in advance."

The required notice for a job is two hours. The dispatcher in the tug company office calls the tugs on the radio and divvies up jobs to get enough tugboats to each ship. "It's a juggling match. Things can get jammed up," says Kevin. In a typical year, more than 2,500 ships leave Hampton Roads—most of these get handled twice during their visit, once coming in and once leaving.

The standard procedure is that a tug picks up the docking pilot at the pier where a ship is headed. That way he's seen the berth and knows if there's something out of the ordinary there. "I'm aware of the conditions on an hour-to-hour basis," Kevin explains. The tug takes him to the ship, and he climbs up the ladder on the side of the ship to join the group on the bridge. The state pilot tells him anything he needs to know about the vessel and what's going on—her draft, current rudder and engine orders, and any unusual handling characteristics. In Hampton Roads, the state pilot stays aboard, as there is no convenient way for him to leave the ship, but he backs out of the way, perhaps to settle in with his newspaper. (Undocking a ship in Hampton Roads, both pilots board at the pier, and when the tugs aren't needed anymore, one takes the docking pilot from the ship.)

Kevin has to size up how the ship handles in the conditions and figure out what tugs are needed. "That's the most difficult call, what is the least we can use and not get into trouble." It all comes down to money. The tug companies like having their own pilots because independent pilots have no incentive to minimize tug use.

One would think that language would be a problem, with most ships carrying foreign registration and manned by people from many nations. The ship might fly a Panamanian, Liberian or Norwegian flag, and have a Russian captain, a Greek mate, and Filipino crew (or Croatian, Korean, Indian, Pakistani . . .). Captain Bill Abbott, who has worked as a Penobscot Bay pilot for more than fifty years, says, "Piloting is the greatest job in the world. You get to experience the whole world's culture without ever leaving the bay." But Bill and other pilots agree that language usually isn't a problem.

According to David Galinas of Maine's Penobscot Bay Pilots Association, someone does always speak English, which is the official language for all ships (and aircraft). "There are only a few commands, anyway, and they're universal: left rudder, right rudder, five, ten, fifteen, ahead, astern, full or half. I've never experienced a time when they were completely unable to understand a normal command," says David.

For practical purposes, every ship in the world is run about the same. They have the same hierarchy. Every captain knows what the pilot is expecting, and every pilot has the same requirements. "It only gets complicated," David says, "when you start explaining the way the local dock is laid out, or which line to fasten first, or how to get to Staples to get the best deal on a computer."

Docking is a tricky matter, and trickier the bigger the ship is. The biggest ships in Hampton Roads are the bulk coal carriers, 1,000 feet long and 150 feet wide, and when they're loaded to sail, they draw fifty feet. Their deadweight tonnage (the carrying capacity of all cargo, fuel, and provisions) can be 150,000 tons or even 200,000. "We're at the opposite end from an airline pilot," Kevin says. The speed may not be much, but that's a lot of momentum. Approaching a pier at two or three knots can be terrifying. "The fastest thing in the world is a ship that's almost stopped," he says. (It's also said that an unmoving barge is actually faster. Depends on the viewer's job, no doubt, and in any case, the concept is similar.)

"Everything I do relies on sight, a seaman's eye," explains Kevin. "Visual references. Forward speed of the ship, sideways speed. Trying to land gently. Or if you can't land gently, land flat." If you hit with one end, you are likely to hurt both ship and pier. "You can hit hard and not do any damage, if you land flat."

And for a container pier, the expensive part isn't repairing the physical damage, it's the loss of revenue while the pier is inoperative. "You knock a crane over, and it's out of commission for six months. That's a tremendous loss, and they will seek damages.

"Everyone says if you do the job long enough, you're going to have a big accident." Kevin hasn't had his yet. "Knock on wood. I've had a few dents and dings, but I've never taken anything out of service."

Every port has its own way of doing things. Each evolved in its own way. "Portsmouth is a unique area for docking and piloting," says Captain Christopher Holt, a member of the fourth generation of Holts to work New Hampshire's Piscataqua River. "The current and the narrow channel are a challenge every time," he explains.

Three full partners and an apprentice—that's Christopher—make up Portsmouth Pilots, Inc., the company Chris will buy in when his uncle retires. He wishes he'd been able to work with his father for a while. "If I'm ever a third the pilot he is, I'll consider myself to have done a good job. Grandfather before him, and great-grandfather before him. It's quite a family legacy to live up to."

"You have to have four letters in your name to be a pilot in Portsmouth," Chris's father, Captain Shirley Holt, jokes. The one man who's not a Holt is named Cote.

On the Piscataqua River in Portsmouth, New Hampshire, the tug *Carly A. Turecamo* assists the tug *Penn No. 4* with barge *Potomac*. AUTHOR PHOTO.

Shirley admits that many people are afraid of the river, but explains his own ease: "I grew up on it. I used to row on the river—I learned to play in the eddies and currents, learned when to row and when not to row." He swam in the river, rowed on it, fished it, lobstered there. "You grow up on it, it doesn't bother you," he says.

Perhaps Christopher didn't have as much time in the river as a kid as did his father. He did run tugs in New York Harbor for several years, which many tugboaters feel is about as difficult as it gets. "I was thinking I was pretty good at what I do, but coming here to Portsmouth taught me a little humility. You have to respect the Piscataqua or it'll eat you for lunch.

"It's a tidal port," he explains. "The currents zigzag off the banks. It's all cross-currents, eddies. Inbound, we like to be approaching the berth around slack water, and you want to come through the Sarah Mildred Long Bridge with a favorable tide."

Most people, when they refer to a "favorable" tide, mean a tide going the same direction as the boat. "For me," says Christopher, "a favorable tide usually means a head tide, especially when loaded—I can take my time, use the ship's power to steer through the current. But with a loaded tanker, drawing over thirty-two feet, you have to come with a flood tide." The flood tide will be from behind as a ship goes up the river. The Long Bridge is built on an angle to the current. "You have to be aware how the current sets you, and the wind," explains Christopher. "The visual is a big deterrent—it'll shake you up a little."

When he was a student at Maine Maritime, Chris rode with his father and was impressed by the approach to the bridge. "You're going sideways till you get up close, and then you line it up and shoot it through. You might have only ten feet on either side, and the bridge abutments are of the finest New Hampshire granite. Watching, not knowing what's going on, you're sure you're not going to make it." But with thirty-eight years of service, Shirley has no tales of mishaps. "It's second nature," he says. He does admit that two or three men have come to try their hand at piloting on the river and couldn't take it. "Some people have a knack."

The port and the work there have changed in his lifetime. When Shirley's father, Chris's grandfather, first piloted in Portsmouth, the tugs were steam-driven. "Everything was small in those days, you realize. There were a lot of little small four-hatch ships coming in, and wooden coal barges. It wasn't until after the war that we got bigger ships."

"It's a unique port to be in. I'm not saying any pilot has an easy job, but this one is more of a challenge than other ports I've been in. If you do a job you haven't done before and do it reasonably well, you get a nice feeling of accomplishment," says Chris.

Sometimes conditions aren't textbook pure. Pilots and tug captains alike deal with things as they come. Captain Corliss Holland tells of running the tug *Security,* decades ago, to dock a ship in the Penobscot River, when he lost his steering. "I could turn the wheel one way. Bill Abbott had the ship. 'You get out in the middle and tie on,' he said. So I went up and threw a line on and made up to her, and we docked her with no steering." The tug provided power, and Bill managed the steering with the ship's rudder.

Captain Dan Alexander tells about the first time he saw Bill work. "I think he was just playing around." It was a quiet day, and they were taking an Irving tanker into the Bangor & Aroostook Railroad dock at Searsport. Instead of tying the tugs onto the ship on the outer side of the turn to shove the ship around, as they'd usually do, he put both tugs on the inside of the ship, no lines, pushing just enough to keep her off the dock as she made the turn into the slip. "It's my job to drive the ship, not tell you guys what to do," Bill Abbott has told Dan. Pilots should use the tugs for little corrections, he believes, or to hold the ship against the dock, and of course to turn the ship around, but they should use the ship's engines, rudders, and momentum—make full use of the ship. "Most good docking pilots are old tugboat captains anyway, and know what they can and can't do," Dan says. "They have to realize the limitations, too."

One attempted undocking that didn't go as planned demonstrates the impor-tance of leverage. It was blowing twenty or twenty-five knots, and a light tanker was tied up on the leeward side of a narrow slip-berth, preparing to back out. Her bow was protected from the wind, but her stern was fully exposed. There was one tug on the bow, and another as far aft as he could get, but because of the boat's shape, he was still a little ahead of the bridge. While the wind tried to move the ship sideways, the tugs were holding her onto the dock while the lines came in. Presumably out of concern that they might end up in the propeller, the stern lines were let go first—and the ship started swinging, pivoting from the bow and threatening to pin the after tug against the pilings on the other side of the slip. That tug was hooked up (pushing with all she had), but the stern still was coming down on him. The tug's skipper called to the pilot, "I'm full here, and if you're not gaining, I'm leaving." He was ready to cut his line before he was crushed into the pilings when the pilot ordered him to let go. "I put the boots to her," says the towboater, and he scooted out from the pinch.

"It's a leverage game," he says. From partway forward on the ship, he couldn't push enough to hold her, but he went around the stern to the windward side and told his deckhand to throw his head line up onto the after corner of the ship, snugged up tight. From there, he had the maximum mechanical advantage he could muster, and, backing full astern, he pulled on the ship with all he had. His flanking rudders let him steer his sternwash and stay straight and out of trouble, and he managed to pull the ship back into the dock. They tied her up again and waited for the wind to die.

Occasionally the pilot makes a mistake and it's only luck that determines the outcome. A young mate I'll call Charlie describes such an undocking. He says pilots may be confident and capable—or they may be cocky. This one was cocky. They were backing a ship out of a northeastern harbor—he doesn't want to identify which, not wanting to upset anyone. There was a tug at either end of the ship. Charlie was on the stern and he had let his line go. The stern tug slid along the hull as the ship backed by, so that when she got into the turning basin, both tugs would be on the bow and could push her around to head her outbound. As she was backing out, the ship lost her engines.

Anytime there's a loss of propulsion, steering, critical navigation instrumentation, or electric power, or if there's a grounding or a spill of hazardous materials, the Coast Guard must be called, and they are supposed to determine the procedure. Not this time. "The radio conversation was something," describes Charlie. "The Coast Guard said, 'Well, Cap, what do you think you can do?' He's still underway—he can't anchor—if the ship swings a certain way, he might fetch up on something. Cocky guy says 'I can take her out. I got two boats.'"

But the two tugs were only 2,000 horsepower apiece, and the ship was light and therefore offered a lot of windage, so she was a lot for them to handle. The pilot made up the other tug back by the house on the port side of the ship, on the hip, the way you would on a barge. Charlie's boat didn't fit as well under the curved chines, so they put a line onto the starboard bow. At that point they were in a deep, open basin—safe. They could have put the ship back in the dock—not easily, but they could have done it. Or they could have gotten her into another dock. "Or we could have held her there—with two tugs you can keep it sitting there, wait for someone to come, get another tug to help. To go out to the anchorage, in the dredged navigation channel, it's limited what you can do. But we were bringing her out.

"The boat on the port side started easy. A little more, a little more, is this gonna work, or not?" The disabled ship had to be at enough speed for her own rudder to be effective—but the more speed she made, the harder it would be for the tug on the bow to get out at an angle where she could push the ship around. The ship herself would have had ten or fifteen thousand horsepower to call on and would have been making nine or ten knots coming out, but the tugs had only four thousand between them. And there was a crosscurrent at the last turn.

They got the ship up to four knots headway. Charlie's boat was pushing full on the bow, trying to push it around but starting to roll as the ship pulled her sideways, and the tug on the port quarter was backing full. The ship's rudder was hard to port. The turn was coming right up on them, and it wasn't at all clear that the ship would come around.

"The pilot was scared, you could tell in his voice on the radio. He didn't think we were gonna make the last turn. He even said that on the radio, which maybe wasn't the smartest thing." There's always the issue of liability on everyone's mind.

If the ship didn't make the turn, probably her grounding would be relatively harmless, as groundings go. She would make a soft landing on the mud alongside the dredged channel. But it would be considered a major grounding, and it would turn into a salvage operation, if only for legal and liability reasons. And if she was holed and was dumping bunker C into the flats, "then everyone would go after the pilot, and after the captain of the ship. Foreign crews, language barriers—all that would come up in court, and it would all come down to how good the lawyers were." But luck was on the side of the pilot. They made it out of the channel and into the anchorage.

The instructions a pilot gives to the tugs under his control must be clear, and they very nearly always are. Captain John O'Reilly holds pilot's credentials for ports and connective routes from New Jersey to Rhode Island plus Portland, Maine, and he tells a story of one serious miscommunication. A good friend of his was chief engineer on an assist tug, moving a dead ship from anchorage to a berth in New York Harbor. There were four tugs altogether, two on the bows and two on the quarters. The docking pilot was on the bridge of the ship. There was a man on the bow, who heard the clear order on the radio: "Drop the anchor!" Assuming there was some kind of crisis, he let go of the brakewheel and dropped the anchor—right down through a tugboat, which sank on the spot. The men on deck got off, but the engineer, below, went down with her. It happened that another ship maneuver had been using the same radio frequency, and the order was for that vessel.

How does one become a pilot? An Unlimited Master Mariner in the fourth five-year renewal of his license, Captain O'Reilly says he's spent three months in examiners' rooms getting pilotage credentials.

Perhaps surprisingly, a person who would like to be a pilot need not have any other ticket, not even a seaman's document or a junior license. To be sure, in order to qualify for a federal piloting license, a candidate must show knowledge of regulations and ship-handling techniques and rules of the road, and, according to John, "the test will be a back-breaker" for the previously unlicensed applicant. He must also demonstrate the local knowledge needed to dock a vessel, and he must have made the requisite number of trips in and out of the particular harbor. The number of trips depends on what other experience he has. A newcomer or a junior officer with no previous pilotage has to have made fifty round trips before he can sit for his license, while a Master or a person with a first-class pilot ticket elsewhere needs only a dozen. A person with more experience is assumed to know what effect a certain sea bottom will have on a ship, for instance. But all candidates have to have made at least one trip within the last five years—things change—and they also must draw, from memory, the chart of the waters in question.

The would-be pilot may bring with him to the test a tracing of the chart with the outline of the landmass, a North arrow and scale. Bridges may also be on the drawing—the idea is that anything you can identify on radar is fair. The inspector checks the paper for extra marks or pinholes that might give unauthorized assistance, and then the candidate fills in the rest. John lists what may be included:

Courses, distances, channel widths, channel depths, buoys, beacons, day-marks, ranges (in some cases both natural and man made), anchorages, pipeline areas, cable areas, geographic names, arcs of visibility, vertical and horizontal bridge clearances, any lines of demarcation, the vertical clearances of overhead cable and pipeline crossings, magnetic variation, and blue water outline (blue color on the chart normally indicates the three-fathom curve, but that varies on some charts).

In short, "Anything that is on the chart is fair game. Most testers like to see general depths or a depth where every buoy is. The depths are the only thing that need not be repeated in the quantity they are represented on the chart.

"Believe me," he adds after enumerating this list, "I know I have forgotten something." And that's just how you feel when you are getting ready to hand the test in.

The test grader takes the completed drawing and overlays it on a real chart. His judgment can be subjective, pilots say. The rules say simply "sketch" and "convey knowledge of the area," but O'Reilly knows of one person who was failed because he used the wrong color pencil. Personally, John makes every effort to make his drawing look like a photocopy of the official chart.

"I have a friend, a northeastern pilot, who's the most irritating man. He gets in the car with the chart, and he can memorize it while his wife drives him to the test." It takes John between two and four weeks to prepare, and he may draw the chart two or three times for practice. He memorizes the positions for everything by ranges and distances from prominent points on the tracing.

Even that is boggling to a neophyte.

2
The Business
Side of Tugboating

Tugboating is a business, like any other. Certainly some of the people involved in it love it—love the boats or the jobs they do or simply the adventure of the sea—but the fact is, by far the greatest number of them are in the business to make a living. Historically, a good living could be made in tugs, whether by owning them or running them or simply working on deck. Many companies over the years were started by a single guy with a boat—or, in the case of McAllister Towing, one of the bigger American companies today, by James McAllister with a boat and a horse during the Civil War. It was a rowboat that gave the huge West Coast company, Foss Maritime, its start. Today, most companies have multiple vessels, if not multiple offices in multiple ports around the country. "The office" is a place all captains are very familiar with; in this day of cell phones and super-radios, they check in there regularly, to keep management informed as to their status or to report issues with boat or personnel or job, or to request parts or materiel needed by their vessel.

Within the office are the usual staff people to be found in any business—managers, secretaries, marketers, bookkeepers, computer and web site gurus, and so on. Many of these people have moved ashore from the boats, enjoying regular hours and desks that stay put, and others look at the job as simply work, just as if it were in an insurance company or widget manufactory. In the bigger outfits there are also specialists: people with mechanical expertise, people who develop new technology for the boats, people who work on regulatory matters, and people to handle legal issues that sometimes come up.

An essential part of any tugboat office, the person on the spot for day-to-day operations, is the dispatcher.

"Dispatching was fun for me," says Dave Boone, who for twenty-two years was responsible for sending Curtis Bay Towing Company tugs to work in Philadelphia. "I couldn't wait to get to work." In the 1970s and '80s, Philadelphia was a busy port, with fifteen or twenty ships a day. "Every day, a new set of ships, circumstances always changing. You were responsible for a lot. It was always a challenge."

Ships were handled by contract, and the agents would let the company know a day in advance when a ship was expected to come in, where she was to dock, and how long she was going to be at the pier. It was the dispatcher's job to assign tugs to each job, jockeying ships around to fit and modifying the plan whenever anything changed, for instance, when a ship broke down and was late. "I'd begin the day with Plan A and see what plan we'd get down to before the day was over," Dave recalls. He had worked on the tugs and knew how things actually worked on the water, so there was mutual respect between dispatcher and the guys on the boats.

There were 150 different places to dock on the Delaware River, and Dave had to know each one, what cargoes it handled, how the tides and currents affected it, when it could and when it couldn't handle a ship. The sugar ships, for instance, could only go into the piers at certain tides, and tankers had to dock on a rising tide. Timing of dockings and undockings had to take all that into account, as well as the availability of tugs. Once in a while an odd consideration had to be made, such as when a containership captain insisted that his vessel be docked by the *Reedy Point*. No other tug would do. "What if she's out on a job already?" Dave asked him. "Doesn't matter, I've got to have the *Reedy Point!*"

Union rules came into the equation, too. Tugboat crews were paid by the hour, then—it's by the day, now—and it was the dispatcher's job to schedule the boats so the crews didn't go into overtime and triple time. "It was like a game of chess, making moves and planning them. It took a pretty sharp individual who could think on his feet." Every boat had to tie up for eight hours each day too, to rest the crews. Sometimes Dave would work "swaps" with the other companies. If he had two tugs waiting for a job at 2000 hours, he would ask the dispatchers at the other docking companies if they had any late work. If one had a job at, say, 2200, and agreed to swap, Dave could tie up one of his tugs and the other dispatcher could tie up one of his, and they'd share both jobs, saving overtime hours for both companies. "Some nights you would have three or four swaps working with all the companies! Ask a dispatcher today what a swap is, and he'll look at you funny. Rookies!"

Dave says it takes five years of dispatching to run into most of the situations you might confront and all the various weather conditions. "My first five years, if something ever went wrong, it was on my watch. If it blew up, sank, or ran aground, it was when I was on." There were, in fact, two explosions, one from a collision and another a discharge mishap. And for a long time, he was the only dispatcher in the company who actually lost a tug on his watch.

It was Election Day, 1975, a harbor tug holiday but business as usual for everyone else. A ship launching was scheduled for the early afternoon. Dave was the only guy in the office, and he was listening to the VHF radio as they positioned tugs where they wanted them for the launch.

Dave heard the pilot explain about the drag chains on the starboard side of the ship, which were to slow her up and prevent her from shooting across the river and going aground after she splashed. He told the tugs to stay away until the chains were dropped, and then come into position. The *Sewells Point* was to be on the port quarter of the new ship. "Get two lines up as soon's you can," the pilot said to Vince, the captain of the *Sewells Point*.

"OK."

Then came the call on the radio that everyone was waiting for: "Here she comes!"

The next thing Dave heard was from George, the pilot. "You all right over there, Vince?"

The ship was afloat and coming quicker than they expected. There was no answer from Vince. "She's coming around awful fast, George," said one of the other tug masters.

"I can see that," said George. The ship was turning. The drag chains stopped the stern, but the bow was still traveling. "It's like a dog on a leash," explains Dave. "You yank on the leash, the head comes to you but the body whips around." On the ship, the bow whipped around.

Sewells Point. COURTESY OF DAVE BOONE.

"Uh oh. We got a problem with the *Sewell*," someone said.

The tug on the starboard bow could get out of the way, but the *Sewells Point* had no place to go. The ship hit her broadside, hard, and she fell onto her side, halfway submerged. The little yard tug on hand to pick up the dunnage after the launch was able to pull alongside the *Sewell* and get the crew off. They were taken to the hospital because they'd inhaled some water and oil and quickly gotten chilled in the November water, but fortunately there was no serious injury and all were released.

The lawsuits started. The shipyard sued the towing company because the *Sewell* put a dent in their ship. Curtis Bay prevailed with the argument that the yard's ship had struck their tug, not the other way around. The tug was doing just what it was supposed to be doing; it was the yard's engineering of the launch that screwed up. The towing company was paid for the tug, which they sold for a dollar to a local salvage company "as is, where is." The salvors raised her, repowered her, and sold her on. Now named the *Fort McHenry*, she's working out of Mobile, Alabama.

While he was at Curtis Bay, Dave was one of three dispatchers. The rest of the staff consisted of an operations manager in the office and a night watchman on the pier. Between them, these five men covered every hour of every week. At night, whichever dispatcher was covering could work from home. The watchman could handle things on site. The dispatchers' jobs were treasured—nobody ever left one of those positions save by retiring or dying. With eighteen years in the job, Dave was still the junior dispatcher. In 1992, he became the operations manager, but the world was different by then, he says. After the Philadelphia strike in 1987, a year before New York's union-breaking lockout, the boats no longer had the same dedicated crews they used to. "The companies had replacement crews waiting, ready to go. It took the wind out of the strike. The union had no bargaining power, and went off with their tails between their legs." There were no more holidays or triple time; crews were paid by the day. The companies said, "Enjoy it or find other things to do," and a lot of the old crews did just that. "It changed the industry forever," Dave says. "It ceased to be fun anymore, for everybody."

And by then dispatchers were different, too. The people Dave had worked with had retired or left the business, and the new guys just didn't seem to care as much. The industry had changed in other ways as well, with new regulations and requirements. Dave didn't feel that equipment was being kept in as good condition either— ironic, considering all the burdensome new governmental rules. "There was no pride anymore, it was just a job," Dave says. He didn't stay much longer. But he had loved every minute of his days dispatching.

Not all offices are as big as the one Dave worked in. Smaller companies continue with fewer employees and less formal ways.

Arthur Fournier, who has made his living in tugs since he was a young man, has for years had an unusual situation: his dispatcher stays in Belfast, Maine, while he and his towing companies move around.

In 1982, when Arthur was running the Penobscot Bay Towing Company in Belfast, he hired a young woman named Jolene Abbott to do his paperwork. He ran the boats, and she ran everything else. From an old building on the wharf, she dispatched the boats and handled all the paperwork for the company, using a manual typewriter, a copying machine that used special paper, and no computer at all.

When Arthur sold the Belfast business and moved to Portland, he asked Jolene if she would move down there with him. No, she wouldn't. But she would continue to run the office from Belfast, and that she has done, in an only slightly more upscale location. Fortunately, cell phones came in just about the time he made the move to Portland. Arthur's endeavors grew—he started Portland Docking Masters and bought a little railroad in Cleveland—and still Jolene ran the businesses. She and her assistant, Sheila Dassat, were in communication with Arthur constantly through the day; they faxed information back and forth and talked on the phone, but the only listed number for Portland Tugboat & Shipdocking Company was Jolene's office in Belfast, two hours up the coast from Portland. There was no sign on the door, so no one who didn't know Arthur and his company would ever stumble into his office.

A contract for three years of Jolene and Sheila's time went with the deal when Arthur sold the Portland tugs to McAllister, which formed Portland Tugboat LLC, with Arthur's son Brian as president. Arthur still owned Portland Docking Masters, and couldn't stay out of tugs for long—he bought a few boats and started working at the Cape Cod Canal. Jolene now dispatches for McAllister's Portland operation as well as for Arthur's Docking Masters and Canal Towing and Assist. She also does various bookkeeping jobs for McAllister, the railroad, the docking masters, and for the canal company. She talks to Arthur twenty-five or thirty times a day by phone, and only ten or fifteen times to Brian. "He isn't so vocal," she says. "It's nice when they're both on jobs, like they are right now," she added, savoring a moment of peace and quiet. She certainly has a lot to do, in between phone calls.

One Tugboater's Story

Many tug companies have been built up by rough-and-ready entrepreneurs, one man of little means with a single boat. Captain Arthur Fournier is only one of the more recent men of this stripe to build considerable personal success in the field. On December 21, 2001, he sold seven tugs with over 27,000 horsepower between them, and all the equipment and assets of his Portland Tugboat and Ship Docking Company, to McAllister Towing. "That includes this luxurious office complex," said Arthur of the cluttered, paper-filled barge that served as his operating office in the Maine harbor for the previous ten years. His son Brian says Arthur sold him with the company—part of the deal was that for a number of years, Brian would be president of the company McAllister formed to run the operation, Portland Tugboat LLC.

When I first spoke with Arthur, the sale was not quite finalized. He was eating his lunch at a desk that looked as if it hadn't been cleared in many years. Lunch was Honey Nut Cheerios, raspberry-flavored chocolate, and mineral water. His phone rang several times, and he always answered it with a fast, loud "Yeah!" and quickly dealt with the business at hand.

Several times people came in to update Arthur on the status of the electrical system or hydraulics in one tug or another or to report on the weather—a job was awaiting the fog to lift. "We haven't got scale enough to do it," Arthur said, referring to the low visibility. Once he sent a young man off to the photo store to pick up pictures of the 3,000-horse Z-drive tug he was getting as part of the deal. Always there was a brisk jocularity in the communications between the men, and always Arthur picked up his narration where he'd left off, running down his career since its beginning. Each of the many segments of the story he documented clearly with dates and the names of people or vessels involved (in depth or cursorily), and he illustrated it all with suitable photos, some posted on the wall, others pulled from a corner or a file. He rummaged in the front pocket of his baggy corduroy trousers for something one time, moving a pistol from that side to the other. "Never leave home without it," he said in passing, and his own tale demonstrates that on at least one occasion, he was right to follow that philosophy.

Arthur likes the phrase "horsepower in the wheelhouse," which he attributes to an old Boston towboater. It sums up his approach to towboating: it's not just the hardware that's important in tugs.

Fournier's career started in 1947, when he worked as a deckhand on coal barges for the Sheridan Transportation Company, of Philadelphia. He came up through the ranks through one venture after another, and today, a wealthy man, he remains the senior docking pilot in Portland Harbor while he embarks on various other projects.

At fifteen, he was on the 385-foot barge *Blanche Sheridan*. They'd loaded coal in Norfolk, Virginia, taken it to Chelsea, Massachusetts, gone to the nearby shoe-manufacturing city of Lynn to pick up a load of leather (piled as high as the sky,

Arthur says), and taken it to Norfolk. There they loaded the barge with fertilizer for Havana, Cuba, which is where he spent his sixteenth birthday. In Cuba they took on tobacco leaf for Richmond, Virginia. "That's how it was, then," he says. You might carry anything anywhere.

Along the way on this trip, Arthur was promoted to donkeyman, the middle-ranked of three men on the barge: captain, donkeyman, deckhand. Under way, they steered the barge; many of these barges were simply old sailing vessels, their masts removed. As donkeyman, Arthur's job was to build steam up on the barge's donkey engine, which hauled the anchor, pulled in the hawser and did anything else that required force. He was still sixteen when he moved onto the tugs but, whenever a crewman for the barge was drunk, didn't show up for work, or was fired, Arthur, as an agile young man, was sent back to the barge.

The one detail Arthur didn't remember is the date of the terrible weather that beset them on their way to Searsport with two barges of coal in the spring or fall of 1948. "There was no gyrocompass then, no radios. There wasn't shit," he explains. They'd run from Norfolk to Providence to Boston, dropped barges off there and picked up the *Blanche* and the *Rockhaven*. The old *D.T. Sheridan* was towing the two barges behind, in tandem, and Arthur was on the *Blanche*. "The weather was twenty-five to thirty-five knots from the south-southeast. Horrible. The barge captains that weren't drunks knew where we were just's good as the captain of the tug did, even though they were just following." He lists off the buoys from Boston to Monhegan. "When we got to Monhegan, it was daylight but we couldn't see the barge behind us. The *D.T.* was the most powerful boat they had—1,200 horsepower—the pride and joy of Dan Sheridan, who owned the company. We were listening for Monhegan—the fog signal is actually on Manana island, a half or quarter mile west of the light on Monhegan.

"All of a sudden, the *D.T.* is blowing the danger signal: *blat blat blat blat blat*. The captain says to me, 'Go forward and let go the anchor,' and the *Rockhaven* let his anchor go the same time. And there's the *D.T.* broached sideways on the beach. We ran headfirst onto the beach but didn't turn sideways—our bow was on the beach and our stern in 75 feet of water, and the *Rockhaven* was in 140 feet. His anchor down kept us from swinging sideways." They put their dory overboard and got the guys from the tug and brought them back to the *Blanche,* and the lighthouse keeper on Mon-hegan notified the Coast Guard.

"The *D.T. Sheridan* was a total loss within a week. I couldn't believe it," Arthur concludes, listing what tug came from where to take the two barges to which ports and how soon. If there's anything the man has forgotten, it probably doesn't matter to anyone.

Arthur's first tug of his own was the *St. Theresa*, a forty-five-foot wooden boat that had been sunk for a couple of years when he got her. He was nineteen years old. He raised her, took her behind his mother's house in Somerville, Massachusetts and rebuilt her. He installed the engine from a wrecked Greyhound bus, and his father borrowed $500 against his life insurance to buy a marine transmission for the boat.

Arthur attributes his education to Daniel J. Boylan, a self-made man who owned Boston Sand and Gravel Company as well as a couple of dredging companies and two shipyards. Mr. Boylan hired the *St. Theresa* to tow sand scows from the mouth of the Charles River. To have a regular job "and not be kicking doors looking for work" made all the difference in starting out, Arthur says. Working for Mr. Boylan, he had the opportunity to run cranes and backhoes and front-end loaders, as well as to work his tug, and he learned about running a marine contracting business, too. The job only lasted a short time—Mr. Boylan died before four years were out—but Arthur asserts

The *D.T. Sheridan* soon after grounding on Monhegan. COURTESY OF ARTHUR FOURNIER.

The *D.T. Sheridan* a week after her grounding. COURTESY OF ARTHUR FOURNIER.

that in that time he learned as much as he would have in four years in a maritime academy and three at Harvard Business School.

Hurricane Carol hit during the time he was working for Mr. Boylan. Even though the local weatherman was predicting winds of less than 50 knots, they'd reached all of that as Arthur drove back from Fairhaven, Massachusetts, where he'd put extra lines on a tug in Mr. Boylan's shipyard there. Arthur has written up the tale: "As I drove across the Mass. Ave. Bridge to Cambridge, at approximately 11 a.m., the winds suddenly veered to the northeast, gusting over 80 knots. The Charles River instantly had a five foot northeast swell from the old Charles River locks to the Mass. Ave. Bridge and beyond."

Driving along the Mystic River in Somerville, he saw that his *St. Theresa* had dragged her mooring a quarter of a mile and was only three hundred yards from the sea wall. His skiff swamped immediately after he launched it, so he swam to the tug—five-eighths of a mile with the wind and tide taking him up the river at three knots. "As I swam alongside of the *St. Theresa,* I grabbed one of her tires and swung myself aboard. I entered the engine room through the rear hatch and went below. The wind was screeching, the rain was coming in torrents, and the inside of the engine room was soaked. I gave her Gray Marine 6-71 diesel a shot of ether, crossed my fingers, said a little prayer, and hit the starter button. The engine fired immediately and I ran to the pilothouse. I opened the pilothouse door and it smashed back, breaking the window."

He ran the tug up on her mooring but couldn't get slack enough to free the mooring wire off the bitts. "She kept falling off before the wind. I finally had to cut the cable with an ax, while leaving the engine in gear. By this time the *St. Theresa* had closed to within 100 feet of the riprap on Mystic Avenue in front of the Minute Man Car Wash. The seas in the river were breaking over the *St. Theresa* from bow to stern."

With the wind at 100 knots, five- to six-foot seas in the river, and no visibility, he tucked the tug into a slight lee behind the Wellington Bridge. "At about one p.m., the wind without warning veered to the south and was gusting over 140 knots." A friend of his came aboard, leaving his car on the bridge, where the hood blew off and flew over the tug, into the bridge pile, and overboard. A second friend showed up a little later. "As he came aboard, he slipped and fell and hollered, 'There's something running down my leg. I hope it's blood.' No such luck for Ray—it was his half pint of Seagram Seven that had broken in his hip pocket."

Before it blew off, the anemometer at the Blue Hills Observatory in Milton, Massachusetts, showed the wind gusting to 165 knots.

By three-thirty, the wind was dropping and had backed to the west. "We left the bridge and sailed up to the Winter Hill Yacht Club. Every boat that was moored there was sunk or thrown up on the marsh or had beat itself to death on the riprap on Mystic Avenue. We were able to help re-float about six of the stranded boats but those that hit the sea wall were turned to kindling wood in a heartbeat.

"All my life I wondered what I would have done or how my life would have changed if I lost the *St. Theresa* to Hurricane Carol. In 1954 I didn't have a penny to my name. Everything I owned or hoped to own in the future was in the *St. Theresa*."

During the few years that Arthur worked for Mr. Boylan, he made more than 1,500 trips with sand scows to the sand plant in the Lechmere Canal, which has been filled in long since. "As I towed back and forth with the two loaded sand scows up the river, through five narrow bridges each way, often I would see Mr. Boylan parked in his car, watching. One Saturday morning at his 0700 staff meeting, he looked over at me and said with a smile, 'You've done a great job these last six months, Captain Arthur. I have great confidence in you and the *St. Theresa*. You've hit everything except the Registry of Motor Vehicles—keep up the good work!' He got a great laugh from the guys. I just said, 'Thank you, Mr. Boylan,' and was happy to run outside and load a truck."

The term "sand man" has nearly disappeared from the tugging lexicon, but as long as Arthur's around, it will have meaning. It describes a particular type of tugboater during his early career, and he was one. "Highly skilled in close quarters, scow and barge handling, we plied the rivers, creeks and canals of major cities with small 150-horsepower tugs, always towing astern sand and gravel scows, unassisted." Only a few years ago—five or six or eight, he says—he was on the tug *Amy Moran* as bridge pilot, taking her and a coal barge through the Million-Dollar Bridge in Portland, Maine. He had an hour to kill while on the boat and headed for the galley, where he found the crew sitting around talking about old times. It turned out that they were all old sandmen from the Bronx. "Shit, *I* was working down there then," he said to the men.

But they didn't remember him. "What was the name of your company?"

"Coney Island Tugboat Company, from Coney Island Creek."

They said they'd been in and out of there every day, but didn't remember him, and they didn't remember the *Peggy*, his boat, either.

Arthur had often brought barges from well up the creek out to the deeper water where bigger boats could pick them up. "You think the good fairy brought all those barges out to the wall for you?" he asked them.

"What color was your boat?"

"Blue and yellow," he said, and suddenly they remembered.

"Holy shit! You're the guy with a dog for a deckhand!"

Arthur says he couldn't afford a deckhand in those days, and talks about crawling along the hawser to get from the tug to the barge as if it was an everyday matter. Someone had to do it, and perhaps the dog wouldn't.

That was during the early 1960s. He'd expanded into dredging around New England and had gone through what he calls an involuntary bankruptcy because he didn't know his way around the court system yet. He'd then gone to work for someone on the Miami River, taking small freighters up through ten bridges in Miami, Florida. He stayed for only six months—he describes the operation as one "destined to become insolvent." After the company didn't take his suggestion to buy the *Peggy*, a steel tug that he said could replace three of the old wooden "shit boxes" they were running, he bought the tug himself for $7,500 down and $8,000 owed. He took it north with a barge headed to Syracuse. On his way back out through the locks at Buffalo he ran into Bob Cohen, a barge broker he knew, who asked him where he was headed. "To Boston to starve," Arthur replied.

"Why don't you take this barge to Jones Beach," Mr. Cohen asked. "You can starve there." But Arthur didn't starve there on Long Island. After one foggy night's layover, he hooked up with a fellow working on jetties who offered him $1,500 a week to move stone and crane barges. On weekends he went into the city, where he found Coney Island Creek with no small tug serving it. He saw the opportunity, grabbed it, and started Coney Island Tugboat Company on New Year's Day of 1961.

By the spring of 1964, the business had expanded. "I was the only non-union tug in New York Harbor, and the union didn't like that I should be so successful," Arthur says. He'd tie up his tug under the Cropsey Avenue Bridge at Coney Island Creek and climb up through a manhole to the streetcar lane overhead. "That's why the union never found my boat," he says.

One time, after he'd moved a brand-new barge with a load of sand, Joe O'Hare, the president of the union, called the owner of the barge. "You got any welders and burners?" O'Hare asked. "Send two of them right now to start cutting up that new barge," he advised. "The *Peggywhore* moved it, and never again will any of us touch it."

It was time for Arthur to leave New York. For the next ten years he was back in Boston, starting with a contract to move and burn construction debris for building and demolition contractors. He took the ashes to Spectacle Island, which he had bought. The island had been the city dump, and the ashes he dumped were just covering sixty years' worth of garbage. "There were subterranean fires there for ten or twenty years," he says of Spectacle, "and I finally extinguished them."

In the winter of 1972, Arthur was ambushed by three gunmen in his office underneath the Mystic River Bridge. He was shot twelve times, and himself got four shots into one of the intruders. Ironically, he and his assailant ended up in adjacent rooms at Massachusetts General Hospital. Arthur still claims to have no idea of the reason for the attack (someone told me it was a dispute "over some obscure point of ethics"). By this time he knew the right people to know in Boston, and got twenty-four-hour protection. But he didn't identify anyone to the police, and his hospital neighbor claimed that three guys had jumped *him* as he got out of his car. The two kept running into one another in physical therapy and, in fact, Arthur eventually gave the other man a ride home. "How could you ever?!" his mother demanded to know, and for the rest of her life—another fifteen years—she never let him forget about it. Arthur says the escapade is known as "the great shootout at Pier 50."

His life seems never to have been simple, particularly in his home port of Boston. The rubbish business was going well for Arthur when Captain Adams, the captain of the port, stopped by. He was in one car, and there were two more cars behind his. "Well, Mr. Fournier, you've been here almost a year now, and you've done better than I thought you would. I expected you to burn the city down." After a little more chat, he called his support troops, and ordered Arthur to close his burn yard on Spectacle Island immediately.

"After two years of brutal attack every time I turned around," Arthur says, "one day my wife told me she'd heard that a tugboat captain had been indicted by the grand jury.

"'Oh? Who?'

"'You,' she said.

"They came to my house and arrested me, cuffed me and took me away, charging me with the deliberate attempt to sabotage the port of Boston."

When the case came to court, Adams testified that on a particular date, Arthur brought a barge into the harbor, fully ablaze. For forty-five minutes, he listed the entities from Gloucester to the Cape Cod Canal that Arthur had endangered.

"Then it was our turn," says Arthur. His lawyer showed a picture of a barge passing under the Mystic River Bridge.

"Oh, but it wasn't like that," Captain Adams said. "There wasn't just a little smoke coming out like that, it was full ablaze."

"And did it endanger the bridge?"

"Yes! Yes, it did," Adams said, grateful that Arthur was adding to his own charge. "It put the bridge in jeopardy and could have killed all the people on the bridge. Oh, it was terrible!"

"And as you were standing there looking at it, did you find it necessary to call in a fire alarm?"

Well, no, he hadn't. . . .

The judge dismissed the case immediately.

Arthur had moved into salvage work by the 1970s, and in 1976 he got the job of refloating the *Musashino Maru* off Searsport, Maine. It was a reefer ship that had come in to pick up a load of frozen potatoes and been blown ashore in a sudden gale. Penobscot Bay pilot Bill Abbott remembers Arthur's first trip into the area: "He wanted a pilot. I wondered why. All he had was two old barges—he didn't have to have a pilot. But what he wanted was information. He pumped me all the way up the bay, and when we got there, he asked me 'How much?' and he paid me in cash."

Arthur had called on a couple of local companies to provide assistance on the *Musashino Maru* project, and early in May 1977 the owner of one of those companies, Clyde Holmes from Belfast, called and offered his Eastern Maine Towage for sale. "There he was, dealing like a Scollay Square hooker," says Arthur. Turned out his employees had struck. Arthur paid for the assets of the company, including $1,000 for the phone number, and that was the end of Eastern Maine Towage. On advice of labor lawyers, Arthur immediately took the Holmes tugs to Rockland and put two of his own tugs in place in Belfast, starting the Penobscot Bay Towing Company. At first, the local pilots weren't sure they could operate with just the two tugs, being accustomed to having more at their disposal, but the horsepower was much greater on the Fournier tugs, and soon they were content to work with him.

Captain Jim Sharp, a schooner captain during the summer months, went to work for the Penobscot Bay Towing Company in the off season. Not everyone could get along with Arthur, Jim says. "With Arthur, you never had any crew. Sometimes he'd get a kid, and then he would raise hell with him and then he would quit or he would fire him." But Jim worked for Arthur for eight winters. In part, he attributes their getting along to his own age, but the two men had more than age in common. "He always kept his expenses down to a minimum," says Jim, himself known for being careful with his money. He laughs about the rations on one of Arthur's boats. "Many's the time I've taken a tug out, taken a tow or something to do, and he's said it was all provisioned and ready to go. Then you get down in the galley, and nothing's there but Ritz crackers and a jar of peanut butter. That's the way Arthur ran 'em—on a shoestring."

But it is clear that Arthur respected Jim, who prided himself on taking care of the equipment under his management. Running the tug *Pauline* under the stern of a ship on one job, Jim bent the pipe bow rail. The next day, he brought his toolbox and started straightening the rail. "What the hell are you doing up there?" Arthur hollered.

Seeing what his employee was up to changed Arthur's attitude toward him, Jim says. "He was explosive, and he was always blaming someone else for anything that went wrong. 'How did that wheel get bent on that boat? How did that ladder get broken? How did this happen—how did that happen?' he'd holler. 'I know Jim Sharp didn't do it, because he'd have been here the next day fixing it, if he did.'"

When there was a shortage of crew, Jim says, Arthur just did for himself, same as he had done through his entire career. "Sometimes he'd get one boat started, then we would tie the two boats together, and he would start the second boat while we were going out. He never gave 'em time enough to warm up. Oh, he couldn't be bothered with that. So it was always tenuous whether they would start or not, because they were all sooted up from running cold. But by the time we got to the ship, they'd be warmed up enough to use them."

"We went through an awful lot of tugs," Jim recalls. "I ran twelve different tugs working for Arthur. God, what that man taught me. I like to think I learned in spite of Arthur's language. You could tell what kind of a day he was having by the language—on a good day, every other word was a swear word, but on a bad day, it was just a slobber of profanity. But he had a way of putting things that you remembered them." And Jim enjoyed the variety of tugs he ran for Arthur: "I ran bell boats, old converted steam boats, direct-reversing boats like the *Mary Holmes*."

Running a Direct-Reversing Boat

Of all the tugs Captain Jim Sharp ran for Arthur Fournier, the one he enjoyed most was the old *Mary Holmes*. "That was the hardest boat in the fleet to run. Arthur gave her to me, and thank God he did, because I loved it." She was a pilothouse-controlled direct-reversing boat, which meant the captain did everything himself and didn't rely on the engineer. But it wasn't like a modern boat with gears—or controllable-pitch

Mary E. Holmes.
COURTESY OF STEVEN LANG.

propellers—to change direction. The engine actually had to turn in the opposite direction.

Jim describes the pilothouse controls: "You'd have a wheel, of course, and there was another lever for your throttle. And there was another great wheel, all polished brass like the old days, with a pointer-handle on it. That wheel was marked Stop at twelve o'clock, Start Air Forward at eight, Forward at ten, and Reverse at two, and Start Air Reverse at four o'clock.

"It was like patting your head and rubbing your belly, because you'd turn the handle on the brass wheel around to inject the air to start that engine, and when you heard the air get her rolling, you had to tickle the throttle ahead a little bit so she'd take. Then you'd move the lever back to the run position and make sure she kept going. Meanwhile her propeller's turning and she's jumping ahead, so you're trying to turn the wheel in the direction you want to go, but you have to stop her before the hawser takes up or you run into the ship or whatever it is you're doing. So you return the handle to straight up until you hear the engine stop, and then move the thing back to the Reverse Start Air position, give her a tickle on the throttle and hear her start in reverse, and move the handle to Run again. By then she's probably backing more than you want, so you go back to Stop and repeat the process for Forward again. All this while you're trying to spin the wheel to steer her. You needed three arms to do it. Ship-docking, you were as busy as a monkey falling out of a tree. And in the middle of all that, somebody would call on the radio or you would have to pull the whistle to answer the pilot.

"All these things to do in that boat—it was more fun! But any modern towboater wouldn't enter that pilothouse. They've got lever steering now. They've got these little controls that run everything. You can go from full ahead to full astern without hesitation, no problem. Arthur had some of those boats. They're good, but nowhere near as much fun to run."

The Balance of Power

In any given harbor, there's only so much work for tugs, and there's an equilibrium. It makes no sense for a company to come into a market that already has all the boats needed—unless the owner intends to chase other boats out. And that happens from time to time in harbors of all sizes. In a place with higher traffic and more than one towing company, rates are kept in line by the competition, but people who would like to come in keep their eyes out for a particular niche they might fit into, hoping to expand from there. Overhead, by necessity, must be kept low in a one-company port; a small port can only charge a certain amount or someone else will come in, under-cutting their fees, and drive them out.

While Fournier was working out of Belfast, he became a docking pilot on the Kennebec River, where Bath Iron Works had a yard full of ships under construction—a piloting contract worth $300,000 a year. Moving a couple of tugs there so he could provide BIW with towing service as well upped his earnings by another million dol-lars annually.

Before long he expanded into Portland, where he saw more opportunities with the then-new BIW drydock. Moran had tugs there at the time, but within a few years, Moran had abandoned Portland. "I took over part of their crew and one tug. That reads pretty well, and is pretty close to the truth," he told me. To his son, who hap-pened by the office as he had finished telling the story, he said, "You'd never know the true story, judging by how low I told it."

"Just as well," said Brian. (But hang on; there's more to the story.)

For more than fifty years, up into the late 1980s, Moran Towing provided tug services in Portland, Maine. Portland was a busy port, although smaller than others Moran worked, and they were the people to call for ship handling. When traffic dropped off in the middle of the decade, Moran raised their rates significantly—that's the only way they could cover their overhead—and in response, shipping agents in Portland contacted Arthur Fournier, who had tugs in Belfast and Bath at the time. He moved a couple of tugs into Casco Bay, announced rates lower than Moran's, and, by docking the *Mando V* on August 15, 1985, started the war.

"Arthur was willing to lose money for a long time," says John Worth, who ulti-mately bought Fournier's Belfast business. "He didn't care if he had to live in a shack until it was all over. Moran never got that. They're a regular company, with the union, and mortgages to pay, and their people did care where they lived." Being a "regular" company with plenty of productive work elsewhere, Moran eventually saw no need to hang on in a port that represented a small part of their business and a smaller part of their profit.

Nevertheless, it was a long run, going into years—years filled with shenanigans and game-playing and other ploys. At two o'clock in the morning, Arthur would call London to see what ships were headed to Portland so he could call their agents and strike deals before the rest of Portland was out of bed. He ran his 1,600-ton dump scow up and down the river in Portsmouth, also Moran's port, to accumulate the requisite number of trips in and out to get his pilotage papers there too, so as to put further pressure on Moran. And who knows what deals he made with whom, shaving a dollar here or a thousand there, or making outright payments to companies to get their business. Finally, in the spring of 1988, one of Moran's higher-ups called Arthur and asked to meet him in Nantucket. They'd known each other since they were kids together; things had not always been comfortable between them, but Arthur speaks of him with nothing but respect. Moran was planning to pull out of Portland, the fellow said. "I want to have your word, not as a gentleman, which I know you're not, but as a man, which I know you are, that you won't piss on us in Portsmouth. And then I'll make it happen sooner rather than later."

In the middle of the night on September 30, 1988, Moran moved their tugs out of Portland in formation. Arthur's acquaintance at Moran later told Arthur that he'd waited all weekend for him to call. "I wasn't gonna call you. I was afraid you'd turn around and come back," said Arthur. The fellow then asked that Arthur take good care of Moran's customers. "And don't gloat."

By far the greatest share of ship-assist work in Portland Harbor has been Arthur's since that time. In 2001, Arthur made the arrangements to sell his company to McAllister Towing.

The balance of power is a tenuous thing. Penobscot Bay, with its docks at Searsport, Bucksport, and Brewer, has not had business enough in the last fifty years to support two companies. Maineport Towboats has to keep its rates low enough that no one else can come in cheaper. The Cape Cod Canal also has limited demand for towboats, but not long after he sold his Portland operation to McAllister, Arthur Fournier—again, Arthur—took a boat to that area. C&M Towing owner Harvey Church had provided services there for fifteen years. "One of us will leave," Church predicted at the time. "I'm not too concerned about it," was Arthur's reaction. Three weeks after that conversation, C&M's *Waukegan* showed up at the Portland tug muster wearing Fournier paint, and C&M was no longer. Arthur's Canal Towing and Assist had taken over the beat.

But sometimes the balance of power is more complicated. A large towing company has ways to maintain its monopoly. It doesn't have to personally threaten the owners of an upstart outfit, although that has happened. Instead, it can simply let shipping companies know that nothing but an exclusive contract is available for *all* ports where the towing company has tugs. Or alternatively, it'll allow ships to sign up with the new tugs and then raise its rates in other, unchallenged harbors, thus eating up any savings made by the shipping company.

Either way, it's bye-bye, newcomers.

The larger cities—New York, Norfolk, San Francisco, Seattle and Los Angeles/ Long Beach, for instance—are home to two or more large towboat companies, and often there are smaller companies at work too. In New York and Boston, Arthur Fournier got his own start in such situations. The big companies scrap and fight, sometimes bitterly, for their share of the work, and sometimes the little ones can benefit from that. There have been changes in several major ports in recent years, including San Francisco, Seattle, and Long Beach.

In 1987, Harley Franco saw a niche in Puget Sound that he didn't feel was being adequately filled by the two big West Coast companies, Foss Maritime and Crowley Marine Services. Franco believed he could offer better bunkering service (taking fuel to ships in harbor), and one large shipping company was willing to give him a shot. "By the time the big towing companies got us on their radar," says George Clark of Harley Marine Services, "it was too late." Bunkering in Puget Sound was theirs.

In the last fifteen years, Harley has grown from one tug and one barge by buying existing companies and building their own boats. The company now has fortyeight vessels working along the West Coast. In Dutch Harbor, Alaska, they're doing assist and escort work, in Seattle and Portland, they've stuck to bunkering, and in LA/Long Beach, bunkering is solid and they're expanding into ship assist work and escort work. "The other companies have seen us before," says George. "They've slashed prices and done everything they can to keep us out." But to date, Harley's doing fine.

Toward the end of his career, George Kraemer worked for McAllister in New York. He speaks of the ferocious competition there; as a matter of economics it was sometimes a nasty fight between the rival companies. "But the strange part is, you depended on the competition for help." Whoever gets a big contract looks to the other companies for additional boats to do the work. "For Op Sail and the International Naval Review, we couldn't have handled it without Moran, Turecamo, and Red Star."

Choking Out the Union

A recurring theme in tugboating almost everywhere is unionization—union-forming and, even more, union-breaking. In big ports or small, the subject comes up. And for many of the stories I've been told, either the tellers asked that they not be identified or I would feel uncomfortable in identifying them. Most of the tales are from the point of view of sailors who had been, were, or would have been unionized. Obviously, as there always is, there's another side to the story. In the case of tugboats, the small, independent companies that ran on a shoestring couldn't have existed had their employees had the pay scale that the unions were able to demand for a time.

In one particular non-unionized, one-company port a few decades back, times had been hard. The owners of the company asked their employees to stick with them, even though they couldn't give raises, saying that when the economy turned around, they'd treat them right. Three years went by, business improved, but not a single penny more was offered to the captains or crews of the tugs. Unionizing looked good to them; they joined up, and struck.

But the union didn't look so good to the owners. They hired outside people to run their boats. Pretty soon the business had been sold. There went a good old towboat company. A while later, a local businessman approached one of the former towboat captains and asked him what he had done to the "poor" company owner. The captain had known the man most of his life. "Let me put it to you this way," he said. "If I was working for you and had six men under me, what would you expect to pay me?" The man named a figure. "Well, if I'd been getting half that, I'd been happy," he said. No one ever questioned him about the "poor" owner again.

In the big-city ports, unions have been around for many decades. In New York, it is the International Longshoremen's Association Local 333. Career deckhands used to make big money, collecting time-and-a-half on Saturdays, double-time on Sundays, and serious regular overtime pay to boot. They knew their jobs and the workings of the boats. Often a deckhand would run a tug down to where they were to pick up a barge, make up to the barge, and get ready to cast off, and only then would the captain take over. Everyone aboard the boats then belonged to the same union, and it represented their interests well, according to some of them today. Too well, say others, who feel that by the late 1980s the union had allowed its members to get lazy, and the companies weren't getting their money's worth any more.

In 1988, contract negotiations were coming up in New York. The companies wanted to eliminate the cooks from the tugs. It was an easy money-saving measure, reducing manning costs in one simple action. Of course the union objected, but the companies never came to the table. It happened to be a time when international oil prices were so low that the Louisiana oil fields couldn't compete and had shut down, so hundreds of merchant mariners there were out of work. The New York towing companies hired licensed people from the Gulf to come up to work in New York Harbor. Some of them signed on as deckhands or cooks, hoping to work their way back up again. Others, the companies sent around the harbor on charter yachts to learn the waters.

Then armed guards and dogs would appear on the tugs in the middle of the night, throwing union crews off the boats. (For some of these men, their tug had been their second home for twenty years.) And so the companies now needed new mates and captains, and—wow, what a coincidence!—they had a bunch of licensed guys all ready to step in! They paid them a fraction of the union wages, but it was good money for the laid-off guys from the Gulf, who had families to feed.

The union offered some contract concessions, which were not accepted. Their only choices were to cave to what they felt were unreasonable demands, or to strike. They struck. But no tug was tied up. Work went on as usual under the Gulf masters and mates, some of whom had had no idea that they were coming on as scabs when they went to New York. One mate-in-training I'll call Joe came from the oil patch not knowing the New York situation until he was in it. He quit his job after hearing a voice over the house-radio frequency. "I have you in my sights," said the voice, and then described what Joe was wearing.

One union man says that while he was on the picket line, he noticed that, even though the strike was about cooks, there were no cooks on the line with him. This didn't make him happy. Gradually, he and other guys started coming across the picket line, though they were nervous to be seen by their peers at first, and sometimes arrived hidden in the trunks of cars.

The union sent a boat out with a big public address system to harass the scabs, and more serious threats were made, too. There were reports of pilothouse windows being shot out, and it could be interesting running a garbage tow through Gasoline Alley between Staten Island and the gas refineries on the Jersey shore, where tankers are loading all the time. At least once, someone—from which side of the dispute?—shot a flare into a loaded scow. "There you are, going by the refineries with a fire on board. I grabbed the fire extinguisher in the pilothouse—dead. Then the extinguisher on the engine room door—dead. I told the engineer to fire the fire pump up—he didn't know how. Finally we attached a hose to the crew's shower head." The fireboats came along, but it was scary for a time there.

According to one source, the companies did play with flares. From a bridge, someone dropped flares onto oil barges, fortunately without disastrous results. The press blamed the unions, but police traced relevant license numbers to vehicles rented by a security company from Florida hired by the three major towing companies.

During the strike, at least one company kept unusually close track of their tugs not at work, keeping them made up into one unit, lashed together, with only a few lines onto the pier and a skeleton crew on one boat: engineer, deckhand, captain, and a watchman. If there had been a threat or a fire on the pier, they could cut the lines and tow the whole flotilla out into the river.

The replacement deckhands were inexperienced or worse. One fellow had crack-heads on his watch, and says he couldn't take his boat close enough to the piers to put a line ashore to hang out because the deck guys would go ashore for a fix and leave him shorthanded. "You couldn't fire anyone, because you couldn't hire anyone. It was perilous work as a scab."

The situation was also perilous for the local people working the harbor. One mariner, long familiar with New York Harbor, considered himself fortunate to be working at this time as mate for a non-union company. We'll call him Charlie. He tells of an incident while loading gasoline onto a small motor tanker at Tremley Point. It was a heavy ebb tide, and he looked up to see a southbound tug and barge coming directly at him with the current behind them. Charlie told the dockman to stand by the valve—"That guy's getting too close to us."

"No, no, he's coming into the north berth."

Charlie didn't see it that way. "Shut me down!"

The fellow didn't want to shut the valve, but given the direct order, he had no choice. They got the tank tops closed, but there was no time for Charlie to run back and warn the rest of his crew before the barge hit them—*smack!*—aft by the cook's dry stores. The impact knocked the captain square out of his bunk, and it made a mess in the galley. "The cook was ticked!" There wasn't serious damage, fortunately, but it could have been horrendous. "They don't provide parachutes on those barges."

The guy on the helm of the tug had never been around Tremley Point before. He didn't know the current was apt to be a knot and a half or two, or that it would set him toward the dock.

Another day, in Newark, Charlie watched a tugboat coming out from Sun Oil turn around by cutting across the flats, completely out of the channel. "It was just going *thumpa thumpa thumpa,* the propeller hitting the bottom, throwing mud up out of the water. He's looking around like he's wondering why the boat isn't turning. In another hour, he would have stayed there. At low tide, if you see a seagull out there, he's walking." Another case of lack of local knowledge.

Insurance claims by the tugboat companies are said to have gone up tenfold during this time, as former oil-field crews who had no familiarity with New York Harbor drove underpowered, single-screw harbor tugs in place of the high-powered, twin-screw rig tenders they were accustomed to.

The strike didn't work. In the past, strikes had been backed by longshoremen and other people working the docks, but this time there was no support from anywhere. At the end of Reagan era, the whole country was in an anti-union mood. Petroleum was moving; people had gas in their cars and their houses were heated, so no one cared. The only ones who made out were the shipyards, repairing all the damage.

A tugboat engineer, who shall also go by the name Charlie, was at a dinner party held to benefit some historical group. There he ran into a high muckety-muck from a big tugboat company who was crowing about what great things he was doing in the towing industry. "There were some tense moments," says Charlie, "when I told him how many of my friends he was putting out of work, how many had lost their cars and were having their houses foreclosed upon. Had he been a younger man, it might have come to blows."

The strike theoretically lasted seven years, but as one towboater says, "You can't call it a strike when all the union members who wanted to work were back at work—it was only the union that was on strike." And, say many, the strike had only been called in the first place because the companies wouldn't come to the table to negotiate in good faith.

The federal government eventually forced the companies into accepting the union back, declaring the situation to have been a lockout, and assessed fines in the millions of dollars, but in the meantime, the New York Harbor tugboat scene had changed permanently. Local 333 had lost its bargaining power, and many good, up-and-coming officers with four or five years' training went ashore and never came back. Older men, too, left the boats. Says one man, "I retired before it got really bad. Gunfire and everything else. Cars shot up. All for nothing."

One mate was thirty at the time of the strike, the youngster on his boat; the captain was seventy-two, the engineer sixty, and the deckhands were both in their fifties. The deckhands had been making $180 a day, plus time and a half for weekend work, and were building up time toward a union pension: $25 a month for every year they worked. Today they are making $186 a day, with no overtime and no accumulating pension benefit. That mate was making $45,000 a year at the time of the lockout. Five months later, he was thirty-five feet off the ground setting a ridgepole on a house, with no medical insurance, when he realized this was not what he wanted to do for the rest of his life. "I drive tugboats for a living." He went back to work on the boats for $29,000 a year.

The union pension fund closed in 1988, so the retirement benefit hasn't increased since then. They can put money into a 401(k), "but," says one, "that's my money, I have to take it away from my family. The owner is putting five thousand a year into it—but what the fuck is five thousand dollars?"

Not all the employees were forcibly taken off their boats in 1988. A member of the union then and still today, a man I'll call Harry, had worked for Moran out of New York for ten or twelve years when the company approached him and very politely asked him to get off the boat and take his crew with him. "I didn't believe they'd do that," he says with incredulity today. "I was hurt by that. I thought I'd done good work for them, and all of a sudden they threw me out like garbage. I think they could have worked it out, been more diplomatic." He feels lucky to have worked in the tow-boat industry during what he calls the Golden Age, the 1960s and 70s. He places the blame for the decline equally on the union and management. The union got too strong—but the companies allowed it to. And then management changed everything too quickly, too violently, instead of negotiating.

In 1957, Harry was on a 135-foot tug, 1,800 horsepower, with ten or eleven men on it. Today the boat he runs is also 135 feet long but 6,000 horsepower, and she carries five men. And he doesn't want more people aboard: "If they add another man, we'll all get less pay. They're not going to pay any more money; it'll all come from us."

Everywhere, boats have fewer men aboard, and there's constant turnover. Some run with only four: just captain, mate, and two deckhands, their engine rooms entirely automated. Many of the crew are inexperienced, perhaps don't speak English very well. "Taxi drivers and truck drivers, fishermen looking for a new career," is how one tug captain sums it up, and many immigrants, says another. In the seven years before the strike, he worked with a total of ten guys, and nowadays he goes through twenty a year. A popular sport for some of these short-term employees is said to be suing the company for an injury, settling for far less than might be granted by a jury but a sum that is a significant nest egg in their home countries.

One captain today speaks out clearly against the union in New York. "These people that rode around in the union became a really lazy bunch of slack people, and the companies weren't getting value for their dollar. The guys were making good money, but they were abusing the situation, hiding behind the power of the union. That's why the union got smashed—and rightfully so."

There's a lot of grumbling. "The shipping business is an ugly, ruthless industry," says one former tugboater, "and tugboats are one step farther down than that." Maybe there is always grumbling, but some feel the opportunities in tugboating are not what they once were. In New York Harbor today, some of the big companies are union, some are not. Says one tugboater, "Three-thirty-three's a joke. But don't quote me."

On the West Coast, unions remain healthier, at least from their members' point of view. But even where the unions aren't what they once were, there is still a dedicated core of towboaters who can't imagine themselves doing anything else.

The Loopholes

Part of the reason tugboats are such a common part of the American maritime world is that they do jobs that no other vessel can, but also, regulatory loopholes make tugs and barges more economical than ships in some cases. These loopholes have to do with manning and piloting requirements due to tonnage, and with the regulations governing construction. American regulations allow owners of vessels under 200 tons—which includes nearly all towing vessels—much more latitude in how they man and operate their vessels.

All vessels are given a tonnage rating that is based on a theoretical measure of their volume. There are various means of determining this figure. The International and Panama Canal Tonnage measures relate to the actual eyeballed size of the vessel, but the United States has its own esoteric measurement system. Sometimes this measurement is not only esoteric, it's spurious.

In theory, for these purposes, a ton is equal to 100 cubic feet and is measured by a formula that takes into consideration the highest continuous watertight deck, a definition which itself can be fooled with. As an example, a structure with a watertight door can be included in defining a watertight deck. But if you take the very same door, mount it in a flange, and bolt that flange into the same bulkhead with a very large number of bolts, then even though it functions exactly the same as it used to, the compartment is not considered watertight and isn't included in the computations. The vessel can carry as much cargo just as safely as it would if the door were not on the flange, of course, but the volume of the compartment behind that door doesn't count in the total tonnage.

Just about all tugs are rated under 200 tons—and some older ones are grandfathered—which allows them to be skippered with a simple 200-ton Operator of Uninspected Towing Vessels ticket. And that tug can have a barge with her—even one that is all but permanently attached—that, as long as it is rated under 10,000 tons, doesn't count for tonnage regulations either. That barge may be carrying as much as 190,000 barrels of petroleum, and tug and barge together might add up to a total length of well over five hundred feet, and she still may have only an Uninspected Towing Vessel (UTV)-licensed captain in control.

The requirement regarding pilotage is odd too. A vessel over 1,600 gross tons must carry a First Class pilot into a harbor—but a barge of under 10,000 tons doesn't count for that requirement either.

For comparison, a small motor tanker, such as the 321-foot, 2,800–gross-ton *Great Lakes,* on which Captain John O'Reilly has served as pilot, has to have both a master with an unlimited license and a First Class pilot aboard even though she carries only one-fifth the petroleum cargo of some of the tug-and-barge combinations. The tug and barge, though, may be guided into port by a person whose sole qualifications may be that he or she is at least twenty-one, has spent sixteen hours in the exam room taking a restricted mate's exam, and claims to have made a certain number of round trips from the port in question, including some at night. The last is done on the honor system.

Manning requirements for vessels under 200 tons differ from those for larger ones, too. While a larger vessel must have three watches if she's licensed for coastwise travel or for oceans (as opposed to lakes, bays and sounds), one of under 200 tons need only need two watches, no matter where she's running and no matter what she has in tow. That's hard on the crew, particularly the captain, even aside from the obvious stress from the greater amount of time required of each man to be on watch. If anything goes wrong during the captain's off-watch, he must be awoken. "You don't like to interrupt his sleep cycle, but you have to," says John. "It leads to exhaustion." And an engineer need have no license at all on such a vessel. "Just a social security card," John says, "and a Merchant Mariner's card, the Z-card." (One of the recent regulatory changes made in an effort to increase safety at sea is that any merchant mariner who will go more than three hundred miles offshore has to have completed a Standards of Training, Certification, and Watchkeeping for Seafarers course (STCW) covering basic safety issues: personal safety, basic fire fighting, basic first aid. It is also more difficult to get an entry-level position at sea because the courses cost money.)

I was told of a large ocean-going tug whose U.S. papers showed her to be 198 tons, a very convenient size to be. Her International rating was more than 800 tons. The American computations showed the height of the interior to be seventeen feet from the keel to a deck that didn't even exist on the boat. The International computations were based on a depth of hull of twenty-two feet, two inches, where there was in fact a deck. The captain drew this interesting peculiarity to the attention of his company's port captain in hopes of getting more manpower aboard, but by the next time he was on the boat, the form that showed the calculations had mysteriously come up missing.

Constructing new ships is far more expensive than building tug-and-barge units—perhaps as much as double the cost. Requirements are more stringent for ships than for either tugs or barges. As one simple instance, a tanker has to have an extensive fire-fighting system with an elaborate design and constructed to certain standards. No fire-fighting system is required on a tank barge. (In fact, if a company chooses to put some kind of fire apparatus on a barge, they have to be careful about nomenclature. If they have a fire hose, Coast Guard regulations say they have to maintain it in a specified and cumbersome way. Much easier to simply have a wash-down hose, built in such a manner that it could be used as a fire hose. Just don't call it that.)

The loopholes are defining the bulk of non-passenger shipping jobs in the United States of late. In 2000, there were approximately 5,400 coastal and inland tugs and towing vessels, and only about 120 cargo ships, 1,500 passenger vessels, and 1,400 workboats. While the actual number of tug and towboats has decreased more than ten percent in the last ten years for coastal, Great Lakes and inland use, the carrying capacity (deadweight tonnage, dwt) of barges, particularly dry cargo barges, has increased tremendously. Tank barges, too, are increasing in tonnage. In the same period, the total dwt of the domestic fleet of liquid-carrying ships has dropped by a quarter and is projected to drop considerably more in the near future.

There's another aspect to the loophole that some feel is significant for the people working on the Uninspected Towing Vessels. Because a UTV need not be inspected, the standards are far more lax, which may lead unnecessarily—and unreasonably—to less safe working conditions than are found, for example, aboard a similarly sized oilfield support boat, which does have to face rigorous inspections. The design, construction, modifications, and repair records of an inspected boat are all scrutinized for seaworthiness and stability, and the boats are limited to those routes for which they are deemed safe. They must carry survival craft, have regular man-overboard and abandon-ship drills, and carry fire-fighting systems and ground tackle. Even a pleasure boat must carry flares or other distress signals. The uninspected towing vessel need have none of these things. American Waterways Operators has established voluntary safety and environmental policies and procedures, but far fewer than half of the 1,100 U.S. towing vessel operators are in that program. A 1994 report estimated the fatality rate in the towing industry to be six times the national marine industry average. And perhaps some of the 15,000 people working on UTVs don't know how much more dangerous many of their jobs are compared to those of other mariners.

These loopholes make tug work far more economical—hence, profitable—than other marine endeavors, so there is pressure to leave the regulations as they are. It's all about the bottom line—unless, of course, you're one of the people whose very life may be in jeopardy while working on an unsuitable vessel.

Looking to the Future

Perhaps it's just the ubiquitous older-generation-worrying-about-the-younger thing, but many people I talked with in the industry are worried about its future. The new Coast Guard licensing regulations are making it more difficult to enter the field, and they're also causing some older towboaters to leave.

Captain Jack Colomara has been in the business for forty-five years and is on the ninth renewal of his ticket. "I'm sixty-three years old, and have my Master of Oceans license. I've just renewed it, but to keep it next time, I would have to go to about fifty-five schools." He exaggerates—but the concept is very real. It's not that there hasn't been any notice. He's known for years that he would have to get a number of endorsements to his license to demonstrate that he knows things he's used for years, radar and firefighting equipment and so on. "They're gonna tell me I'm not qualified?" he asks rhetorically. "I'm not gonna do it," he says. "It's not worth it." He feels that the Coast Guard has made a terrible mistake. "Losing people like me—they should have tried to grandfather some of us in. The people coming in are coming mostly from the academies, and they'll never do the kind of stuff I could do with a boat."

The other day, he heard a couple of guys talking about towing three pieces of dredging equipment at the same time. The young guy said you can't do it—it's impossible. "I didn't say anything to him, but I've done that—I towed a dredge and two other pieces from New York to San Francisco. They're so afraid of safety—but there was nothing unsafe about it."

I keep hearing about how no one is coming into the industry, or how those who do only want office jobs. Everyone agrees, there are two kinds of people—Academy people and hawsepipers—and everyone agrees that, regardless of your training, there's no substitute for working as a deckhand in order to understand the towboating business. An unlimited third mate's license, such as many maritime academy students graduate with, gives no preparation whatever for the day-to-day work of a tug-boat. "It's best for tug guys to come up through," says Dan Alexander, who himself grew up on a cruise schooner and has worked on tugs from the deck up. Although he has his master's ticket, he is still running as mate, due to his relatively young age. "You gotta know what's going on around you, what the deckhand is dealing with. If you're not paying attention to that, it's the best way to kill him or lose him over-board." Many new licensees do realize this and take jobs on deck in order to learn how the vessels operate.

It used to be hard to get on a tug without knowing someone in the business. "Hamming" or "hambone" referred to the practice of going aboard for the experience underneath someone, often paying grub money to the cook. Then when a job came open, the mentor would ask the union boss to let the trainee join the union.

The "steersman" system still is in existence on the Mississippi river system, where a young person trains under a pilot, drawing pocket money from the company, which then gets a share of the earnings of the new pilot's salary for a few years after he gets his license. (On the rivers, a pilot is a person who stands a watch, either the master or the person in the wheelhouse on the other watch, the equivalent of a licensed mate on the ocean.)

But at this time, everywhere in the U.S., there's a shortage of manpower, both in the wheelhouse and, even more, in the engine room. Captain Steve Rhodes thinks the industry is going to die within ten years. "Salary's gotta come up," he says, "and I don't mean like baseball players'!"

But others view the scene differently. "I'm always gonna think I'm underpaid," says Captain Bob Peterson, "but I make a good living. I can support my family on my salary and only work six months a year. I come from Maine, and I broke my ass fish-ing 365 days a year to starve to death up there. This is pretty good." The only rea-son he feels he's underpaid, he says, is because of the responsibility he holds. "Before lunch, they've entrusted me with a hundred million dollars' worth of equipment, so I think I ought to be paid a pretty good sum." And he believes that pay will go up. "They have created a huge shortage, and it's hanging in the balance—if I have a tug-boat company and I need a captain and I can't find one, I'm gonna steal one from you. That's when the wage goes up."

Steve doesn't feel that he is treated as a professional. Like many of the older captains, he resents the increased requirements of the Coast Guard. In the United Kingdom, he says, once you get your Master's license, it's good indefinitely. "I know how to do it," he says, undoubtedly correctly. "Put me in a tugboat, and with the radar, I can take it anywhere in the world and not even open my eyes to look out the window."

Steve is a hawsepiper. "But I finished college so I have a semi-part of a brain," he says. He spent a year and a half on deck and then moved into the pilothouse. "I don't know if it's the industry, or the people, or the Coast Guard, but now it takes years to make the transition." And then, in the next breath, he says that he doesn't know of any mate that's ready to move up. "I know that both my mates can't handle the rig, so I set sailings and dockings for real close to my watch time so I don't have to get up at three o'clock in the morning to dock the boat. "

There's a matter of talent, which many feel a boat handler either has or doesn't have. "You can tell if he's got it or not by looking at his barge and the pilings," says Captain Doug O'Leary.

Of one nameless tugboat master I was told, "He has a tendency to bump into things." The trouble was that in his case each incident was inexcusable. He hadn't thought the particular situation through fully. "With your talent level, you have to have a crutch," my confidant once told this fellow. And the best crutch is simply to pay attention to detail. "Winging it is unprofessional," he says, "and doesn't work for him."

It does work for some skippers. The same master said to me, "Some people are born to be good boatmen. They just do what feels right, and often they can't say why they do what they do. It's an inner gift. When you watch them work, you know which ones they are. They're like Michael Jordan, they're not like the rest of us. The rest of us have to learn. We have to pay attention." For example, he said, you might observe that there is a two-knot current in the river, and you'd know that you'll have to make the effort to check it out the next time because then it might be different, and affect the tug or barge differently. Without paying attention, you have nothing to base decisions on.

Steve Rhodes used to work for Maritrans, which had a name for this necessary level of attention: situational awareness. Steve defined it this way: "Being aware of your situation: the wind, the current, your deck. How knowledgeable is your deck crew? How dependable are your engines, the clutches, the machinery, and so forth—all the forces that can work against you?"

Another fellow speaks of talent from the other side of the fence. "Boat handling is my forte. Any good sailor can tell you, you either have a knack or you don't. It's an art. You can learn all about side-thrust, and propeller rotation, and cause and effects, but there's an artistic side, and I have been gifted with it."

The artistry is a recognized aspect. People remark on it when they see it. They say, "The boat was an extension of himself—he didn't have to think about it." Steve Rhodes gives an example: "It's an art when you can run something 640 feet long and you can dock it in 642 feet—that's pretty good."

Steve says that it's "the young ones" that scare him. "They'll take a chance unnecessarily—I'm not gonna do that. It's because they don't understand the danger yet, not only the danger of hurting somebody but the danger of losing your license. When I move my vessel, that's in the back of my mind. How can I move this thing safely and efficiently, taking everything to my advantage?"

Paradoxes abound. Just about all the guys with decades of experience are glad they spent their lives in the business. "I enjoy it. I've seen so many sunsets, sunrises, so many fish," says Steve. "It surprises me why younger people don't want to get in it." And then they fume about the changes, the liability, the requirements, the testing, the low pay, the lack of respect, and the lack of future for the industry or for the few people they foresee being in it.

I had always assumed that the market would take care of the problem; if companies weren't able to hire people at the rates they were paying, they would have to increase what they offered. But there are people in tugs today who believe that it's only a matter of time before the Jones Act is discarded because of pressure from business interests. The Jones Act requires that any vessel used to transport merchandise between U.S. points, either directly or via a foreign point, must built in U.S. shipyards, owned by U.S. citizens, and be documented by the U.S. Coast Guard for such carriage. I am not about to enter the discussion of the pros and cons of the Jones Act, but it's safe to say that, if it were eradicated, the world of tugboating in the United States would be changed forever. Certainly it would be hard to find anyone actually working in the industry, from deckhand to personnel manager, who believes that revoking the Jones Act is an acceptable answer.

I've heard it said that of every ten people who make a first trip on deck, six or seven never come back—some don't even finish the one trip. "It might not be anything more than seasickness. It's too dangerous for some. Others don't like to be gone," says Captain Dave Riddick. "There are all kinds of reasons not to be out here if you don't want to be."

Says engineer-turned-office-fellow Bob Mattsson, in the business for forty-odd years, "Some people love the work—others can't stand being away, do not like the close quarters or the lonesome night watches."

But all the same, some believe tugboating still offers real opportunities to the right people. "This is a good industry for a young man not inclined to go off to college and become a professor or something," says Bob Peterson. He feels that the hawsepipe is still open. "Just like all those guys I grew up with who went fishing offshore. For the right kind of person just done with high school, he can jump on a boat, and in five or six years he'll have his steering license." He believes that the wage is now as low as it's going to be. And he loves the business. "For someone like me, I've died and gone to heaven. I work for two weeks, they give me a nice, big, powerful boat all wrapped up in rubber, and then I have a two-week vacation and I go home. Best thing ever happened to me."

3
Working In and Near Harbor

When most people think of tugboats, they think of harbor work—in particular, ship handling, the guiding of big vessels into their berths and helping them set sail again. That is certainly a big part of many tugs' lives, but there are other harbor jobs, notably moving barges around, and even the offshore tows end up in a harbor. The ratio of terror to boredom inside the harbor is probably higher than offshore, where the weather usually offers the most serious threat. In the harbor, everything is out to get you: other vessels, currents, piers and sunken obstructions and shorelines, the wind, and the regulations.

Captain Doug O'Leary has spent a lot of time in a tug with a barge on the head—the tug is tied into a notch in the stern of the barge with a line off the tug's nose and wires that run aft from the after corners of the barge to the stern of the tug. Docking of these rigs can be tricky. "What you have to know," he says, "is you're guiding the whole goddam thing. You have to have a 3-D view of everything happening." Offering a special challenge are petroleum barges, and he's pushed around a lot of those. "Liquid cargo has inertia. You back the shit out of her, and she's s'posed to stop. And she does stop—but then the inertia takes over, and she'll charge right ahead again. "I always tell my new mates, 'Now, for God's sake, you can always come ahead, but you can't stop her. Don't ever forget that!'

"Sometimes you have to ram in there because of the current. The oil companies, seeing as we're not handling ships anymore, by and large have decided we don't have to wait for slack water—because we have TUGBOATS! So you get the goddam barge in there." That situation is one of the frightening ones. "That's where the grommet puckers, or you rip your pockets out of your trousers. God forbid you should show absolute terror.

"You get burnt once in a while, land her a little hard—you have to, sometimes. The worst thing in the world is a fair-tide landing. The current up your rear end and the inertia in the cargo. Little-bitty towboat and a great big barge, deeply loaded—you know what a deep vessel does in a current. You put that four or five thousand horsepower full astern and say, 'Hail Mary, full of grace, the Lord is with thee.' *Bang bang bang!*

"It's not a matter of horsepower or no horsepower," says Doug, "it's the way you're rigged up. There's two wires off your quarters to the barge, and that's it! You jerk 'em wrong and they part, and you're in a heap of trouble. When you start backing that son of a bitch—boy oh boy—you're thinking, are these the new cables? Did they put the new cables on?"

Captain Pamela Hepburn used to run the classic tug *Pegasus* from New York. She made a few coastal trips to Wilmington and Atlantic City, which she described as being like a vacation, easy until you get to the harbor entrances. "The inlets are a challenge," she says. "You have to time it right, and sometimes you have to do three things at a time, with no room—what do you do now?" She was towing three barges on her first trip into Atlantic City, where there's no real dock, "just one falling-down affair." She called a friend who worked for a big dredging company and asked him about the entry. He told her to shorten up the tow by the sea buoys and to go in just before the ebb tide. "That much I'd figured," she says. Then he told her how to work her bow into the mud banks on the right-hand side before the bridge, almost like an

An empty hopper barge on the nose in New York Harbor. Author photo.

anchor, while the barges stayed out in the stream, staying behind her till she wanted them. "I don't know if the Coast Guard would call it moored," she says.

"All that stuff—when you do it the first time, it's a blast. You're never sure it's going to work. With any kind of boating business, especially in close quarters, you have to be ready to alter your plan—like if you're sailing into a dock and suddenly you get in the lee of a big building." Particularly with a light barge high off the water, sudden wind changes alter everything.

Engineer Gary Matthews spent time in New York Harbor too. He liked the up-close tug work with barges too long to make the corners of the creeks they were working in and out of. "You had to be completely under the rake," he says of some long barges Reinauer Transportation owned. "Really neat, fantastic towing. It's a condition of creek towing. Nerve-wracking at first, but when you know what you're doing, it's really fun."

Not all harbor work is elegant, but it's all about leverage. Captain Dan Alexander describes a recent job where they were unloading the cargo from a ship out in the anchorage and transferring it to shore. "We were lightering a coal ship and had to dock a loaded coal barge, me and a deckhand only, and there's no one on the dock. It's pouring rain, and I'm feeling bad for the kid, so instead of waiting around, I drive the bow of the barge right up to the dock, stop it right there. (The dock helped me do that, unfortunately—not very hard, but we did bump.) Tie it up there, you know it isn't going to go anywhere." Then he could back around, pushing the barge alongside the dock, and tie up the other end. "That's the name of the game, leverage."

New York Harbor is still one of the busier harbors in North America, but it's nothing like what it once was. Captain George Kraemer describes the harbor when he first worked it fifty years ago: "You used to be able to walk from the Battery to Governor's Island across barges and tugs." Whether it originally came by ship or rail, once cargo arrived in port, almost all of it was offloaded onto barges, which then took it to the Manhattan piers, from which it was delivered around the city by truck. "There'd be trucks lined up from downtown New York up to Forty-Second Street," says Kraemer.

And railroad cars themselves were transported across the harbor on barges; in the 1950s there were a dozen or more railroads, more than a hundred railroad tugs working, and perhaps a thousand railroad "car floats." Now there is just one company carrying rail freight cars across the harbor, the New York Cross Harbor Railroad, which takes railroad cars between Jersey City and Brooklyn. Captain Hepburn worked for them for a time. There were many challenges associated with the job beyond the little matter of getting paid, which seemed problematic too. "The car floats were going across prevailing traffic—Jersey to Brooklyn—across ferries, tugs and barges going to the Gate or up or down the Hudson. You had to weave across."

Railroad car floats in New York are usually about three hundred feet in length, with three tracks down their length, and can carry fifteen regular boxcars. In earlier days, a tug would moved a pair of these barges, but Hepburn's tug usually took just one across the harbor at a time since there wasn't demand for more than that. "You'd make up [tie the tug on] in the middle of the float, because they're so skinny that they'd want to dive off on you all the time," says Pamela. There are advantages to their narrowness, though: "You learn how to wiggle them. They pivot easily." That's how things are on the water. "You figure out what's going on, use things to your advantage that might seem to be an obstacle."

Sometimes she did shift two car floats at a time, taking them to side-by-side racks (pens) at the float bridges, the car floats' connection to the land. She'd have one barge on each side of the tug. In addition to the usual straps (spring lines), head lines and stern lines, there also would be a bow breast line strung between the two barge bows.

As she approached the float bridges, the deckhand let the bow breast line go. With the tug still moving slowly ahead, the natural response of the floats alongside was to open up, spreading enough to head for their respective racks. "Then you start to back, and the inclination of the barges is to close together again. You're still drifting ahead into the racks, but backing enough so they are just closing and therefore staying in shape." When all works as it should, one float quietly slides into one rack, and the other settles easily into the next one.

Once in a while, she'd push a car float from astern when there wasn't room to get alongside. Her predecessor at Cross Harbor said it was like balancing a pencil on the end of your finger. They both enjoyed seeing if they could get across the harbor in that configuration sometimes, though they had to come alongside the float to dock. For four of the five years she worked with the car floats, she ran her 1907 tug *Pegasus*. "It's traditional work, so it was kind of fun to be running the *Peg*," she says. "Everything's so old and funky and big and medieval-looking."

Captain Kraemer had some interesting harbor jobs in New York, including towing a billboard on a barge up the North River and down into the East River. He did that for only a short time, though, because drivers were paying more attention to him and the huge Ford Motor Company ad than to their driving, and he was causing accidents on the West Side and traffic jams on East River Drive.

Steam tug *Transfer No. 15* landing two car floats, September 1935.
FROM THE COLLECTION OF ARTHUR FOURNIER.

Looking down on a loaded car float. COURTESY OF DON SUTHERLAND.

Tug with a gravel barge on the hip in New York Harbor. AUTHOR PHOTO.

George was working in the tug company office when his son's fifth-grade class was on a Circle Line tour. "I grabbed a tug and was laying off the pier when the Circle Line came out and started down the North River." George, on the starboard side of the tour boat, saluted with three whistles. The Circle Line boat answered with a whistle, "and all of a sudden, all the kids run to the starboard side and she takes a list." Over their loudspeaker came the request, "Now hear this. Will the little boy whose father is on the tug please wave bye-bye, so we can get back on an even keel?"

Captain Dan Alexander enjoys his occasional trips to New York from Long Island Sound. "It's always fun to go to the city, as long as I'm not being asked to do anything too crazy. I like to look at all the lights, boats, people—check it all out. The container ships start at two a.m. from the anchorage at Ambrose, all coming in in single file. You can see them on the radar, all lined up. Docking tugs from the Moran and McAllister companies and anyone they've chartered come out of the kills and drift down and meet them at Verrazano Narrows Bridge. They have their own docking pilots with them, and they go to the first ship and put the pilot aboard and then move on to the next, and the next—then they all go up and take a hard left through the kills into Jersey."

Almost anyone who's ever worked tugs in New York Harbor, at least until very recently, has stories about garbage scows and the kills. It was not a romantic duty, but it was certainly memorable. Before 1934, the scows simply took the stuff to sea and dumped it. For the second half of the last century, the Fresh Kills landfill on Staten Island received it all, bargeload by bargeload. Just terminated in 2001, the regular dumping peaked in the late 1980s, when each of several tugs took eight to twelve thousand tons of garbage to Fresh Kills every day, adding up to an average of 27,000 tons each day. (Within months of the official closing, the site was opened again after September 11 for debris from the World Trade Center.)

Captain Chris Kluck describes the operation in the 1980s as "a view into surreality." For miles and miles, there was nothing but landfill, thousands of acres, mounded two hundred feet high in places. During this time, New Jersey sued New York because of the garbage blowing across to the Jersey shore. To contain the loose trash, the landfill was surrounded with huge nets, which became festooned with dead gulls. Sodium vapor lights lit up the area where equipment was at work; it was the biggest strip-mining equipment available, though here the huge trucks were adding material, not taking it out. The tug crews shot rats for fun while the barges were unloading.

All harbors have their share of tricky passages, and the garbage tugs dealt with most of New York's. Older tugs were used on this detail—going into Fresh Kills, a vessel's draft was limited to twelve feet. They were all single-screw boats and none had a surplus of power. They'd pick up the loaded barges in creeks usually just wide enough for a single barge alongside. "It was like operating a full-size tug on a pond, and there's not a lot of clearance under the bottom, so the boat doesn't react well," Captain Christopher Holt recalls. "And if you weren't in a creek, you were in the East River or the North River, bucking tide all the time. You can get caught in a current you don't want to be in, and get set too close to a dock or to an anchored ship.

"Between the Brooklyn piers and Governor's Island there's a passage called the Buttermilk. Going east on a flood tide, if you don't come off the docks, it'll set you right on, and with the single-screw tug, there isn't much you can do.

"Running up and down the East River, it was great training ground. It really taught you how to handle a single-screw tug and how to build up your nerve doing that."

There are ways in which New York is different from many other places. One captain I spoke with—we'll call him Joe—said that in most harbors to be captain of a boat was to be godlike. "When he spoke, you better be doing what he said. Every boat I was ever on, that's how it was." Not in New York, however. There was the time when Joe was bringing a single-screw boat into the dock, and a fellow I'll call Giovanni caught the line for him. Giovanni came from Brooklyn, "right out of *The Sopranos*," says Joe. "A big, goofy guy—tattoos, accent, the whole bit. If he isn't throwing lines, he's probably stealing cars somewhere." When Joe was ready to go, he said to Giovanni, "OK, Giovanni, let her go." Giovanni let her go, and then Joe saw the company boss coming down to the dock. "Hold on, Giovanni. Catch that line again. We gotta come back in." Giovanni caught the line. Then the boss took off again, and once more Joe was set to go. "OK, let her go." But then the boss was waving at him again, and with a single-screw boat in a running tide, he couldn't just sit there. "Giovanni, you gotta catch the line again." Giovanni was unhappy now. He looked up at Joe and said, "Let me tell you something, Cap. You got one more fucking line today—no more. So don't waste it!" Joe cracked up. "OK, I'll try to use it wisely." He hadn't been around that kind of attitude anywhere else, but he liked it. "Any boat I'd been on before, they'd stand there throwing lines all day if I asked them."

Joe enjoyed New York and its contradictions. "The stupidest son of a bitch, if he comes from the streets of New York, he's smarter than almost all these other people because he's been exposed to so much. I've been with guys, they could hardly speak but they liked classical music. And when they go shopping for grub in New York, they go to all the little delis and bodegas and come back with all this wonderful stuff you don't get anywhere else. Anywhere else, you're gonna live on Wonder Bread and bologna."

New York is just one of several busy harbors in North America. The last two years Captain Bob Glover was in tugboats he spent doing harbor work in Puget Sound. "I loved that. Two weeks on, two weeks off—and during the two weeks on, you were apt to do every facet of tugboating." One afternoon he'd be docking container ships and then moving barges up and down the stream from one dock to another, and the next he'd be on the stern of a barge, pushing the way you would on the Mississippi. "It was very engaging. Your sleep cycle is nonexistent. You might work four hours, sleep two, work sixteen, sleep four, work again, take a catnap." Even then, of course, this was in violation of regulations that say no one may work more than twelve hours in twenty-four, and Puget Sound is hardly the only place where this happens.

"You might have to run up to Port Angeles, fourteen hours, for a ship job and then run over to the oil refineries. You'd make up to a barge a hundred feet wide with a tug thirty-six feet wide plus two feet of tires on each side—a hundred and forty feet altogether—and have to go through a railroad bridge a hundred and fifty feet wide. And the barge is two hundred and fifty feet long. When you make up to a barge with the tug on the quarter, it crabs sideways. Approaching a bridge like that, you've got to get the bow though first and then jockey the stern around. There was a railroad bridge followed by a road bridge, separated by six hundred feet. Soon's you get through one, you have the other. You'd be doing it in the middle of the night, or in the rain. . . .

"They say when you tow offshore, you rot. In the harbor, they work you to death. But it never even bothered me. It was so fun to go to work every day."

Docking with Single-Screw Boats

One of the primary jobs that harbor tugs do is help ships get alongside or away from docks, and it's an essential job. Most docking is done by twin-screw vessels, which are a clear improvement on tugs with but a single engine, but there are plenty of single-screw boats still docking, and, increasingly, tugs with azimuthing drives and Voith-Schneider cycloidal drives are being used.

On the Great Lakes, just about all docking is done with single-screw boats. "Why would you want twin screw?" asks Captain Franz VonRiedel, of Zenith Tugboat Company in Duluth. "They have twice the moving parts, twice as much to go wrong. Singles do the job just as well." Then, only slightly tongue-in-cheek, he gets to what may be a large part of the essence of the issue, saying, "As these companies out on the ocean are forced into this new twin-screw conspiracy, we will gladly go out and buy all their old singles for pennies on the dollar. To us, a new tug was built after World War Two."

The tug *Vermont* on the stern of a ship in Duluth, showing the typical Great Lakes short hawser off the tug's stern. Note how much she's being pulled over!
COURTESY OF ZENITH TUGBOAT COMPANY

Great Lakes Towing Company, the big player on the Lakes, is a company that can be credited with timely performance and a strong safety record. Great Lakes has thirty-eight docking tugs, most converted from steam, and the newest one was built in 1952. (Although she is still fully operational, they no longer work the *Wisconsin*, launched in 1897.) The boats have a low profile that looks odd to people accustomed to ocean tugs, and they have relatively low horsepower, often only 750 horses apiece, and rarely more than 1,200 horsepower. A baker's dozen of them are diesel-electric. Often they work from directly ahead and sometimes directly astern of the ships they're assisting, on lines that are so short they're nearly vertical. When working ahead, the lines are run from the tug's stern bitts, as is common in Europe but not seen on traditional tugs on the coasts of North America. The rig itself is provided by the ship, rather than by the tug as is common elsewhere.

Much of the ship-assist work in the Great Lakes is in tight turning basins or rivers where there's barely enough room for the ship itself. "We couldn't use a longer line if we had to—there simply isn't room to maneuver," says Franz. "We dangle off the ends of the ship with the tugs and work them from side to side, sometimes literally wrapped around the bow or stern, leaning over with the tug's gunwale in the water. These are the conditions where you would think twin screw would be mandatory." But, he says, the system works, "so why change it? When they were built, the tugs that are used on the Lakes were assisting three-hundred-foot, six-thousand-ton freighters. Now they are out there docking thousand-foot, sixty-thousand-ton-plus freighters, and they do the job just as well. Same tugs." One does need to point out that the freighters often have their own thrusters now, which help them make the turns.

"If you brought a twin-screw tug to the Lakes," says Franz, "the boys wouldn't know what to do with it. They'd be running only one engine and trying to figure out why she's walking with a limp."

On salt water, the tugs work differently. Captain Dan Alexander started his work in tugs in Maine's Penobscot Bay, docking in what he describes as the "big, awkward," single-screw ship-docking boats of Maineport Towboats. "I learned to work with a loose, sloppy line," Dan says. "Just to get a line up onto the deck takes ten feet—more if she's light. It's impossible for the line to be tight. It'll stretch out, and all of a sudden, it might be twenty feet long. Depending how much nylon there is in the line, there'll always be some amount of stretch." Dan often chooses a looser line. He'll either instruct his deck hand to make it up that way or he'll land aft or ahead of the chock, making his own slop.

"If you know you're going to make a real hard turn, you want as much leverage as you can get," Dan says. The bow tug wants to be well forward, as every foot of leverage is critical. "You cheat forward on the ship," Dan says. But you can scare the pilot if you're screwing around getting in position, he adds. "You don't want to affect the ship except as directed—that may make the pilot unhappy. You have to know when you have the opportunity to sneak up or back."

Leverage is particularly important with a boat of lower horsepower, as most single-screw boats are. "If I had 4,000 horsepower, I'd have all the nuts I need— I could put it to her and make a lot of black smoke and not have to worry about sneaking forward."

The ship's stern is a particularly good place for a single-screw boat, Dan says, provided the ship's not going to go backward. On the East Coast, the tug usually runs a single line up through the bullnose to the center chock on the ship's stern, if it has one. Unfortunately, one of the economies of shipbuilding is to minimize the number of chocks. The tugboater just hopes they're where he needs them. Cruise ships in particular are apt to be short of chocks, Dan says, and this can be a problem. And, unlike with most freighters or tankers, their sides are not strong enough to handle a tug just anywhere alongside. "You see labels on the side of the ship saying 'Tug Here,' but they may not have a chock placed within twenty feet on either side." The tug has to work where it's supposed to—or "you'd walk right through into some dining room."

Newer ships sometimes have stern chocks only on the quarters, for that's where they are used most often when tying to docks. A tug working behind such a ship

The single-screw
Cape Rosier shows
a sloppy line.
AUTHOR PHOTO.

would have to run two lines up, one to each corner. This holds it more nearly in one place, with the only slack coming from the stretch, and that can actually be preferable, particularly when there's much height from the bullnose up to the ship. With two lines, as the tug tightens the load on one, the other can be snugged in, "and eventually you're nailed down," Captain John Worth says. "Then, as soon as you're asked for something, you can give it right away." That's more important for heavy horsepower boats, as suddenly putting a lot of horsepower onto a slack line could cause the line to part when it fetches up.

With a single loose line on the stern, the tug can get more angle across the stern. Dan repeats the common phrase in tugs, that leverage is the name of the game: "When it's time to put the ship on the dock, if the line's too tight, I can't get fully across the ship, so I'm pushing the boat up the dock and not into it." With a long line, he says, "If I need to hop around on the stern, I can. It's handy sometimes, if I'm pushing the port side of the stern and suddenly he wants me to work her off, I can let the boat fall back. It'll take up the slack and stretch the line out and then I can slingshot to the other side."

Sometimes it's necessary to move the ship ahead a little bit along the dock, for instance to line up the manifolds on a tanker with the hoses on the dock. "If you were to give a kick ahead with the ship's own engine, it'd jump ahead twenty or thirty feet, where a tug can nudge it ahead two or three meters—slowly creep you up there."

The pilot has to be used to having a tug on the stern. "He can back over you," Dan says. "And once the pilot loses track of you, you're gonzo." Often the best pilots have run tugs themselves and understand the issues facing the tugboater. The captain of a tug must learn his situation, local conditions, what the dock's like, and the weather. And he must know his pilots, know what the pilot's trying to do, and know whom to trust. No tug belongs behind a ship if the ship's going to make any sternway. "If you get flopped, you'll roll, and the propeller can slice you open like a can."

Twin-Screw vs. Single-Screw

Whether on the ocean or the lakes, single-screw tugs still are working in many ports. "Ship handling in the best of circumstances can be done in a very gentlemanly fashion," Dan says, and, because he grew up with them, he's comfortable in the one-screw tugs. "But," he adds, "if you have problems, the last thing you want is a big, old single-screw boat."

Most tug work nowadays is done by twin-screw vessels, which have the obvious advantage of having a fall-back should they lose power in one engine. Captain John

The single-screw *Mary L. McAllister* alongside a loaded tanker, ready to do as the pilot orders. AUTHOR PHOTO.

O'Reilly tells of making an approach to the Sun Oil Company dock in Paulsboro, New Jersey, with a single-screw boat and a 25,000-barrel petroleum barge. "I went to back down during my final approach, and all I got was a red light and a buzzer—not much solace there!" There was only one engineer on the boat, and he was asleep, though not for long. "I knew that he knew there were problems by the sound of doors slamming throughout the boat. I didn't go check, but I imagine that that engineer was a blur down there in the pit." John says it seemed like two hours before the boat was back up and running, but it was probably less than a minute. "We managed to miss anything of importance." Nowadays, single-screw boats aren't permitted to push petroleum barges specifically because of situations like the one John describes.

Most important in the average day's work, twin-screw boats are more maneuverable than a single-screw tug. Dan Alexander enjoys the twin-screw boats he's running now in Long Island Sound. They certainly can make the job easier. "They allow me to do any cheating, dancing around, that I want without interfering with the situation." Translation: he can move his boat from one angle to another and not put any pressure on the ship. "And a single-screw is slower—you have to be going ahead for all maneuvers to get steerage. Twin-screw can twist, turn around. You don't have to move."

On a twin-screw boat, one propeller can go forward while the other is reversed, allowing the boat to turn around in her own length and make far sharper turns, or even inch herself sideways for a short distance. She can hold herself at right angles to the ship she's handling better than can a single-screw boat, particularly with a relatively low ship speed. She can also perform this maneuver more safely; using a lazy line to keep a single-screw boat perpendicular to the ship has led to many a tug being tripped.

Tractor Tugs

But it is the tractor tugs that have truly revolutionized ship docking. Captain Bob Power was a harbor pilot for twenty-seven years in Halifax, Nova Scotia, and worked with all manner of tugs. He says that a single-screw tug can push or tow well but isn't so good for backing up. A twin-screw rig has less pull per horsepower than a single-screw boat but is more maneuverable, and that's what's important for ship handling. But, he says, "as a pilot, if you have two Z-drives when you're going alongside a dock, you don't have to worry about a thing. The tug is always in position—it can give power in whatever direction you want."

When Captain Power retired from his pilot's job in Halifax, he started running tugs himself again. He enjoys his semi-retirement—he can say no anytime he wants to. But he never does. He loves driving the Z-drives. "It's mind candy," he says.

Pilot Bill Gribben, of Portland, Maine, describes the azimuthing tractor tug *Vicki M. McAllister* as a sports car with a lot of tricks. She has a pair of Z-drives mounted aft, and the two thrusters can be used together or in opposition to one degree or another, permitting the tug to go in any direction. As in almost all tractors, the captain has all the controls in the pilothouse, controlling both engine room and winch operations. He can move his boat in any direction he chooses simply by twiddling the joysticks that control the direction and force of the thrusters that have taken the place of propellers and rudders.

The real key to the Z-drive boat, Bill says, is that it can hold a ship sideways and move with the ship at the same time. "She can stay head-on and ready to work while still going ahead or astern."

Captain Mike Hickey, of Boston Towing & Transportation, runs the tractor tug *Freedom*. He spent ten days with Foss Maritime in Long Beach learning the tricks of tractor tugs. He started running them on his second day out there, and says that by day nine, he didn't want to leave. "Every time I heard the engines run, I was up in the pilot house." He has brought many of the western stunts back to Boston, and enjoys the outrageous moves possible with a tractor. "You gotta think outside the box," he says. "I'm always pushing it."

The panel on the helmsman's left on the azimuthing-drive *Freedom,* including hawser winch and Z-drive controls, autopilot, and navigation program. Although there are electronic versions, some feel that a printed tide schedule is still the easiest to use. Author photo.

The mate on the *Freedom* is Dave Black. When he realized he didn't like his engineering job in plastics, he got a job on deck at Wilmington Tug, which has used Z-drive tugs since 1977 and has no conventional boats. Dave got his master's license as soon as he could, and it wasn't long before he was asked to use it. He is unusual in that he has never run conventional tugs.

Boston's Chelsea Creek is the access to a number of tank farms, and while it's short, it is tight and twisty and there are two bridges to pass through. Both Mike and Dave like the opportunities it offers to play with the tractor's capabilities. Mike chuckles about the way they handle the second bridge, which is too narrow for a tug

Freedom tails a tanker through a tight spot on the Fore River, Boston Harbor. Deckhand Steve Santos is painting—he's not one to waste time. Author photo.

to stay alongside a ship going beneath it. They run a line from the tug's bullnose through one on the bow of the ship, then push sideways on her hull to get her lined up for the bridge. Then they scoot ahead, turn the tractor around, and run backward ahead of the ship, still tied on, as they go beneath the narrow bridge. It's just not a thing a traditional tug could do.

"The docking pilots enjoy it when we're on. We have a can-do attitude," Mike says. "The pilots know there's nothing Dave and I can't do with the *Freedom*."

"I like it when they say, 'You want to have fun tonight?'" adds Dave.

Ship Docking Modules

Seabulk Towing, in Tampa Bay, has the ultimate docking tugs to date: Ship Docking Modules. Captain Preston Barco runs one of them, the 4,200-horsepower *Suwannee River*. "If you can think it up, these boats'll do it," he says of these most-specialized and maneuverable docking tugs. The SDMs are ninety feet long and fifty feet wide, with semicircular ends. Their Z-drives are placed one forward, one aft, both off-center so the wheelwash of one drive won't interfere with the other. It doesn't make the slightest bit of difference to an SDM if it's going frontward or backward. Sideways, it does slow down a bit. Captain Barco says, "You can go from full-ahead mode, 12 knots, and stop within a hundred feet. You can turn around in the same axis, slide over a little bit, and go in the opposite direction. Or you can go from full sideways, 6½ knots, which is unheard of in a tugboat to start with, and go the opposite way full sideways. Or you can go full ahead and spin 180 degrees—or 360—and go back the other way." He admits that some of these tricks aren't applicable to the work the tug does, "but they give an idea of what you can do with the boat."

John Collins, operations director at Seabulk, enjoys Preston's demonstrations. "He likes to come full-speed toward the dock, and a couple of feet off, start making squares."

The SDMs and other tractor tugs have more options than a traditional tug as to where to come alongside a ship. The flare of a ship's bow looms out over a tug working forward; the visors of older conventional tugs are often bashed in from contact. But most of the tractors have relatively narrow houses, set well in from the bulwarks. A tractor can land almost anywhere on a ship. The well-protected pilothouses are nearly all glass and have angled corners, so they offer excellent visibility.

"You can go in either direction coming alongside a ship. I come backward. I run it forward and backward—doesn't matter. I use the ship as my reference," says Preston. "The engineer can put up the line where it's most convenient, or keep it from getting wet, or get under a bad counter on the stern—I can come along forward of the chock instead of behind it. Then the pilot can see you easier and doesn't wonder what you're doing."

Preston points out one of the difficulties with the new tractor tugs—language. Pilots forever have asked assist tugs to move forward or back, but these commands make no sense to the tractors that can move in any direction at all, and which may have landed on the ship in some non-traditional direction. Which way is "forward?" An effort is being made to standardize language, with directions to be given with reference to the ship. Other commands are also being standardized, like the terms for the degree of power being asked for—"full," "half," "easy," and "dead slow"—in place of local phrases and some that may not be so distinguishable over the radio.

And there's a story going around about how Crowley's tug *Captain* had to be renamed. "Come ahead, Cap'n," is a common-enough command for a pilot to issue, but it might refer to any of the people running assist tugs, or it might mean that particular boat. This innocent ambiguity caused confusion, so the tug was renamed *Admiral*.

The SDMs are the ultimate in their ship-docking specialization and are dedicated to harbor work. Their extreme proportions make them less suited for rough waters.

Ship Docking Module *St. Johns,* sister of the *Suwannee River,* showing off her tricks.
COURTESY OF SEABULK TOWING.

Preston brought one across the Gulf of Mexico in six- to eight-foot seas and says it wasn't a fun trip. "It's like riding a five-gallon bucket—every time you pitch or roll a little, it's like reaching down and scooping up some water."

Harbor Work—Docking an Oil Tanker in Searsport

The most photographed occupation of tugboats is probably ship docking. Everyone has seen the photographs of the first *Queen Mary* surrounded by six or even eight tugs, pushing and pulling as they guide the huge ship into her berth. Nowadays, cruise ships usually have their own thrusters that allow them to dock themselves, or at least get by with minimal help. But freighters, tankers, and other commercial ships still rely on tugs to dock them. Docking is the primary job of Maineport Towboats, until recently a partnership between Captains John Worth and Duke Tomlin.

Maineport Towboats operates four single-screw tugboats from Belfast, Maine. The company also does some coastal towing of construction equipment for bridge-work or other projects. They move the occasional fireworks barge, and have the con-tract to move the Maine Department of Environmental Protection's emergency barge from Bucksport if an oil spill should occur along the coast somewhere. "Ninety-eight percent of our work is ship docking in Searsport, Bucksport, and occasionally Win-terport," John says. "Very rarely, we go to Bangor. We only get involved there if there's an anomaly—like when a twin-screw ship only has one engine [operational]."

Four boats is a good number for them. Most jobs take two boats, though Duke likes to use three for the larger tankers in Searsport now—the recent pier construc-tion has made for stronger currents. Having an extra allows a rotation. Or, if all are up and running, they can do a ship in Searsport and a barge in Bucksport at the same time.

I visited Maineport Towboats on a busy Saturday in May when both a tanker and a tug-and-barge needed assistance docking. "It's unusual to get two at once," John said. "It makes it look like we're a busy place here, but we didn't do anything last week." This day, both assist jobs were in Searsport, and only two tugs would be required.

John was running the tug *Verona* for these jobs. She was in the middle of her spring painting, but "when you're outfitting, you don't have the luxury of staying in the harbor," John said. Life goes on for a tug, paint or no paint. The 120-foot tug has a 27-foot beam and draws about fifteen feet aft and nine feet forward. Originally steam-driven, she was built in 1913 by the Hamburg American Line to dock its ocean liners. In the 1940s she was converted to diesel-electric, one of the earliest diesel-electrics to be fully controlled from the pilothouse. She has a single 1,800-horse engine that turns a generator creating electricity for a motor that drives a ten-foot-diameter wheel with a 99-inch pitch—meaning that for each rotation of the drive shaft, the propeller has taken a 99-inch bite out of the water (and, because of vari-ous inefficiencies, has moved the vessel forward somewhat less.)

"She can step right out if you want her to," John said. "She can do 13 1/2 knots, but she burns sixty gallons an hour at that speed." With no apparent effort at all, she cruises at 10 knots, using fuel at half that rate.

The second tug on the job was the *Cape Rosier,* with Captain Pete Graham at the wheel. Originally a railroad tug, she first worked in Chicago. Like many tugs, she has had a succession of names: *Chicago, Accomack, Staten Island,* and finally *Cape Rosier.* She is a little shorter and a little shallower than the *Verona* and is also diesel-electric. Both tugs normally operate with two people aboard, the captain and an engineer/deckhand.

The 650-foot tanker *Reliance* had offloaded half her cargo of No. 6 industrial fuel at Portsmouth and was expected to arrive at Mack Point in Searsport at six p.m. on

Saturday of Memorial Day weekend, but John received word that she'd be an hour early. (Setting out again on Sunday, she more than lost any time she saved herself or the tugs on Saturday. First she was going to go out at eight-thirty in the morning, then nine-thirty, and finally she sailed at about one. "This is a lot of what we do," said John afterward, "sit and wait.")

Searsport gets more than its share of weekend and holiday ships, John said, because it's a relatively inexpensive port. In New York, the docks will unload at those times, but ships pay dearly. Searsport is happy for the business, whenever it comes. (This has long been so. The logbook for Christmas Day, 1967, shows Maineport Towboats' predecessor's *Security* heading out at 1100 to dock the *Vishva Pren*, but the ship was late. The men tied up the tug at 1340 and came back early the next morning to finally dock the ship.)

Working with *Verona*, the smaller *Cape Rosier* handles the bow when ships come into the Sprague dock at Searsport because quarters are tight between the two long piers. She made up to *Reliance*'s starboard bow with two lines forming a V. (This con-

Swan Point and *Lambert Point* work a ship in the 1970s. Both are now fish condos, as the tugboat people say—at the end of their careers they were sunk to form part of a protective reef off the Maryland coast.
PHOTO BY SYDNEY S. SUSSMAN PHOTOGRAPHY, FROM THE COLLECTION OF DAVE BOONE.

figuration compensates for the longer lines needed to reach the half-empty ship, which floated high in the water. Had *Reliance* been loaded and riding lower, *Cape Rosier* would have had sufficient control with a single bow line.)

Normally, the *Verona* would have been pushing directly on the transom, but the *Reliance*'s transom was too high off the water for the tug to reach, so she tied onto the starboard quarter.

While docking, all three vessels (the ship and two tugs) were under the command of the pilot who, in this case, came on board the ship at Monhegan three hours before her arrival in Searsport. As he guided her up the bay, the pilot suggested commands directly to the captain of the ship (who passed them on to his crew) and made them directly to each of the tugs by VHF radio. The tugs confirmed each command either with their horn or on the radio. Pete acknowledged with the *Cape Rosier*'s horn.

"*Cape Rosier,* half on one." (Half throttle, forward. "One" signified "ahead.")

Toot.

"*Cape Rosier,* stop."

Toot.

"*Cape Rosier*, half on one."

Toot.

"Gee, I hope we're gonna get to do something," said John, leaning back in his chair aboard the *Verona*. He explained about "cheating," swinging the tug out to 90 degrees to the ship to have more leverage when he's called on later. In this instance, being tied on the stern quarter, he could use the wash of the ship's propellers to slide the *Verona* out. "I'm gonna cheat out here a little," John said to the pilot on the radio as his tug's stern floated away from the ship.

"*Verona,* one quarter on one, please."

The *Verona*'s horn was down, so John repeated the command back to the pilot on the radio. "One quarter on one."

"*Verona,* easy."

"Easy."

"*Cape Rosier,* stop. Come into your line, and a half on two."

Toot toot (acknowledging the "two" command to back).

"*Cape Rosier,* minimum on one."

Toot.

"*Verona,* a little more on one. Look ahead about a forty-five."

"Looking ahead," said John, indicating that they were pushing the ship up into the dock a bit.

Everything was very smooth as the ship settled into the pier.

"John, we've got all four lines on back there. When they've got them all tightened up, we can let you go."

No one knew which tug would be called on to assist the coastwise tug *Tarpon* and her barge coming in at the other dock that day, but the job fell to *Verona,* since she was released from the *Reliance* first. The *Tarpon* is about the same size as the *Verona,* but twin-screw and powered with two or three times the horsepower. She has a towing machine that allows her to maintain an even tension on her towing cable even in a big sea. She also uses the winch to hold herself in the notch on the stern of the barge when she's in push mode, as when she approached the dock on this afternoon.

She could do docking work, and sometimes towing-boats do get into the docking business, John said, but *Tarpon*'s high wheelhouse—great for seeing over the barge—might get in the way here. She also isn't as well-armored with tires as is a harbor tug, because the fendering would ice up offshore. Tires are noisy and throw water on the deck, too.

The barge carries perhaps a hundred thousand barrels of oil; the tanker *Reliance,* when full, would carry twice that. John estimated that, together, the tug and barge carry six or eight people compared to the eighteen or so on the *Reliance.* (Not so long ago, the tanker would have had a crew of thirty, but, because of automation and the development of synthetic rope of lighter weight for equal strength, fewer men are needed now.) This saving in manpower is one of the advantages of transporting petroleum products by tug and barge.

Sometimes the tug-and-barge guys don't call for help when docking, John said, and they rarely need help to undock. They try to keep assistance to a minimum because of the expense. Although there may be a pilot aboard, the tug captain usually gives the commands, and the pilot simply gives advice about local conditions. This particular tug and barge came in from Canada and picked up their pilot at Matinicus.

The *Tarpon* and the *Verona* got the barge into the dock and tied up in a half hour, finishing up not long after the *Cape Rosier* was released from the *Reliance.* Both Maineport tugs headed for the other side of the Sprague dock, where they would stay overnight to be ready to undock the *Reliance* the next day. Their deckhands organized the lines so they could tie up side-by-side. The two tugs were hitched together and docked as a unit, with John giving the commands to the *Cape Rosier.*

"I always wanted a twin-screw tug," said John.

Old and New in Portland

I got to sit in on an entirely different operation in 2003 when the tractor tug *Vicki M. McAllister* docked the square-rigged training ship *Eagle* in Portland Harbor for Labor

Day weekend. She spent Thursday night at anchor in the harbor, and was scheduled to meet the 210-foot Coast Guard cutter *Seneca* at Portland Head on Friday morning and arrive at the Maine State Pier at ten o'clock. Portland Tugboat LLC was hired to dock her, and Captain Brian Fournier ran the lead tug.

Brian and his crew had docked a tanker into the crude-oil pipeline terminal at eleven o'clock the night before, taken another ship into the Merrill Marine Terminal at three in the morning, and sailed a tanker at six. But they'd caught little naps in between, and this morning they were watching *Today* on the galley television until time to leave the dock. Much of the galley on the *Vicki M. McAllister* looks like any home kitchen; their side-by-side refrigerator is a standard model, with ice and water dispensers in the door.

The docking pilot, Bill Gribben, came aboard at seven-thirty, as scheduled, and Brian backed the *Vicki* out of the slip. He stood in front of the helmsman's chair, looking aft, one hand on each of the small and nearly circular handles that control the two azimuthing drives. "Where I point her is where she'll go," Brian commented, showing that her simple controls had become part of his automatic reflexes even as he remarked that he was still learning her capabilities.

Brian didn't seem particularly enthusiastic to be doing this job, perhaps because it was a freebie—Portland Tugboat's contribution to the city's Labor Day festivities. Also, the pilot had mentioned that the old sailing ship offered challenges a modern ship three times her length would not. "She has all kinds of stuff sticking out," Bill explained, "and she's white everywhere you touch. Her steering gear is antiquated—it takes two people to turn the wheel, and she has a small rudder. Low horsepower, and she's heavy. The visibility on deck is horrible. There are a lot of people standing around watching, and if you make any little mistake, everyone knows." But Brian and Bill clearly weren't afraid of the task.

One of the two cell phones by Brian's right hand rang for the first of what seemed like fifty times during the morning's work. "I've just gotta find a way to get my pilot on here without doing any damage to this thing," he told the person who'd called. The *Eagle*'s spars were squared to the centerline, looking very handsome but pointing directly toward the tug's approach. Before *Eagle* raised anchor, Brian brought the tug in head-on between the fore and main masts. Though the *Vicki* has tremendous visibility forward, aft, and to both sides, from the pilothouse her helmsman can't see the tug's own mast, which holds her vast array of antennas and lights. A deckhand was on the bow acting as spotter for Brian. In addition to the cadets and Coast Guard officers on the *Eagle,* there were dozens of civilians all over her decks. "That's why these jobs are hard," said Brian. "You're under a microscope." Bill climbed aboard.

Brian grabbed a handful of Hot Tamale candies. Sugar junkie? "Just a little. I don't drink coffee—have to do something. Usually I have a pound of M&Ms." And why isn't he as big as a house? "I work out," he said. "Steering boats." (Steering the *Vicki* takes less than three ounces of effort from each hand.)

Brian backed the *Vicki* away from the ship and headed toward an empty chunk of water away from everyone else to show off the boat's tricks. She can make about thirteen knots ahead, Brian said; he didn't get her nearly to that speed this morning, but his full arrest was impressive nonetheless. "Did you ever see a boat stop that quick?" Brian asked. He explained that he did this by setting her drives opposed to one another, directed outward. Next, he spun her in place, one way and then the other, and showed how she can move sideways, although he admitted he wasn't fully fluent in that maneuver yet. The only time he has had occasion to walk her sideways was to get under the bow of a ship whose anchor line was fouled with lobster gear. "Trial by fire," he said.

Three radios are on all the time, their microphones hanging around Brian's head. One is set to a working channel on the boat herself so he can talk with his engineer and deckhand. The second radio is tuned to channel 13, the bridge-to-bridge channel, to catch calls from other commercial vessels in the harbor. This day, the third radio was set on the channel the Coast Guard had chosen for communication between *Eagle* and the tugs. In addition, Brian had his two cell phones. There are two GPS receivers and a radar screen overhead and a big compass mounted near the floor in front of the helmsman's chair. On each side of the chair are consoles that hold the controls and many buttons and lights. On the port side, two lights were covered by a box constructed of cardboard and duct tape. This boat was originally built to dock Navy ships in Puerto Rico, and when McAllister lost the contract, she was sent to Portland. "That box is a Puerto Rico special," said Brian. "She came with it." The lights it blocks are too bright at night.

When *Eagle* raised anchor and headed back out to Portland Head, the *Vicki* followed along behind. Right on schedule at eight-thirty, the 210-foot cutter *Seneca* came in from seaward and met the *Eagle* at Portland Head Light, her crew lined along her decks to honor the old square-rigger. (Brian suggested that he could drive right up between them and salute them both with the water cannons, but he didn't carry out the plan.) *Seneca* headed in, and *Eagle* continued out to sea. She wasn't due at the dock until ten o'clock. The *Vicki* just hung out, waiting for *Eagle* to come back.

Brian recollected taking a group out to Portland Head to admire the ships coming in for Op Sail a couple of years back. "We were on the *Boys*," he said, referring

Captain Brian Fournier "in the office" on the *Vicki M. McAllister.* Author photo.

to the tug *Fournier Boys,* "and we got out to here, and there was a four-foot swell. The caterers were down in the galley throwing up. People were in tears." He took them back into the sheltered water. None of it bothered him—all the more lobster for those who still wanted it.

He told also of the time that an Aegis destroyer was coming back to the States from somewhere. Her captain was from another local harbor, so they made an unscheduled stop there for two days. (The captain said he wanted to get his boys some ice cream.) The Portland tugs went out to help her. "It was OK with me," said Brian. "We made about thirty grand out of the deal. 'Any time,' we said."

This September morning, the sun made dramatic the bright colors on the boat. Looking over the bow from the wheelhouse, the rails gleamed white against the green upper deck and red foredeck. Black bitts, their ends and tops highlighted with yellow, stood out against the tan bulwarks capped with black, as did the top of the white canvas that had been hung over the rubber bow fendering to protect the white topsides of the *Eagle.* The deckhands wore bright orange lifejackets, and even the

Spectra head line shone blue. Looking aft, the colors were just as brilliant, but the silver paint on the stacks looked shabby.

"Look how bad your stacks are peeling," Brian teased Junior, the young deck-hand. "Did you use the wrong paint? You use high-heat paint?"

"I did, but I thinned it. I won't do that again," the kid said.

"Guess not," said Brian.

Eagle finally turned back and made her security call before entering the harbor. (Security calls are radio announcements to let nearby vessels know your intentions. They are required by the Coast Guard of vessels at certain ports, but are voluntary in Portland Harbor.)

As she passed Portland Head, Brian turned on the fire monitors. The *Vicki* can pump 1,500 gallons a minute through her fire hoses. She was saluting *Eagle* with nearly that much, rainbows shining beneath the water streams. It seemed sad that there was no one to watch the show, not at Portland Head Light nor at Spring Point Light. Was no one aware that *Eagle* was in town?

A second Portland tug, the *Justine McAllister,* came out to help with the docking. "I chose the *Justine* because she has those rope fenders," Brian explained. "And she's pretty gentle."

Gentleness was key. The *Vicki*, held in place on the *Eagle* by the Spectra head line leading through a chock forward on the ship, helped the big ship make the turn into the dock. The pilot gave his orders in a quiet voice, each acknowledged by the tug's whistle, an alto *wheep* from *Vicki*.

"Brian, ahead gently."

Wheep.

"Just barely. Very very very easy."

Wheep. Brian's hands moved nearly imperceptibly on the controls.

"Stop and hold."

Wheep.

"Very gently."

Wheep.

Throughout, *Vicki* stayed perpendicular to the ship as it moved forward through the water. "This is a big, powerful, massive tug," Brian remarked, "but she can be very very gentle. Even so, she's not like the *Captain Bill,*" he said, referring to the old diesel-electric boat back at the dock. "I could drive thumbtacks with the *Captain Bill.* You'd have to give me eight-penny nails for this one."

"Hold there."

Wheep.

The *Vicki M. McAllister* salutes the Coast Guard training ship *Eagle*.
COURTESY OF PHIL ROBERTS, JR

Heaving the line to *Eagle*. (The glass of the pilothouse received its share of the salute.)
AUTHOR PHOTO.

The big ship was nearly parallel to the dock. "Sammy, are you in a place where you can come in on the port quarter?" Bill asked the *Justine*'s captain. *Justine*'s whistle is shriller than *Vicki*'s. She shrieked a short reply and slowly moved in on the *Eagle*.

Bill differentiated the orders by the captains' names.

"Brian, ahead easy."

Wheep.

"Keep working easy now, Sam."

Skreek.

"Small push right now, Sam."

Skreek.

"Brian, just back real easy."

Wheep wheep. Brian acknowledged the order to back.

"Just ahead, Brian, just a touch."

Wheep.

"Keep touching her, Sam."

Skreek.

"Again ahead just a bite, Brian."

Wheep. The *Eagle* moved slowly forward and sideways toward the pier.

"Another touch, Sam."

Skreek.

"No push, Sam."

Skreek.

"A little bit back, Brian. Just a baby."

Wheep wheep.

"Stop, Brian." *Wheep.*

"Touch in, Brian. Baby touch."

Wheep.

"I'm driving the *Justine* away with my wash," said Brian to the people in the pilot-house, "making his life more difficult, so I'm just using one drive now. Means a little more maneuvering on my part," he said, but it wasn't apparent. The fingers on his left hand made small movements with the handle while his right pushed the button for the whistle.

"Done pushing, Sam, I hope," said the pilot. "Baby touch in, Brian."

Wheep.

"Good."

When the square-rigger was in place on the dock and the lines were ashore, there were two more orders to Brian: "Very easy."

Wheep.

"Stop, Brian," and a final *wheep.* The pilot released the two tugs. It was ten o'clock on the dot.

The *Justine*'s stern was swinging over toward the *Vicki.* "I'll shape you up," Brian radioed to Sam, and he sent the wheelwash from his right engine toward the *Justine*, who responded by swinging slowly perpendicular to the *Eagle* again, and Sam backed her out. *Vicki* followed and, after a quick tour of the river, Brian sidled her into place next to the barge that serves as his office.

"What do you think is next?" the pilot asked Brian on the radio. They had a ship to dock at midnight. More immediately, Brian said, was nap time.

Shifting Barges

For many tugs, moving barges around is probably their most common and least glamorous job. Other than handling ships, a tug isn't good for much without a barge, and any working waterfront is littered with barges of all kinds, inevitably in the wrong places. On the breezy May day that I was aboard, Donjon Marine's 151-foot *Atlantic Salvor* was waiting for a dredge scow to be filled so she could take it out off Sandy Hook to dump. But the dredging was going slowly, so the tug was given fill-in work at one of Donjon's two dock areas in Port Newark. The big tug was called to the shop

A small barge of containers moving in New York Harbor. AUTHOR PHOTO.

area first so the port engineer could make some repairs to the towing winch, and then she was sent over to the other pier to shuffle barges.

"Take these, flip 'em over, slide 'em down the dock some. *Chris* stays on the dock. Put the *106* outside the *Columbia,* get the transformer, and then put the *106* in the hole there." Those were the instructions. Noon came and went between the time the *Salvor* left the first dock and reached the second, so John Woods, the mate, had taken the watch from Captain Dave Riddick and was on the helm. Everyone knew what was meant by the orders. There were a number of barges along the pier, including the little deck barge *106* laying inside the *Chris,* a bigger hopper barge. They were to turn those two barges around in place and push them along the pier, leaving a hole between them and the other barges. They would tie up the *Chris,* take the *106* up alongside the crane barge *Columbia.* There was a transformer on the pier next to the *Columbia;* they'd load the transformer onto the *106,* and return the *106* to the hole.

John pushed the button that switched the compressed-air controls to the star-

Off-watch on the *Atlantic Salvor,* Captain Dave Riddick helps William Johnson on deck. He's freeing the double-wrapped line from the barge *Chris.* AUTHOR PHOTO.

board-side bridge wing, where he could see what he was doing and communicate with the deckhand. In front of him were the two engine throttles, a joystick for steering and the bow thruster control. He told Allen, the deckhand, what the plan was. Allen easily jumped from barge to barge and onto the pier to release a line and off again while John gently moved the bow of the *Salvor* just above a bitt on the barge. Allen took the head line from the tug and dropped it over the bitt with a turn. "That's good," he said. "Leave a little slack so I can get away from it." Allen scampered back to the inner barge, the *106*. John asked him if the lines holding the two barges together were good. Yes. OK. A short quick back on the *Salvor* pulled the corner of the pair of barges away from the pier, turning on the one line that still led ashore.

"Think you can get the head line off even though it's wrapped?" John asked the assistant engineer on deck. "I'll try," said the AE, but the off-watch captain was right there and flipped the line's double loop off the bitt on the barge. Everyone in the tugboat industry agrees that no one should work in the wheelhouse unless they've worked the deck and understands it. And deck skills don't leave you.

Allen Searle is on the barge as the *Atlantic Salvor* maneuvers it into place. Author photo.

"This is where the swearing usually starts," John said to me. "Especially on a windy day." But, quietly and without fuss, he nudged the barges in this direction and that, signaling to Allen when to let the stern line go from the barge and all the while telling me about people I ought to interview. The two barges smoothly turned around parallel to the pier but now in reverse order. He looked to Allen again. "Can you get a line on that corner?" From up high, John could see that the barge was about to hit the pier. "Watch the bump," he warned Allen, who balanced himself without apparent effort when the barge hit with a little lurch.

John once again addressed me: "Big boats and little barges don't work." You couldn't tell by this exercise. "Allen, now you can let them go, I'll slide them down. I just don't want to get under the bow of the *Chessie*," he said, referring to the overhanging bow of the largest barge of all, with not only the largest crane in sight but the largest on the East Coast, tied further along the pier. It can lift 1,000 tons. "I'm gonna slide back a little toward the *Chessie*—I want to leave a bigger hole, is all."

When another tug came by, he told me about her. "The *Cynthia Moran* is identical to the two up in the yard that Donjon is scrapping out," he said. "Okay, Allen, any cleat you come along, grab it there." He turned back to the assistant engineer. "Doug, want to take that head line so I can get Allen on? Stay right there, Allen, I'll get you." The line was a quarter of the way forward on the *106*. "This is either gonna make me look real good or real stupid," he said. "Watch the bump!" he again warned Allen. "This is a finesse," he said to me. "Little barges can make a fool out of you. And definitely, one thing this boat wasn't made for is handling little barges smaller than itself." (Captain John O'Reilly also knows this boat. "*Salvor* can really be a bear with a small barge," says he.)

Could have fooled me. There were two more barges to shift, and the rest of the moves were made just as easily. Perhaps "easily" is the wrong word—but that's how it looked.

Hazards of the Trade

Not always is a helmsman so careful to warn his deckhand to watch the bump. Captain Richie Bates tells of a time when he was just starting out and working the deck. "I was a young guy in good shape, fortunately." It was 1978, just before Christmas. Taking barges into the dock, they bumped and he went into the river, falling through ice. "There I was standing on the bottom of the Hudson River under the ice, all my clothes on and no life jacket," he says. "They tell you to look up to see the hole, and it's true—you can see it. I pushed off and swam for the hole." He was able to swim up and climb back aboard the ribbed-sided barge. "I walked back to the boat, and I'm gonna kill the captain. He'd told me it was gonna be all stop, and I was working the docklines. 'Course he said he didn't bump me—for some reason I just fell off." The kindly old cook aboard walked Richie to the shower and gave him a shot of brandy, and then they sent him home. "I was all scratched up and bruised, and I was very frightened," he says today, and the fright is still in his voice.

Towed objects offer external hazards, too. Captain Jim Sharp says that simply moving his wheel a half a spoke could have demolished the Million-Dollar Bridge in Portland, Maine. "Sometimes, there are things that you do without stopping to think about 'em. You just do what you have to do. If you bothered to stop and think, it would just complicate things. You trust your boat, you trust your gear, and you just go for it. If I had thought about the damage I could've inflicted on that bridge, if I'd connected with it with that ungodly barge piled high with mushroom anchors and gobs of chain, it might have rearranged my mental outlook. It should have. It didn't."

Arthur Fournier had the job of towing Bath Iron Works' drydock from the Boston Navy Yard to Portland, where BIW would use it to finish the Arleigh Burke–class destroyers they were building in Bath. Jim was running the 1,800-horsepower tug *Bronx*—now the *Verona*—for Arthur. "The tug was half a ship, she was so big," says Jim. She's 120 feet long, only a foot and a half shorter than his own former Glouces-ter fishing schooner, *Adventure*.

The drydock, more than two football fields long altogether, came in nine sec-tions, each 80 feet long by 256 feet wide, with wing walls at each end that not only towered over the tug but interfered with both visibility and radar. Each wall's sail area was tremendous. "It was a challenge to maneuver," Jim says in understatement.

He describes the pendants they rigged to tow each section. "We used inch-and-a-half stud-link chain—hernia work—you could hardly pick up a single link of it." They flaked the whole chain out on the fantail of the *Bronx*, and a little yard tug would take a line connected to the chain and steam away, drawing the chain up over the bollards of the section of drydock. "But you have to stop the tug at the right time—if the chain gets beyond its gravity, it'll roll off the barge and fall down in the water again.

"There was a lot of ship handling just rigging this thing."

And the whole process had to be done nine times.

The tug could only average two knots on this job. "We'd get out there on a great long hawser with this huge thing behind us, and if we had a headwind, we'd only make a knot and a half—if we had a tailwind, maybe three or three and a half," Jim says.

"We had to pick our weather carefully. Then, of course, you'd get to Portland half the time working in fog. Once it was dungeon-thick fog—and I could only see the radar out one side, so I had to judge the distances from the one side—it was a navigational challenge! This was before GPS and all that. Thank God we had radar! With those huge massive wing walls, the compass was all deviation. I was flying by what I saw on the radar."

Delivering the drydock took nine trips, and then the final part of the job was moving the barge with all the ground tackle, chain, anchors, and gear to secure the entire drydock. "It was loaded down with all that chain and the mushroom anchors. There was an enormous pile of it, mounded up as high as the tug, and it seemed as if there musta been forty anchors, each maybe five thousand pounds. I have no idea how much all that weighed, but it was an ungodly heavy load." Jim brought that barge and another with a big gantry crane on it down to Portland and tied up at the old pilings at the foot of Franklin Street. Arthur had told Jim to take the chain barge up to the Cianbro construction company, whose dock was just the other side of the Million-Dollar Bridge. Jim had agreed before looking at the chart—"and then, God, I looked at the bridge clearances. Wow. Ninety-eight feet it was. The barge with its great pile of chain was maybe sixty feet wide, and the tug was twenty-five feet wide, and with about eight feet of oversized-tire fenders, that all let me out to over ninety feet of width.

"When you're pushing a barge on the hip, you can't push straight in line because it'll skid off sideways," Jim explains. "You have to push kind of kitty-cornered, which increases the width of the tow even more. So I knew I was pretty damn close to the width of that opening in the bridge." And with all the weight on that barge, it wasn't about to stop even if it connected with the bridge.

"Well, I didn't think about all that until after I started. I had a fair tide, unfortunately, for that meant I needed more speed to maintain steerageway. I had to aim the leading corner of the barge right toward the piling of the bridge opening, and when I got up there I had to quickly straighten her up and shoot through. Thank the Lord we didn't connect, 'cause if I'd torn that bridge outa there, I'd have been in jail forever, and Arthur would have blamed me.

"It was more than a little scary," Jim admits, the more so since when he got through the bridge, they were making four knots. "I went right into reverse and was backing her full, backing her full, backing her full—all the way till we got to the dock." He finally got her stopped and skidded her over and got her tied up.

"When I think back on how close we came to connecting with that bridge, I have more respect for guys like Arthur who have done it all their life. Boat handling is a kick, though—I love the challenge of it."

The *Adriatic Sea* coming through Hell Gate light tug (with no barge).
COURTESY OF DON SUTHERLAND.

New York's Hell Gate

They say that tugboating is endless hours of boredom punctuated by moments of sheer terror. Some of the time a tug spends in port, she's just biding her time until the right window opens up for a job, and when that time comes, life may get interesting. While I was aboard the *Adriatic Sea,* her assignment from K-Sea Transportation was to take a partial load of gasoline from New York to New Haven. There was no terror in my trip, which was all right with me, though I imagine the crew of the *Adriatic Sea* found most of my forty-eight–hour visit to be pretty dull since we sat at anchor most of the time. But we did face Hell Gate, once we were under way.

There were only two issues with the voyage: when the dock would be available to discharge the fuel, and the timing of our passage through Hell Gate. There, the Harlem River joins the East River just as it jams into a narrow, S-curved channel before expanding into Long Island Sound. Given this topography, the name Hell Gate seems appropriate, but, in fact, it comes from the Dutch *helegat,* meaning "bright passage." In New York, this channel is simply known as the Gate.

Mariners have to be careful when they pass through the Gate. With each change of tide, the current reverses direction, and it can run at five knots or more. When the tide is going out, all of Long Island Sound on the east tries to force its way into the City through the Gate, and when the tide's coming in, the water of New York's harbor pushes for the Sound. It is usually dangerous, if not impossible, to make passage with a loaded barge at these times. Fortunately, there is a slack time between tides. "For a brief minute, there's no current at all," the *Adriatic Sea*'s Captain Vernon Elburn explained. There's about an hour when the current is easily manageable by any vessel. Vernon will tow a light (empty) barge from the Sound to the harbor at any tide at all; with forty-five years' experience in tugs, much of it passing through these waters, he knows where each eddy and current is. "You stay on the outside, and you're OK," he says. "If you go on the inside, the barge wants to pass you." A barge going by its tug can pull the tow wire off to the side and "trip" the tug—capsize it.

Other tug masters also know the Gate. Captain John O'Reilly, for one, has been going through it for a quarter of a century. "I have a pretty good idea of what the currents are doing where I'm going. I look at the stage of the moon and see if I can make it through. Sometimes you can't, depending on the vessel's handling characteristics, the time of the month, and so on. The inexperienced guys get stuck in there and can't go forward and can't go back. You can see the fellow's eyeballs bulging in fright if he doesn't know what he's doing."

Captain Christopher Holt remembers the Gate from his time on the sanitation run. "You have to come through Hell Gate on the right tide. On a 1,600-horsepower tug, even with everything you've got, it's not enough when the current is running full bore. I've heard of people hitting the river wall and breaking the tow. There's always a light tug [a tug with no barge] around somewhere you can call for assist. You just hope you don't take out anything on the way. I was blessed."

Any sensible mariner will be cautious. "You don't go through the Gate hooked up," says Dan Alexander, using the tugboating term that means "at full throttle." "You always want something in your pocket. You go as slow as you can so you have a lot in reserve. You never know when you're going to meet someone—maybe some clown in a Hatteras [a sport fisherman]. Then there are the tugs coming down from the sewage plants, making a milk run—they just go—no security call, no nothing."

"You do your best not to meet anybody in the Gate," says the *Adriatic*'s Vernon. Whoever's running with the current—whichever way it's going at that moment—has the right of way, but unless one vessel is very small and can just stay out of the way, commercial vessels do not meet in the Gate.

Under the center of the Triborough Bridge, which crosses both the East River from Queens to the Bronx and the Harlem River to Manhattan, there's an eddy. Tug operators try not to run through it when there's a strong current. "I came through many years ago in a strong fair tide in a small tug, light barge, and went through the middle of the whirl," says Vernon. "It was such a whirl the boat dropped a couple of inches—it was just sucking us down. I always remember about that whirl, and stay out of it." It also matters which side you're on. "If you get to the right of it, you get a strong right-hand set into the rocks, so you try to stay just to the left of center."

Our own trip through the Gate was originally scheduled for midnight, which disappointed me; I'd been looking forward to seeing our passage. But because the *Adriatic*'s opening in the berth at the other end was twice delayed, the passage was postponed to the next day. We finally went through on the slack that came at six p.m. while there was still daylight. With Vernon at the helm, I experienced nothing the least bit alarming. Even the potentially terror-filled times on tugs can be quiet, if not boring. No one complains.

The "Houston Chicken"

"If you don't know the Chicken, you don't want to be in Houston," says Captain Steve Rhodes. "If you read the *Professional Mariner* magazine, in almost every issue you'll read about an accident in Houston." The shipping channel is very narrow, and there's a lot of traffic: small barge traffic, ships, and tugs-and-barges like Steve's articulated unit. "Let's say I'm in the channel headed up and a ship's coming out. We head right at each other. We'll have our radar set on the quarter-mile ring, and when we get there, I turn to my starboard and he turns to his, and as soon's we're amidships on each other, we turn back. That way you minimize being out of the deep part of the channel. You better be sure you know how fast your boat steers!" Sometimes a vessel actually bounces off the water squeezed between hull and bank. Bank effect, that's called.

Steve says the Houston Chicken is common practice there, but it's a maneuver made nowhere else in the world that he's ever seen. "The first time I did it, I freaked out," Steve recalls. "The pilot said, 'OK, steer at him.'

"I said 'What?'

"'Steer at him. Steer *at* him!'

"It's unique, but it works. If you don't do it, you're not going to make it."

Of course it's not always foolproof, but few of the irregularities are serious. The channel is lined with soft mud, and no damage is done by bottom-touches that in the Northeast would send vessels into the yard for new propellers.

Dredging

Ever since there were people in boats coming and going from harbors, the harbors have been just a little bit wrong. Often a channel doesn't exist, isn't deep enough, or used to be all right but has silted in so it no longer can handle the traffic that would like to use it. An anchorage or docking area may be too shallow, or a particular obstruction may be deemed dangerous. Permits from the Army Corps of Engineers in hand, the dredgers arrive with their barges, cranes, and tugs. (Actually, there are also specialized ships that do dredging, but they're not my topic.)

Dredging is a job with little romance but some appeal nonetheless for a towboater who is tired of the always-on-the-go nature of most harbor work. The dredging tug's job has a lot of hurry up and wait to it, and it is yet another of the environmentally touchy projects, such as moving petroleum products, that tugs are often involved with. In this case, the issue is the disposal of the materials dredged up. Sometimes they are taken to sea and must be dumped precisely in a designated area—and you can count on it that the Army Corps of Engineers is paying attention.

"Dredging is tugboating at its best and its worst," says Captain Bob Peterson. "The good thing about being on the towboat is they forget you exist. As long's I'm doing my job, the company doesn't care if I'm dead or alive." Bob runs a tug for Great Lakes Dredge & Dock Company, the largest dredging contractor in the United States. He came to tugs from commercial fishing, where he worked three hundred days a year to make about as much money as he now makes in six months. But by its nature, dredging has its hazards. It is almost always done in shoal water where there's some kind of a problem that they're trying to correct. "Normally, it's in a traffic lane, and normally that's gonna be up in some bay or a harbor with the current jumping around doing weird shit to you," says Bob. Their present project is on the Cape Fear River, North Carolina. "Fast currents, high winds, narrow channels, and a lot of yachts" is how Bob describes it.

And, he says, "It's not like in the oil industry where, if you go to put a barge to a dock somewhere, you call an assist boat, and you grandma it in there and take your time." He tells of taking a couple of scows up the Cape Fear side by side and landing them in a dock in Wilmington, on the tow wire. "You never even consider doing that in any industry other than dredge." (In fact, in the Pacific Northwest, chip barges are often moved three at a time. But he's right that it's unusual.)

"We do an awful lot of barge handling, more so than in any other business I'm aware of. Other businesses do a lot of shifting, but it's the nature of this business to take the load and get rid of it as quickly as you can and get the barge back, because you don't want that dredge to ever have to stop." The dredging equipment represents a lot of money to be just sitting around.

Essentially, all dredging jobs are Army Corps of Engineers projects, and there's usually a deadline in the bid specs. In any case, time comes into the financial picture. The faster a job can be finished, the sooner the equipment can go onto another project. "We're hooked up all the time. I get on that scow, and as soon as I'm safe, I push it to her."

In the most recent projects Bob has worked, the dumping ground has been twenty-five to fifty miles from the dredge site. Depending on the wind, current, and sea, they might make twelve or thirteen knots or they might only make five, but he says they can average about eight knots, including the dumping time. That often makes for an all-day run out and back. "They leave me alone as long as I'm towing their mud. Nobody calls me, nobody checks. It's beautiful—it's like my own business."

The scows hold between 3,500 and 6,500 cubic yards of material. While they used to have barges with bucket cranes to unload them, now the big outfits use split-hull dump scows controlled from the tug. "Hit the button, she's gone," says Bob. The barge jumps right up when the mud drops, going from a twenty-foot draft to three feet in seconds.

The dumping is carefully managed by the Army Corps, which sends an inspector along on every run. For each project there's a dumping ground identified and charted out with individual cells; each load, depending on the type of material dredged up, is destined for a particular cell. The inspector not only makes certain that the load is dumped where it is supposed to be but calculates the volume of material on each load, keeps track of the pressure in the scow on the trip to be sure it's not seeping or leaking beyond a certain tolerance, and keeps an eye out for marine life that might be affected. He records all this data on his computer, and with a GPS program keeps track of the location of the boat and scow so he can give the official okay to dump. He may be on line directly to the Corps headquarters—"There's some schmuck in an office somewhere actually watching me as I either fuck it up or don't fuck it up," says Bob.

The software on the inspector's computer is extraordinary. Not only does it permit the engineers on shore in Rhode Island to keep track of the location and direction of movement of the boat and of the scow—if they should become separated, the office will know—but it can tell how deep in the water the scow is riding, and therefore whether it is fully loaded. It allows the inspector to check weather conditions and specific data from the weather-reporting buoys spaced along the United States coastlines—if there are high winds or heavy seas at a particular and relevant buoyed location, they will know it.

The people who created the software can also look over the inspector's shoulder and correct any problems that should arise on the computer right then and there. That there's a live human being on the boat alongside that computer is important too, says Ned Clement, an inspector. "My job is to be sure the equipment is running, and also to be sure what they're taking out is what they said it was, not smuggled oily rags or untreated sewage waste—that that there's no funny business going on." But there's more than simply a policing effort being made. Inspector Joe Giquinto says that everyone on the boat helps one another as much as they possibly can, that the crew respects what he does, and he respects what they do. "I rely on his knowledge," he says of the captain, "and he relies on my communication."

It's sometimes tough to dump the load exactly where it's supposed to go. Bob speaks of a job in New York. "Last time we were working there—now mind you, I gotta do this on a wire. I can't round up on the scows and get them alongside because it's too rough. And we had scows that were sixty-five foot on the beam, and the cell was only a hundred yards square. So you gotta dump it on a gnat's ass, and then everybody gets all red in the face if you happen to miss or you circle around all day, so there's just an ongoing argument about the process."

Even so, Bob admits, dredge work has an advantage over transporting petroleum products. "Hauling mud, if I screw up and dump a load the wrong place, they're going to be a little upset but they're not gonna crucify me."

In dredging, the familiar tugboating theme recurs: "When it's boring, my job is good," says Bob. "It goes from sheer boredom to way too much excitement, too quickly. I don't like them nail-biters—it kinda puckers you up in the ass a little bit. Makes it interesting." He speaks of coming up the Hudson River to the cruise ship piers in Manhattan, where Great Lakes dredges year after year. "You come in with the dump scow on the wire very, very short—pulled right up on your ass. Then you let the scow go, detach altogether, and step around the scow to get it alongside the tug. If you miss that thing, there's ferry traffic, yacht traffic, docks, wharves—everything. So that keeps you awake."

In spring, the freshets coming down the Hudson increase the current. "Runs like a bastard on the ebb current," is how Bob describes it. "You have go up into those piers with much more headway than you want to be carrying because, if you slack off, the current's gonna smack you right into the leeward dock there. So you go around the corner screaming, and as soon as you get into that slip you start backing like a son of a bitch, hoping to Christ you don't end up on the West Side Highway."

The Cape Fear River is a challenge too. "Once you're used to it, it's OK," Bob says, "but getting used to it is a nail-biter. It goes from channel depth to two feet very quickly, and if you stuff that tug, the scow is going to roll right over you."

Having plans and backup plans is essential in any kind of situation like this. "You go in saying, 'Well, this is what I'm planning on doing, and if that doesn't work, I'm gonna try this, and if that doesn't work, we'll do this other thing,' and after that—Jesus, hold on."

He describes an incident that happened to a fellow on another boat in New York not too long ago. He went to move the dredge and a scow in the Kills and got caught in the current, and ended up on the wrong side of his tow. "He tried to get on the other side and collect the whole mess up. Once he got there, he couldn't stop it, and the current bashed him into a rock, going backwards, and busted everything to hell."

You get fooled by a barge sometimes. "I'll tell you," says Bob, "you look at that thing, and it doesn't seem to be moving, but you maneuver your tug around, and that thing's swinging like a son of a bitch, and you didn't see it." As a fellow from Moran Towing told Bob once, "The fastest thing in the world is a scow dead in the water."

One of the biggest concerns of any tugboater is collision with another vessel. One time the Coast Guard called Peterson on his tug on the Cape Fear River. "That boat you ran into," they started to say, but Bob interrupted. He couldn't imagine what they were talking about.

It was a moonlit summer night, flat calm, clear as could be. Bob was headed outbound on the Cape Fear River, towing a loaded dump scow up short, on maybe a hundred feet of wire. A few miles back, he'd seen a little power yacht and tried to call him on the radio. "As usual, he didn't respond." Yachts don't monitor the radio much. "But I'm watching the guy, and he's on his side of the channel and I'm on mine. I walked over to the side to look at him. It was a pretty little boat—little round fantail." Bob watched the boat go on by him, "and then I was setting up for a turn in the channel, so I went back to what I was doing."

Two or three miles down the river from there, the Coast Guard came out and circled around Bob, who called them and asked what was going on. Could he help them? "There was a collision on the river between a tug and a yacht," they told him. "Did you see anything?"

"No. I think I'm the only tug on the river, and I only saw one yacht. He went by me on my port side."

The Coast Guard went its way and Bob went his, and by Bald Head Island, the phone rang, and it was the Coast Guard. "Well, Cap, that boat you ran into—"

"Whoa, hold on a minute! What are you talking about?"

"Let me rephrase that," the Coastie said. "That boat that ran into you." But Bob still had no idea what they were talking about. "There was a yacht that passed you along about Sunny Point," they said. "He said that he thought the running lights on your scow were channel markers, and as soon as he got by your tug, he ran right into your scow."

"You're kidding me!" Bob said, but they weren't. He asked if the guy was all right, and they said he'd cracked his boat up pretty good and ran it up onto the beach, but he was OK. It was an old guy and his wife. "He obviously didn't know what he was doing. They checked me all out, and of course my light configurations were correct.

"The deck lights off the tug illuminated the tow wire all the way back, and the head log of the tow was illuminated. I can't imagine how the guy got that confused. If it were me, it would have been my last day of boating.

"He's lucky he's alive. *I'm* lucky he's alive. They'd have taken me and thrown me in jail. Wouldn't even have asked me for an explanation. On I go with the paperwork, all the while wondering if they're gonna come with a ball and chain. We're always wrong—we're the licensed people. Seems they'll always come after the guy with the license because they have no hold on the other guy."

Bob came out of it all right other than the nuisance of the paperwork, as did a guy coming out of Boston a while back with a loaded dump scow on a short wire at midday. A sailboat slipped between the tug and the barge, which ran right over him. "Gee," the yachtsman said later, "I didn't think that thing was connected to you."

"If there's one message you can get out there," Bob says to me, "it's to tell yacht people in general to find out where the commercial vessels are working on the radio—usually it's channel 13—and at least have the courtesy to communicate with us. That doesn't mean you have to get on with all kinds of radio banter, but I would be happy to talk with you and let you know what I want to do, what I'm going to do. When I call someone and they answer, it makes my day. Often they're intimidated, think we don't want to be bothered, but I would rather be bothered than dragged off in chains."

Escort Duty

A relatively new job for harbor tugs developed as a result of the increased concern first about oil spills and now terrorism. The Coast Guard now requires that petroleum tankers be escorted into many harbors, including Prince William Sound, Puget Sound, San Francisco Bay, Los Angeles/Long Beach, and San Diego. Even the newest double-hulled tankers with fully redundant propulsion, steering, and navigation systems must have one escort. In other ports, oil companies themselves have required escorts—for instance, coming into the pipeline terminal in Portland, Maine. Sometimes the requirement is local. Fear of terrorism has put cities on alert when what they perceive as particularly dangerous cargoes enter their waters; in Boston, for example, the liquefied natural gas tankers are given tremendous protection.

It takes extremely powerful tugs with particular capabilities to provide the degree of safety expected of an escort. Tractor tugs have become the boats of choice, with their particular propulsion systems that allow them to move, push or pull in any direction. These may be Voith-Schneider cycloidal units or azimuthing systems.

The first Voith-Schneider propulsion unit, installed in a European tug in 1954, started a revolution in tug design and operation. Since then, tractors have become increasingly common in Europe, and have recently become better known in North America, too. The West Coast's Foss Maritime was the first company in the United States with tractors; they built their first Voith-Schneider cycloidal propeller tugs twenty years ago in anticipation of the need for escort work. More recently, Foss has also added boats with azimuthing stern-drives, but they continue to opt for the Voith system for most escorting. Crowley Marine Services is also a major player in the West Coast escort business. They too operate Voith-Schneiders predominantly but have recently built some azimuthing boats as well.

Originally designed as assist tugs for docking ships, at which they excel, tractor tugs have proven themselves particularly capable in their more recent role as escorts, especially if the hull was designed for escort work. The idea is that an oil tanker going through a vulnerable passage can be attended by an escort or two so the tugs could take over, stopping, holding, or turning the tanker should it lose its own power or steering. But the momentum of a big ship that suddenly can't steer itself is tremendous. With the engine shut down, the distance she might travel on her own would be measured in miles, not feet. She has a great desire to go in the direction she's already moving, and the trick is to save her before she bumps into something.

In Puget Sound, tankers are limited to 125,000 deadweight tons (this includes ship and cargo), and while this tonnage isn't very large by contemporary tanker standards, it's still a very big object for a tug to handle, particularly when it's moving. Nonetheless, the Foss people say their Voith tractor tugs can manage such a ship at the permitted speed of ten knots and even up to twelve. Because of the length of the

Voith-Schneider escort tug *Nanuq*. COURTESY OF CROWLEY MARINE SERVICES.

Strait of Juan de Fuca, the entrance to Puget Sound, shipping companies naturally want to maintain speed as long as they can. From where a tanker picks up its escorts, it still takes several hours to get to the refineries near the Canadian border, and ten or twelve hours to reach a refinery at Tacoma.

In tricky or narrow places, at the end of the escort, or whenever an oil company's policy calls for it, the tug astern puts a line up onto the tanker, thereby becoming a "tethered escort." "You're the brakes and the rudder if there's a failure," explains Mike Hickey, who escorts in Boston. If a tanker were to suddenly lose power or steering, she would sail on for a long way on her own. If a precautionary line were not already in place, a tanker would move a significant distance during the time it took to get a line up from the tug. Or it might be that the ship simply has to stop more quickly than she can on her own, as happened in the summer of 2001 in Valdez Narrows, when a fishing vessel was setting a seine net in the traffic lane and didn't respond to hails on the radio. Fortunately, the escort vessel *Aware* was on the tether and could pull back against the ship, bringing it to a complete stop within two ship-lengths—amazing, but still, that was more than 1,500 feet.

The most effective way for an escort to slow a tanker at speed is by opposing it indirectly. In a Voith boat, the tug is set perpendicular to the movement of the ship, and its big skeg aft provides tremendous drag, becoming in effect a huge sea-anchor. Early azimuthing-drive boats were best able to slow a ship from behind with a transverse arrest, directing full power of each unit outboard. Once the ship has slowed to six knots, the nozzles can be turned to pull directly against the ship's movement. More recently, a box keel on the forefoot of some Z-drive tugs allows them to mimic the Voith's sideways positioning. Oriented perpendicular to the movement of the ship, the added sail area beneath the water provides great slowing force to the ship and stability to the tug.

"Opposing, the tractors (drives) push a huge wall of water," explains Captain Preston Barco of Seabulk Towing. "It's like someone dragging you through the water by your feet, and you're OK until you put your arms out—the water will actually bend them." He has seen tank tests showing stern-drive tractor tug models being dragged sideways and at forty-five degrees. Water came over the bulwarks and halfway up the house, but the boat never changed attitude. "With traditional boats, water over the bulwarks will roll a tug, or make you cry uncle and turn into it."

Aside from any additional stopping power that a Voith boat might offer, the controls are generally considered more intuitive and easier to master than those of an azimuthing drive. But the Voiths do require more boat per horsepower than do the Zs, and more horsepower per unit of bollard pull. A Z-drive is also considerably less expensive to build than a Voith. Although Steve Kimmel, port captain for Foss in Seattle, appreciates the Voith boats, he sees the Zs as the boats of the future and says they will replace most conventional tugs in time. "They handle so much better than conventional tugs."

In Boston, the new Z-drive tugs *Freedom* and *Liberty* were built specifically for the escort business. The city requires tug escorts for ships carrying liquefied natural gas (LNG) into Boston. (The ships are also accompanied by city, state and environmental police, fire and Coast Guard vessels, and a helicopter. Under Coast Guard and FBI direction, a tremendous number of protective and security measures are taken. Traffic is effectively stopped in and over the parts of the harbor the LNG ships are passing through, and personnel aboard or involved with the vessel along the way are carefully tracked. No one is permitted aboard one of the escorts without full security clearance.

Never mind that a tanker of gasoline is actually far more likely to explode than is the super-chilled LNG. Certainly if the LNG were to go off, it would be disastrous.)

Freedom and *Liberty* both come from the Washburn & Doughty yard in Maine, and were designed for Boston Towing & Transportation Company and its contract with Tractebel LNG Shipping, which brings all LNG into Boston. Their hulls are basi-

Although this tanker is carrying relatively innocuous product, *Freedom* here has a line up onto her transom, tethered aft as she would be on a ship loaded with liquefied natural gas. AUTHOR PHOTO.

cally the same design as the rest of Bruce Washburn's 92-foot tugs but they are fitted out specifically for this duty. Propelled by two 2,200-horse Caterpillars, they have two 3,000 gallons-per-minute fire monitors and two big winches, all of which can be run from the helmsman's chair. The tension on each winch is displayed on gauges in front of the helmsman, both graphically and digitally.

Captain Mike Hickey worked on various Foss Maritime boats when he was training in Long Beach. "That *Marshall Foss* is a beast," he says. "As long as *Freedom,* eight feet wider, and 2,500 horsepower more." He describes escorting a deep-draft supertanker with Vic Schisler as pilot. Mark Walsh was captain of the *Marshall Foss.* The escorts into Long Beach and Los Angeles are always tethered; the *Marshall Foss* had her line stretched out 150 or 200 feet through the center lead of the transom. As they came up on a turn where he knew that Vic would want to take headway off, Mark told Mike to watch the tension meter.

"OK, slow me down," said Vic.

"Mark put the boat into a transverse arrest and stood on it," says Mike. "He rung it right up," using the leftover lingo from the days when bells communicated with the engineers below. "You felt that tug come alive," he says. "It showed 110 tons on the meter, and you could see the knot meter coming down. It was phenomenal."

Having the two tractor tugs available has changed escorting in Boston. Boston Towing used to take six traditional tugs to the job. Because it's a Tractebel requirement, they still take four, and they're all tied on, but the two tractors are generally the only ones working.

The harbor work that tugs do varies, as do the configurations of the boats themselves. Increasingly, they are specialized for their particular jobs, but the challenges they face are always the same—winds, currents, undersea topography, and other vessels. A tugboater has to be alert at all times.

4
Coastwise Work

A large part of the work that tugboats do is coastal towing. They take barges from one port to another carrying petroleum products, building or other raw materials, dredging equipment. They pick up small loads of containers to make full loads for overseas passages, and they distribute containers around after they've arrived in the States. They're never far from land, and their masters need not have the big licenses that are required for offshore work. Many companies in smaller harbors may do mostly harbor work but take on coastal towing when the opportunity arises. Many tugboat operators love distance towing; many hate it and prefer to stay in the harbor. It takes all kinds.

Moving barges is serious business. Out of control, a barge can trip or run over its tug—or it can drift off sideways and end up aground, maybe holed, maybe spilling its contents. Hawsers can snap, jump around, or otherwise attack unwary deckhands. The master of a tug must always be aware of his barge.

Captain Steve Cobb tells of a near-miss back in the 1970s when he was mate on the tug *D.T. Sheridan*. This was the second tug of that name, built to replace the one that went ashore on Monhegan. She was twenty years old when Steve came aboard, and her engineer had been on her since her launch.

Steve says she was very similar to the original, one of the last of the old-style tugs, with one big direct-reversing, slow-turning engine and lots of joiner work. She had a regular run taking bargeloads of corn meal gluten to San Juan, Puerto Rico (where the longshoremen made a secondary industry of sweeping up the loose meal and selling it as rose food). "We steered every inch of the way," Steve recalls. There was no autopilot nor much else modern aboard. "The thing I liked about that boat was that it was sort of the last of the old style, where there was a lot more seamanship involved and not just mechanics."

There was no air conditioning, says Steve, "so you'd leave the windows open, and the draft would come up from the engine room and out the pilothouse windows and you were breathing engine room all the time. Not exhaust, just oil, warm steel, and bilge water."

They brought the barge back light to Tampa. There they loaded phosphate rock and took it to a place above New Orleans called Uncle Sam Bend, where there was a phosphate rock rendering plant. "That turned it into phosphoric acid, which was used for fertilizer, rust preventatives, and Coca-Cola," Steve says. "Then we'd go up to Baton Rouge, where there was a cleaning facility—they'd come on with high-pressure hoses and high-suction hoses and clean out the barge."

They were southbound off St. Petersburg with a load of corn meal one time when they lost a cylinder ring. "The chief engineer was so attuned to the sound of the engine, he could tell that it was going to get worse, and real quick, so he shut her down." The tug was a deep-hull ocean-going towboat, quite narrow, and immediately when the engine stopped, she stopped herself. The barge was carrying 12,500 tons of corn meal and was on a 1,200-foot hawser. It did not stop. "Just as straight and true as an arrow, it kept coming, right at us." The captain—our own John O'Reilly—called the engine room "for a chat," says Steve. The chief didn't want to start the engine, but John wanted to get out of the way of the barge. The chat got loud, but John and the engineer came to an agreement, and the engineer fired the engine up just long enough to scoot out from in front of the barge that was about to run them down.

"Then we only had the length of the hawser before the moving barge would pull us around and cause trouble." If the hawser was thrown across the stern of the tug-boat and the tug couldn't swing around in time, the barge could trip and capsize her. So they had to let the barge go, and quickly. That meant getting the seventy-five-pound shackle aboard. The hawser was shackled to the tugboat on the end of a chafe chain that rode back and forth on the stern of the boat, saving wear and tear on the rope hawser. (In this arrangement, the rails get chafed instead, and are periodically rebuilt with welds.) Also attached to the shackle was a messenger line that came back aboard the boat and could be run around the capstan. They heaved in on the messenger and brought the shackle aboard on the end of the gob chain. The shackle had a big nut, four inches in diameter, with welding rod acting as a giant cotter pin. They freed that, got the bolt out, and the hawser was free.

They let the messenger go. "It was a rope hawser with a big heavy thimble, and it sunk straight down, much deeper than the water was, but it didn't seem to slow the barge down. That thing just kept sailing.

"We wallowed for awhile, and the chief engineer commenced to take the engine apart—while it was still hot—and got the piston out of the cylinder. This was an opposing engine, with a top and a bottom piston for each cylinder, so he's working on his hands and knees on the floor in the engine room, inside this hot engine," recalls

Steve, describing how the engineer pulled pistons out, put new rings in, and put it all back together again. He started it back up again about two hours after the initial shut-down, and it was just fine.

"Then we went to lasso the barge, which was practically out of sight. We'd kept track of it on the radar, but it went for seven or eight miles before it finally got slowed down by its own hawser. We had to come alongside. The seas weren't huge, five or six feet, but enough to be enough." Some of the seas were coming aboard, and the men had to leap from the boat deck onto the barge.

"It could've been a lot worse. It was nighttime, but it wasn't raining, and it wasn't cold, and the weather wasn't really horrible," says Steve. "It was dark, that's all. The bad part was jumping aboard and going down below in the bow of the barge and groping my way around with a Bic lighter, trying to start the generator.

"There was a big capstan on the barge, and the bridle on the front of the barge was made of two chains with long legs, sixty feet each, with a huge, big bar in the middle. That all had to be heaved aboard just to get to the hawser. Then we had to get the hawser aboard—end-for-end, the whole length of it—to get the tugboat-end of it.

"This is a twelve-inch hawser, better than four inches in diameter, and it's laid rope." Nowadays they use braided rope that's easier to handle. "This was a nylon rope and it was full of Portuguese man o' wars' tentacles. So you have to wear gloves, which makes it more difficult and uncomfortable. You still get those stinging tentacles all over your wrists and develop hives, and they itch like crazy."

They got the whole hawser aboard the barge and threw a monkey's fist on a messenger down to the tug, so they could hook it all back up again. "We got back on board and went on our merry way. The whole thing took about six hours."

As a young man, Captain Richie Bates was aboard a Hudson River tug that got tripped by its barge, though that story too came out all right. A hydraulic steering line broke on the *Cheyenne*. The boat lurched hard to starboard, caught on one of the gatelines, and rolled onto her side. Richie, off watch, was lying in his room. Water poured in the open portholes and filled the whole room. It's a myth, he says, that you can't open the door in that circumstance. "I went out and climbed on the rail with my life jacket in my hands, and saw that the barge was running us over." The captain had been sleeping at the time, too, but he ran to the stern of the tug and released the taut gate line. "That righted the tug, popped it right up, and then the barge was no longer running us over. We repaired the hydraulic line and proceeded down the Hudson River as if nothing had happened."

Most tug trippings aren't so fortunate. "You cannot believe how fast a tug can sink," says Dave Boone, whose career was with the Curtis Bay Towing Company on

the Delaware River. "When you are in one that is going down faster than you are try-ing to get out—fighting not only the water coming in but everything else that has broken loose and is blocking the way—it is a scene of sheer panic, with every man for himself. Most times the boat is upside down, and along with everything else that is happening, your sense of direction is all screwed up."

A fatal accident took place on May 12, 2001, in the C&D Canal off Reedy Point, Delaware, when a 280-foot barge overtook its tug, the *Bay Titan*. The barge, loaded with 835,000 gallons of liquid sugar, was under tow, headed north on the Delaware with the tide behind it. There were six men aboard the *Bay Titan*. Save for the young master, they were all in the galley, eating lunch.

Barges under way want to keep moving, and usually in the direction they're going already. It's a hard left turn from the Delaware River into the C&D canal, and the *Bay Titan* made the turn, but the barge's momentum took it straight up the river, right on by the tug. It then veered back, and actually tripped the barge from the port side. The *Bay Titan* went under, stern-first. The captain and four of the men got out before she went down. The other man didn't make it.

Coast Guard investigators felt the tug had been going too fast to make the sharp turn safely. Perhaps the tide was also a significant part of the problem. Some cap-tains go on up the river, turn around, and approach the canal from the north, which has the double advantage of a less-sharp turn and, in these tide conditions, an oppos-ing current to allow steerage way at a slower speed over ground. Perhaps if the watertight doors had been closed on the tug, the added buoyancy would have given the men a little more time to get out of the boat. Any amount of second-guessing can take place, but the fact is, the tug went down and took a life with her. Her captain, only in his mid-twenties at the time, will live with that for the rest of his life. Barges will trip tugs, and care has to be taken.

Working the Intracoastal

The Intracoastal Waterway system extends more than a thousand miles from Boston to Key West and then, after a gap on the west coast of Florida, continues another eleven hundred miles along the Gulf of Mexico to the Mexican Border. Sheltered by barrier islands nearly all the way along each stretch and with the occasional canal, the ICW provides protected passage between coastal ports and rivers. The Atlantic Intracoastal is used mostly by pleasure boats, while the Gulf Intracoastal carries far more commercial traffic. Much of the commercial cargo consists of petroleum prod-ucts, and most of it is moved by tugs and barges. "The guys who work the Intracoastal in the Gulf coast area are the best boat handlers in the world," asserts Captain Zach Thomas.

Most barge work on the Eastern seaboard is offshore, using oceangoing tugs and big barges. Still, there are always a few tugs at work on the Atlantic ICW, and Zach ran one of those for a couple of years in the 1980s. They are running in a narrow, shallow channel with many turns, pushing very long barges, and the barges aren't the best. Most are gravel and chip barges making shorter hauls, usually for local construction work. The Atlantic ICW changed following a fatal incident in Alabama in 1993 involving a misplaced tug and barge, a bridge, and an Amtrak train. What's amazing to Zach is that there were so few such incidents during his time there. "We were mostly hauling very low-value cargoes. Most companies on the Intracoastal are mom-and-pop operations; the big companies don't want to waste time on it. Once a barge was no longer fit enough for the ocean or anywhere it was actually required to float, it was turned into a gravel barge for the Intracoastal," he recalls.

He tells of loading gravel onto one barge that started sinking under the load. "You never know where the holes are," he says. "The barge started filling up, and we put a pump on—and another, and another—and it kept sinking. Finally we had five pumps on, and it wasn't enough. That barge sank to the bottom. We had to take all the gravel off, and when we got the barge over to the yard we found it had humongous holes in it."

Most of the Intracoastal Waterway is supposed to be dredged to twelve feet deep, ninety feet wide, but with so many inlets continually bringing in more silt, it's not possible to maintain that. Often it's closer to eight feet deep and sixty feet wide. In most places, when a commercial ship goes aground you call the Coast Guard, but on the Atlantic Intracoastal "there was no point in doing that, you went aground so often," says Zach. "Grounding a barge or tug didn't hold the same fear it would normally— it was a daily event. You were more than likely going to get stuck and have to break the tug off and pull the barge, or do whatever you had to do to get going again."

Not only were the barges on their last legs, the tugs too were often not the best-equipped. Some ran with no compass, let alone radar; their crews went completely by eyeball. "When the weather obscured your vision, you were flying in the dark."

And fog is very common on the ICW. When they did use radar, the ICW captains would set it on the lowest range and use it to keep themselves in the middle of the channel as best they could. "It was like a video game with race cars, and the sides of the road close on each side. You couldn't see very far ahead on that scale, so you had no idea what was ahead of you.

"Most of those guys grew up in the area and knew the waterway like the back of their hand," says Zach. "Just like pilots, they'd have it memorized. These guys knew hundreds of miles, every bend—there's a marina around the next corner, it generally gets shallow over there so you have to stick to this side—it was real piloting experience."

Often, those tugboat men didn't have formal educations; they'd just learned the route riding as deckhands, storing it in their memories as they went. "It was fascinating to me," Zach says. "They were outside the realm of decent society. They did what worked, the way everyone had done it in the past—not necessarily what was legal or proper. You ended up doing some crazy things.

"Actually, I was very lucky. Other than going aground all the time pushing huge loads, I didn't have much go wrong." The biggest loads were on 200- by 50-foot deck barges, and they would push two of them in tandem. "The tug was 65 feet long, so in essence you were driving a 465-foot vessel, 50 feet wide." Not only is the channel narrow, shallow, and crooked, but there are six hundred bridges between Virginia and Florida, most of them on bends, usually with only sixty or eighty feet of clear span. "You've got ten feet on either side, sometimes cross currents, nearly always the wind to deal with. It's like threading a needle with chopsticks ten feet long.

"Some spots were much worse than others, but the stress level was always very, very high. You have to line everything up perfectly—you can't just stop the barges, you're totally committed. And I never did hit something.

"That's the amazing thing—there are guys doing that day in and day out, and you never hear of accidents. That they do it well enough so they don't hit anything is incredible."

Zach does tell about one trip where things did go "a little wrong," as he puts it. They did a lot of work in Chesapeake Bay, going from Norfolk to Baltimore or Washington, D.C., usually carrying cement products for bridge or shoreside construction projects. This particular contract was to tow a bargeful of bridge pieces up to Washington. "It was one of those Erector-set bridges, all riveted together." They were taking the old bridge apart piece by piece and replacing each one, and Zach's job was to take a load of new pieces up the bay. They had come in by ship from Texas to Norfolk, where they were loaded onto the barge. As captain of the tug, Zach checked the 100- by 35-foot deck barge, which was all loaded when he got there. The bridge pieces were 40-foot-long I-beams, which for some reason had been loaded standing on edge instead of stacked flat. They were a couple of feet across, bottom and top, all lined up like twelve-foot-tall dominoes.

"In general," Zach explains, "when you're hauling cargo around, the shipper will have hired a professional to make a stowage plan, and a surveyor will come and check it all out and say it's a good plan and secured properly." Zach saw that the securing wires were all tight, and he assumed all was in order. "I took it as good to go."

At one point, the channel they were following took a left to go up into the Chesapeake. "It was blowing twenty-five. There was a three-foot sea coming in, and we were going right into it." He was towing the barge a thousand or more yards out on the wire. "Everything seemed to be riding well, so we went to make the turn. Everything's all set, and I turn around to look at the barge—and there doesn't seem to be anything standing up on the barge anymore. There are pieces hanging over the side."

Zach made an immediate note of their position, told his crew to start shortening up the wire, and called the Coast Guard. "We may have a problem," he told them. As they got closer to the barge, they could see that not only had the I-beams fallen down, but they only had half the cargo they'd started with. Zach called the Coast Guard again to report that they'd dropped some pieces.

His great fear was that the huge steel pieces had fallen into the channel, which served as the main thoroughfare for naval vessels, submarines, and aircraft carriers, as well as all the commercial vessels. "It was hard to say where it had dumped—I wasn't watching, and the barge was pretty far behind us. I couldn't pinpoint a fix for them, but I gave them the coordinates the best I could.

"My next fear was the pieces hanging off the edge. God knew if the barge was going to flip over."

Gingerly, he brought the barge—its huge steel cargo still hanging over the side—back to the pier where they'd started. He knew it would be a trick to land without hitting anything, and without the barge flipping onto them. He decided how he was going to approach the pier when he noticed that he had a large welcoming committee awaiting him.

"Brass bands," he says figuratively, and adds more literally, "neckties, epaulets, all that.

"So we got things tied up, and the youngest guy there is forty. I'm twenty-five at the time and have long hair. I'm pretty scruffy. We'd picked up the barge at four in the morning, so I'm still in my pajamas, or close to it. Typical Intracoastal attire—less than spiffy. I step out of the wheelhouse, and everyone's eyes rolled up into the back of their heads. I'm thinking, 'This could be the last day I work anything to do with the water.'"

Holes had ripped in the barge-top and sides, and pad-eyes had ripped out, and the friction had been so great when the I-beams fell that there were burnt spots.

"Carnage," Zach describes the scene. "The pieces of steel were huge, so it's not surprising, but it was impressive to see the damage." Surveyors from every interest climbed onto the barge to look—people from the company that owned the material, the owner of the barge, the people who loaded it.

The surveyors of course all started spouting opinions on whose fault it all was. Meanwhile, the Coast Guard came to check Zach out. "It became obvious I wasn't drunk and hadn't done anything out of the ordinary. They didn't have anything to say to me—they just gave me an accident form to fill out and send in. But it was a long day, a nervous day for me, thinking 'You're done, brother.' But it all turned out fine. There were lawsuits of course, and I had to go to depositions, but it turns out that no one had ever drawn up a stowage plan. They just secured whatever looked good, and never checked it out. So the people responsible for stowing got the bill.

"But I'll never forget finally getting the barge tied up at the pier—the quintessential moment for a mariner."

And other than that, Zach's experience with barges on the East Coast was wonderful. "Bumping barges around tight spaces. Doing wonderful, neat things. With a lot of horsepower, running a tug and barge is like being a cowboy in complete control of his horse, herding and making cows do just what he wants. I really enjoyed that."

Cowboying in an Earlier Time

Perhaps the quintessential cowboy of forty years ago was Captain Corliss Holland, who ran the towboat *Security* out of Belfast, Maine. *Security* is long gone—she died in Boston, Corliss thinks. And he's been out of tugboating for nearly thirty years. These days, he likes to go faster on the water, and as owner of the racing lobsterboat *Red Baron,* he's had plenty of opportunity to do that.

By far the largest share of Eastern Maine Towage's work was docking. "Docking's all right, but it gets kinda boring," says Corliss. He liked outside towing best. "Outside, you're doing something different all the time, always going somewhere different, seeing different things." (It's funny—all the people who work tugs say that the particular job they prefer offers different jobs and different sights. In my experience, most people at the wheel like harbor work best. Corliss is an exception, but his reasons for his preference are the same.) He admits that you do have to watch the weather, though.

He came aboard the *Security* in 1958 as a deckhand. The company was hauling gypsum out of Walton, Nova Scotia, to the North End of Rockland, Maine. They asked Corliss if he'd go on the barge with Captain Bradley. "No, I ain't gonna be towed all over hell." So he stayed on the boat. And then, on the first trip, they had engine trouble and had to get towed in. "Ain't this a hell of a deal—we're a tow boat and we're being towed."

Over the next fifteen years or so, Corliss worked in every position there was aboard the *Security:* on deck, in the galley, in the engine room, and finally as captain.

The ninety-foot wooden *Security* was built in Damariscotta, Maine, as a mine-sweeper for the U.S. Navy during World War II but never saw action. She had a 450-horse Fairbanks engine. "Up today and down tomorrow," Corliss calls it, referring to the very slow rate at which the engine turned. "She was underpowered—you had to watch what you were doing."

Corliss made a dozen trips hauling pulpwood to the mill in Bucksport, Maine, from the island of Grand Manan, New Brunswick. "One trip was clear, and the rest was fog, fog, fog," Corliss says. On one particular trip, he couldn't find the paperwork for the customs officials in Bucksport. "We're going to get you for smuggling," they told him.

"If I was gonna smuggle something, it sure as hell wouldn't be pulpwood!" Corliss told the customs people. Corliss still doesn't hesitate to say what's on his mind, though he often can see the humorous aspect of otherwise annoying situations. That was true years ago, too.

Corliss and the *Security* also took barges of granite from Stonington, Maine, all over the New England coast: Block Island, Newburyport, Provincetown. On one trip, he ran into a sou'wester, blowing hard, and decided to change course for Portland to tie up. His log book quietly notes, "Found cargo shifted, some overboard."

Only once did he have to call for help from the Coast Guard. He was on his way home with a barge and ran into a gale off Seguin Island. Water was leaking down through the deck. The electric pump shorted out and cut off. Water was welling up onto the engine room floor. When Corliss called back to the office, his boss asked, "You'd better be thinking about leaving that thing, hadn't you?"

"I ain't leavin' while she's afloat."

"Well then, let the barge go."

Corliss told his superior that he wasn't going to let the barge go, either. "That was my lifeboat. As long as the old bird was afloat, I was gonna stay with her." The mate was fussing about what to take with them if they had to abandon the tug, but Corliss told him not to worry about flashlights and all that. "I wasn't going to abandon if she went down. I'd 'a brought that barge alongside, wouldn't even 'a took the hawser off it, because I'd 'a been anchored already."

A helicopter came from the Cape and dropped a pump down. That soon ran out of gas, but before the tug was in serious trouble again, a Coast Guard cutter caught up with them. It's difficult to get two boats together in such rough weather—it takes a lot of boat handling. One Coast Guardsman can thank Corliss for his life; he was reaching down between the boats when they started coming together. "I grabbed him and flung him right into a steel door, but he was alive. Woulda cut him right in two."

The longest trip Corliss ever made with the *Security* was to Buffalo to get a grain barge and bring it back, empty, to Rockland. The trip took a month, down the St. Lawrence Seaway and into the Great Lakes.

"Coming through the locks on the Seaway, I had two pilots aboard. The lockmaster said you gotta have someone on all the lines. I said, 'I can't do that, there's only seven of us on this thing to start with, and at least one person has to stay on the boat.' I put the pilots on the barge, handling lines.

"The lockmaster says, 'Can you ballast that barge?' 'Yeah, I can, but I ain't gonna.' 'Could you if you wanted to?' 'I could sink that thing if you wanted me to.' Well, that followed me the whole length of the canal. Everyone heard about it.

"'I'm going to restrict you to twenty-miles-per-hour wind,' he said. 'Finest kind. That's all right with me. That's good.' Light ships blow around a lot—hard to handle in the locks."

After a stop in Rockland, they took the barge to Cargill's in Norfolk, Virginia, where it was loaded with corn. "They loaded it heavy by the head. Jesus, didn't that thing handle mean. So I thought, 'Well she's got ballast tanks, maybe I can get her on her feet.' After we'd pumped a while, I thought, 'Jeez, I don't know if I'm pumping into the ballast tanks or into the corn. If it's the corn, she's gonna blow.'"

The barge was still down by the bow and handling badly—but hadn't blown up—when they finally got to New York City. "We had a little tug going along with us till we got through Hell's Gate—that's a mean place with a barge that's not handling good." But then the other tug left, and Corliss was concerned about the Cape Cod Canal. He called the people at the canal. "In case I need help going through, can I get some?"

"Can't get any help till eight o'clock."

"'Oh hell, I'll be through there on my own by then," he told them, and he was.

He got to Rockland at dusk. Because it was the first load of grain coming in to the new facility, they asked him if he could wait till morning to dock the barge so they could take pictures. "I been gone a month now, and no, I ain't gonna wait for no pictures," Corliss told them.

He never let a barge go at sea but he once came close to it, approaching Providence towing a scow with a crane. "The *Security* was underpowered, and we were drifting toward a ledge—Brenton Reef, I think it was. Getting closer, closer, not making any headway. 'If we're gonna get any closer, we're gonna let that barge go, 'cause I ain't goin' ashore,' I said. But just as it got real close, she picked up headway."

They weren't clear of trouble yet, though. "We picked up that crane in Massachusetts, and it was going to Block Island. Half or two-thirds of the way to Block Island, when I came up for my watch in the morning, there was the guys on the barge waving an oilskin. The barge looked pretty deep." It had torn a plank off and was sinking, crane and all. Corliss brought the towboat alongside, moved the hawser to the stern, and towed the barge backward to take the water out of her. "Yeah, it worked. You gotta think of something, you know."

He called ahead to Block Island. "Be sure to have someone there to pick her off," he told them. "Well, there was no one there. Circled round and round—had to keep moving or she'd sink."

At Block Island, the sand shifts and needs to be dredged often. Another time when Corliss was headed in there, a little boat come running out to the *Security*. "You can't go in," he told Corliss.

"Why not?"

"There's a nine-foot spot ahead."

"You get outa my way, and in just a few minutes you're gonna have twelve feet. I'm gonna dredge it for you." He chuckles. "It did slow her down a little."

Perhaps all towboaters are independent cusses. Corliss certainly is. There was the time in Boston when he took a ferry boat in tow. His job was to take her to Baltimore. Another tug had brought her down from Grand Manan—that was her name, the *Grand Manan III*. Corliss thinks she might have been going to be scrapped—she hadn't been in use for a time. Because the ferry had come from a foreign port, Corliss told the boss he had to officially enter her into the country, go through customs.

"It's all right," said the boss, "just go."

"All right," said Corliss, "it ain't no skin off my nose." Then, when he got to Baltimore, the boss told him hang on for a day so he could come in when there weren't any customs officers on duty. But Corliss liked the weather and said no, he wasn't going to wait.

And sure enough, he had a hassle with the customs office. "You got to enter," they said.

"I ain't got to. My tug ain't been out of the country," Corliss told them. They told him he'd be fined. "It's all right with me," said Corliss. "I don't care."

One time Corliss took the *Security* to Portland to pick up a scow for a fellow from Bar Harbor who was going into the marine construction business. Corliss looked at the scow, and said, "I don't want to put a hawser on it."

"Why?"

"It'll never see Bar Harbor, that's why." The barge was a decrepit old thing. There was no bitt on deck—to tie on, you had to crawl down through and latch onto something down below. But the owner insisted on making the trip, and he and another man were going to ride the scow. "OK," said Corliss, "but I'm telling you, it won't get there. You got life jackets?"

They didn't, so Corliss provided those from the tug, along with a little rowboat that he made them take. "We didn't hardly get out of Portland harbor, and there they were, rowing off." The fellow asked if he could use Corliss's telephone to call the bank.

Corliss knew the seller. "You're too late. The guy you bought that thing off, he cashed your check before you ever left."

They had to cut the cable with an axe, because they couldn't get down into the scow to let it go. "They put an article in the paper about me putting that skiff on there. Hadn't 'a been for that, they mightn't have made it. Wish you coulda seen that scow. No one in their right mind woulda put a hawser on it.

"It's always in the winter when you run into that stuff," he adds.

He took a barge of granite to Cuttyhunk one time. "There ain't water enough to put that scow in there," he said to the guy expecting the granite.

"It's a misprint on the chart," the guy there said.

Like hell, Corliss said. He called the boss and said he didn't want to go in there. "Ain't water enough."

"Go," his boss said.

"Sure enough," says Corliss, "we went aground. I didn't care. It was low water— I was gonna float her off pretty soon. The Coast Guard came out to see if I wanted help, but I was OK, I told them. They said they wouldn't file a report and they wanted to put a line on. They damn near run into us getting that line on, and they had a report in before I ever got home. They don't put too many mistakes on the chart. The ironic thing is, for some reason the guy in Cuttyhunk didn't want that load of granite, and we had to take it all back out again. Had quite a time to get turned around without touching the shore—wasn't ninety feet across in that little harbor."

It was bad weather one time when Corliss came into Rockland Harbor. "Fog and blowing and whatnot." The deckhand wondered if Corliss was going to anchor. "I don't like to anchor. I'm goin' into the dock," Corliss told him.

"What if you don't find it?" asked the deckhand.

"That's all right. When we hit the bank, she'll stop."

As a young man on the gypsum trips, Corliss learned a great deal about working with the tides. Walton, where they picked up the gypsum, is at the head of the Bay of Fundy, past Cape Split in the Minas Basin. "Going through the Split, the tide run so hard you were actually going astern. When it turned, you went through in a hurry. And when the tide come in, you wanted to be ready 'cause it wasn't there very long." It took a day and a half to get to Walton, longer to get back—loaded, they didn't make more than 4 or 5 knots. "I got used to going slow. I've made up for it since."

Before Corliss got on the *Security,* he took over running the *Pauline Holmes* for a time. Captain Clarence Nickerson describes the *Pauline* as "another woodpile," like the *Seguin,* which he ran in the 1960s. Clarence wasn't on the *Pauline* much, though; he says he was only called in occasionally when her regular skipper wasn't feeling well. Corliss is more direct about the boat's former master: "He got into the sauce a little heavy. He grounded her out in the Muscle Ridge once, and they had to wait for the tide to come and float her off." Another time, he was showing some teachers how to handle a tug over in Searsport and put her under the dock. And once he ran almost half of the *Pauline* into the old steamboat dock in Bucksport. The deckhand said he thought *he* could do as good as that, "which he probably could," says Corliss. He suspects the skipper might have been in the tea a little on each of these occasions.

Finally the company relieved the fellow of his position—put him on as deckhand—and gave the boat to Corliss. "I thought that was pushing it a little too far," he says. Things weren't always smooth with Corliss at the helm either. He'd been running the *Evelyn Holmes,* and the *Pauline* handled a lot differently. "The *Evelyn,* you'd get fairly close to a ship and put her in reverse, and she'd stop. The *Pauline,* I got fairly close to a ship and put her in reverse, and she had no intention of backing down. Ran right into the ship." But, he says, you learn your lessons quick.

The old skipper committed suicide—shot himself. A little while later, Corliss's engineer from the *Evelyn* also shot himself. "If this is a trend, it's gonna stop right here, because I'm not going to shoot myself," Corliss said.

The *Pauline*'s Last Run

The *Pauline Holmes* had been built in the early 1940s in Cambridge, Maryland, for Moran Towing to use on the Erie Canal and the rivers of New York State. She wasn't finished until after the war, as the materials were all needed for the war effort. When Eastern Maine Towage brought her to Belfast, she had a low pilothouse designed to

The *Pauline H. Holmes* on the railway. Courtesy of Steven Lang.

pass under the inland bridges, but they built her a higher pilothouse. Arthur Fournier bought her with the rest of the assets of Eastern Maine Towage in 1977.

Jim Sharp remembers getting aboard the *Pauline* one night to head to a ship docking. She wouldn't start. "Arthur did everything he could—weasel pee [diesel starting fluid], everything." Finally he tied her up alongside the other tug and headed out toward the ship. "He literally got the shaft running by inertia through the water. He jump-started her! I couldn't believe it would ever work, but it did!" And then she wouldn't steer: "I was going in circles out there." They lashed the two tugs back together, and Jim drove while Arthur went down in the engine room. He got the steering going before they reached the ship.

But Arthur didn't keep the boat long. He sold her to a fellow who said he was going to take her to Florida to move barges of fresh water across to a resort in the Bahamas. Hugh Curran tells the rest of the story. He's a lifelong mariner who makes his home in Camden, Maine. Arthur hired Hugh's friend Cyril Weinstein to deliver the boat to Florida. Cy asked Hugh to go along, but as Hugh had just come back from Africa and eight or nine months away from home, he didn't want to make the trip.

Pauline H. Holmes.
COURTESY OF STEVEN LANG.

"Well, at least come down to Rockland to get the engine started," said Cy, and Hugh did. He was curious to know how the trip went, though, and he informed himself about the rest of the story after the fact.

It was in the winter. Hugh describes the buyer, a man named McCrory. "He was a mysterious, distinguished-looking gentleman in his fifties or early sixties, and he had an assistant with him, a younger gentleman who deferred to Mr. McCrory, almost like a military aide."

The weather was pretty cold. Hugh started up the little heating unit and pump that circulated warm water through the water jacket on the big Cooper-Bessemer main engine. "I told the assistant to allow that to run until he could put his hand on the water jacket while he said 'Now is the time for all good men to come to the aid of their country' without burning himself, and then to start it up. It worked."

Since the *Pauline* was designed for rivers, there wasn't much freeboard in the first place, and once she was 98 percent loaded with fuel, there was just about *no* freeboard. Hugh was concerned because from the steering room—where the electric motors were that ran the hydraulic pumps that steered the boat—"you could look up through the whaleback, and, as the old sailors used to say, you could throw a cat through the seams." He told Cy he wouldn't want to be going offshore in that boat.

They got a provisional insurance classification that said it was OK to take her to Florida as long as they treated her as a small craft. She wasn't to be out if small craft warnings were posted, and they couldn't tow anything; otherwise, the insurance wouldn't cover her. Before they left, Mr. McCrory and his assistant took Hugh out for coffee. They wondered if he was a resident of Maine. Yes, he was. Would he do them a favor? Would he buy them 1,500 rounds of 9-millimeter Parabellum ammunition? (That's wartime ammo for machine guns like Uzis and MP-5s. Not your everyday product.) "I'd been around in the military," Hugh says, "and Mr. McCrory and his aide looked like what in Vietnam we used to call Christians In Action—CIA. But I had no idea what was intended for the tug, and I didn't get them the ammunition."

To go along on the delivery, they hired a young guy named Jerry, just out of the Navy. Cy, Mr. McCrory, the assistant, and Jerry made up the crew starting the trip. Cy said he'd feel it out, and make up his mind later about whether he'd make the whole trip.

When they got into Narragansett Bay, the wind picked up to twenty or twenty-five knots, and they were taking green water on the back deck. As Hugh had predicted, water dripped down through the deck and shorted out the steering motors, leaving the *Pauline* with no steering. They rigged plastic over the motors and lucked out; they were able to get the motors started back up again. They pulled into Newport, and Mr. McCrory got a big bunch of roofing shingles that he and his assistant nailed all over the deck to fix the open seams. An elderly wharf-loafer told them that the first time they went out in a good breeze, the shingles would blow right off. "Don't worry about it," said Mr. McCrory.

It was all a little too weird for Cy, so he went home, though Jerry stayed on. (And it was Jerry who later filled Hugh in about the rest of the trip.) McCrory, despite not having had any sea experience, took over as captain. He hired a dockside hanger-on to go along. Like many such fellows, this guy needed an occasional drink to steady himself. "Sometimes he got so steady he couldn't move," says Hugh.

They sailed from Newport for New York. Despite the insurance classification restrictions, they took an empty petroleum barge in tow, headed for the Delaware and the Intracoastal Waterway. Offshore, a northeaster blew in, and the *Pauline* lost her steering for real, along with the rest of the electric power on the tug. They had no radar, and they were lost. McCrory tried to back the tug "in some obscure maneuver," Hugh calls it, and wrapped the hawser around the propeller. The guy who liked to steady himself said, "You're gonna get us all drowned," and McCrory pistol-whipped him, right there in the wheelhouse, just like in a third-rate movie. "And in the midst of this psychodrama, the weather deteriorated even more," Hugh says. Jerry thought they were going to die.

Suddenly they heard booming surf. They were at Ocean City, Maryland, being driven up on the beach. The *Pauline* grounded, the barge too, but a hundred yards of vicious surf still separated them from land. Coast Guardsmen fired out a messenger line from the shore. Jerry got it secured on the tug, and he and the drunk and the aide hauled on the line to reach the attached hawser, only to discover that the Coast Guardsmen had forgotten to secure the hawser to anything on their end. For the second attempt they affixed the hawser to the bumper of a pickup truck.

Jerry was the first to go across. He took all the clothing he could pack on himself and jumped into the water. He held onto the line and tried to pull himself in, but the sea kept ripping him back along the line, skin tearing off his hands. The Coast Guardsmen formed a human chain and managed to haul him ashore. The three men remaining on the boat wouldn't try repeating Jerry's feat.

Then the sea drove the barge in at right angles to the tug, positioning it just like a gangplank from the tug to the beach. The others all got ashore without getting their feet wet.

The *Pauline* was wrecked, and presumably without hope of any insurance payout. Jerry never got paid. The last he saw of McCrory was in the Ocean City hotel where the Coast Guard took them. "If you know what's good for you," McCrory said to him, "you'll keep your mouth shut."

Hugh's only involvement—fortunately, as it turned out—had been as a consultant to tell them how to start the engine. He's glad he avoided helping them buy any ammunition. "And to this day," he says, "I don't know who those guys were."

5
Connected

There are several ways to connect a tug and barge. The tug can tow the barge on a hawser, it can take it "on the hip" (tie on alongside the barge), or it can put it "on the nose" (push from behind.) When sea conditions warrant, pushing is the most efficient, allowing a third more speed. Because it's hard to line up a tug exactly on the centerline of a barge's stern and get the wires out so she stays there, it was inevitable that people would design barges to make the process easier. The first notches in the sterns were just shallow indicators of where the tug should nudge in. But it was such a good idea that, before too long, the notch started growing longer and longer until it enveloped most of the tug. It was later that rigid connections with the tug developed, allowing the tug to stay in push mode through nearly all weather conditions.

Pushing Deep-Notch Barges

"I used to look young, but I don't anymore because of seventeen years in push tugs," says Captain Rick Clarke. He was among the first two or three masters of tugs running "in the notch," in the then new tug-and-barge pushing units. A five-hundred-foot barge that draws thirty-two feet and is eighty feet wide is a nice solid object to hang onto, "although when it gets rough, you'd be surprised how much that big object can bounce around," says Rick. And it's a wholly different game when you're towing: "Things jump all over the place."

Rick worked for Bulkfleet Marine carrying gasoline in the Gulf of Mexico. The barges could carry as much cargo as a small to medium-sized ship—30,000 deadweight tons—and had a deep V-shaped notch in the stern into which the tug settled herself. For thirteen years, he was on the 140-foot tug *Valiant,* which nearly disappeared in the 85-foot notch in the stern of her partner, the 502-foot petroleum barge *Pennsylvania.* He spent another four years on her sister, *Victory,* with the barge *Texas.*

At the time, there were no guidelines about operating such a rig. They were making it up as they went. "We were learning by Braille, feeling our way along," he says. "It wasn't pretty."

The boats had upper wheelhouses that also were not as well developed as they've become since. Some of the older upper wheelhouses were similar to phone booths atop telephone poles, with an external ladder to get to and from. "Pushing a barge in rough seas, the vibration, noise, and movement could be unnerving," Rick says. A helmsman sitting alone up there for four or six hours would certainly feel the precarious nature of the construction. "On the *Valiant,* as with most, there was no head, so nature's call meant getting someone to stand by, then running down four decks and back again. Who needs a Stairmaster?"

They were also working out how strong the tugs needed to be to work in the notch and how to hold them there. During the first year of their careers, the *Valiant* and the *Victory* both went back to the yard to be beefed up in the bow; they were too light in the fender area, and crumpled like tin cans in rough weather. "They still weren't as heavy as the barge, so when they came together, the tug suffered." Other early issues included towing gear that was too light, so pennant wires and lines and bridle chains were all replaced.

To hold them in place, they simply used a head line—a big line, to be sure: three wraps of nine-inch circumference, three-strand Dacron, run from the bitts on the tug to the bitts on the barge—and wire backing lines from the quarters of the tug onto the corners of the barge. The wire lines turned out to be unnecessary. "Everyone was afraid that the unit would get disconnected, that you'd need to back hard and—

The tug *Valiant* deep in the notch of the barge *Pennsylvania.* COURTESY OF J. BARRY SNYDER.

whoops!—you'd disconnect, but then we figured out that wires or no wires, the tug wasn't coming out of the notch by accident. They did away with the wires because they tore themselves and their turning blocks in a sea."

In a sea, there is a lot of movement between the tug and the barge. The tug would be bucking up and down, and it didn't matter how heavy the bow line was, it would break. Then all hands would have to come on deck to get the line out of the way and end-for-end it and make it fast, or else hook up a new line. Then they had to cut off the broken end and re-splice it, ready for the next time it snapped (which they knew it would, perhaps in another thirty minutes.) The captain would be in the upper wheelhouse, and the crew would all sleep on the floor in their slicker suits and life jackets in the lower wheelhouse, from which place it was a simple matter to get onto the bow. There was no sense in going down into their rooms.

There is no written rule about when to come out of the notch and tow—when is that point? It's to everyone's advantage—usually—to stay in the notch.

"Obviously, you don't want to hurt anyone, and you make better speed pushing," says Rick. "On a six-hundred- or thousand-mile trip, towing might change your ETA by twelve or thirty-six hours. They don't want to hear *why* you're late. You say you're towing, and they say 'What are you towing for?' 'It looked like it was going to get rough.' 'And is it?' 'Well, no . . .'" Rick says the office was understanding, but impatient with slow towing speeds or overcautious towing decisions in marginal weather conditions.

To pick up the tow with the *Valiant* wasn't simple, particularly when done in open water with too much sea. In theory, they were always ready to make the switch to towing. A pennant wire was attached to the towing bridle on the front of the barge. The wire was stowed wrapped around the bow and outboard on the starboard side, lashed to the deck edge, ready to be pulled off. A heavy floating line shackled to the end of the pennant ran all the way down the starboard side of the barge and dropped onto the tug. When the time came to tow, someone had to go onto the barge and ready the pennant to release. He would put cuts in the manila lashing so when the tug yanked on the pennant, the lashings would break. "We'd back out of the notch and, even though we'd separated ourselves from the barge, we're still attached to it by the line to the pennant wire. It's just a matter of easing up to the barge, picking up the slack floating line until we reach the wire, pulling the wire over onto the back deck, and shackling into it.

"It sounds easy," Rick says in a voice that shows it isn't. "In real rough seas, there's so much that can go wrong—and did. That's a pretty good way of doing it, but not with fifteen-foot seas washing over you. A lot of times a big wave would come up and throw all the floating line into the lifelines or bulwarks and get it tangled. So we've separated from the barge, and we're pulling on this thing to get to the pennant wire, and we're not going to get there because it's now wrapped around something."

On tugs that tow all the time, the back deck is kept as simple as possible, with few things for the shackle to hang up on. It's clean, with rounded surfaces. Not so on the *Valiant*. "On a lot of big push tugs they forgot all those basics, and the back deck is full of cleats and fairleads and bitts and access hatches to the steering room."

And then, a push tug isn't ideal as a towing vessel. It's nice to be able to see over the barge, so an upper pilothouse is one of the compromises made in order to maximize the tug's ability to push—but it makes her top-heavy. The bow, with its vertical surfaces, is better suited to pushing in the notch than to braving the sea on its own. Still, sometimes towing is the answer. Through trial and error, Rick and his crew learned that the *Valiant* should be towing the loaded *Pennsylvania* in any sea more than fifteen feet. With a light barge, eight to ten feet was plenty.

Making the switch from push to tow in rough conditions means the crew gets exposed to the elements at their worst. Rick admits to pride in his ability to evaluate forecasts. In good weather, it took them four or four and a half days to get around Florida and across the Gulf to Corpus Christi, their longest regular trip. He describes a common situation: "We'd have good weather for the first three and three-quarters days, and the last day it would be slowly building up out of the southeast in front of a cold front. We'd know it was only twelve hours to go, and if we towed and it came in too rough, we couldn't get back into push gear, so we'd push on through.

"Sometimes we'd get steel-on-steel in the fender area. We'd take a couple of really big hits and the whole crew would be uneasy—we all knew there might be an All Hands to tow in rough conditions." There was never any need to actually call the crew when it was time to tow after having pushed to the brink. No one, feeling the tug lurching oddly, tug and barge thumping together, would be asleep. "Go to sleep? Not hardly. Waiting for the call, feeling the tug start to bump and grind and pitch then suddenly fetch up, briefly jammed in an awkward position, and then do it again, only worse. . ."

In the last fifty miles, the water shallowed up and the seas got easier. "We'd get over the hump and it would start to lay down, and we'd know we'd made it."

A lot of times, Rick could tell a day or two ahead that they weren't going to beat the coming weather and would change to towing while it was still relatively calm.

He feels fortunate to have had only one time when it was really tricky—"and damn scary"—getting out of the notch. "We were eastbound, into a strengthening easterly wind, and I knew that when we got close enough to Florida, we would get the benefits of a lee of land to reduce the seas. Unfortunately, that day I gambled wrong on the forecast's accuracy." The more the seas built, the slower they went. "I could hear my seventh-grade science teacher: 'If you consecutively move half the distance to your destination, in theory, you never will arrive.'" They weren't getting there, either. They were still a couple of hundred miles off, making four or five knots over the bottom even though the engine was turning as if they were making eleven. The seas reached twenty feet, and finally Rick had to come out of the notch.

"When you're pushing, you're forced in, and there's no free movement, but in order to back out, you have to stop the engines—that takes ten seconds—and put the engines astern and back hard—that's another thirty seconds. The *Valiant* was direct-reversing, with no clutches." You stop pushing, then you're vulnerable. A little misjudgment, or a swell coming along at the wrong moment, and it's easy to do serious damage to tug or barge.

"I kept one engine ahead and stopped the other—I wanted to have the first engine backing before stopping the other. And then the barge turned and we had the wind on one side, which slowed her turn, but it's so loose and jumping around, and we had an eighty-five-foot run to make.

"We let the barge go and stood by. We were completely disconnected from the barge now, and 150 miles from anything. The closest was an oil platform. We drifted forty miles in thirty hours—in the wrong direction. But as long as nobody got hurt and the barge wasn't damaged, it didn't matter.

"They were upset about the delay, and there was an investigation about how to do things differently next time, but I didn't feel bad about it."

That may have been his only really frightening incident getting out of the notch, but often, Rick says, they only just made it. And then there's getting back into the notch.

Because pushing gives tugs so much more control over the barge, tugs always push when going into port. Even when Rick had to switch over to towing for part of a run, he needed to be pushing when he finally docked the *Pennsylvania*. It's far simpler, though, for a more traditional tug to get its barge back on the nose than it was for the *Valiant* to hook back into her deep notch. While the *Valiant* might leave the harbor, pushing, six hours after a smaller tug with a barge in tow and blow by the other tug eighteen hours later, she could lose all that advantage if she ran into weather that required getting out of the notch. She might have ended up jogging around outside the sea buoy at her destination, waiting for a break in the weather to get back in the notch. The *Valiant* and the *Pennsylvania* together, even on a very short hawser—a couple of hundred feet—were nearly a thousand feet long and needed sea room to come back into push mode. Meanwhile, the small tug might have come back past since it could go into more protected water before coming around into push gear.

Rick describes how another captain in the *Valiant*'s sister tug got caught by staying in the notch too long. "He chose to stay in, no matter what, and it was slamming hard." Slowly, the steel sides of the tug dented. One particularly big slam tripped the generator out. "Then they're in the worst position. It shut the main engines down, and they had a dead tug in the notch." Subsequent hits ruptured one day-tank for the generator, and diesel fuel was everywhere. "It's a very dangerous fuel hazard. You just need the right ignition source—like an eight-hundred-degree engine exhaust, for example. So there they are, trying to get the other generator on, slipping in diesel fuel." With astounding efforts, the engineer got the other generator started, and they managed to get clear of the barge. "They very nearly sank, and they were just lucky not to have a fire."

A barge can break loose from its boat, too, as the *Pennsylvania* did from the *Valiant* once. "It was Pearl Harbor Day, 1983. I got a letter of commendation for my actions that day," Rick remembers. "It was more fun than anything else, because I was young, straight out of college. Taking risks was what I was all about, back then."

They were coming from Delaware Bay, towing a loaded barge, headed to Boston in a terrible blow from the westward. Off Block Island Sound, the tow wire broke on a wreck on the bottom. In rough seas, they chased the barge overnight as it drifted thirty miles at two knots toward a little island off Martha's Vineyard. The Coast Guard was standing by, but no one could do anything. The towing winch on the *Valiant* was disabled from the break, anyway. "We were a lame duck." recalls Rick. In the morning, a helicopter brought a guy out from shore, picked Rick off the tug, and dropped them both on the barge. Another tug came out to help. Rick and the other fellow helped the second tug capture the barge and get it under way. They rode the barge to Providence, where *Valiant* picked it up. "We saved the day," he says. "The barge was within a half mile of going aground with 200,000 barrels of gasoline."

Rick sums up his years in the early days of deep-notch pushing: "We're lucky we went through that learning curve and nobody got killed, and we didn't have any serious disasters." He credits excellent crews and great fortune. There was only one time that someone got hurt. "He got washed around a little bit," Rick says. "He broke some bones in his foot. He's fine now, he's not limping or short in one leg or wearing a patch, but you can't help but think about it sometimes."

Pushing Shallow-Notch Barges

"A shallow-notch boat requires the most boat handling," says Captain Steve Rhodes, presently captain on the *Ralph E. Bouchard,* which connects to its petroleum barge with soft lines (rope). A deep-notch boat like the *Valiant* when Rick Clarke was running her stays solidly in place with no more than a bow line out because her pivot point is within the notch. When she turns, she's pressuring the barge to turn too. And, in general, the deeper the notch, the more weather the pair can stand. The disadvantage to a deep-notch barge, of course, is the loss of payload.

The pivot point on a shallow-notch boat is outside the notch. "When you have to steer the vessel and turn hard, if you're not rigidly connected, you'll pop out of the notch," says Steve.

The *Ralph E. Bouchard* is held in the barge's shallow notch with 200 feet of 18-inch circumference Samson line, nylon braid. "That's the strongest as far as nylon goes. It can stretch forty percent without weakening." Their towing winch has two

The *Adriatic Sea* comes into the shallow notch on the barge *KTS 135.* Deckhand Trevor Campbell is ready to throw the head line over to waiting barge mate Dan Bruton.
AUTHOR PHOTO.

drums, one side for the towing wire—three thousand feet of 2 1/2-inch wire—and the other side for the pushing wires. These go from the drum around sheaves on the stern of the tug and outboard, where they're connected to the soft lines on the barge. Those lines stay permanently on the barge, which is manned; two men are on it all the time.

He describes the maneuver of getting out of the notch, no easy feat in either kind of notch boat. "When I go from pushing to the tow wire, that's the most dangerous, hardest part." He drops his soft lines and the barge crew hauls them up its stern. (If the barge were unmanned, the tug's crew would have to haul in their own connecting lines and pick up a trailing emergency line from the barge.) "I back out— actually, I get thrown out." Now the barge is adrift, there is no longer as much as a line connecting the two. "I go to the bow of the barge and come alongside, pointing in the same direction as the barge." Anyway, he tries to go head-to-head, feeling it's easiest for himself and the guys on the back deck, who end up with the barge giving them a lee from the wind and sea.

"Sometimes you can't do that, if it's really rough and the wind's blowing me into the barge, or the barge is turning too fast, or whatever. It has its own mind, sometimes." Barges differ, but most of them turn into the trough. "Then I go heads to tails, my stern where his bow is, my bow pointing at his stern. I have enough fendering to protect me."

The bargemen lower the pennant to the tug, where the crew shackles it onto the wire. The hard part is to get away from the barge, and this is where boat handling comes in strongly. "I've got to turn my bow to the barge, bring my stern out, then I have to back real hard, real fast, on my inside engine to pull my stern away from the barge. Then slack the tow cable real fast to give me the room to back or it's just going to pull me back into the barge. Slacking the tow cable, it's going around a bitt on the stern and back to the barge. I back full until I get far enough away where I'm safe—eighty feet, say—and I stop my tow cable and start the twin screw—the tow cable will pull my stern around. To keep the tow cable from getting caught in the propellers, I've got to pull the tow cable in, and then I've got to take off. It's real tough, man, let me tell you. A real pain in the ass, because it's dangerous."

There's plenty of chance for things to go wrong while coming out of the notch, and occasionally they do. Steve is careful not to blame anyone, but there was a time things had gone bad on the mate's watch and Steve took over. He had to push the barge around and go head-to-tail. "It was nasty and rough. I got it connected, and I'm still kinda thinking about how we got into this situation, not how to get out of it, so I started backing without thinking about the shackle. The shackle is huge. It's always on deck when you make it up to the pendant, and you have to pay it over the side. This time—my fault—I didn't put the shackle over the stern and started backing on it. Looked onto the stern, thought 'Oh my God,' threw my engines out of gear—but it was too late. The shackle got hung up and it ripped part of the bitt out, and then that socket flew up in the air. Busted a fuel vent and a couple other things. Damaged the tow cable. Luckily, I always clear the deck—tell the guys to get outa there when I'm going to do that kind of maneuver. Eventually we got under control and proceeded to West Palm Beach. I had to call the company and say 'Hey look, I need somebody to come. I had to cut fifteen feet of tow cable off, and I need to solder another socket because I damaged it.'"

The other time Steve tells about was in Boston Harbor in the wee hours of the morning. He got the shackle hung up between the stern bitts and the house. "You don't want it there, you want it on the stern. It's heavy, and you can't lift it up. So we had to rig something to lift it up with. Meantime, I'm floating down the channel and it's three o'clock in the morning, and a ship's coming in." But they got themselves clear and got out of the way of the ship. There was some damage to the outer hull of the barge that time.

"There's a lot of opportunity for disaster. But do it right, do it smooth, do it slow—it works every time," says Steve. "I've done it a hundred times in my life, and only twice had trouble."

The *Ralph Bouchard* is a big, fast, comfortable tug with a lot of power. She has inboard-turning wheels. Twin-screw vessels' propellers always turn in the opposite direction from each other; they can turn inboard, or outboard. Outboard-turning wheels give better handling, and the boat can walk sideways, which is very handy coming on or off a dock. Inboard-turning wheels give better power, fuel economy, and speed. "They handle like a tug," says Steve. "To leave the dock in a normal tug, you turn your bow into the dock and let the stern come out and then you back out, and you have maneuverability. That's what we call tugboating. If you tried to turn your bow out, the stern would suck in to the dock and stay there, and you couldn't get away from it. Anchor handlers and the like out on the Gulf have bow thrusters so they don't have that problem."

Getting back into a shallow notch is another chore. Steve likes to connect while heading into the seas. He slows to three knots to shorten the tow wire as the barge starts catching up with the boat. When he gets some slack in the wire, the guys can pull the pin and disconnect the wire. Then he comes around to the stern of the barge and tucks into the notch. "As soon's I get in, I give a lot of power—have to, or you bounce in and out and in and out. The barge is going slow, and when you apply 6,300 horsepower, the barge isn't gonna pick up speed for awhile but the tug is gonna be pretty much stuck in there. That gives us the thirty minutes we need to connect the soft lines. Then we go back to the tow winch and stretch the lines out—*boinnggg*—run the winch engine at full speed for three minutes to get all the stretch out, and there we go."

Hooking up the push gear is dangerous too. "Double line, eighteen inches, two hundred feet long. It's wet, it's extraordinarily heavy, and at either end there's a giant thimble, fifty or eighty pounds apiece, plus the shackle and the pin and the nut on it, and a welding rod to keep the nut from backing off, and the thimble on the wire—it's a lot of weight. Setting it up is slow going, and if it's rough and you're bouncing up and down, the guys are in danger. It's a dangerous thing."

Underway, like any towboater, Steve faces challenges all the time, too.

At Mesquite Point, outbound on the Sabine Pass below Port Arthur, Texas, there's a stretch of river going due east, and all of a sudden there's a 100-degree turn to the right, to go south. A big lake opens out to the channel at this point, and there are a couple of islands where people often get ensnared. Steve had made this turn about thirty times before, but on this one trip the pilot wanted fifteen degrees port rudder as he approached the turn.

Steve was getting ready to turn right. "You mean right?"

"No, port rudder."

"I'm gonna run into the bank!"

"No you won't. Trust me."

Steve did as he was told, and the cushion of the bank kept him from hitting it. The pilot said that at a certain point—he'd tell him when—he'd want Steve to mid-ships the rudder. The moment came, right where the outflow from the lake came in, and the pilot gave the command.

Steve centered his rudder and flew around the turn. "Incredible!" he said to the pilot. "You just taught me ten years' worth of knowledge in one trip!"

That pilot told Steve to look up a book published by a Sabine Pass pilot in the 1940s or '50s called *Shiphandling in Narrow Channels*. It took his librarian six weeks to find it, and Steve was only permitted to keep it a week, but during that week he learned about bank cushion and bank suction, which are key concepts not only in narrow channels but when meeting deep-draft ships too.

A narrow channel such as at Tampa makes the fellow at the helm pay attention.

The *Adriatic Sea* in a shallow notch, preparing to discharge her payload in Portsmouth, N.H. AUTHOR PHOTO.

The channel narrows to about four hundred feet, and there might only be a hundred feet or less between his unit and a ship going the other way. It's important to know how the two vessels will interact. A ship with a big, bulbous bow drawing thirty-five or forty feet and moving along at ten or eleven knots pushes aside a lot of water. When Steve approaches, his barge drawing only twenty-six feet, the displacement of the ship pushes the barge's bow away. "So when I get to him, I steer into him ten degrees, like I'm going to actually turn into him. That'll offset the push. When I get amidships of this guy, I'll midships my rudder. Then when I get to his stern, the stern sucks you in—exact opposite of what happens at his bow." So he steers ten degrees away from the ship. "That way I can pretty much run down his side without getting sheared. But if I'm not ready, he'll suck me right in and make me do a one-eighty.

"Sometimes I'll slow down. I'm doing eight or ten knots, and if I slow down, it does two things: I get a little bit more time, and if I need a little extra power to compensate, I can speed up. Sometimes power helps, sometimes it doesn't—it just depends how you use it.

"These techniques take time to learn, but it's stuff like that that makes a better boat operator out of you."

He gives another example of non-intuitive tricks of the trade. "I let my mate dock the barge today. We were coming in on a face dock, and we had to make a one-eighty to dock port-side-to, facing out." On the starboard bow of the barge was an assist tug. The mate expected to come in at an angle, bow facing the dock, stern way out in the channel. Steve told him there was a better way: "Come in parallel and get your stern in real close to the dock. When you stop and turn around, that's going to push you away from the dock. The closer you are, the easier it is to stay in there."

Steve explained that he would have the assist tug back on the starboard bow. The mate thought that would pull the bow to the dock, but Steve said no, because he'd turn the helm to port. His tug was stronger than the assist boat and would off-set him. But the assist tug would hold him still and change the pivot point on the unit. "You're going to walk your stern toward the dock. That way, you'll be parallel when you turn around, and it's going to be an easier job." Steve let the mate experience it, giving the commands to the assist tug for him.

"That's another point, learning how to use your assist tugs correctly. It was a guy in Florida who taught me that: back your tug and go offset rudder, and it's like a car with four-wheel steering, you can parallel park. "I love these tugs, because you learn so much about boat handling."

The mate thought he'd done a pretty sloppy job of docking, but Steve corrected him: "You did good—there was no accident report."

"I'm going on thirty years in the wheelhouse," Steve says, but he's relatively new to the *Ralph E. Bouchard*. His counterpart on the other crew has been on the *Ralph* for eleven years. "I'm not afraid to ask the other guy for advice. He's got so much more shallow-notch time than I do." But Steve's ready to get back on an artic-ulated tug and barge. "I've been on an ATB before—love 'em."

There are times when Steve wonders if he wants to be in this job anymore. "The other day, coming through the tropical depression, I couldn't see the bow of the barge." He says the radar on the *Ralph* isn't absolutely the top of the line, and there are probably five hundred oil wells in the Gulf, many of them not lit, some nothing more than a big pipe coming out of the ocean. The radar doesn't pick them up in the rain all that well. "If I have an accident when I'm doing everything right, they'll yank my license for a year, maybe longer. If I'm smoking dope—yeah, go ahead and take my license forever. But if I'm doing everything right, they shouldn't have that ability. Times like that, I think it's just not worth it."

But then he talks about another boat handling job and gets enthusiastic again. "These are the sorts of things I find interesting. Been doing it thirty years, and I'm still intrigued by the job. It still excites me. I take an almost childish pride when I get on a unit and can handle it in a safe manner."

Tugs and Barges United

There are a number of valid reasons for having a rigid connection between a tug and her barge. In addition to making the connection stronger and saving the trouble of hooking up wires or lines, the unified tug-and-barge units have regulatory and economic advantages over ships. Because the power and the cargo sections are sep-arable—at least in theory—the Coast Guard regulations for both construction and manning are less stringent than would apply to a tanker. The units are about half as expensive to build as a similarly sized ship, and the savings on personnel can add up to a couple million bucks per vessel per year. Little things such as canal charges make a difference too; they're based on the total tonnage of a ship but only the ton-nage of the barge for a tug-and-barge unit.

A couple of different approaches have been tried, *integrated*—solidly attached—and *articulated,* with a jointed connection. In common usage, the two terms are often used interchangeably, or sometimes with specific meanings different from those I'm going to use, but there are two distinct systems. The Coast Guard decided to differ-entiate them with the terms "Pushing Mode ITB" and "Dual Mode ITB," referring to the capabilities of the tug in each case. (At this writing, the Coast Guard is consid-ering changing these names.)

On a Pushing Mode ITB, which I shall call an integrated tug and barge or sim-ply an ITB, the tug is attached rigidly to the barge. Basically, the unit becomes a ship, and the tug actually bears no resemblance to a tug. In most cases, it is built like a catamaran, with two hulls that straddle a specially designed section of the barge. The sides of the tug are flush with the sides of the barge. From a distance, in fact, it's difficult to see that the unit is not a ship, a good-sized one at that. The ITBs run by United States Shipping LLC—until recently, Sheridan Transportation Company—are seven hundred feet long.

Not many ITBs have been built. Although the original idea was that the tug would unhook from one barge at its destination and pick up another and be on her way with a short turnaround time, unhooking proved to be a far trickier thing than expected, and the tug isn't stable on its own. Only in a yard situation or some seri-ous emergency would the tug be pulled away from its barge—and it's just not possi-ble in most cases. On her second trip, an early ITB, the *Oxy Producer,* ran into rough weather off the Azores, causing enough movement between the tug and her barge that holes opened in the tug. Her crew tried to disconnect in order to repair the damage, but the tug was so unstable that she rolled and sank. Fortunately her crew was able to get on the barge, and there was no life lost. The conclusion after the drawn-out series of lawsuits that inevitably followed that event was that improper mating of the vessel caused the sinking and that the vessel was unseaworthy on delivery.

Disconnecting just doesn't work with an ITB, and even if it did work, it turns out that it takes longer to discharge one than normal, to boot. "It was a hare-brained idea," says one fellow who has spent time on one. United States Shipping, the company, however, is happy to have them. In effect, they are among the very few Jones Act (American) tankers left.

Tom Balzano, now First Engineer on the *Philadelphia,* one of the six U.S. Shipping ITBs, is very happy in his job. "It's one of the largest tugs—19,400 horsepower—and can push a 340,000-barrel barge at 16 knots," he says. "It's a tug in name only, though. In no way, shape, or form is it like a tugboat."

On the other hand, in an articulated system—a Dual Mode ITB, an ATB or, as designer Bob Hill refers to them, an AT/B—the tug is joined to her barge with a locking mechanism that allows her to pivot on one principal axis, pitching independently from the barge but rolling and yawing with it. And she can back out of the notch and tow when necessary, hence the Coast Guard's term "dual mode."

A number of companies produce the couplers. The first system available, Articouple, was made in Japan. Due to patent issues, they stopped offering the system in the United States before one was actually installed here. Bludworth's system uses lubricated hydraulic pads that push out from the sides of the tug along with a grip on the bow that clinches onto a bar on the inside of the notch. In several of the other systems, including the Intercons, hydraulic pins push out of the tug's sides just above the waterline and mesh into notches in a "ladder" on each side of the barge's

The ITB *New York.*
COURTESY OF
UNITED STATES SHIPPING LLC.

notch. These boats are known familiarly as "pin boats." The pins on some more recent models operate on air, rather than hydraulics, and are lighter in weight as well as less expensive than earlier ones. They also retrofit more easily, and this is a route many companies are taking.

Articulation is still expensive when compared to simply tying the tug in the notch, but the results are far better. Captain Steve Rhodes is looking forward to getting back on a pin boat. His experience has been with Intercon systems, which he describes as "the Cadillac." "It enables you to push in anything up to twenty-five-foot seas. If you get caught in something, you can get through it." The motion is better than that of a towboat with a barge on the string. At seas of sixteen to twenty feet, another captain reports, "We didn't make real good speed, and there wasn't a lot of comfort, but it's the lesser of two evils."

"It's a dual-edged sword," observes Captain Rick Clarke, who ran boats with Intercon systems for Penn Maritime for a time. "It's unnatural to have a fifty-inch-diameter hole at the waterline. Two of Penn's tugs have watertight doors to that room [where the hydraulic pins mechanism is] and two don't. It makes for interesting possibilities," he says.

Disengaging pin boats has occasionally been a problem in the past. Tug and barge have to be lined up just so to align the pins, or rams, and the ladders, and the pressure required to move the pins in or out is immense.

Aside from the specific hazards of the actual disconnection, the difficulties of getting out of the notch with an ATB are the same as those for vessels simply tied into the notch. The interval when the boat has let go of the barge but is still in the notch is dangerous no matter what the system. The *Undaunted* tried to leave the notch of her barge *Pere Marquette 41* during a squall on Lake Michigan, holed herself in the process, and damaged the barge too. The barge lost its cargo and deck equipment, but fortunately there was no injury to crew, and the tug stayed afloat.

Steve Rhodes isn't concerned about disconnecting under way; he won't do it. "That would be the last thing you'd want to do," he says. Another ATB captain says he's not worried about the system either. He says he could get out if he needed to.

Everyone agrees, though, that with an articulated system, you can't push a light barge. There's too much pounding. You have to have a ballast system or else tow. But, unlike the ITBs, an ATB tug is a seaworthy vessel in her own right, and can tow when asked to. Increasing numbers of petroleum barges now are double-hulled—by 2015, all will be—and the space between the two hulls is used for ballasting the barge so the tug can continue to push even when the barge is empty of cargo.

On an ATB the balance between tug and barge must be maintained. While loading or discharging, the tug is always disconnected, and as she pushes, the tug must be ballasted to make up for fuel expended. The engineer is aware of how much fuel the tug is using, and once or twice a day he balances her up with seawater pumped into her ballast tanks. If he hasn't kept up, the pin bushings let you know when it's time to change the ballast. "They start making a squealing noise like an elephant in heat. A four-foot diameter bushing twenty feet long, bronze—it's really loud," Steve says.

On August 10, 1993, Tampa Bay was the site of one of the messier accidents in recent time, though fortunately there were no lives lost. The outbound Philippine freighter *Balsa 37* collided with two inbound ATBs, the *Captain Fred S. Bouchard* with the *Bouchard 155* carrying No. 6 fuel oil, and the *Seafarer* with jet fuel, gasoline, and

The *Kara Sea* has a JAK coupling system, developed in Finland. Here the pin is extended as if it were in the ladder. COURTESY OF K-SEA TRANSPORTATION PARTNERS.

The ladder in the notch of the barge *Spring Creek*. COURTESY OF K-SEA TRANSPORTATION PARTNERS.

Headed out, lightly ballasted. The barge draws about five feet completely empty, and here it appears to be drawing six. COURTESY OF K-SEA TRANSPORTATION PARTNERS.

diesel fuel in the barge *Ocean 255*. The Coast Guard concluded that the accident was caused by incomplete communications between the bridges of the three vessels, and to one degree or another criticized the masters and pilots of all three. In any case, severe damage occurred to all the vessels involved, and some 328,000 gallons of heavy fuel oil ended up in the water, blackening seventeen miles of beaches and killing or endangering a variety of birds, sea turtles, mangroves, salt marshes, sea grasses, bottom sediments, water column biota, shellfish beds, and sand beaches. (For comparison, the *Exxon Valdez* spilled eleven million gallons.)

The *Seafarer*'s barge and the freighter came together first, generating sparks and a great deal of heat, and leaving the *Ocean 255* in flames. The captain attempted to disconnect his boat from her tow but, from the wheelhouse, couldn't withdraw the rams. He attempted to ground the barge, sounded the general alarm, and made a second unsuccessful attempt to get out of the notch. The Intercon system—and ATBs in general—came in for some criticism after that, but people on them now say that disconnecting is possible even in stress conditions.

Captain Joe Hopkins, then mate on another vessel, was aboard the *Seafarer* as an observer while his own boat was in the yard. He was asleep, and wasn't aware of any of the events prior to the general alarm. *That* he heard. "I could feel the boat backing down. I threw on my shorts, a shirt, shoes, grabbed my lifejacket and a survival suit. I could hear the captain saying it wasn't a good thing going on." Joe started to go out the hatch by his room, but the heat of the fire drove him back. "I mustered up the courage to look forward—and there was the fire on our barge, probably two hundred feet high—huge."

Joe and the rest of the crew that were below ran out to the main deck and to the stern. "It was like opening the oven door and the heat hits you in the face," he says. "You could hear the fire just roaring. The smoke was black, black, and there were cinders, like when you poke a piece of wood on the fire. Those cinders falling on us were three feet wide—big old cinders from the rubber and paint and things on the barge. It was HOT, very hot. You'd try to walk to one side and the heat would drive you back, and you'd try the other, same thing. There was a water hose back there, and one guy had it and was spraying everybody off."

Joe had heard the captain say earlier that they needed to get off the boat, and he was ready to jump overboard. "I was on the stern hollering, 'Hey, guys, we gotta get off the boat!' They were saying, 'We gotta wait for the captain.' I stayed back there till I couldn't stand it no more—I knew if I didn't do something, I was gonna die—and then I straddled the waist on the tug and put my foot in the water. I wanted to make sure there was no fire in the water and there wasn't, so I jumped in with my life jacket on and started swimming away."

He yelled back, "Y'all come in. The water's good!" and swam about two hundred feet away, and then there was a big explosion, "*Ka-POOM!* I put my hands over my head, afraid metal might land on me. None did, so I started swimming again, and I hear splashes now, everybody's jumping in. Then there was a whistling, more and more intense, more and more, till there was another explosion. It was like Vietnam or World War Two movies. You see a bomb and then you see a shock wave. I could feel it go through me like nothing I'd never want anyone to deal with. You're not really thinking, you're in instinctive survival mode.

"I covered my head again, and I thought, 'I'm gonna die right here.'" The rest of the crew was yelling that everyone should get together. "Yeah, you come over *here!*" Joe hollered, but he swam back to them, and felt gasoline in the water. "Now there's fire on the water, and I could feel it."

One guy on the boat had had his son with him, a boy of twelve or so. In the water, the kid kept climbing on his father, who asked Joe to help him. "Come here, Stevie," Joe called, and then Stevie jumped on Joe's back. "My instinct pushed him off. 'Go back to your dad!' It's something I'm not proud of, but it gives an example of the flight-or-fight instinct, the survival mode we were in."

The pilot boat *Manatee* came to rescue them. "I saw it over there a ways, and I started to go for it. The other guy said, 'Joe, don't leave me!' I turned back around and called, 'Come on, Stevie.' When he came to me this time, I grabbed him by his collar and said, 'Don't jump on me!' and I kinda shook him and said, 'Swim with me.'" Joe got the boy onto the boat, and then started grabbing the rest of the men.

"People say, don't worry about a loaded barge, it won't explode, but they do. They blow up. There's a certain amount of distance between the deck and the top of the product, where vapors collect. It might not explode as much as an empty barge, but it does explode."

An event like that is bound to have a lasting effect on anyone. "Sure, I had post-traumatic stress," Joe says. "Everyone dealt with it differently. I went back to work right after, but ended up going on disability for a few months. Talked with a shrink, read books, and I'm the better for it now. Before, I didn't have any empathy. I never put myself in anybody else's shoes. Now I appreciate life more. I'm more caring for other people than I was.

But, he says, "Nobody left the business because of the accident—nobody I'm aware of."

Designing Tug-and-Barge Units

Naval architect Bob Hill, who with a partner developed the Intercon coupler, has been fascinated by tugs since he was a boy in Troy, New York, where tugs were constantly bringing barges into the four petroleum terminals. He hung around the boats and talked with the men working them. "To a man, they said, 'You don't want to work on these, you want to design them.'" Bob took their advice and taught himself to draw. He says he picked up his first job, with Matton Shipyard, because he was the cheapest help Matton could get. His first independent project was fabricating a sewage retention tank for the tug *Margaret Turecamo*. "I measured it all up, and it was going to fit like a glove." Marty McGeary, the yard foreman, said so too. But there was a problem. "You see how big that door is?" McGeary asked young Hill. "It's a great tank, it fits perfectly, but I can't get it in the boat." The door was twenty-four inches wide and the tank was fifty-seven inches—so it had to be cut into three sections.

"I was devastated!" Bob was certain he'd get fired over this blunder. Bart Turecamo owned the shipyard at the time, and it was part of Bob's job to drive him to and from the airport. When he heard about Bob's mistake, he spent one trip reaming out the young man, every other word four letters long. "I thought I was doomed. I had to take him back to the airport that afternoon, and he was nice as pie. In today's environment, I could have sued him for some of what he said—but I still had my job."

Today, Bob is one of the last self-taught naval architects in the business of commercial design. He credits the elderly, knowledgeable gentlemen he had the opportunity to work and talk with as he was learning the business—Merit Demerest, Dan Berg, Joe Hack, John Gilbert—and says he picked up the engineering in dribs and drabs. "I'm fortunate in the clients I have had over the years. They had enough faith in me to give me a chance. Nowadays such a chance would be hard to find." He certainly knows his stuff, but he started out without the advanced degrees that most people in his position began with, which meant he could not testify in court as an expert witness—an inability that, to this day, he doesn't mind a bit.

It was in 1972, while he was working for Matton Shipyard, that Bob did his first serious work on a tug. This was the *Mobil 1* (now the *Zachary Reinauer*), designed by Merit Demerest. The *Mobil 1* was interesting because she was taller than most boats of the day, with her wheelhouse a half a deck higher than normal, and she had twin screws. "That was becoming the rage at the time."

In 1980 Bob first got involved with the field he now specializes in, the articulated coupling of tugs and barges. He was working for John Gilbert when an inquiry came in from Sun Transport, for whom they had done a lot of engineering work, stability testing, and barge modifications and the like. Sun Transport wanted to carry chemicals to Puerto Rico, but they didn't want the cost of a ship and they didn't want a towed barge. They wondered if it would be possible to design a tug-and-barge unit like the integrated tugs and barges that had recently been built, but able to separate and function independently. Matton designed a tug and barge to utilize the Japanese Articouple system, and the plans had gone out to bid, when suddenly Sun sold their refinery in Corpus Christi and the project was killed.

But from then on, it was in Bob's head that this was the way to go, although people in the American petroleum industry didn't see the value of the new idea for a few years. In the meantime, Bob had been pondering a better design. He went to the Intercontinental Engineering and Manufacturing Corporation in Kansas City, whose people he knew well. A good share of their business already was marine in nature. Their towing winches, capstans, and other equipment were at sea on many vessels. If anyone had the machining ability to make the gear-driven screw-drive connection Bob had in mind, it was them. The patent for the Intercon coupler that is one of the primary coupling systems in use today has Bob's name on it, along with that of Clare Kuhlman, the chief engineer at Intercontinental, as co-inventor. It was Bob who created the term *Articulated Tug and Barge,* or AT/B, which refers generically to the system now being adopted by most companies. (He has trademarked the abbreviated name with slash.)

The first application of the new coupler was in 1986, a retrofit of the Maritrans— then Sonat Marine—tug *Intrepid* and her barge *Ocean 250*. Their first trip out of the yard was pushing into fifteen-foot seas, a job a traditional tug couldn't have managed while tied flexibly into place behind the barge. When the *Intrepid* had been running for six years, Maritrans ordered three more refits.

By 1993, articulated systems had taken off. In that year, Bob formed a company in Massachusetts, Ocean Tug and Barge Engineering Corporation (OTBE). A year later, Penn Maritime ordered the first new builds using the Intercon system. OTBE designed the structure to hold the Intercon connection, modified the Halter Company's standard hull shape and planned the installation of the coupler, and provided the engineering for installing the system aboard the barges Alabama Ship was building for Penn.

Now many tugs being built to move petroleum are made with articulated systems, and some companies are retrofitting their boats and barges to take advantage of the new technology. Bob has gained respect from the entire industry, and there are now more than two dozen tugs afloat that he either designed in their entirety or where he engineered the installation of couplers. Failure of one of those installations while handling a loaded petroleum barge could be costly in both environmental damage and dollars. "Oil transporters literally entrust me with their future," he notes.

His boats have a distinctive look, obviously developed from a traditional tugboat—he remarks that people in 1910 had it right—but graceful and unmistakably his. Shipyards are constantly pushing for simple lines and flat steelwork—no curves, and don't bend the metal. Naturally, they want to save money, but Bob holds out when he can. "From Merit Demerest, I learned the best word in the business: No." Not only are the curves of his boats extraordinarily beautiful, they are functional.

He designs his tugs with a single helm station, up high. On the *Nicole Leigh Reinauer,* the height of the helmsman's eye is fifty-five feet. The wheelhouse must be round. "If you stand at the conning position, you have the same view angle from every window." Not only does that give a better view of the ocean around you, but it

The Bob Hill–designed AT/B *Mohawk.* Courtesy of Bob Hill.

allows you to see the deckhands on the quarter bitts or on the foredeck. From a square wheelhouse you might see one of them, but not both. The tower tapers inward as it rises, and the pilothouse overhangs it, allowing good visibility and making a far more attractive and spacious boat than those with the pilothouse up on stilts. At the same time, the side windows of the pilothouse cant outward, allowing the helmsman to see down without having to get his head out in the rain. "It's the kiss of death if you can't see the deckhand. You go to back down, and he's still got his arm in the bight. . . ." This is how a deckhand could lose a limb or worse. From that height you don't feel the boat the way you do when you're closer to the center of gravity, so seeing everything is even more important. The helmsman can see the alignment point of the coupling pins, too. (There are boats on which the captain sees neither the front deck nor the coupling devices. Everything is done by radio.)

Bob's next boat, the *S/R Everett*, built for Mobil Oil Company and launched in 2000, was designed to a particular set of requirements: she had to function as an AT/B, able to lock into a petroleum barge to push at sea, but she also had to be able to take a barge alongside because some docks require that. She would also need to be able to do some shipwork, and had therefore to be under 120 feet in length or she would stick out too far into the channel. She had to have smooth sides and fendering in order to push on ships.

The end result is a different-shaped tug, with each distinctive feature driven by the requirements. Her propellers are fairly well inboard so as not to interfere with a ship. The weight of the fenders and the added displacement from them required that the chines be fattened a little. There are no big blisters on the side from which the connection pins extrude; she could neither take a barge alongside nor dock ships if she had blisters.

The *Everett* and her barge have recently been purchased by K-Sea Transportation and renamed the *Lincoln Sea* and the *DBL 140*. (As if by magic, the unit has now apparently become an ITB; that is because K-Sea uses that term to refer to Dual Mode ITBs.)

A new design from OTBE has the more traditional stacked, straight-sided house. It still permits the view available on the *Nicole*, the *Everett*, and their sisters, but the vessel is less expensive to build. "It's less roomy and not as pretty," says Bob, but he's added little details like tapered bulwarks that give the impression at least of a real sheerline.

Due to changes in the industry, new construction has slowed. When Bob started in the business, oil companies wrote twenty-year contracts with the transporters. In the late 1970s and early '80s, when oil companies were no longer keeping their tank

PENN MARITIME 6,000 BHP
ATB OCEAN TUG

OCEAN TUG & BARGE ENGINEERING CORP.

This recent, plainer and more economical design was commissioned by Penn Maritime.
COURTESY OF BOB HILL AND OCEAN TUG & BARGE ENGINEERING CORPORATION.

farms topped off, five- to seven-year contracts became the norm. That was still a long enough period for a tug company to warrant building a boat to fill a known demand. Now contracts are only for a year at a time, and may get shorter yet.

The petroleum companies themselves are now qualifying the tug-and-barge companies. Beyond the physical requirements of the Coast Guard and industry safety programs such as ISO 9002 and the Responsible Carrier Program, they are establishing high standards for record keeping and reporting incidents. They are looking into accident rates and making root-cause analysis of any spills. "That's a new discipline," Bob notes. "They say there's no such thing as an accident. Everything is someone's fault. You have to dig and excavate to get to the root cause."

As an example, Bob gives a theoretical case of a fast mega-yacht barreling into a tank barge in the dark. There's a big spill. The captains testify that they saw each other, had radio contact, and each had an idea where he was going. But somehow they hit. Root-cause analysis says such an event is not an act of God. It's not because someone's radar malfunctioned, even though that may be the case. If the radar wasn't working right, how come? They might find a failure of a particular circuit board. But why? An assembler left something off the board. Why? Interview the workers on the line—aha! The parts come in a bin, and it's easy for the board to go by and the person might not grab the right part. So what is it about the assembly bin that causes the problem? How might they do it better? "It's a micro-forensic investigation."

In an actual case, an oil barge bumped a dock. The root-cause analysis led back to quality control of the casting procedure for the engine. "In the past, we'd have said it was a failure of the engine and left it at that."

In the case of any spill or collision or incident such as a steering or engine failure while approaching the dock, the oil companies require that the tug and barge companies do that kind of analysis.

Once an oil company has qualified tug companies, they know that whoever they choose from their list will provide good equipment and good service. Every year, the contracts come up, and every year, someone has an underutilized boat and they offer a low rate. "At various times, all companies have been guilty of this," Bob says.

Water transport faces other competitors, now, too. More and more bulk oil product is moving by rail. A tank train has been developed with connected cars holding up to 33,300 barrels apiece that pump out from one end. Mobil's canal business from Albany to Plattsburgh, New York, has been hijacked onto rail. The Illinois Central Railroad is connecting the Gulf of Mexico and the Midwest, and the Union Pacific is taking lube oil from the Gulf to the West Coast.

In 1970, the cost of shipping a barrel of gasoline from New York to Boston by water was forty-six cents. At this writing, it is about fifty-three cents. "Doubling the rates would add scarcely two cents a gallon," Bob says, "but the oil companies see those pennies as so many billion dollars a year."

Meanwhile, the cost of equipment skyrockets, for both construction and maintenance. "Everyone who builds is building on spec," Bob says. A thirty- or forty-million-dollar decision is based on a company's confidence that it can keep the new boat working beyond the current contract.

"A tug-and-barge unit is a very dynamic structure," Bob explains. The stresses on an Intercon or other coupling system are huge, a thousand or fifteen hundred tons in one dimension alone. "It takes a tremendous beating. Everything will fail eventually—nothing is immune. We design with the intention that each component will go through fewer cycles than it will take to make it fail." Computer modeling predicts the cycle life of each element, and when that cycle life comes near, the parts are replaced or rebuilt. "It's just the same as in a diesel engine—you change the pistons at a certain time interval because, predictably, that's when they will start failing."

Some years ago, Bob designed a series of 125-foot articulated tugs. The first few performed beautifully, but then the rudders fell off four of the new tugs, all in deep water where they couldn't be retrieved. "As the naval architects, we were the people they looked at first," says Bob. But on inspection of the rudder on a boat still under construction, they found that it hadn't been constructed the way OTBE had drawn in the plans. Neither the welding nor the steel were as called for. All the boats that had lost their rudders were built by one shipyard, which had in turn subcontracted the rudders to a particular machine shop, which had for whatever reason unilaterally elected to change the design. Normally, once the American Bureau of Shipping has stamped a plan Approved, that's final. It's not clear why these were not built to the original specifications. It was then necessary to call back the other boats and be certain they were all right. "You can't take anything for granted," Bob says. "Fortunately there were no accidents." The rudders are so big that even though one boat must have run for a week on only one, her captain said she maneuvered just fine—the only clue they had was that they had to hold a couple of degrees of rudder to go straight ahead.

AT/Bs have been accused of being rule beaters, but Bob explains that, while of course they are chosen over ships because of the lower operating expense, they aren't rule beaters. They are instead boats that the rules allow. "They are built to take advantage of the envelope that the regulations allow. We're not going to the rusty edge of what's allowed and stretching it," Bob says. Not by a long shot.

"The hardest part about being a naval architect," he says, "is that every once in a while it dawns on you that people are riding around in your boats in all weather—you're responsible for these people. You hear of a casualty somewhere, and think, 'There but for the grace of God. . . .'"

6
Pushing Petroleum

While tugs push barges containing all manner of materials and products, one of their primary longer-distance jobs is the moving of petroleum in its various forms. There are pipelines—for example, pipelines carry crude oil and other petroleum products from the Gulf of Mexico to Philadelphia and to New York refineries and terminals, and there is one from Portland, Maine, to Montreal. In Alaska, a pipeline runs from the Northern Slope down to Valdez. Some petroleum goes by rail, too. But where

Viking pushes a loaded petroleum barge past the United Nations building.
Courtesy of Don Sutherland.

there are no pipelines or rails—and even where there are, depending on cost—petroleum is moved by water. Only a third of that coastwise transportation is by tanker. The rest goes by tug and barge.

Engineer Gary Matthews used to work on tugs moving petroleum, but is glad to no longer be doing that. "I can sleep at night, not pushing large bombs around."

This matter of bombs isn't total exaggeration. Asked what was the most frightening experience she has ever had on a tugboat, Captain Melissa Terry doesn't hesitate. "A near collision in Long Island Sound in the fog," she says. Working as a deckhand, she was off-watch, asleep in her room on a 3,900-horsepower, twin-screw tug with an empty 100,000-barrel manned barge that had been carrying gasoline. The vapors left in a light barge make it far more explosive than one with a full load. Headed back into New York, they were towing the barge up short, with the shackle almost over the stern, but they couldn't see the barge in the fog just eighty feet behind the tug. "That's always unnerving," she says. It was even more so because of the high traffic in New York Harbor.

"What woke me up," Melissa says, "was a sharp boat lurch and then a turn, and then I felt the boat going over waves." She says that even asleep, you're always half aware of what's going on. She knew where they were, and knew that there should be no sharp turns. What was *that*? She ran up into the galley. "Part of the crew was sitting there with their eyes like saucers, white as a sheet." They told her they were lucky to be alive. They had just missed a tanker—by ten feet.

Melissa says that the other deckhand, her counterpart, was in the wheelhouse with the captain, providing another set of eyes. He heard the captain's communication with the pilot on the ship—they agreed on passing port to port, half mile CPA (closest point of approach)—and knew they saw each other on the radar. Everything looked fine, so the deckhand had come down into the galley.

Then came the lurch. He looked out the window—and all he saw was red bottom paint. He estimated that the ship was making sixteen knots and the tug ten. A twenty-six-knot closing speed is tremendous. Later, the guys on the barge said they could have jumped from there to the ship.

"From that point onward, whenever it was foggy, we were *all* up in the wheelhouse—we didn't trust the captain. Nobody said anything on the radio. There was no notation made, nothing. Everyone zipped their mouths.

"It's pretty hard to miss a seven-hundred-foot ship, and our barge was four hundred feet long. Our tug to the end of the barge was nearly as long as the ship.

"It's scary, after the fact, just knowing what could have happened," says Melissa. "Not that I'd have known anyway."

The *Amy C. McAllister* with a light barge on the East River, towing up short. AUTHOR PHOTO.

Environmental concerns and ensuing regulations have meant that fewer and fewer of the myriad small terminals that used to dot the coast still exist. Today, big tank farms serve as regional distribution centers. Gasoline, diesel fuel, home heating oil, aircraft fuel, bunker C, and various other petroleum and chemical products most people never hear of make their way from place to place in barges.

Since the *Exxon Valdez* incident, everyone is taking petroleum movement very seriously. The federal government, the Coast Guard, the industry itself, all are developing standards for safe transport and loading and unloading. Among other things, the Oil Pollution Act of 1990 established a timetable for eliminating all single-hulled ships and barges. They will be phased out by 2015.

Safety training requirements are continually being increased. There are no fewer than five governmental or quasi-governmental national organizations involved with licensing and inspections and accidents: the Coast Guard (with responsibility for licensing of personnel and for the operations and safety of inspected vessels), OSHA (apparently with responsibility for safe operation on uninspected vessels), the FCC (radio operations and licensing), the EPA (on-scene response and clean-up of environmental incidents), and American Bureau of Shipping (hull and engineering design and integrity—shared with the Coast Guard.) State agencies and local groups such as harbor commissions and fire departments add their own regulations.

Penn Maritime's *Tarpon* pushes her barge into Searsport. AUTHOR PHOTO.

American Waterways Operators is the national trade organization representing owners and operators of tugboats, towboats, and barges. It promotes the long-term economic soundness of the industry in part by developing standards for safe, efficient, and environmentally responsible transportation. AWO requires that its members comply with the standards it has established in its Responsible Carrier Program. Members' vessels are subjected to certified third-party audits. It is not AWO's intent to duplicate the regulations enforced by the Coast Guard or other entities but rather to create a sensible program based on the experience and expertise of people in the industry itself.

AWO's standards include such things as hull inspections in drydock at least every three years, with all openings, piping systems, and tanks checked annually. Firefighting, life saving, and towing equipment are covered by particular standards. Maintenance records must be kept, and safety policies and procedures must be in place for personnel, operation of the boat, and proper handling of various types of cargo. Also addressed is the fatigue factor. The Federal law says that a licensed operator is limited to only twelve hours of duty in twenty-four—a rule that is consistently broken on two-watch boats, though AWO members agree to honor that policy. Training is also spelled out for particular positions.

Three hundred and seventy-five member companies have agreed to AWO's Responsible Carrier standards, although a few companies chose to resign their membership rather than comply with the audits.

Despite all the efforts being made by all these different agencies and organizations, there are people in the industry who are skeptical of the whole thing and feel that there is no coordination whatever at this time. They say a complete overhaul is needed, with one industry-wide set of rules and regulations being applied fairly and consistently.

An oil spill is now considered a criminal offense, and a whole list of charges can be filed after a spill incident. According to several people I've spoken with, the Department of Justice won't be happy until someone goes to jail. If there's one dead bird, then you're guilty of violating the Migratory Bird Treaty Act. And there's the Refuse Disposal Act. It was intended to prevent people from tossing garbage around, but now, if there's the least bit of oil in the water, that act too can be used against the evil perpetrator. Tugboaters aren't blasé about oil spills—far from it—but they worry that their own careers may be ended by an overzealous bureaucrat. "It's a notch in somebody's gun to send people to jail," says one captain.

The transport companies are making an effort to be less visible, just in case something does happen. When Harley Marine Services started up, the Yellow Pages people tried to sell them a business listing. "We have four customers and three competitors," they said. "We all know who we are. We don't need advertising." As George Clark of Harley told me, "We want you to never know our name as well as we all know Exxon's."

And Exxon's name will not again be plastered as loudly all over the newspapers in connection with an incident, either. Its name no longer shows up on any vessels. Their transportation business was moved to a new subsidiary innocuously named SeaRiver Maritime, Inc., and now that company too has disappeared. To be sure, when awards are given out—and SeaRiver got its share for environmental excellence—ExxonMobil sent out the press releases in their own name. But there will be no more *Exxon Whoevers* on the rocks. The *Exxon Valdez*, banned from Prince William Sound, was renamed the *SeaRiver Mediterranean* and carried oil uneventfully in foreign waters until recently, when it was decided that she was no longer profitable. At this writing her future is still undetermined. Her sister ship, the *SeaRiver Long Beach*, continues to sail the Alaskan waters for which both boats were designed.

There have been other spills since the *Valdez* incident, though none of that scale. One of the best known took place in Rhode Island during a storm in 1996, when a fire in the tug *Scandia* caused her to lose control, and she and her tank barge, *North Cape*, ran aground on Moonstone Beach. Attempts to anchor the barge before it grounded failed due to improper stowage of the anchor. Three million gallons of home heating oil were safely taken off the barge after the grounding, but an estimated 828,000 gallons spread throughout a large section of Block Island Sound. Large numbers of birds, fish, lobsters, and other aquatic life died, and 250,000 square miles of the Sound were closed to fishing for several months.

It can be said that this spill had nearly as much impact as did the *Exxon Valdez*, partly due to its visibility and partly because the Feds wanted to establish a precedent of criminal prosecution for oil spills. Hold someone responsible—it feels better. The state of Connecticut had some demands of its own—the governor threatened Donjon Marine's salvage master with jail if the barge wasn't removed within twenty-four hours, despite 50-knot winds. (Apparently reason later prevailed on that one.)

In a plea bargain, the captain of the *Scandia* and an official of Eklof Marine Corporation, the owner of the tug, both admitted negligence for ignoring storm warnings as well as not having adequate fire suppression and anchoring equipment aboard. Eklof Marine was fined a total seven million dollars and agreed to donate another million and a half to The Nature Conservancy for remediation and land preservation. In addition, they agreed to make a million dollars' worth of safety improvements to their fleet. The captain was fined ten thousand dollars and placed on two years' probation. No one spent time in jail, but it was the end of the Eklof company—the owners sold the business to a group of employees and others, who created K-Sea Transportation.

Although Eklof pled guilty to the various charges, they certainly cannot be held up as an unusually irresponsible company, and they were in violation of no Coast Guard rules. They had developed an internal safety program and had voluntarily adopted the AWO Responsible Carrier Program standards. Still, fire equipment was not present that might have made containment of the fire possible. As an uninspected towing vessel, the tug was not required to have a fixed fire-fighting system, nor automatic or remotely operated ventilation dampers, nor a remotely operated fire pump, nor fire suits and self-contained breathing apparatus. And while the barge had an anchor, which was not required either, it might as well not have been there, as there was no windlass and the crew was unable to undo the lashings securing the anchor.

As a result of the *Scandia* incident, the Coast Guard banned single-screw boats from handling petroleum barges or tankers. It has also beefed up some of its regulations about anchors and fire detection and suppression on uninspected towing vessels. Before a barge is allowed to sail, it must have a functioning anchor, and tugs now must have fire detectors, although remotely operated fire suppression devices are not yet required save on new boats and those formerly owned by Eklof (many of K-Sea's present fleet). In other words, you have to know the fire's there, but you don't have to have a way to put it out. When it comes to sensible regulations, there's a ways to go yet.

Incidentally, I have heard that the *Scandia* fire started when a cigarette lighter in a crewmember's pants pocket ignited in the dryer. Such a simple mistake, and such ramifications!

(Many would think the *Scandia* was a bad-luck boat. In 1983, as the *Helen McAllister*, she was flipped by her oil barge off Portland Head, killing the mate. She was raised and returned to work as the *Scandia*, and thirteen years later was in trouble again. Arthur Fournier, ever the seeker of advantage and a deal, bought the remains of the *Scandia* after the Rhode Island incident. "It was a burned-out hull. Had to start from scratch." What sort of a project is that? "Six months." The only thing salvageable was the reversing-reduction gear, which was rebuilt in place. He put a factory-rebuilt 20-cylinder EMD engine in her and felt he had a brand-new boat, only the hull remaining from the old *Scandia*. She's now the *Fournier Girls* and back in the ownership of the McAllister company. Arthur and the men running her today agree that she's a good boat. But she has had more than her share of trouble.)

Attention to tow wires was increased after an incident a few years ago when the tug *Emily S.* left Puerto Rico with the tank barge *Morris J. Berman* on a cable known to be bad. The cable broke once, and the crew retrieved it, jury-rigged it back together, and went on their way. It was a short crew working long hours. The word is that the mate fell asleep on watch and no one noticed when the cable broke again. Several hours later, they learned that the barge was aground and spilling. The failure to replace a $9,000 cable left some 800,000 gallons of No. 6 oil on the beach, required over a million man-hours to clean up, and resulted in the largest fine in history: $83.5 million. (This works out to about $100 a gallon. The fine in the *Exxon Valdez* case just a few years earlier and in a far more remote location was $2.27 per gallon.) Now there are regulations about maintaining the history of every tow wire.

"The way it goes in this industry, you're gonna get in an accident," says Captain Steve Rhodes, who has been pushing petroleum for fifteen years. "It's not *if*, it's *when*. It happens. If a guy comes to me and tells me he has fifteen years' experience and no accident, he's a liar—ain't no way. Or he runs stuff that's so small that when he has an accident, nothing happens." (To be fair, there are captains who say this is overstated; they themselves have had no trouble and plan to continue in that manner.) The barge Steve runs today carries five million gallons at 6.6 pounds apiece. "My barge hits the dock at a half a mile an hour, it's gonna knock the dock down.

That's how big it is—it's ungodly. You can't afford to run aground or get caught in the fog. When the fog comes, I'll drop my anchor as soon as I safely can. I don't really care about getting there as quickly as possible—too much liability."

Steve's only spill took place in New York Harbor in 1998, and, as it happened, during the Million Man March. "That's why the heat didn't go on me. It was on them instead," he says. Sixty-six barrels, about three thousand gallons, went overboard, and although there were various contributing factors, Steve accepts responsibility for the spill. "They docked my license for three months. I couldn't work or make a living. And now, every time I go to do something with the Coast Guard I have to re-explain what happened. I've done my time. I had to go back to school, take a three-weeks training course. I did what they asked me to do, but I still have to go through this."

Today there are captains with big licenses and a lot of experience who have elected to work as mate rather than carry a captain's level of liability. "It's a criminal offense now to spill oil," says one. "Take an airplane pilot—he can be flying four hundred people, and he could crash that plane and be negligent and walk away from it and not go to jail, but if I spill oil in the Gulf or the Atlantic Ocean, and I'm not even negligent, I'm going to jail. Instantly. They take me to jail first and then they ask questions. Something's wrong there."

Captain Bob Peterson no longer pushes oil at all. "When you're a licensed mariner, any level, but especially in the wheelhouse, you carry the weight of the world on your shoulders. Everything's good till you make a mistake. They can name you personally in a suit, and you lose everything you've worked your whole life to gain. You screw up, if there's anything you could be found negligent on—even if there's a navigation buoy out of place—you're in trouble." By law, captains are required to keep their charts updated from the weekly local Notices to Mariners. "If that buoy was knocked out of place by a yacht that just went through ahead of you, and it hadn't been reported yet, you might slide by—but certainly you're gonna get overhauled in the process. It's gonna cost you a lot of money at least, if not your career.

"I was on a boat hauling oil in Puerto Plata [Dominican Republic]. I was off-watch, and the mate had actually been in and out of there more often than I had. He put the boat on a reef. I didn't put it there, but I was the captain—we both got fired. I looked back on that and thought how bad it could have been, and I decided I'm not gonna do that anymore unless I'm starving to death."

I've heard of more than one captain who has switched ownership of his house, car, and any other significant assets to his wife's name in order to protect them should he run into trouble. Others don't even carry insurance, assuming that anyone filing a suit would go after the deepest pockets. "And I sure don't have deep pockets!" exclaimed one mariner.

Each incident brings on more regulations, but also more attention to safety. AWO's Responsible Carrier Program is making the companies pay more attention, and the threat of being held personally liable is making tug operators more careful than ever. Everyone is aware of the serious damage potential posed by the products they are moving. The inspections are forcing better maintenance—the tendency to patch up and get by is far less than it used to be. The trend is toward towboat owners hiring third-party companies to do major maintenance instead of depending on

Tasman Sea pushing a petroleum barge in a shallow notch. COURTESY OF DON SUTHERLAND.

Beaufort Sea towing down Penobscot Bay after offloading her cargo. AUTHOR PHOTO.

their own engineers. The outside engineers give a warranty. Their reputation is at stake, while the liability of the boat's owners is lessened.

One advantage of the petroleum transportation business is that it provides steady work. In bad times, it's a good job—people always need the commodity you're moving. Lenny Greiner has a captain's license but is working as mate on the *Adriatic Sea.* "If you were to take it all too seriously," he says, "you couldn't do this. The regulations, the liabilities—you couldn't drive this thing around. You'd be all choked up."

The *Adriatic*'s Captain Vernon Elburn worked for a coal company for five years but the rest of his forty-five years in tugs has been oil-related. "It's all I've done my entire life." Of course, years ago, the liabilities for a captain were less. But the advantages of staying with the job have outweighed the negatives for Vernon. "Where you got a steady job and the pay's good, you stick it out. Your benefits, 401(k) and retirement, build better if you stay the same place, and you get comfortable with the people you're working for. Some of us hate to make changes." He's nearing retirement anyway, and says, "I'll stick it out."

I met Captain Elburn and his crew one Monday in October of 2002. A bit before midday, I stood on the dock at K-Sea Transportation on Staten Island, which was surrounded by barges and tugs and strewn with all sorts of material and equipment, much of it, to me, unidentifiable stuff. I watched the *Adriatic Sea* nose in between the corner of a barge and another tug's bow. I was led across the other tug—"Watch out for the grease!"—and, as soon as I was aboard, the *Adriatic* was backing out again. Though she was assigned no job before the trip to New Haven scheduled for late that night, the pier was busy, with the *Beaufort Sea* and the *Falcon* shifting barges in and out. The *Adriatic* was told to go sit with her own barge, the *KTC 135*, already on anchor in the Bay Ridge anchorage, loaded and ready to go. The plan was that she'd leave New York Harbor in time to make the midnight slack tide through Hell Gate.

Mate Lenny Greiner showed me around the tug and introduced me to the rest of the crew as we came across them. It was nearly watch-change time, so everyone was around. Most were in the galley, which is at main deck level, the lowest of the four house-levels. "Life revolves around that steel box right there," said Lenny, referring to the refrigerator. He's a wiry fellow in his mid-thirties, not very tall but strong-looking and with a symmetrical, aquiline face. He wants Tom Cruise to play his part in the movie (of *my* book?), and it's not a bad choice. The union contract has requirements for refrigerator and freezer space, as well as televisions for the crew and linen service if there's no washer and dryer. The *Adriatic Sea* has laundry facilities, as well as a particularly good galley, including a dishwasher. "You know you've hit the big time when you have a dishwasher on a tug."

Eleven-forty-five and watch-change time. Lenny led me past the crew's rooms, up a ladder to where the officers' rooms (and mine) were, and up another ladder to the pilothouse. He was about to take over for Captain Elburn, a rugged man with silver hair slicked back from his forehead who speaks with a gentle Eastern Shore dialect. Vernon told Lenny that Donjon Marine was working to raise a sunken barge ahead—earlier, they'd had a diver's flag out. "OK," said Lenny. "I'll keep an eye out for that." Vernon told him the office hadn't yet come up with any other jobs for them. In the morning, they had taken a barge out to lighter a ship because the ship had too much draft for the dock she was to go into. The *Adriatic Sea* isn't ideal for shifting barges, Vernon told me. "She doesn't handle very well in close quarters. She was built for long-distance towing and pushing." She has Kort nozzles, giving her increased thrust, particularly at slow speeds. The tradeoff is in maneuverability. As Lenny describes it, "Moving little bunker barges with the *Adriatic* is like a gorilla trying to take care of a kitten."

Lenny took the helm from the captain and quietly guided the tug into the notch in the *KTC 135*. "Let Traffic know you're standing by here," said Vernon.

Mate Lenny Greiner in the *Adriatic Sea*'s galley, the most important part of a boat, according to many. AUTHOR PHOTO.

Tying into the notch. T John Kanoute is handling the line; you can tell he's an engineer by the ear protectors. AUTHOR PHOTO.

The Coast Guard's Vessel Traffic System—known as "Traffic"—keeps track of all the commercial vessels in New York Harbor. No move is made without telling them, and by radar they watch everyone at anchor, too, to be sure no vessel impinges on anyone else's swing circle or into the shipping channel. In the *Adriatic*'s pilot-house, three radios chatter constantly when she's in the harbor: Channel 16 is monitored by everyone all the time and is where any emergency call would be made. K-Sea uses 18 as their company channel, and Traffic is on a third channel. (On one of the radios is a sticker that announces 77 as the emergency channel—for the boat, it means. If there were trouble on the *Adriatic Sea,* the onboard communications would be on 77 with portable radios.)

While the barge was alone on her anchor, one of its two crewmen was responsible for monitoring Channel 16. (Not too long ago, the Coast Guard hailed a barge on 16 and got no answer. The barge was fined $500 for not standing radio watch. The real concern is that someone should be alert for a dragging anchor.) On arrival of the *Adriatic,* the barge was relieved of that responsibility. "I gotta listen to the foolish radios now," said Lenny. He doesn't stop his conversation for their benefit, however. All those guys have a third ear attuned to the name of their vessel, and whenever the name *Adriatic* came over any of the radios overhead, Lenny immediately picked up the appropriate mike and responded. There is also an internal telephone that requires no electricity; a hand-cranked ringer can direct a call between the wheelhouse, the engine room, the galley, the upper wheelhouse, or the captain's room.

The manned tank-barge *KTC 135* has its own cooking and sleeping facilities (and its own TV). It is 435 feet long, 80 feet wide, and 37.5 feet deep and can carry 135,216 barrels of petroleum or chemical product. K-Sea uses it primarily for coastal routes—New York to Philadelphia, Albany, New Haven, Boston, and the like—but it is marked with an ocean load line and can go offshore if need be. It carries two people, captain and mate, one on watch at a time. Each has a Coast Guard PIC (Person in Charge) document. Until recently, this was known as a tankerman's credential, and in common parlance it still is called that, but political correctness demanded the change in title. The license shows that its holder has been trained in handling dangerous liquid cargoes, and it is the job of the PIC to load and discharge cargo from the barge.

Most of K-Sea's barges are manned. They do have one or two unmanned barges, which a shore-based tankerman loads and discharges. They also are increasing the number of "pinboats"—articulated tug and barge units whose barges are unmanned—on which members of the tug's crew will have the endorsements to manage the barge duties too.

Barge Captain Bill Howe has been working on barges for twenty-three years. He admits he likes the job in part because of the time off. He also likes the quiet of being on the barge and waiting for the boat to come. "It's nice when you only got two guys. There are too many people on the boat," he says. "I like it quiet. People leave you alone on the barge." He says, smiling, that his mother is from Georgia and his father from New York and that may be why he likes it quiet. It doesn't matter to him where the barge goes, or how long it spends in one place or another. "I'm here for two weeks. I don't care what we do—I'm camping out anyway. I go camping every two weeks. And I get to see a lot of places." The facilities are tight, yes, and inevitably, your partner on the barge gets on your nerves sometimes, "but when you get cramped, you just go outside and do something on the barge.

"We try to get along. He's got the same thing—he's out here for two weeks, too. I do the same things he does. Rank's not important, not to me." He admits it's not always that way and that sometimes you just can't get along with the other fellow. "Then one of you's gotta go." Dan Bruton has been on the *135* with Bill for three years, which is unusual.

As on the tug, the barge keeps regular watch hours. As tankermen, they may be in the middle of a job, loading or discharging, when the watch changes. "I just pick up where he leave off at," says Dan. "We transfer information, and then he get his rest."

Bill wants to be around people when he's home. His son is grown and shipping out himself, six months at a time. His wife has a hairdressing shop and can arrange her own schedule. When he's home there is nothing to prevent them from enjoying themselves, spending time with friends, going places, taking mini-vacations. Life is good for this barge captain.

The *135* and the *Adriatic* were adapted specifically to one another by Maritrans, their former owner. The *Adriatic* has big rubber-clad "blisters," protective pads on her sides, shaped to fit snugly into the notch in the stern of the barge. Hanging with the barge on the anchor, waiting for the order to get going, the crew had simply run out the bow line onto the barge without attaching the wires that would hold the two solidly together under way. Connected just by the bow line, the tug would be ready to detach quickly if called on for some other job by the company in the meantime. She was just a little loose in the notch. When one of the Staten Island ferries passed, the tug rattled with an odd, sharp motion as she hit one side of the notch and then the other. The *Adriatic* has bigger blisters further aft, too. She used to work with a 190,000-barrel barge with a 90-foot notch that engulfed the tug to the end of her main deckhouse.

The blisters used to sit tighter in the notch than they do now. Vernon spoke of brushing tallow onto the barge where they rubbed so they wouldn't get stuck. Even now, the rubber still sticks once in a while. The last time they pushed into Boston, it got a little rough and they tightened the cables again after the tug had been surging and twisting around. Although they slacked the cables when they started pumping out the cargo, the boat rose right along with the barge. "When it got high enough, it broke loose, and the boat musta fell three feet. The chief wasn't used to that, and he come running up on the bow to see what happened."

Vernon started as a deckhand when he was seventeen. He was born and raised in an Eastern Shore Maryland fishing community and had always worked on small boats. "A friend went to work on a tug, and I was between jobs—it was between seasons—and he asked me to come along. I was gonna make one trip, just till I found something else," he says. "I'm still looking." He was in charge of a boat before he was twenty, and now it's forty-five years later. He compares his job to fishing. "It's easier than working outside on the water in the cold and ice. I can be inside the wheelhouse, usually."

"When Captain Vernon started," said Lenny, "they had no radar, just spotlight, compass, and stopwatch. Now, if the computer's down—" he made a face. "'Specially me."

Captain Vernon Elburn writing in the log. AUTHOR PHOTO.

"We used the whistle a lot," said Vernon. "In good weather, you'd steer a course, check your time, and figure your speed. Then in bad weather, you'd have notes, so you knew," Vernon explained.

Nowadays they run navigation software that combines with the GPS to place the boat directly on the chart on the computer in the wheelhouse.

"To me, lighthouses are just scenery," Lenny added. "But to him . . ."

"If it was very foggy, I'd think, 'We ought to be abeam of that lighthouse now' and sometimes we'd shut the engine off and listen for it. And we had a lead line to check the depth of water."

The tug *Mary L. McAllister* sailed by. "She sank off North Carolina," Vernon told me. (Tug people always know about all the other tugs around.) The *Mary*'s history demonstrates how tugs lead complicated and sometimes circular lives. Forty years ago, the boat (then called the *Marjorie McAllister*) was caught in a storm and her whole crew was lost. She was raised eight years later, rebuilt, and put back to work. After stints with two other companies, she returned to McAllister and was given her current name.

A tug with a railroad car float on her hip passed. Vernon spoke of years in the past when car carriers were common. They all went across traffic in the harbor and they all assumed the right of way. When it was time to go, they'd untie their lines and just go, sounding the whistle to warn everyone to get out of their way. "They'd take their lines in, bear down on the whistle, and put the lines down again." The ferries do the same thing, but at least you can always see the ferry terminal and have an idea of what's coming. "The car floats were in at the top of long slips, and you couldn't see them coming out."

Captain Elburn was tired. "I'm going to go put my feet up," he said, and headed below. Lenny started talking about crew change, which was coming up Wednesday. The men on the boat and on the barge work two weeks on, two weeks off. The question is always where will the boat be, come Wednesday. "That's another real important aspect of this job—crew change," said Len. "And you try not to talk to each other when you're off. I don't want to hear anything about a tugboat when I'm home. My wife doesn't understand when I want to go sit in the living room by myself, all quiet. I tell her, 'You try being penned up in our kitchen for two weeks with the lawnmower running.'" Even while we were just sitting on the anchor there was a steady hum of diesel engine as the *Adriatic* ran a generator.

Lenny started talking about Captain Elburn again. "He's the best. I'm not just blowing smoke. Not only can he manage crew better than anyone, he can handle the boat the best. He's never upset. He knows what's going on three steps in advance.

I've worked with a lot of people in a lot of ships, and he's the best. When he's awake, everything in the world is at peace.

"Every trip we come across something where I don't know if it can be done or not. Last trip—it sounds minor—but we let the barge go and put it on the wire and picked it up again in Newark Bay, a turning basin for freighters. It's a big boat—if we don't do it right, something will go aground or into a container ship—but Vernon said we could do it. Well, it happened that the time to do it came on the watch change, so I watched Vernon do it—like tying his shoes. If Vernon says I can do something, I know I can."

Vessel Traffic System came on the radio asking the *Adriatic Sea* to move a little to the south. Her swing had encroached on a tug-and-barge unit behind us. "The *135* has been here since last night," Lenny said. "What I want to know is, did our anchor drift or did they come in on top of us?" But to Traffic, he politely agreed to move. He called the engine room and asked Assistant Engineer T John to start her up, and then he called the barge and the galley and asked Dan and Trevor to raise anchor. "More than likely, when I move and re-anchor, Traffic still won't be happy."

As do all things in this business, hauling the anchor took a while. The thing is a 4,000-pound Danforth, each fluke five or six feet tall. Lenny says it doesn't hold very well at all. It's on a cable but would be better with a quarter-shot of chain. Chain lies on the ocean floor better and makes the pull on the anchor come horizontally instead of at an angle, which tends to loosen it. When the barge was rigged out, it wasn't anyone's intention that it would have to anchor. They didn't actually plan for it to stop at all, other than to load and discharge. That probably explains why the hydraulic system for raising the anchor isn't as rugged as it might be. When the men on the bow of the barge finally reported that the anchor was clear of the water, Lenny pushed forward a ways and called Traffic. "I've moved six hundred feet south," he told them. "How's this looking?"

"Your bow is pointed south?"

"Yes, sir."

"How many shots are you going to put out?"

"Three, three-and-a-half."

"One moment, Cap. Stand by." And before they came back, the tug and barge had drifted out of place. "Oh for Chrissakes," said Lenny, his finger off the transmit button on the radio. "I had it perfect to let go. . . ."

"We're going to ask that you move to the west," Traffic told him.

"If I move to the west, I'll be within a quarter mile of that Reinauer boat," Lenny said.

"When you get in position again, give us another call, and we'll take another look at it."

"You gotta roll with the punches," Lenny said to me, but he was still grumbling as he maneuvered the tug and barge over. "It's amazing how we did this all by ourselves before they came here, eight years ago. The entire port used to run with everybody using common sense." Lenny believes the VTS people are sitting in a room with computers that automatically flash a warning signal if one vessel comes within a particular distance of another. "They ask you to move a five-hundred-foot barge full of gasoline so their light will stop flashing."

Once again the unit was where Lenny thought it ought to be, and Traffic seemed happy, but the anchor cable had twisted. Finally the anchor went overboard and lowered to the ocean floor. "Is it bouncing?" Lenny asked the guys on the barge bow on his handheld radio.

"Yup, jumping a little bit. It's still going up and down."

"OK, start heaving," Lenny told them. Up again.

Traffic came back on the radio. "If you're having trouble anchoring, we've got another spot for you."

"OK," said Lenny.

"We've got an exemption for you to go to the top of Stapleton," they said. "There's plenty of room for you over there." Stapleton is an anchorage reserved for ships. (Actually, in the notch as she was, the *Adriatic* is long enough to qualify, Vernon said when he came back to the pilothouse later, but Traffic didn't seem to realize that.)

"This is terrible," Lenny told me. "Now I'm going to miss *Oprah*. I don't watch *Oprah* at home, but I watch her religiously on the boat." (The television is always on in the galley, and some of the programs selected seem like odd choices. At five in the morning on Wednesday, I came into the galley to find two of the guys staring at the local news from Chicopee, Massachusetts. They live in Pennsylvania and Virginia themselves. The captain on the other crew brought his satellite dish with him but he didn't pay for the sports package, which Lenny says makes it pretty well useless. It only works at anchor or on a steady course, anyway.) But Lenny was still hopeful he'd get the anchor down by four o'clock. "I'll tell the deckhand that I'll cook and he'll do anchor watch."

His personal phone rang. "Maybe my boat caught a tuna!" he said. Lenny has a sport fishing business at home; a friend runs the boat for him while he's on the tug. No tuna today, though. The fellow's wife looked close to having their baby. Lenny was more concerned about tuna than babies. He radioed Traffic. "*Adriatic Sea* shifting from Bay Ridge to Stapleton with loaded barge on the head," he told Traffic and New

York Harbor. He called to Trevor on the bow and asked him to come back and tighten the head line. "I've got T John to start the capstan. You copy me, Trevor?"

"Yeah, he's on his way," said the barge mate on the bow.

"Too much stuff going on here," said Lenny. The head line had gotten slack from all the wiggling around trying to position the boat to re-anchor. "It would have been better to have had the wires out with all this BS, specially going across the channel," he said. "But you don't know if you're gonna be asked to do something." If the boat had been sent off to shift a bunker barge, for instance, then the wires would have had to be let off again. "None of this moving around was necessary, anyway."

Slowly, we crossed the shipping channel. Lenny kept talking but was checking the situation in Stapleton at the same time. "T John says Vernon's going to be in the Tugboat Hall of Fame." He added that there is no such thing.

"I was sitting right here in the fog, bunkering a tanker, when another ship hit us," he remarked matter-of-factly as he planned where to drop the hook this time. K-Sea does a lot of bunkering, fueling ships from a barge while they're at anchor or waiting to go into the dock or unloading. This event took place seven years ago, before Lenny was on the *Adriatic*. "The ship we were fueling was full of gasoline. I was asleep, and woke up just when the bow of the oncoming freighter poked out of the fog—like, Right There! The captain ran down and got us all up—we weren't getting out of bed quick enough. He was hollering and screaming, and we knew something was up. We ran out on deck in our underwear.

"One of the top engineers at K-Sea now was cadet on the ship that hit us—he's port engineer now. The two of us got very, very close to being smoked at the same time that day, before we ever met, but the freighter hit the tanker in the engine room compartment, and not a cargo tank. It rolled the ship on anchor, and our lines went *keek, kyeeeek, keeeek*, getting ready to break. But there was no damage to us. The freighter's bow got bent up, and the tanker's engine room was all broken up—you could see the engineers through a big gash in the side."

Lenny got the tug and barge where he would like to anchor. "OK, how do you like this?" he asked Traffic.

"Looks better. Let me know when you're fetched up."

"Roger that."

The anchoring went smoothly. Lenny let the engine room know he was through with the engines and asked Trevor to come on up to the wheelhouse when he was finished. Trevor brought along instructions for Lenny about the potatoes and carrots for the stew he was making for dinner. Lenny only missed a few minutes of *Oprah*.

The office called the *Adriatic*. The berth in New Haven, which was supposed to be available at nine Tuesday morning, had been put off until Wednesday morning at eight. "Stay down here. Hang loose tonight," they said.

"That's how this business is sometimes," Trevor said. "You don't know what'll happen." He rang Lenny down in the galley and told him to call the office. He wasn't going to tell the mate himself that they'd be putting off their trip for another day and that crew change would have to be rearranged. After *Oprah*, Lenny returned to the pilothouse, and before long, Vernon came along too, ready for watch change again.

"I see we've moved," he said, and Lenny told him of the changed departure plan. "One thing about tugboatin', nothing's ever certain," said the captain. "This morning we were all set, I had my crew-change message and everything." Oncoming crew members call an 800 number to know where to meet the boat. The uncertainties of crew change were the subject of much talk for the next twenty-four hours.

Lenny remarked that the office makes up a schedule and they always follow it unless something goes haywire, "which it usually does."

Normally, the owner of any vessel wants her to hustle off, discharge whatever cargo she's got, and head back for more. They make more money that way. Sometimes the shipper pays by the job—and the hustling scenario fits—and sometimes by

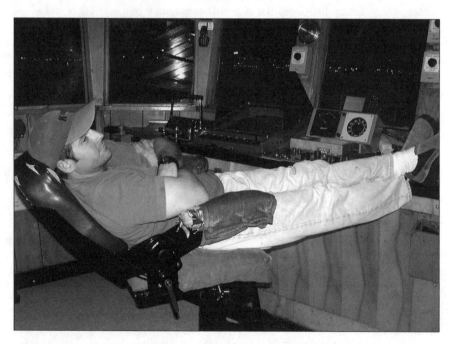

Anchor watch. Lenny's watch from midnight to six in the morning doesn't look strenuous, but someone has to be awake and ready to act at all times. AUTHOR PHOTO.

the boat's time. I'd guess this case must have been one of the latter. It certainly seemed that K-Sea was in no particular hurry to get the *Adriatic* to New Haven; she was sitting and everyone appeared happy, except perhaps the crew of the tug. "Oh, my, I'd rather be moving," said Vernon.

Traffic in the harbor slowed down after dark, but never stopped, and though there was no moon, there was plenty of light. The barge's deck is kept lit when it's at anchor, the various lights on passing vessels at least identify them by type, and the buildings of the city never seem to turn their lights out. The Staten Island ferry runs into the night, albeit less frequently. But I retired to my room early, watched some TV—nice to have one's own TV—and soon was gone. Twice during the night I heard the main engines start up, but we didn't go anywhere. The engineers like to run them periodically so they don't cool off entirely and are ready to start right up and go to work if need be.

Tuesday morning I awoke at about five and climbed up to the pilothouse. It was still dark out, and the only light in the wheelhouse was from the radar and GPS. Lenny was leaning back in the helmsman's chair, stretched out, talking about fish with Trevor. The radios were nearly quiet. A flashing yellow light marked a tug and barge heading up the channel on our port side. Lenny took the binoculars and in the dark identified Donjon's *Mary Alice* with a crane barge on her hip.

Watches come and go, the quotidian rhythm quietly flowing along, people coming and going, eating, working, sleeping, little note made. The harbor runs the same way. But, sitting at anchor, anyone would be glad to get off watch. This was a classic case of the extra-boring aspect of tugboating—not that people prefer the extra-stressful times. Five-thirty in the morning Lenny pronounced as the magical time of day. "It's time to call the boys, Trevor. The captain likes to have a peck on the cheek."

Trevor didn't call Matt, the other deckhand, though. "Give him extra time to sleep," he said.

"It's quiet now," Lenny said. "Everything's gonna break loose soon."

Just after six it was a little bit light and Vernon had taken over for Lenny. The container ships and freighters started in toward the docks. Stevedores get overtime after four p.m., so container ships want to be on their way by then. Vernon said that a tanker will take thirty or forty minutes to tie up, but a container ship can do it in ten minutes; every line is on a winch and operates quickly. "Speed is money."

Brian Garrett was the chief engineer on this trip, filling in for the regular fellow, whose mother had passed away. Brian is very apt to wear his ear protectors even when he's not in the engine room (where they're essential). He'll stand in the galley watching TV with the muffs covering his ears. Brian grew up in Illinois and worked on farms in summer as a youngster. He chose going to sea over the only other alternative he saw available to him—standing in one spot in a factory, pushing the same button year after year, as his brothers were doing. He's had twenty-three years on the water, in the military and in the private sector.

Brian was new to K-Sea when I rode on the *Adriatic*. He'd just moved up from the oil patch, the Gulf of Mexico, where he had been on a 275-foot rig-towing boat with 11,000 horsepower, eleven diesel engines, 370,000 gallons of fuel and water, and only four engineers to take care of it all. He was pleased to be working for K-Sea, which has a good reputation and, operating from New York, pays on the northern pay scale. "It's the company that makes the job the best," he said. In the oil patch, pay is proportional to the size of the boat. He took a bit of a pay cut coming to K-Sea, but only because he'd been on the biggest boat down there. On a boat the size of the *Adriatic,* the money would have been a lot less down in the Gulf.

"The more south you go," he said, "the more the pay drops off. You might as well go where you make the most money—it's the same job, and you can't go home at night anyway." Down there too, the rotation is two-for-one; he had been working twenty-eight days on, fourteen off. "I'm never gonna be a Rockefeller," he said, but he wants to spend more time with his family.

Brian gave me a tour through the engine room and the back deck. The *Adriatic Sea*—formerly the *Diplomat,* and before that the *Lamco VI*—was built in 1978 in Louisiana for North Sea oil-rig work, although she never did that. She's 126 feet long, has a beam of 34 feet, and draws 16 feet. Maritrans bought her in 1979. They raised her wheelhouse four feet and added the upper wheelhouse and blisters. Eye level in the main wheelhouse is twenty-three or twenty-four feet off the water; from the upper, it's sixty-three feet. "She's a pretty good sea boat," Vernon says. She originally had another fuel tank under the engine room deck, but that has to be in permanent ballast now because of the increased weight above. Maritrans also changed the cooling system for the air conditioning, which now uses the water in the ballast tank, avoiding the clogs caused by debris around the docks. She uses about 5,000 gallons of fuel a day towing a loaded barge, and can legally load 65,000 gallons for offshore work.

With her barge loaded a little light, the *Adriatic Sea* can tow at seven and a half knots in still water. With help from the Gulf Stream, Vernon has seen her tow a loaded barge at more than twelve knots for short periods, and average ten and a half or eleven for a couple of days. But it's not always so easy: "Towing back from the Gulf, we came into a north-northeast front blowing thirty to forty—a day and a half of eight- to twelve-foot seas. It was miserable, but we kept going. No place else to go."

In a short chop, four or five feet, she can stay in the notch and not have to switch to towing. "In a long swell, you're lucky to hang on in three feet. Over two feet, I don't even try," Vernon says.

She has a double-drum towing winch, which allows for a towing wire to be on one drum while the wires they hook up while pushing are on the other. The wires are two inches in diameter. "It's only single-screw boats that do hawser work with rope anymore," says Brian. "This is cream puff work here with a wire, compared to a hawser. That's back-breaking work, particularly in the winter when it gets iced up."

One of the best aspects of the *Adriatic Sea*'s engine room is the air-conditioned and sound-protected booth in the background.

She has two main engines, sixteen-cylinder EMDs, and two generators, 6-71 Detroits such as might themselves propel many a good-sized fishing boat. One generator runs all the time, even at anchor. In tight quarters—the East River or Hell Gate, for instance—both generators are kept running although only one is on line. If the one should fail, the other can immediately take over by the flip of a switch.

What makes the *Adriatic* special to her engineers is her control room. The engine room is by necessity a loud, hot place, but central in the *Adriatic*'s engine room is an air-conditioned, glass-walled little booth that allows the engineer on duty to sit comfortably at a desk and keep track of the myriad dials and gauges that tell him the condition of the machinery under his jurisdiction.

Brian and I settled in the galley after the tour. "Coffee and crew change, those are the most important things on a boat," said Brian.

Matt was roasting a chicken for lunch. Since we were just sitting on the anchor, he had nothing else to do. "Get a picture of Julia Child over there," Brian suggested.

"You keep the engines running," said Matt, "and I'll keep you fed."

An elevator runs from the lower to the upper wheelhouse, some forty feet higher. It's a little grey steel box in a shaft that *chug-chug-chugs* up or down as long as your finger is on the appropriate button. I worried that I might feel claustrophobic in the thing, but with one side open to the shaft, it's not uncomfortable—as long as you're less than XXL in size. I'm sure it's disconcerting to be in the elevator in weather as you can't see what's coming. And, of course, every story you go up increases the roll.

There's an outside ladder as well, with a cage around it.

Vernon suggested I go on up while we were sitting at anchor Tuesday morning. He warned me about the peculiarities of the elevator, like that the floor stops about two inches short of the upper wheelhouse floor and that there is a big clunk when the elevator hits the plywood floor and lifts it up out of the way. (It *would* have been alarming had he not warned me.) When you're at the top, you push a button again, on the outside, to send it back down. Its weight aloft wouldn't help the motion of the boat, and the piece of floor drops into place again, increasing the floor area of the wheelhouse by twenty-five percent. When you're in the upper wheelhouse, you hear the elevator coming for what seems like a long time while you wonder who's coming up.

There's room for a comfortable chair for the captain. The computer running Nav-Tech navigation software sits on a table, with a stool next to it. All the controls, gauges and instruments of the lower wheelhouse are repeated up top, and the same battery of radios is mounted on the ceiling. There's an AM-FM cassette player, too, and heat and air conditioning. Just as below, there's a little wooden platform in front

Looking forward over the barge from the *Adriatic Sea's* upper wheelhouse. AUTHOR PHOTO.

of the helmsman's chair where the captain sets his own laptop with the navigation program so he doesn't have to turn around backward to read the charts on the boat's computer. The boat steers with little levers from whichever station the helmsman may be, so the steering rig takes negligible space in the wheelhouses.

The upper wheelhouse is known as the "telephone booth," not only, as I thought, because early ones were as small as a phone booth, but also because cell phone reception is considerably better up there. Several times while we were at anchor, one crew member or another took the elevator up to make a phone call.

While I was in the upper wheelhouse, Vernon called the office to see what was going on. They promised to call him back in ten minutes, but long after I was back down again, he still hadn't heard anything. "Yup," said Brian, "that's tugboat time. Stand by to stand by."

The boat was obviously not going to have time to discharge and leave New Haven before crew change—that run takes sixteen hours more or less—so the captain retaped the phone message to alert the relief crew that they had to get to New Haven. "Well, that part's on there. We'll see how long it is before they change it."

The *Adriatic Sea's* back deck, seen from the upper wheelhouse. AUTHOR PHOTO.

The NavTech software on *Adriatic* not only shows the charts and the position of the boat but also contains a tide book. Vernon printed out the tide table for Hell Gate. We would have two opportunities to pass through the Gate, around six p.m. and again after midnight. Either would get us to New Haven in time to make the dock at eight in the morning. I had been hoping for a daylight trip up the East River.

Once again, the dock time changed. Now the barge wouldn't be unloaded until three in the afternoon on Wednesday but they could take the barge up and anchor up there. Vernon arranged for the company van to be available at the yard at nine-thirty a.m. for the oncoming crew. They would drive the van up to New Haven, and his gang would take it back again—except for Brian. His counterpart was flying in from Florida and wouldn't get to New York before eleven. No one can leave the boat before his relief shows up. Brian wasn't happy, but Vernon and Lenny were even more unhappy. That engineer had pulled this before.

Just before noon, the watch changed quietly, as they always do. A group of men took over and one by one the others disappeared into their rooms. The rhythm of the boat is steady and quiet and continuous. I was the only one keeping anything like normal shoreside hours, up all day and asleep at night, though I too took a nap mid-afternoon. My companions just changed from time to time. In the afternoon, Dan, from the barge, was fishing on the back deck with Trevor. "It's all part of the job," he said of hanging around.

Finally it was three o'clock, time to hook up the wires to the barge. The three men on Lenny's watch, coincidentally, were all dark-skinned. This is unusual. There aren't many blacks in tugboating, but not because there's any prejudice, Lenny told me. No one contradicted him. Of these three, only one was African-American; Trevor Campbell is from Tobago, and T John, whose name is really Thiadane Kanoute, is Senegalese. He is a graduate of a West African maritime academy, has sailed on foreign ships, and is, said Lenny, the best electrician in the company. But he can't sail as chief engineer until he gets his citizenship and can sit for an American license. He speaks seven languages: French, five regional African dialects, and, most recently and fully fluently, English. He had another year to go before he could get his citizenship.

Unhurriedly, purposefully, deliberately, Dan, Trevor and T John hooked up the wires. After spending thirty-six hours on anchor in New York Harbor, the *Adriatic Sea* was at last preparing to push her barge to New Haven. Barge Mate Dan threw the heaving line from the starboard quarter of the barge to deckhand Trevor on the tug's back deck. Trevor pulled it and then the heavier messenger line across from the barge, then dragged the big messenger to the rotating capstan near the towing machine and used the capstan to pull the barge's wire up through the scupper while Assistant Engineer T John took up the slack. Moving the massive shackle on the end of the starboard pushing wire into position with a long crowbar, Trevor attached the eye in the barge's wire to the shackle on the tug's wire, slid the shackle pin through the shackle, and screwed its nut down. The messenger he led back toward the barge and then threw the heaving line up to Dan, who hauled both back onto the *KTC 135*. They repeated the whole process on the port side, and T John climbed up onto the boat deck with its doghouse controls for the towing machine. While Trevor stood by below, T John winched the wires up taut. Finally, with a long iron bar for leverage, Trevor turned the big wheel that sets the brakes on the towing machine.

Conditions were ideal. Tug and barge were motionless, anchored in the quiet harbor. No extra steps were taken, nothing was said, no unnecessary moves were made. It was hard work but flowed smoothly as each man played his part. I could only imagine how difficult it would be outside in a big sea.

"That's good," signals Trevor Campbell. AUTHOR PHOTO.

Lenny's next task was checking the emergency steering. They are required to run the test and log the testing regularly; they make the check every time they start a voyage. Then Lenny's phone rang. His boat had caught a tuna! Six hundred pounds. His concern changed from whether they'd get one to how much they'd get paid for it. Sometimes a tuna that size can pay all the boat's expenses for the year. Other times, it brings but a few dollars a pound. The last one he caught was on the low end—the Japanese economy was down and they were importing less.

Multiple calls to Traffic followed. Lenny informed them the *Adriatic Sea* was preparing to get underway with loaded gasoline barge *KTC 135* in push gear. He gave the length and draft of the unit and announced his intention to head up the East River for Hell Gate. Traffic ran down the list of vessels in his path, but he didn't pay much attention. "They'll say it all again when I check in after the anchor's up."

Lenny switched the steering to the upper wheelhouse. "The rudder—you only forget that once." He switched on the running lights: port, starboard, two mast lights, stern. "Gotta look that up. Two ambers?" He flipped open a Coast Guard book by the computer. Yes, two ambers. He took the boat's phone up with him "in case these clowns call me" and left his own below. "I got enough distractions." On the VHF he talked with Trevor about raising the anchor, and set foot in the elevator. "I'll send it back down for you," he said to me. "We have a stool up there we keep for pilots and authors of books and other special guests."

Once in his chair in the upper wheelhouse, he called the barge. "*One-thirty-five, you hear me, Dan?*" Dan acknowledged him. "We're going to go ahead and start heaving. Trevor's up there, and we're working channel 5."

Heaving the anchor is another slow, deliberate, steady job. "I have to constantly slow my pace down and not get in a rush, while Vernon is as patient as a human being can possibly be," Lenny said. "I'm thirty-five now; I can't blame it on being young."

From the bow came reports and requests of the helm: "Come ahead. . . . Hold your own. . . . All stop. . . . Two shots to go." (The anchor cable is marked every ninety feet. Each ninety-foot shot is connected to the next with a link that can be disconnected.) "Straight up and down. . . . We can see it."

On that word from Trevor, Lenny said he was going to switch off and report to Traffic. "You guys have a good one," he said to his crew.

He told Traffic that the *Adriatic* was under way at this time, and repeated all the stats. They replied that there was a southbound container ship at a particular buoy ahead, and no other immediate traffic. Lenny then started the series of security calls that he—and later Vernon—made at regular intervals to let surrounding vessels know of his whereabouts and intentions. "Security, *Adriatic* leaving Stapleton. Going to be turning around off the Navy pier and heading for the East River."

It was rush hour on Manhattan, a solid wall of cars on the FDR Highway as we passed up the river. It was peaceful where we were, running upriver at a little over eight knots with just the occasional tug and the Coast Guard cutter *Sturgeon Bay* coming the other way and a city sludge tanker going past us northbound. The only sound I heard—other than the radio—was the *Adriatic*'s own engines, and they're pretty quiet from the upper wheelhouse. The vessels coming down the river called the *Adriatic* on the radio to confirm passing plans. "Seeya on one," said Lenny, referring to the single whistle that means "pass port side to port side."

At quarter to six, the sun had set behind the Manhattan skyline. The elevator made its chugging trip up the chute, and Vernon appeared. Lenny let him know what traffic was coming, told him what else was going on with the boat. "I guess I gotcha," Vernon said, and took the helm. He called the captain of the other crew about the personnel change and the van in the morning, and hung up, saying we'd gotten to Hell Gate so he'd better start paying attention. Passing through the Gate, he told me about its vagaries, but there was no one coming at us, and all was quiet.

It had gotten dark, and someone called from the galley. They'd put my steak in the microwave for me. I went down and took the plate from the microwave, grabbed a fork and a glass, filled the glass from the water fountain, and sat at the table by the television. "You're one of the gang now," said Lenny.

"An honor," said I, sincerely.

Later, for a half hour or more I sat in the dark in the lower wheelhouse with Matt. There wasn't anything to say. We just watched the lights of the occasional boat and the city go by, fewer and fewer and at greater distances as we got farther into Long Island Sound. The radar showed the buoys and the occasional boat coming our way; after a while there was nothing showing at all inside the mile-radius display. The engine was steady, unchanging. The GPS kept us informed of the speed and course, but I paid little attention. Eight knots and a bit, usually. I was tired from the day—an intense one for me, quiet and ordinary for the *Adriatic Sea* and her crew. Sleep came before the end of a TV show I actually was interested in.

I awoke again as we were approaching New Haven Harbor. I rode the elevator up to the phone booth, where Lenny was again at the helm. He pointed out the channel

Beaufort Sea looks small ahead of her light barge as she tows down Penobscot Bay.
AUTHOR PHOTO.

markers on the radar screen and out the window, and the range lights on the shore that aided in a straight approach into the harbor, which was formed by breakwaters.

In the dark they anchored the barge and disconnected the wires. The windsock on the barge showed that the wind was coming crossways across the deck of the barge, but the tug and half-loaded barge, still deep in the water, are little affected by the wind and instead line up with the current. A note was posted on the galley white-board: Please call T John at 10:30. The van from New York would be there soon after that. Lenny told me that the wife of the man running his fishing boat at home had had a baby last night. "He can give Mom a kiss and get back down on the boat today." Lenny's mind was already home. He and I were getting off the boat at 6:30.

When Vernon came up into the pilothouse, Lenny told him that T John was all worried that when they drove down I-95, they wouldn't stop and let T John out when they went by his house. "Tell him to have his baggage in hand, and we'll slow down to thirty mile an hour, and he can jump," said Vernon.

"I told him, no way are those guys gonna stop in the Bronx," said Lenny. (Of course they will.)

"Seems like this day's been a long time getting here," said Vernon. "The older I get, the longer the trips get and the shorter I'm at home and the less I get done while I'm there. Used to be, you looked forward to getting back to the boat. This was your life. But now I'm just looking forward to when I can retire. I've seen everything, been everywhere."

Vernon and his wife are raising a granddaughter. He has been with the *Adriatic* for ten years, coming with her when K-Sea bought her from Maritrans. At the time of my ride, the *Adriatic* was due to be converted to an articulated unit, fitted with pins to connect her to a new double-skin barge. Then there would be just a six-man crew for the tug and the barge together: a captain, two mates who'll steer and do cargo, two deckhands, and an engineer. There will be two people aboard with tankerman credentials, and no one on the barge. She may well move onto long runs to the Gulf. "I really don't think I need that," said Vernon. "I may step down to one of the smaller boats and work the old way." He intends to run tugs until his granddaughter has graduated from high school. Then he's done.

"When I was twenty-five or thirty, you couldn't get a better job than this except if you were a top executive. Now, the bill-payers in the office get more than we do."

7
Offshore

"Endless days of boredom punctuated by five seconds of sheer terror." That is how offshore tugwork is described by Captain Doug O'Leary. It's a variation on a theme one hears again and again throughout the towboating world. His son Brendan agrees. He's now mate on a coastwise tug and works for a paving company when he's home. "That's to get back for having all that relaxing time on the tug," he says. But when things happen on a tug, particularly offshore, they're apt to all happen at once, and no one can let his guard down.

Whenever time isn't critical, carrying cargo by water is very economical. United States coastwise traffic is required by the Jones Act to take place in American-flagged ships, and more and more often that means by tug and barge. As but one example, 90 percent of the coastwise petroleum transport in this country moves this way.

There is also traffic in bulk cargo—sand and gravel, cement, grains, and the like—and containerized cargo also moves by tug and barge, particularly to Puerto Rico, Alaska, and Hawaii. There are always vessels or awkwardly bulky objects such as drydocks and oil-drilling rigs that need to go from one place to another, and towing is the easiest way to move them. In its advertisements, Moran Towing Corporation says it has "the resources and personnel to tow virtually anything, anywhere in the world, safely and expeditiously." And one of their former employees says he has towed about everything that floats.

Some towboaters live for the long-distance traffic that leaves the relative civility of the bays. Others avoid it as much as they can. According to Captain Vernon Elburn, "Offshore, it gets monotonous—you just take whatever the sea dishes out." Another towboater says if you've seen one wave, you've seen them all. Christopher Holt says that being at sea for twenty days at a time plays tricks on your mind. "The best thing to do is to get into a routine and stick to it." Offshore, the usual watch system is four hours on, eight off, and the captain often stands a watch. "If he didn't, he'd go crazy—or drive us crazy, and we'd kill him." With nine people, three would be on the bridge, three would be sleeping, and three would be milling about. "Part of my routine was to walk on the upper deck for an hour for the exercise," Chris says.

Wind certainly is a hazard faced by tugs with barges, and Captain Jack Finney, who tows for Foss Maritime from Seattle, says that in Alaska he's often seen the anemometer at 100 knots. In northern climates, icing of the vessel adds its own danger. Too much ice makes the boat top-heavy and threatens its stability. Combine severe cold with a good wind, and it's even worse. "We turn around and hide somewhere if we can," says Jack, "or we grin and bear it." Hiding is a part of dealing with weather in any vessel, but for a tug with a barge it's a particularly attractive choice if it's available. "No sense being out there doing one and a half knots—backward, sometimes," Jack points out.

According to Jack, a tug can take on four tons of ice in an hour, and you have to slow way down to minimize it. He says he's never been in really bad icing—nothing that couldn't be handled by several hours with a baseball bat followed by shoveling ice over the side a couple of times a trip. Clearly, he defines bad icing differently than some might.

Lines can be hard to deal with in winter. They've had to use axes to break the ice off bollards before they could tie up. And if a line gets wet, it freezes solid and becomes very difficult to bend around a cleat. On cargo barges on Alaska runs, there's often a temperature-controlled container for the lines, marked KFF (Keep From Freezing), set to stay at sixty degrees.

Ordinary snow can be a problem too. Captain Bob Glover tells of the Hydrotrain run, a regular run from Seattle to Whittier, Alaska, in Prince William Sound. There'd be two barges, each with seven or eight rows of train cars on tracks. It was a great run in the summer, he says, but unbelievably miserable in the winter. They might get freezing rain or snow crossing the Gulf of Alaska. "You'd get two feet of snow on the barges, and have to dig out the snow to get at the turnbuckles and lashings for each car. Thirty-five or forty individual boxcars or tank cars on each barge, each with four turnbuckles and four chain binders. It would take a day and a half or two days to get ready to offload. You could only work four or five hours at a time, it was so bitterly cold."

"Warm, sunny days? Gentle rolling seas?" asks Captain Jack Finney. "Yeah, we have those occasionally. You relax, open the door, smell the fresh air!" And go fishing. Doug O'Leary tells of a petroleum tow between Marcus Hook, Pennsylvania, to Jacksonville, Florida, on which he worked as a mate and always enjoyed. Coastwise work usually is run on two watches, with the captain at the helm for the watches from six to noon or midnight, and the mate on the twelve-to-six watches. Early in the morning, the flying fish would be jumping aboard and flopping around on the deck. "I used to strip down to my skivvies and go out and gather up breakfast." But one morning, the captain got up earlier than usual. He was not pleased to find that Doug wasn't in the pilothouse, and forbade him to fish on watch.

In the best of times, traffic can be an issue, and in the worst of times it's even more significant. Captain Jim Sharp tells a traffic-complicated-by-weather story. He says he was "guarded by an excellent weather forecast" but adds that you can't always believe those guys. He was out with a mundane barge job one January night when the weather people had gotten the forecast totally wrong. Off Cape Ann, Massachusetts, he had just passed Thatcher's Island but hadn't seen a thing of the twin lighthouses nor anything else. "Around the pilothouse windows there was a combination of snow blowing horizontally one minute, and black sea smoke rising up from the cold water around us the next. I was running mostly by the seat of my pants, as there was so much deviation in the compass that north seemed to be somewhere over New Hampshire." There wasn't much sea, and a good thing too, as the occasional dollop of spray froze into icicles on the rails and pudding.

A red blip showed up on the left-hand edge of the radar screen, which Jim assumed was a fish boat crossing his bow. "In the dead of night with hour after hour of sitting in the glow of the instruments and listening to the static on the radio, that little red blip was kind of welcome. It was a reminder that there was another human being somewhere beyond the whiteout. I watched, sort of mesmerized, as the red dot drew closer to the center of the scope." The blip got closer and closer, coming directly toward him. Then it crossed the one-mile ring on the radar, and he realized he'd bet-

The *Peter B. McAllister* shows the evidence of a cold, breezy day at sea, sometime in the early 1960s.
COURTESY OF BOB MATTSSON.

A *Powhatan* deckhand with dinner, a dolphinfish (mahi-mahi). The tow wire passes through an anti-chafe "worm" as it passes over the rail. Her tow, the frigate *Sims,* can be seen in the distance. COURTESY OF JOHN O'REILLY.

ter do something. He slowed to half speed and started blowing the big foghorn. The red dot kept coming. He slowed down a little more and turned on his big spotlight. He got on the radio with a security call. The red dot crossed the half-mile ring, steadily heading toward the middle, toward Jim's boat. He opened the pilothouse window—heat rushed out and freezing cold rushed in—but he couldn't see anything. The red dot got closer to the center of the radar screen. He kept blowing the horn, sweeping back and forth with the spotlight, and calling almost constantly on the radio. The red dot kept coming.

Head poked out through the window, Jim strained to hear an engine. "There was no sound. No answering horn, nothing but static on the radio, and no lights." He slowed to dead slow, running with just enough turns to stay ahead of the hawser. "The red dot disappeared into the center of the screen. I pulled madly on the horn rope—the danger signal—short quick blasts. No answer."

By and by, the little red dot appeared again, coming out of the center spot on the right side of the radar. "My teeth were chattering by this time (but I blamed it on the cold air). And just before I closed the pilothouse window I could hear the whine of a 6-71." He never did know what the vessel was, or how close it came to him. "But I'd lay my bets on a dragger, running on autopilot with an alarm clock to wake him up at the end of the tow. Someday he'll wake up talking to St. Peter."

Not all offshore tug work is towing. Several times in the past ten years, Captain Bill Stewart, of Halifax, has been involved with transatlantic fiber-optic cable work. One of the last times, the communications company had located a break in the cable eight hundred miles out. They can't simply pull the cable up; they have to send a machine down to cut it and then go back to one end—in this case to Europe—and, using a special hook, pull the cable up and do their maintenance as they run along it back out to the break. Then they leave the tug in place, holding the end of the cable they just retraced. This time it was in 12,800 feet of water. "You can only move within a radius of a half mile of where they drop you—that can be very difficult in sixty-knot winds," says Bill. He was on a 130-foot tug, single-screw, no bow thruster but with a controllable-pitch propeller, which Bill describes as quicker-reacting than a standard screw. They kept track of their position using GPS and Loran C. They were out for three weeks, and three times they were knocked around by winds of sixty-knot strength. Meanwhile, the cable ship goes to the other end—on the Canadian side, this time—and repeats the process back toward the tug. "You hand your end back to them—passing a cable back to a ship in 30-knot winds is difficult too—and they splice it back. There's a lot of expense involved, so you try to finish it as soon as you can, even in weather that's not exactly nice."

The folks who go offshore experience phenomena that just aren't part of shore-bound life—the green flash and moonbows, for instance. Sometimes there's a momentary emerald green glow when the sun sets into the sea, just as it drops below the horizon. No one who's seen it ever forgets it. "What you're seeing," explains Bob Glover, "is refraction of the light in the atmosphere. It takes particular atmospheric conditions." He has seen it four or five times.

The moonbow Bob has only seen once, at midnight. The moon was out and, as they dodged through islands in rain showers, he caught sight of a black and white and grey rainbow. "It was fascinating and beautiful," he says.

Although she holds a captain's ticket, Melissa Terry sometimes works as a relief deckhand offshore. It's boring in the wheelhouse, she says of offshore work. If she's running the boat, she'd rather be in the harbor. But she enjoys working the deck offshore. "Chugging off in the night—when you wake up, it's always interesting to see what you see," she says. And she cherishes the sunrises at sea, when "you're all the way offshore and there are no other lights, especially if it's calm—the sun coming up out of the water, unobstructed." People on land never see the dawn in quite the same way.

And you see funny things offshore, she says. On a trip from Norfolk to Boston, they were thirty or forty miles offshore when they saw something and just couldn't figure out what it was. With their loaded barge, they made a big circle just to see what it was, and found a huge bunch of white balloons floating in the water.

"On board, you're making your fun," says Chris Holt, "but for the most part it's business when you're out there. You don't want to get lax, for that's when you find trouble." Bill Stewart also refers to boredom laced with moments of sheer terror. "Thank God there's not much terror. But you set there doing routine jobs awhile, and suddenly you have to give it your all to get yourself and the boat and whatever else out of a situation." And he recognizes the importance of fatigue. "On tugs, if you get fatigued, you've got to get off. With 5,000 horsepower you don't want to be falling asleep at the controls." You may wake up in trouble—or you may not wake up at all.

Political Hazards from Ashore

"Tugboaters like it dull and quiet. Boring is good." So says Chris Holt, who worked for Moran for eleven years. He hasn't always had it that way.

Certainly a trip he made across the Atlantic to Freetown, Sierra Leone, was a memorable one, and not because of the ocean and its difficulties. They were moving a barge full of rice and corn that had been free-dropped into the hold somewhere up the Mississippi River. Twenty-five-year-old Holt joined the tug in Puerto Rico, where she had come in to top off her fuel, water, and grub before setting off to Africa. He was second mate. The tug was the *Marian Moran,* a 126-foot boat with 5,000 horsepower. "She was a good offshore boat, well-handling, big enough that nine people didn't feel overly cramped." The barge was just a barge, he says, a 22,000-ton dry-cargo barge, the *Virginia.*

The trip across the pond took seventeen days. "You can pretty much guarantee at least one major storm in that length of time, but we were lucky and didn't hit anything. A day and a half before we got in, it was rainy, but you don't care much about rain—it's the wind and seas that'll get you."

Two or three hundred people, desperate for food, met them at the dock in Freetown. "It wasn't a pretty sight," says Holt. The U.S. consul came aboard when they arrived, telling them that the country was undergoing a civil war. The army was there in Freetown for the bargeful of grain; the rebels were five miles outside of town, and they also wanted the cargo. "If people want to come on and steal stuff, you'll have to let them," he said. "If the tug is invaded, don't hurt any of these people."

"Are you crazy?" the men on the tug asked.

No, he wasn't. He meant what he said. If they hurt anyone, they'd end up in jail. The consulate wouldn't be able to do anything about it, and jail wasn't a place they'd want to be. He showed them a newspaper photograph of soldiers holding the head of a decapitated rebel. Even if not executed, prisoners were beaten regularly and starved and exposed to all manner of disease.

Moran provided the tug's crew with axe handles to protect themselves with, but no real weapons. They also hired a local man to protect them; the army would protect the barge. "Nobody felt really comfortable," says Christopher. The company did give them full warrant to leave the barge and head home without it if conditions became too dangerous to stay.

It was the rainy season. In the two months of the year that have any rainfall at all, 144 inches of rain pour down on Freetown. For twenty hours each day, rain fell more heavily than in any hurricane Christopher has seen.

The port is relatively small and not very modern. It took twenty-five torrentially wet days to unload, using ten-inch suction tubes that vacuumed the grain from the barge. And each night, a hundred people raided the barge, climbing up the pigeon-holes and stealing all the rice they could carry away. The army shot and injured two of these invaders. "We let go of the barge and sat out in the stream until it calmed down," Christopher says. Later, they found out that the army was in charge of the stealing. The two men who were shot were freelancers.

The last night they were in Freetown, invaders came aboard the tug, trying to steal the lines, and were chased off. But, for the most part, the locals treated them well. Communication wasn't a problem, as English is the official language of Sierra Leone. The crew went ashore in pairs. On their two trips off the boat, Christopher and the chief engineer found a beachside resort where they could have a couple of drinks and meet local young people.

"It was an eye-opening trip, seeing people thankful just for a bowl of rice a day," Christopher says. "There were craters in the street you could lose a car in, and people would stop in the middle of the road and go to the bathroom in them." The gift of a pair of old sneakers made a friend of one of the locals for the duration of his stay.

"The trip was a harsh reality," he says. "At the time I wasn't sure I cared for it much, but I'm glad I made it."

Gulf Majesty's Last Tow

"I was in charge of trying to keep her afloat," says Sid Hebert, "but it didn't work out." Sid had worked on the 150-foot *Gulf Majesty* on and off for three years when she was in the Gulf, and steady for another two and a half years on the East Coast, but on her last trip he was just filling in because the regular chief engineer wanted another couple of weeks off. "I'd gladly have traded places with him," Sid says.

As Hurricane Floyd was building, the *Gulf Majesty* was towing a container barge from Jacksonville to San Juan, Puerto Rico. Three days out, the barge was out on two 2,400-foot wires, and they were trying to run from the storm. The winds were about a hundred miles an hour and the seas were seventy feet. "If you can't imagine seventy-foot seas, kneel down in front of a six-story building," says Sid. "That's water. There's nothing like looking out to see a wall of water coming at you."

At eleven o'clock at night on the fifteenth of September, 1999, the tug started taking on water.

At three in the morning, the crew woke Sid. The tug was listing to starboard so much that when he slipped on some water in the galley, he didn't stop sliding till he hit the other side.

They were transferring water and fuel to the port side, trying to level her up, and the stern was completely under water. "What I think is, she was busted up in the bottom," says Sid, "and she started taking on water in the back. The seas pounding on her started breaking her up internally." The after tanks were filling with water as fast as they could pump it away.

They'd had safety drills every week—fire fighting, man overboard, abandoning ship, any emergency imaginable. "Everyone knew what the procedures were. That helped a lot. It comes natural. You get in survival mode and do what you know.

"We got the list out of her, and ten minutes later, she was listing to port. We leveled her again, and that's when I walked up to report to the captain. He asked what I thought, and I told him I thought that was it. It was time to get off." They called a Mayday and notified the office of their last position, then readied to abandon the tug. Five men, including Sid, managed to get into the life raft before a gust snapped its tethering line. The last three jumped into the water.

"The last thing we seen was the bow of her," Sid says. It wasn't more than fifteen minutes later that the *Gulf Majesty* went down.

The three life-jacketed men in the water had the EPIRB, the Emergency Position Indicating Radio Beacon that vessels carry for just such situations. The signal is picked up by satellite and broadcast to the Coast Guard. But the Coast Guard couldn't do anything—the incident took place three hundred miles off Jacksonville, and the weather was more than they could handle. Sid describes being in the raft, which had a netted bottom and a solid canopy top. "It was cold," he says. "When we'd ride down a wave, it was like surfing, but a bumpy ride coming down. We could tell when a real big one was coming—it would get deadly still, and we knew to hang on. It was coming, and we were fixin' to get slapped. All of a sudden the wave would hit us, and the wind would come back, and the water would hit on top so hard—three times it folded the raft up like a taco shell and threw us all into the center. We were scared the raft wouldn't survive—and I don't think it would have if we'd had to stay in it overnight."

It happened that the aircraft carrier *John F. Kennedy* was also riding out the storm and was two hundred miles from the *Gulf Majesty* when the tug went down. "She immediately come full-bore back into the storm," says Sid. Seventy-five miles from the scene, two Sea Hawk helicopters rose from the carrier into the hurricane winds and began the hunt for survivors. They found the three men in the water first and then ran a search grid based on the winds and currents. A heavy rainsquall took them out of their pattern—and a good thing too: "When they come out of the rainstorm, they flew right over us, just by luck.

"The wind slapping on the side of the raft sounded like a helicopter, but when it got right over us, we realized there truly was a chopper. It was a beautiful sound."

The seas were still seventy feet, the wind eighty to a hundred miles an hour. The conditions were right at the limit of what the helicopter could handle. "He'd never flew in anything like that before, but they done their job. The rescue swimmer had fins on, and was sitting in the door of the chopper, just smiling at us. He didn't hesitate to come out for us. That captain held that helicopter overhead just like it was a calm day while they dropped that cable down and picked us up, one by one—the raft was drifting and he was steadily following."

Sid says that the rescue man expected all five men in the raft to dive at him in panic when he got to them. "But we were all relaxing. We know we're rescued. Ain't no use in panicking anymore. And nobody did panic. Everyone knew their job, done their job correctly, and that's why we all survived. Even inside the life raft, we were all joking—we never lost our sense of humor." One of the guys in the water had his cell phone with him, sealed in a plastic bag. When they picked him up, it still worked. Someone wondered what he'd thought he was going to do with it. "If I'd drifted close enough to the beach, I'd have called 911 and told somebody to come get me," he said.

On the carrier, the tug's crew were all laughing and joking. The navy guys couldn't understand why they weren't in shock. "We survived. No sense curling up in a corner now," Sid said.

When Sid and the other men were taken aboard the helicopter, they had been in the raft for eight hours. They were sixty miles from the eye of the hurricane, on the bad side—being sucked into the eye. They had traveled thirty miles in the eight hours since the tug went down. The three men in the water had floated twenty-six miles in the opposite direction. The helicopter pilots risked their own lives to find them. "When we got on the ship, we told them they were our guardian angels."

On the carrier, they were asked if they were going to give up the sea or continue on. "Continue on," they said, and all but one have done just that.

Sid dismisses it all. "It's the life of a seaman," he says. "I took six weeks off to recuperate, and then I flew to Panama and got on a boat in Ecuador." He had been bruised and sore "but I come out fair. For awhile I had nightmares—a month or two. When I first got back on a tug, I was asleep one time when the sea came slamming on the bow, and it scared the daylights out of me. But then I realized what it was, and I was all right." He started on the sea on shrimp boats when he was ten or twelve and has been at sea in one way or another ever since.

"I've got salt water in my blood," says Sid. He was asked awhile back to take a drug test—the people in the industry are subject to random drug tests. "I said I'd give 'em a urine sample, but there was liable to be nothin' but salt water in it."

Salvage Mission in the Hurricane

The big story was the sinking of the tug *Gulf Majesty* and the subsequent rescue by navy helicopter of the eight men aboard her, but the second story was of the Donjon Marine salvage tug *Powhatan,* which found and captured the vagrant 750-foot container barge *San Juan Jax Bridge* that the *Gulf Majesty* had been towing.

As Hurricane Floyd approached the mainland, the *Powhatan* was in Charleston, South Carolina, awaiting weather to sail. Steve Rhodes was master and John O'Reilly was chief mate. They had hoped to ride out the storm in shelter tied up alongside the pier, but the storm surge was predicted to be fifteen feet above normal, so the port captain ousted the *Powhatan,* along with the other big vessels. "South Carolina's so flat, if the surge hit there, we'd all end up like cordwood across their roads," says John. "As it turned out, with the distress and ultimate loss of the *Gulf Majesty,* we would most likely have gone out anyhow."

The *Powhatan* is a big salvage tug, 225 feet long, with 8,000 horsepower. She was built for the U.S. Navy but, when they cut down on the number of fleet tugs, they leased her to Donjon Marine of New Jersey. The navy had run her with thirty-eight people; as a civilian, she had a crew of ten when the hurricane hit: three able-bodied seamen, three engineers, three mates, and the captain. "The accountants strike again," explains John.

Out to sea she went. John's thoughts about going out into Hurricane Floyd were mixed. "After all, that's what we get paid to do," he says, but he admits there's always concern.

Securing the boat is the first issue. Everything has to be tied down. "We broke into groups and went about the vessel lashing everything we could." The assignments overlapped so that—in theory—everything would be double-checked. "In forty-foot seas, the most innocuous items can become missiles that can do a tremendous amount of damage to either the crew or the vessel." Within a few hours, this was proven to be true.

It was gray overhead and raining when they sailed. As they passed the jetties, the swells started, and soon, like a car on a roller coaster, the *Powhatan* was bucking twenty feet or more vertically and rolling twenty degrees to port and starboard.

Captain Steve Rhodes says he's been in eight hurricanes, and his intention is always simply to make the safest ride. "It was my plan to haul butt and head east to get on the other side of the storm, which was supposed to go north or west." The northwest side of a hurricane is the easiest side, but easiest doesn't mean easy. Except for Steve and John and one deckhand, the crew was inexperienced. Steve kept the big vessel headed into the east wind, and then swinging around as the wind veered. "You have to turn in the direction of the sea," Steve explains. "You don't want to be in the trough."

Getting rest in such conditions is difficult, though necessary. Off watch, John put his lifejacket under his bunk mattress to hold him against the bulkhead, lay down, and held on. "The best thing to do is to hang on with feet and hands and wedge your head with a couple of pillows—that stops your head from banging on the bulkhead." You're taking a beating, and you may get up more exhausted physically than you were when you went to bed. But when you're tired enough, he says, you manage to get some kind of rest.

These guys who've been at sea for decades develop an unconscious feel of what's right for the conditions they're in and will notice a change even when they're asleep. The *Powhatan*'s pattern changed, and Steve felt it immediately. "You're pitching, you're rolling, and you're yawing—three different forces—and all of a sudden you're rolling left and not coming back to the center. It's incredibly dangerous," he

Tug *Powhatan*.
COURTESY OF JOHN O'REILLY.

says. He immediately called the chief engineer. "Are you doing something? Or is this happening?"

"I don't know," said the engineer, which told the captain they had a serious problem. They could not afford to lose an engine, and there was no saying yet what the difficulty might be. "Get your ass down in the engine room, and don't come out till you've got it fixed. You guys come out one at a time to eat and sleep."

The engineers turned up the problem. Despite the careful stowing, a spare chain had broken loose on deck. As it swung, it snapped a fuel vent, and that fuel tank was taking on water—a lot of water. Since water is heavier than diesel, you can drain water off the bottom of a tank. There was enough water coming into this tank that a one-inch line ran twenty-four hours straight to dump the water until they could fix the vent.

Steve and Dave, the one experienced AB, discussed how to make that repair. "What we gotta do," Steve said, "is position the boat in the weather where you have enough time to run out on deck and plug the vent with a giant plug." Dave said he could do it, and the two of them headed aft. (Steve makes it clear that he didn't tell the deckhand he had to do it, Dave volunteered.) "It was like walking on ground that had a thirty-degree list to it. The boat rolled so much that I started sliding down the deck and ran into the handle on one of the steel lockers on the port side. It knocked me down and came within inches of knocking me out. But there's nothing you can do about it—you gotta keep on keeping on." Steve didn't know it at the time, but that fall caused a compression fracture in his spine. But they got the job done, at least well enough to be manageable.

It was about then that they got a call from the office telling them that the tug *Gulf Majesty* had gone down. "I ran her for three weeks in Egypt and the Middle East," Steve says. "She was a big, coon-ass, 6,200-horsepower, serious ocean tug." The office told them the tug's approximate position and told them to go take a look, and see if they could find the crew. They changed course and ran right into the rough part of the storm, where the seas reached forty feet and the winds a hundred miles an hour. It hadn't been bad enough before. Steve questions how they ever would have picked anyone up if they had found them, but of course they would do what they could. "The wind was on our port bow—we were going almost across it. It was a rough ride," he says.

By midday, they were all glad to hear that helicopters from the aircraft carrier *John F. Kennedy* had rescued all eight men from the tug. "Those marvelous helo pilots from the *JFK* did God's work that night," says John.

But the *Powhatan* wasn't done. Donjon sent her to look for the barge. Now facing truly huge seas as she headed directly into the hurricane, the short-handedness on the *Powhatan* became more of a challenge. Another three or four men would have been good to have, John says, or at least men with more experience. The boat's easy to run—"you could operate it with fewer people if everything was working all right," says John, "but in forty-foot seas, nothing is working right. They're asking you to do something that's really borderline, and extra help is good. Rough weather isn't fun."

"Sometimes you're too scared to be seasick," says Steve.

Eating is difficult in these kinds of seas. Some of the guys just couldn't get any food down at all. "Even if it doesn't want to stay where you are trying to put it," says John, "you have to eat." (Sea-born habits stick with you, too, even at home. "Every so often my wife will catch me at the supper table with my left arm around the plate, glass and silverware, my right arm grasping the table. My feet reach out to hook around the table leg. She gently reminds me that I'm not at work and that the table most likely isn't going anywhere.")

John says that luck is the main ingredient for finding a lost object at sea. "You know where and when it was last seen. You know which way the wind is blowing and the currents are running. You estimate from your experience where you might intercept it," guessing at the speed and course the object might be going. "When you get to where you figure it might be and it isn't, you pick a pattern and criss-cross the area in hopes that you are somewhere close."

They pushed the tug to three or four knots instead of the knot and a half they'd been making while simply trying to stay as comfortable as possible. "We were in our own little world, basically hanging on," says John. They passed through the eye of the hurricane, and all the while the seas kept building. The winds were still topping out at seventy knots. "Of course we only knew that when we got to the tops of the waves."

He tells about seeing the movie *The Perfect Storm* with his wife. "When the giant wave came to finish off our heroes, it looked fake. There was wind chop all the way down the face of the wave. That's not what it would look like at all. Waves that size are flat, glossy smooth at the bottom. There is no wind down there." His wife pointed out to him that few people would notice—most people never see waves that size. Fortunately.

The *Powhatan* kept up her search. The worst part of searching in heavy weather is the course-changing, at the end of each leg of the pattern. "You go through some awful gyrations," says John. One day, two days, into three days, they looked for the barge. Nothing but waves. They radioed other ships passing to ask if anyone had seen the barge—nothing. Navy and the Coast Guard had called off their searches. The insurance company was going to try one last flight, but even satellite imagery had failed.

And then, at 2:30 in the morning on the third day of searching, the third mate spotted the *San Juan Jax Bridge* on radar. "Talk about luck!" says John. The home office told them to try to get it. There was nothing to do but keep track of it until daylight. "You have six or eight guys on the afterdeck of a well-lit boat, trying to see in the dark an object painted black with big pieces of three-inch chain flying around, and wire, too. Something could go egregiously wrong and there'd be no chance of getting out of the way," John explains. And in the dark there's no way to check the barge for damage, either. "You're not going to do anything in a couple of hours, anyway—nothing on a boat ever takes less than a couple of hours. Might as well back off and wait until we can see what we're doing." They circled around the barge for the rest of the night, to keep track of it and to fend off any other vessel that might come by. A container ship did pass fairly close; they warned it to avoid the area. Circling is more comfortable than simply standing by because a vessel left on her own stays with her side to the wind and rolls violently. But the seas were subsiding, and by the time they started their attempt to retrieve the barge, the waves were down to twelve or fourteen feet.

In addition to having mostly a green crew, the *Powhatan* men were very tired; they'd been in terrible conditions for days, searching, getting no rest.

It took them several hours to connect up. They passed a floating line between the two legs of the bridle, grabbed it with a hook, and led it back to their own capstan. They pulled bigger and bigger lines through until finally they could pull a tow wire through the bridle.

John was very concerned about the inexperienced crew members. "My people on deck didn't know the proper side of the tow wire to stand on. Sometimes there's guys standing on top of the wire, and it jumps all over the place. I'm freaked out—somebody's going to get hurt.

"It is never safe to walk on the back deck of a tug with a tow," he adds. Not even in the best of times, never mind in heavy weather conditions. One foot of the main tow wire on the *Powhatan* weighs nearly ten pounds. "It doesn't take much of that to just settle on any part of your body to really hurt." The wire might be under 100,000 pounds of strain, and on the *Powhatan*, with 2,000 feet out, the wire could weigh eight or ten tons. As the tug makes a slight change in direction—intentionally or simply yawing in a seaway—the wire can catch on some imperfection on the rail and the strain increases—and then the wire jumps the snag. "Lightning doesn't move that fast. Even one inch of motion is enough to kill." (John's own first job on a tug was replacing a classmate "who had gotten too friendly with the tow wire." The wire had jumped about an inch and struck him in the hip. The first thing he hit was the rail, twenty feet away. Despite serious bruising through his whole body, it's a good thing he did hit the rail—without that, he'd have gone overboard, with little hope of recovery.)

And the most dangerous time of all is making up or breaking a tow.

The barge was no longer adrift, and in a couple of days of slow slogging, they'd managed to get it within forty miles of Jacksonville. But the barge was still dragging the *Gulf Majesty* or some parts of her, probably a couple of thousand feet deep underneath the barge, and now they were approaching an area where unexploded ordnance had been dumped after World War II. They didn't have the equipment or manpower to cut the cables. And then the remnants of the hurricane caught them again.

There are a number of ways that salvage operations work. Most advantageous to a salvage operator—if he's successful—is the Lloyd's open form, where, in simplistic terms, the salvor owns the retrieved vessel and the owner has to buy it back. The reward to the salvor is determined by arbitration and is based on a number of factors, including the value of the vessel and its cargo, the risk and expense he's endured, and how successful he's been at preventing pollution. Often the captain and crew get a share of the proceeds. Alternatively, an owner may hire a salvage company to work by the day. Steve doesn't know what arrangement his company made with the owners of the *San Juan Jax Bridge*, but to him it was a salvage job like many others he had worked on.

Steve called the Donjon office. He had worked salvage for years overseas, and knew what needed to be done. "I told them we gotta get some underwater divers out here to cut some of that stuff off, and a maneuverable crew boat, and six hundred feet of nylon shock line, and I'll finish the salvage job. As far as I was concerned, I was going to make some money." He reckoned the cargo and equipment on the barge to be worth $40 million. Maybe it was only $20 million. The value was significant, anyway. "That's not including the barge. That was a piece of junk."

Despite his clear request for specific equipment, the owner of the barge, Trailerbridge, hired a relatively small tug from another salvage company to come out to assist. The *Sea Giant* was a 120-foot, single-screw, 2,800-horse tug with oxyacetylene cutting rigs and more lines and towing hawsers and a couple of divers. Joe Farrell, president of Resolve Marine Group of Fort Lauderdale, was aboard the *Sea Giant* as she came out from Jacksonville. "It was pretty damn rough, probably a twelve- to sixteen-foot sea running. We had a heck of a time getting on the barge," he recalls. Access was through a four-foot-high hole at the stern. "It was like trying to jump through a guillotine hole." The tug was moving up and down with each wave, and the barge was rolling hard, as well as drifting sideways at three or four knots. "The *Sea Giant* would get pinned, rolled over about fifteen degrees. We had to put the tug at emergency full astern just to get out from under that barge so we couldn't get capsized."

They managed to get themselves and all their gear aboard, and then they had to lug it some seven hundred feet forward and up two levels on the barge to get to the bow where *Ocean Majesty*'s cables were still attached. "Our mission was to cut the cables free and make up the *Powhatan* to the barge." Cutting the upper cable wasn't all that difficult, but the chain bridle was another matter. The pad-eyes were twenty-five feet below the deck, well back under the rake of the bow. One of the *Sea Giant*'s guys had to take his four-foot torch and hang over the bow in a bosun's chair. With the wind howling and the waves crashing, they got the fellow swinging like a pendulum until he could reach a foothold and cut the chains.

Sid Hebert, engineer of the *Ocean Majesty,* feels confident that the tug didn't break up until she was cut loose from the barge; she was just hanging by her own towing wire, 2,400 feet below the surface, with another seven or eight thousand feet of water beneath her.

Steve was furious that they cut the chains above the flounder plate, and not the short shot of chain below it, because there was then no good way for him to tie back on. (It was all they could do to cut it at all, apparently, but one can certainly understand his frustration.)

The barge was adrift, and once rid of the *Ocean Majesty,* it took right off toward the coast. "It's shallow draft, and nothing but a huge sail," says Steve.

The next step was for the *Powhatan* to come pick up the barge again. "Now I gotta take my connecting line up to the top of the barge," Steve describes. "We've got gravity against us, and it's a huge, heavy line—eighteen-inch nylon soft line with a big thimble. We're chasing them backwards to pass the line up to them from the back deck." They got the retrieving line up to the guy on the barge, but the big line fell into the water and within thirty seconds it was sucked right into the *Powhatan*'s propeller.

Steve took the *Powhatan* and the divers into sheltered water, hoping to cut the rope out of the wheel so they could go back after the salvage. "That's when we found out that the people at Hilton Head are not very friendly," says John. "We headed for the nearest point, which happened to be the golf course, and they were upset to see a ship so close in. There's nothing that says you have to anchor in an anchorage—and all we were trying to do was hide somewhere to get a diver down and cut free." But the divers couldn't manage the mess—four hundred feet of that huge line had tangled into the propeller. The office told him to come home, let the barge go. Steve had no choice but to take the *Powhatan* into port, where it took several hours to free the wheel.

In the meantime, there's the low-powered *Sea Giant* standing off from the barge. It's too rough to lay alongside. "It's getting dark," describes Joe, "and I look over at the horizon, and I see towers. What the hell am I looking at?" Turns out the government had built high antennas off the coast, "something to do with Polaris submarines. And we're headed right for them." says Joe. "We have a half an hour to make a decision. I call Trailerbridge and tell them I'm prepared to take the *Sea Giant* in to the barge." He said it would take half an hour to make the connection, and it would half destroy the tug, with the inevitable crashing between tug and barge. "But it won't hurt your barge too bad."

The *Sea Giant* only had enough power to hold the barge off the towers, not enough to take it anywhere. Joe's proposition to the barge company was that he would make up to the barge, keep it out of the towers, and they'd pay him for the damage to his tug. They'd pay for the repairs plus half the daily rate while she was in the yard.

Joe told the captain of his tug what he'd offered. "I'd rather not," the captain said. "I'd rather not, too," said Joe, "but we don't have any choice. Destroy a six-million-dollar barge and twenty million dollars of cargo, plus whatever the hell the towers cost, versus destroying the tug—that's what we're up against."

Ten minutes later—they were six miles from the towers—the company called him back, agreeing to the terms. They were able to hook up to the two-inch emergency pickup line, but as Joe expected, they did a lot of damage to the *Sea Giant*. Among other things, they destroyed the engine-cooling system so they knew the engine would overheat if they pushed it too much. They were in only four to six hundred feet of water now, and decided to gamble that there were no munitions on the bottom. They payed out two thousand feet of wire, hoping it would hang up on something on the bottom and hold the barge. "It's safer to lose the cable and get hung up than to destroy the engine," says Joe. "We set the engine dead slow until the cable would catch on the bottom, and then it would get loose and we'd go dead slow again. We held it all night long that way, and the next morning a Crowley tug came out for the barge."

They had a difficult time handing the barge over. The seas were still high, and they'd crushed their cutting torch getting off the barge. They had to cut the tow hawser with a grinding wheel. "Then the Crowley tug was able to hook up. They used a nice device, an Orville hook—it floats and picks up the wire." The Crowley boat took the barge in. Five other tugs came out and escorted them in, and the *Sea Giant* went along. "We were able to keep her engine cool enough to get ourselves in." She was hauled out at the North Florida Shipyard, where she stayed for more than two months. The *Powhatan* went on to her originally planned job, but a little while later ran into more trouble because of damage caused by the line in the wheel.

But, as Steve Rhodes says, "The Lord was shining on us, because nobody was killed."

Towing to Izmit

With repairs made and a more experienced crew than she'd had during the *San Juan Jax Bridge* salvage operation, the *Powhatan* went back to the work she'd had to postpone. She made a series of four trips to Izmit delivering retired U.S. Navy vessels to their new home with the Turkish Navy. John O'Reilly was master aboard one of these voyages; he took the *Powhatan* over when she was in drydock in Brooklyn on December 9, 1999. His log and memories give a picture of what a trip like this is like.

Official logs can have two functions, John says. "They can either save your hide or nail it to a tree." In fact, there are three categories of entries: "First, the things you are required to enter, as per the Federal regulations; second, the things the company would want you to enter; and third, the things that may prove to be contentious at a later time, so you'd really like a record of your thoughts and actions."

The log is turned in to the Coast Guard at the end of each voyage. During the month-long period of this Izmit trip, five pages and more were devoted to routine inspections: daily tests of whistles and alarms and the loudspeaker system, weekly stability checks and inspections of valves and their component reach rods, gear actuators, and valve wheels, inspections of emergency power and lighting systems, and regular checks and maintenance of the crane and the Rigid Hull Inflatable Boat, the RHIB. The captain himself made weekly sanitation inspections of the whole vessel and also held safety meetings covering a variety of subjects. There were regular drills, including those for abandoning ship and responding to fires in the galley, in the fueling port, in the crane, and aboard another ship.

Another page records the maintenance of watertight integrity of the ship. Regulations require that watertight doors, cargo ports and the like are kept closed at sea. Each time one of these is opened or closed, a notation is made. There is a page where the draft of the vessel is recorded, and a slop (ship's store) and cash account reckoning, which showed a total of $552.25 handed out to four seamen.

But most of the log is taken up with the day-to-day events of the trip: course changes, injury reports, stability corrections, chafing gear, tow point and wire corrections, significant weather, problems with the tow or equipment, clock changes, medication dispensing, difficulties with steering, pilots coming and going, inspections of the towed vessel. Often in a single line, a captain summarizes a tale that takes him twenty minutes to relate in person.

The master of any vessel has the responsibility not just for the boat but also for his crew. They have signed a contract with him and it's his job to get them home in one piece, properly fed, housed, and, ultimately, paid. He might be fined, jailed, or lose his license for not taking care of everything as he should. "It should be apparent," John says, "that there are many conflicts while wearing so many hats. What may be good for the company might not be so good for the crew. Add to all of this my personal responsibilities at home—it's no wonder my beard is gray and my head is bald!"

The first day the *Powhatan* was back in the water, he faced one of those threats. "The chief mate came in and informed me a small blot of oil had been spotted. A small dot of oil slick—three to four inches in diameter—would appear about every thirty to forty seconds. The law is explicit—it was reported just as if it were the *Valdez*—there is no exception."

The crew deployed a boom to prevent oil escaping. John notified the Coast Guard. "I believe that I spoke to at least one representative from every local, state, and federal agency that gets involved with that kind of thing." Back to the drydock. The log, however, notes only that the *Powhatan* was on blocks with shore power and fire-fighting water on December fourteenth. On the seventeenth at 1600 hours they started filling the drydock, and at 1705 she was afloat. In the meantime, the leak from an adjustable-pitch propeller had been fixed.

A few days late, they reached Philadelphia, where the former navy frigate *Sims* was awaiting her trip overseas. Then there was weather to wait out—winter low pressure systems were climbing up the East Coast. The morning of the twenty-first, they started final departure tests, only to discover that a battery that provided power

Breezy. Behind the
Powhatan, the *Sims* is
taking a different tack.
COURTESY OF JOHN O'REILLY.

to the emergency generator had died. Someone made a trip ashore to get one, and at last they were off to the anchorage where the McAllister tugs would bring the ex-*Sims* out to them. They worked around a problem with one of the throttles at the after steering station, and the trip down the river was uneventful. The twenty- to twenty-five-knot winds and fourteen- to sixteen-foot seas they found off the Delaware Capes, John describes as "really not bad weather for this time of year."

The first gremlin, as John calls it, was a communication problem. He could receive but not send e-mail. Comsat and AOL were fighting, leaving the tug *Powhatan* at a loss.

Then, on Christmas Eve day, the automatic fire alarm system rang. Fire in the engine room! Turned out to be belts burning up on one of the refrigeration compressors. There are two such compressors on the tug, but the other had blown a gasket just the day before. Christmas Eve isn't the time to contact anyone, not that anyone was right at hand anyway. John diverted for Bermuda, three hundred miles to the southeast. Two months' food supplies were worth making the detour to save. But Tom Balzano, chief engineer, showed what engineers are made of, first plumbing the air-conditioner compressor to serve the reefer and then going one better. He was reporting on the situation to John when he spotted the file folders the captain held in his hands. Hmm. The file folder material was a lot like the gaskets for the compressor. . . . Pretty soon, John was missing some manila folders, but the compressor was working again. Course changed again for Turkey.

On the twenty-eighth, weather came at them again, with winds of forty-five or fifty knots, twenty-foot seas. "The problem with towing something like that frigate is that there is no real weight to the thing. It's as empty as it will ever get, and the high superstructure makes it act as a sailboat. When the wind gets so strong, the frigate actually will try to sail past the tug." If a tow passes the tug, the sideways pull can even turn the tug over. Not good. "When all else fails, face into the wind," says John, and he turned the *Powhatan* to a southwesterly heading for the night. Even though they could head east again the next morning, the net gain for the day was a mere twenty-four miles.

On December 30, yet another front came through. The winds reached hurricane force, rain pelted horizontally, and the *Powhatan* faced thirty- to forty-foot seas. "As we would slide down one of the walls of water, we would lose sight of the ship we were towing two thousand feet astern of us—this from a bridge that was normally forty feet above the water." The run for that day was zero miles.

As the sun set, a flashing yellow light on the former *Sims* alerted them to a possible flooding situation aboard the tow. The log shows that the crew shone a search light on the frigate and inspected her as best they could with binoculars. "Floating normally—no unusual trim or list," it reports. The draft marks appeared right, relative to the water. Certainly the weather conditions precluded launching the emergency boat, anyway. Everyone hoped that the float switch was stuck, and the light kept flashing for several days, but the frigate remained balanced in the sea. The light finally went out.

A significant problem was the bottle of ammonia that the storm threw across the galley and smashed. They had to evacuate the main deck and send men in with Scott air packs to clean up the mess. An advantage to being head to the wind already was that the after door could be opened to ventilate the galley.

On New Year's Eve, the weather had eased enough that it was safe for men to get onto the back deck for a tow point change. The "worm" (chafing gear) was mangled, and one of the six strands of the tow wire was severely damaged. Fortunately they'd had enough wire out that they could take seven turns around the drum. "Burying the damage," John calls it.

There was no replacement for the chafe gear. "Chief Mate Jim Moore proved himself on this one." He reconstructed what was left of the chafe gear and banded a piece of rubber hose around it. "Amazingly, it worked the rest of the trip."

There was concern about whether the turn to the year 2000 would cause any of the computers aboard to go down—ship's computer, weather computer, communications computer, the engine room—but only the weather service's machine lost its mind, and a reset took care of the problem.

There are a few medical reports in the log as well. The chief engineer hurt his back during the storm and was given medication a couple of times. The assistant engineer scratched his hand badly and later came to the captain with an infection. "One of the biggest concerns a captain can have is that of illness in the crew when you are in a remote area," explains John. "Well, the middle of the Atlantic Ocean is remote enough for me. Now I was faced with a sixty-two-year-old white diabetic male who had multiple other medical problems." This was a time that the war between Comsat and AOL caused trouble. He tried to get information on drug interactions, but could make no contact. "After fighting twelve hours with that, the AE told me he had his own antibiotic and was self-medicating. That left me with mixed feelings. If the situation had gone on much longer, I would have involved someone like the Coast Guard." The man's hand healed up over the next few days.

Even in good weather, there's always a swell on the Atlantic in winter. "When towing something in the open ocean, there is no guarantee that the tug boat and the object being towed will move in the same direction at the same time." Breaking strain on the 2 1/4-inch-diameter wire is 450,000 pounds, and the *Powhatan* has a tensi-ometer to measure the strain on the hawser. They were trying to keep the tension below 90,000 pounds so as to have plenty of extra should the surges become very strong. On January 8, a very large storm in the North Atlantic, nearly two thousand miles northwest of them, was sending 20- to 25-foot swells, a little more than two a minute. They had to slow down. Slowing releases the tension on the wire, and then the catenary sinks deeper in the water and acts as a spring, smoothing the spikes.

That afternoon, John had just found a break for a nap (he thinks sea captains probably discovered the secret of power naps many centuries before land dwellers did). He can't explain how he knew—there wasn't anything to hear, nor did the tug suddenly accelerate—but somehow, shortly after 1500 hours, he suddenly *knew* that the tow connection had broken. So much for the nap. Instead, he ran to the pilot-house and took over the conn, slowing and turning the *Powhatan* toward the frigate, now sailing free, while the other officers organized what was to come. The third mate woke all hands while the chief engineer started up the engine of the towing winch. The chief mate, in charge of the back deck, assembled the needed rigging and posi-tioned the rest of the crew.

When the end of the tow cable came aboard, they saw that there was some chain attached; a detachable link had failed. "It truly was the case of the *strongest* link in the chain breaking. Either a fault in manufacture or some abuse in its history caused it to fail. I am just glad that it didn't happen in the storm we had earlier."

The frigate was lying almost broadside to the swell, as a ship will when left on her own. John backed the *Powhatan* up to the bow of the ship so the two vessels were perpendicular to one another. It's tricky, keeping two vessels close that are, inde-pendently, moving up and down and side to side as much as thirty feet, five or six times a minute. John describes the process of reconnecting the tow: "One length of chain is hanging from the chock in the frigate's bow. One of the deck hands will hold a long boat hook out past the chain. The chief mate tries to throw a heaving line so that it will get caught by the boat hook. Then the line is pulled around the chain, and a larger work line follows. The work line is brought back aboard and attached to itself, lasso style, by a heavy shackle. The loop of the lasso is left loose and is dropped into the water. With luck it will sink, so we can get more chain up on deck.

"Each link in the chain weighs fifty to sixty pounds. The noise level is high, and it's raining, with the wind blowing—things don't always go as planned. While we were recovering that ship, the chain almost captured one of the crewmembers on deck. Another time, the chain almost grabbed a tank vent and would have ripped it off. Yet another time, the stern of the tug and the bow of the ship rubbed."

The log simply notes "1700 reattached." John credits his entire crew with the ultra-fast recovery, which took less than two hours. "Being a salvage outfit, this company is much better prepared than most to do this kind of work."

While they were passing Gibraltar, the yellow high-water light on the ex-*Sims* came back on. In the morning, after a routine tow-point change, the chief mate, third mate and an AB went off in the RHIB to check the frigate. "They were back aboard in forty-five minutes. With the entire tow about 2600 feet long and having the three crewmen (thirty percent of the crew) off the vessel, I was greatly relieved when they had made it back." They'd found nothing seriously wrong with the ship, just a little water in one compartment that probably came from leaks overhead.

Off Tunisia, a couple of days later, they faced a new kind of excitement. The *Powhatan* had just finished a distinguished career as a fleet tug [ATF] and the vessel they were towing had served as a frigate [FF] for the U.S. Navy. Ships can change color and name, but they seldom change shape. Many seamen can work on a ship for a while and see that ship years later with a different name and paint job and still recognize it as the vessel it once was. Despite her new paint job, the *Powhatan* still looked like the navy tug she used to be.

"After we'd submitted our report to the office one morning, a military anti-sub plane similar to the U.S. Navy's P-3 Orion flew over us. We must have aroused concerns, because by 1100 that morning we had a Tunisian frigate with several smaller patrol boats off our port side. We did have the U.S. flag flying at its proper position, but being merchant marine, that was all we had flying.

"We were asked for our call sign and name five times by radiotelephone. This probably led to more confusion. Though the name had remained the same, the call sign had changed. I really expected to get boarded. Someone, somewhere, must have cleared it up. An hour or so into this game, and without any warning, the Tunisians took their boats and left us."

Good weather was supposed to stay with them while they went through the Aegean Sea, but no such luck. The day before they reached the Dardanelles, once again they found themselves in 65-knot winds, this time with a quick, steep sea and heavy snow and sea smoke. Visibility was near zero. Unfortunately, radar doesn't help much in these conditions. "Heavy rain and snow can reduce the radar picture to an almost useless painting of blots and splotches," John says.

But the passage through the Dardanelles was a lot easier than John had feared. "Our tow pulled a couple of fits, but nothing too gruesome." Then the Sea of Marmara threw yet more heavy winds at them. The local pilots, in fact, notified John that they had suspended service. But in the case of bad weather, no one can deny a vessel entry into a port, and John had been into Korfezi Izmit recently. "Compared to New York Harbor, it is gigantic, with lots of deep water. The only cross-traffic is from ferries that run specific routes." John would keep going. "The Turkish pilot figured I would do what any normal ship—other than a U.S. tugboat—would do and politely go to anchor. Surprise! I ain't normal by his standards.

"In ten minutes the pilot called and asked me to stop because he was now going to try and board us. This proved the man had little towing experience. Yes, of course I can stop. I can reach over and pull back on the bloody throttles anytime I want. There is, however, a slight problem with the object I am towing behind me! If the tug comes to a sudden stop, the tow either runs us down or passes the tug and tries to turn it upside down."

John started shortening the hawser and slowed as much as he could, and the pilot managed to get aboard. The last phase of the trip was to deliver the ex-*Sims* to the Turkish Navy. The log makes no mention of the difficulties with the pilot, but John tells the story: "Both the pilot and I agreed quickly that I would be the one to do the final maneuvers for bringing the ship to where the navy was going to take custody of it. At least, I thought we'd agreed." He had to turn the ship 180 degrees into the wind and tide in order to stop it and let the Turkish tugs get into position. "Then we could knock the pin out of the connecting shackle." But the pilot didn't like John's approach and started countering his orders. John reminded him of what they had agreed. The pilot couldn't seem to help himself and soon started in again.

Two members of a swarm of little boats that took the *Sims* from the *Powhatan* at Izmit.
COURTESY OF JOHN O'REILLY.

John, who stands several inches over six feet, says that the mate on the bridge told the end of the story well: "The old man got red in the face, grew about a foot taller than normal, and growled, 'Go stand in the corner and shut up!'" After that, the pilot didn't say much.

The log notes simply, "Disconnect from tow after performing a visual inspection, which observed no damage on the hull or existing equipment of the ship. The Turkish Navy accepts the ex-*Sims*."

Engineer Tom Balzano comments on his captain: "I have great respect for Captain John. In the Aegean Sea, there were radar targets everywhere, the wind came up, and we had trouble keeping the tow behind us. There was a blinding snowstorm. You couldn't see the bow. There was a lot of traffic and fast ferries. Other guys would be stressed out in four hours, but he just stood there with a cup of coffee, looking at the radar without a reference chart for twelve hours like it was nothing."

Another Former Navy Tug

"The biggest wash it had ever seen was the wake of another ship," says Captain Morris Johnson of the tug *Atlantic,* on which he spent too much of one winter in about 1960. He was speaking of her earlier life as a navy harbor tug. She was an old 110-foot wooden boat built for ship docking during World War II. Mo was aboard as relief captain when her owners took delivery of her in Baltimore. Maybe he should have known it wouldn't be an easy ride because his buddy Dave Watts, who went with him on the trip, said that because her name began with an A, she was jinxed.

The first time they tried to head down the Chesapeake, she pushed up such a bow wave that it seemed she was trying to sink herself. "Down in the foc's'le, you could throw a cat through the hull," says Mo. They had to turn back for some recaulking.

They didn't have much equipment, by today's standards, and what they had didn't work very well. The radio wasn't dependable, and there was no radar, just a compass. There was no towing machine, and they had to pull in the hawsers by hand. They did install an autopilot—"An autopilot is the same as another man," says Mo—but the thing was never operational all winter. The only speed indicator was to measure their own walk against the sea they were passing through—"You had to walk really rapidly down the side, and that was four knots." Not a particularly accurate method of dead reckoning.

Recaulking complete, they headed down the Chesapeake for the second time in the middle of a particularly beautiful December night. "It was so nice, we had all the doors and windows open in the pilothouse," says Mo. It wasn't long before the engine room called. They were still taking on water. The engineer said he was going to take one of the two engines off in order to pump. They were cruising along under one engine when they started to pump, and discovered that the pumps were set up so that instead of exiting through the overboard discharge, the water was going out through the fire-fighting monitors. "We looked like we were welcoming the *Queen Mary,* right there at midnight on the Chesapeake!" Of course the bilge water had oil in it, and the spray that fell on the deck left a terrible, slippery mess. They spent the rest of the whole trip to Florida trying to scrub it back up again. (Nowadays, much more care would be taken to prevent oil contamination. It was a different age then.)

Off the Frying Pan Shoals lightship, the seas kicked up, and once again the boat started taking on water. They radioed the lightship to notify them and to ask about the weather conditions. Seas twenty-five to thirty feet and building. "Jeez, I'm having trouble with the bow in these seas," Mo said. The tug would dive down into the water and have to fight to bring her bow back up. "I'm watching foam go by—not that fast. We're making about a half a knot."

A kid came up into the pilothouse. "Does anyone want anything out of the foc's'le?" he asked. The water down there was up to his chest. It was eleven feet from the foc's'le deck to the keel, which meant that they had over fourteen feet of ocean in the bow. Water was coming right through the planking when the bow was buried down in the sea, "just like a shower," Mo says. Then the engineer called up to the pilothouse again. They had water too, and the shaft was kicking it up onto the electric panel.

They tried to pump using a siphon pump but the screen was clogged up. Mo remembers diving down with a fire ax to cut out the screen. "You can't do that!" hollered the captain, but there was no alternative. Finally the water in the foc's'le started to go down—operating correctly, the siphon pump could dispose of some two thousand gallons a minute. "There were bits of mattresses and everything else going out through the pump," Mo says, "but it worked."

There were six men aboard. The captain and the chief engineer had quarters in the upper level and the other four lived in the foc's'le. "There was not a stitch of clothes left in the foc's'le," Mo says. "It looked like five mad kids had busted everything up down there. We didn't have any clothes or any money, nothing." They took the tug into Morehead City, North Carolina, got some money and clothing, and went on their way again.

They reached Jacksonville on Christmas Eve and had a hard time finding a place to tie up. They got stuck at an oil barge dock and had to get pulled out. Then someone had an idea, recalls Mo. "It was an old navy tug, and still looked navy—had numbers painted on her. So we stripped down to dungarees and T-shirts and tied up at a dock labeled 'U.S. Government only.'" But they didn't get away with that either. Finally, the boss found them a dock.

They spent Christmas Day at the Elks Club. The man there asked them if they'd keep an eye on the club while he went home for Christmas dinner with his family. "A couple of guys came in and we made them drinks, and we all played pool." Merry Christmas.

The first job for the tug was to tow a surplus destroyer from Jacksonville to Southern Scrap Metal in New Orleans. Jinxed or not, the adventures of the *Atlantic* continued. Leaving Jacksonville in a strong current with the destroyer on the hip, they approached a Route 1 bridge. The tug was hooked up, trying to fight her way into the current, when suddenly the spring line parted. "I was on the wing bridge of the destroyer," says Mo. "I jumped down from deck to deck. Dave, on the tug, had slacked off the line, and I tied a great big bowline, put it back on the spring bitt, and we were underway again. We just missed wiping out that bridge by seven feet."

They got the destroyer to the yard with no further fuss, but the scrap company wouldn't pay for the job unless they also brought in a burned-out Chinese freighter from Galveston, so out again went the *Atlantic*. The pineapple-carrying freighter had collided with a naphtha tanker. She had burned for days, and no one ever found the crew. The authorities thought perhaps they had run into the cooler, shut the door on themselves, and perished there. The salvage company sent five men to ride back on the ship. One of their jobs was to be to find the bodies and throw them overboard off-shore. But there were no remains to be found anywhere. "I think those guys were all in California somewhere," Mo says.

Crossing the Gulf with a dead ship was tricky because of abandoned oil rigs. They were charted, so Mo and the crew knew roughly where they were, but they encountered heavy fog most of the way across. Radar certainly would have helped. Only a few of the towers had the required automatic foghorns. The ship was out on a thousand-foot towline and never followed them straight. She'd run off one side and then off the other. "Once in a while a rig would pop up in front of us. If the boat had gone one side of a rig and the ship the other, we'd have been in a world of shit."

The men on the ship had food enough for five days, but the trip took fifteen. "There's nothing worse than a ghost ship anyway," says Mo.

The fog was too thick to enter the Southwest Pass of the Mississippi. As they approached, they kept hearing other ships at anchor waiting for pilots. "They were supposed to be ringing bells, but they were running up and down their decks beating pots and pans. We must have looked like an awful big target on their radar." Mo himself climbed up onto the top of the fire monitors, the highest point on the *Atlantic*, and found himself about head and shoulders above the fog. "I could see the cross-trees of the other ships. I counted twenty-three of them."

Waiting for visibility, they too dropped anchor. "Our anchor wasn't big enough to hold the freighter," Mo says. "The guys on the ship would holler when they could see the beach, and we'd haul them off again."

The fog finally let up awhile, and they headed up the river. Even on a short haw-ser, the ship still wandered from one side to the other. The *Atlantic* got caught in a current. "It laid us back against the ship, and we went sideways out the channel, over buoys and everything," says Mo. "We anchored again." The next time the fog lifted, they started back up the river, but yet again the fog closed around them. Mo and Dave were walking down the deck, and—*whap!*—they got hit across the face with a tree branch. Next instant, the tug was aground. They had to shut down the engines so as not to suck the mud up into the works. The ship was still coasting up the river toward them, and the crew hauled the towline in by hand. "The ship was either gonna hit us or go aground. 'Get ready to run,' I says. If it had hit us in the stern, it would have split us right up the middle." She grounded fifteen feet from the tug.

The next day when the fog lifted, they managed to get themselves and their ship off the mud and back into the river. It was blowing hard. "The ship wouldn't follow—we were taking up the whole Mississippi," says Mo.

They were the subject of much radio chatter. "Jeez, they're all over the place," said one radio voice. "I don't think they have very much control," said another.

"If I'd told them just how much control we did have," says Mo, "they would have turned around."

But it was on that river the first time, with the destroyer, that Mo experienced what he describes as one of the highlights of his career. They had a small assist tug holding the ship's stern up in the 35-mile-an-hour crosswind. The captain of the *Atlantic* got up onto the bridge of the destroyer to guide Mo up the Industrial Canal into New Orleans. As they approached a triple bridge, they could see the captain up on the ship waving his arms around and screaming, but no one could hear anything he said. The bridge-tender opened the bridge and then ran out of the bridge-tender's house, thinking they were going to wipe it out and him with it. "Well, here we go!" said Mo. But they shot through and never touched a thing. Later they checked the charts and found they'd had just three feet of clearance. Tight.

At the time, the most important question in Mo's mind was, where did they have to go next? It turned out the scrap yard was just the other side of the bridge. "Jeez, I gotta stop this son of a bitch!" said Mo. With no time to change the lines leading onto the destroyer, he slammed the boat into reverse. One line tightened up and tore the corner off the galley roof when he backed down, "but it was the only way I could stop it," Mo says. And the wind laid her up against the dock as nicely as anyone could ask.

In New Orleans, they picked up a pair of barges to take to Tampa. Halfway across, the exhaust let go on one of the tug's engines, filling the engine room with smoke and fumes. They had to wrap towels around their faces before going below to pump up the day tanks or check on the machinery. And the engine room was under the galley so smoke leaked up through the galley too.

They got rid of the tow in Tampa and tied up alongside another tug, nicely painted up and looking good. "There's guys in there watching baseball on television, eating ice cream and cake, and I'm saying 'I think we're on the wrong tug.'" The best meal they'd had aboard the *Atlantic* was when they took a sea and the fruit salad fell into the pancake batter. "We cooked it up anyway, and everyone loved it."

The *Atlantic* was a sister to the U. S. Navy tug *YTB 499* in the foreground of this race photograph. The event was at a New York Harbor tugboat muster in the early 1950s. The other tugs are the *C. Stewart Lee* of Curtis Bay Towing Company, the canaler *Dauntless No. 2, Russell 17,* and *NY Central No. 25.*
PHOTO BY HANS MARX, FROM THE COLLECTION OF DAVE BOONE.

Mo and Dave had had enough of the *Atlantic*. The captain started getting a little feisty, Mo says, and they announced they were leaving. The captain told them no, they weren't going, he was, and he was going to give the boat to Mo. But Mo wasn't interested. "We're getting off," he told the captain.

"Not unless you go through me," said the captain. They'd all had a few by then, Mo admits. There was a little tussling, but he and Dave did leave. "We took our matched set of luggage—two pillowcases." With a credit card, they bought bus tickets to Fort Lauderdale to settle up with the boss. They didn't have cab fare to get to the office in Fort Lauderdale, but they told the taxi driver their story, and he took them where they were going for nothing. "You guys have had enough problems," he said. The owner wasn't in Fort Lauderdale anyway. They chased him to a motel in Jacksonville, where Mo was threatening to kick his door down until the motel owners threw him out. "We got stiffed in the end," says Mo.

Was there anything good about that trip on the *Atlantic*? "Boy, you'd have to think a lot," says Mo. But he comes up with something. "It brought some guys together. We had a few good laughs—but they were kinda expensive laughs."

Container Wrestling in the Aleutians

"The last vestiges of the wild west," Zach Thomas calls the Aleutian Islands. In 1991 and 1992, he was there towing container barges from tiny fish processing plants to Dutch Harbor, on Unalaska Island, the only harbor out that way that ships can enter. "It was incredibly dangerous," he says, but then points out the irony that there are many more accidents in the ultra-safe, OSHA- and union-managed port of Portland, Oregon, where he works today, than there were in Alaska.

The only reason to be in the Aleutians, Zach says, is to make money, which means to fish or to process fish. Codfish, halibut, king crab—that's what life's about out there. "Sailing, looking at the mountains and islands, you see nothing but snow and rocks and little fishing stations. Mother Nature only begrudgingly accepting our presence." People are fighting with all they've got just to hold on—and as soon as they stop, he says, "it'll revert back to the state it's been in since the beginning of the earth. It puts your life in perspective."

The company that Zach worked for, Alaska Marine Charters, was servicing Sea-Land cargo, filling and moving containers of fish product from the outports to Dutch Harbor, where they were loaded onto ships headed for Japan or Seattle. "There's nothing there but a safe harbor and a fish processing plant," he says of most of their stops. And at the time he was there, most of the employees in these remote plants were South American. "They were all speaking Spanish. It was too bizarre for words. I can't comment on working conditions—those plants are nothing but knives flying around cutting up fish. They were probably getting minimum wage. But nobody seemed unhappy."

Zach and his shipmates ran tugboats but they also worked as stevedores and gruntmen in those places which had no such services. Perhaps the most unpleasant job, as well as a particularly dangerous one, was loading fish meal from the Soviet processing ships. "You'd smell the ship before you'd see it. Your body would try to do anything not to take a breath."

People would live on those ships for a year at a time, without going ashore. "There was nothing to do there anyway," Zach comments. "They were old, rusted ships, miserable." He felt sorry for those folks. The ships would take the fish byproducts—the heads and bones—and spin them into meal, bag the meal, and call for containers when they had enough bags.

"Loading those was a real trick," recalls Zach. Containers would be stacked on the barge two or three high. They had a forklift aboard the barge that they'd use to load the pallets of sacks into containers. It might be snowing. There was hardly any sun in the winter, and, of course, the dead of winter always seemed to be the busiest time of year. There was a little drop-off at the edge of the otherwise flat deck of the barge, and they had to really pay attention with the forklift.

On one trip, a young relative of the company owner was on board as a second AB, to learn how things worked. Running the lift with sacks on the fork, the young man got over too far, lost a wheel over the edge, and the fork started tipping. "The kid stayed on board, trying to save the forklift, and only jumped at the last second." The forklift drowned; the kid was OK, but soon after this trip, he left the boat. "That was pretty common. We had a lot of people come up for a short time and decide it was not for them."

Zach says they made decent money, but not much more than they would have in tugs in the lower forty-eight. "There wasn't much of a hazard bonus. But the schedule wasn't bad for a young single guy: three months on, three months off. It gave you time on shore to do something if you wanted."

The work was exhilarating. "The ship handling we did there was as intense as you could ever hope for. The docks we were going into at the processing plants were wood—slapped together, rickety. We'd be bringing in a fairly good-sized barge, 320 feet stacked three or four containers high. We had our fair share of storms, crosswinds most of the time, sometimes thirty or forty knots, and all that sail area. If you come along at any rate of speed and hit the dock, it's all going to collapse. And, landing a barge, the tug's alongside, so the captain can't see the dock. The mate's on the corner of the barge calling back commands—he's piloting. You have to think ahead, because of the delay between yourself and that person.

"I loved it. You either loved it or you didn't do it long."

The guys that stayed with it were spectacular at the job. It was a source of pride among them to perform some tricky maneuver better than anyone else. The captain on Zach's boat when he first got to Alaska came from Louisiana. "An RCA he called himself, a Regular Coon Ass," says Zach. "He didn't know anything else. His dad was on a boat, and as soon as he could, he was too." Zach was nervous because most of the captain's previous work had been in the Gulf of Mexico. It's all mud and sand there, and if a barge nicks the shore, it's not the end of the world. In the Aleutians, it's all rock. "He'd make some fancy maneuvers in incredibly tight quarters, but the man was a natural. He never had problems, never even sweated a situation. He was so smooth. Best handler I'd ever seen."

They usually ran with five men: captain, mate, engineer, AB, and cook. Except at Dutch Harbor, where there were container cranes and longshoremen, the men on the tug managed the containers in addition to the tug and barge. This made for continuous, strenuous work, but Zach says that was a big part of what he enjoyed so much about the job.

The closest harbor was eight hours from Dutch Harbor, and that run was the hardest. They worked six hours on and six hours off. If they left Dutch Harbor at midnight, they'd get to the fish plant at eight in the morning. For those on the twelve-to-six watch, "You'd have had an hour of sleep, and then get up and go to work on cargo for ten hours, and then soon it's your watch again.

"It was not unusual to go twenty-four to thirty-six hours with only an hour or two nap whenever you got a chance. If there was a lull between hooking one container and unhooking it, you might see a deckhand leaning on a pole, literally asleep. It was intense.

"If we had a good load on the barge in Dutch Harbor, we'd all jump in the racks and sleep as hard as we could for a couple of hours."

To handle containers in the outlying harbors, they had a crane on board, a track crane with a long boom. Sometimes they'd carry the crane operator with them, and other times he'd fly in. "Most times we didn't know the crane operator. Some guys, it was the first time we ever saw them. You had to have a lot of trust in them. You have a box filled to capacity with 60,000 pounds of frozen fish or crab, whichever season it was, and guys on deck, and he's slinging that crane around in tight spots—any wrong move, you have crushed people." As soon as the crane operator came on board, they'd be taking the measure of the man to see how much they could trust him to do his job well. "Things you do normally, you might not do with this guy" if his competence seemed at all questionable.

In order to pick up a container, the crane hook swings a spreader bar, like a big metal bed frame, out over the container. On each corner it has twist locks that they turned to lock into the container or to release it. "We'd ride the spreader bar to and from the barge—we didn't have men enough to have guys both on the dock and on the barge. There'd be two of us on the bar. The crane operator would lower the bar to a couple of feet above the container, we'd jump off onto the container, and manually hold the bar until the twist locks were over the holes, then tell him to lower it down. On a windy day or if the barge is moving in wave action, the spreader bar is swinging all over the place. It takes everything you've got to get it in position. You time your swing, and when the bar's right over, give a signal to freewheel it—take the brake off and drop it. But you're standing right beneath the spreader bar, a many-thousand-pound object—if he misses, it bounces right onto you. And if he dropped a container on you, it would turn you to jelly."

One particularly breezy day at Chignik, on the Alaska Peninsula, they were doing cargo operations. It was gusting thirty to forty knots. "Riding the spreader bar was definitely a little bit dicey," Zach admits, especially with light containers, which blow all around. When the bar swings, the crane operator swings in the same direction to counteract it, but if he misses his timing, it makes it worse. "He'd been doing a fine job, but he went to make his swing, and a big gust started swinging us out, and he mistimed, and then he stopped. We're moving so hard, on the upstroke it's like being on a ride at the fair—we're hanging on and looking straight down, and then back the other way, hanging on for dear life. White knuckles there for a bit."

This dangerous job was made even worse when they couldn't trust the crane operator. "Then you didn't ride." Instead, they'd spend the extra time to climb on and off the containers and across to the pier, crawling back and forth. "You did what you had to do." On a daily basis, there were a lot of safety decisions. "But it's all fun and games. Until you've been seriously injured, it's hard to picture yourself getting hurt."

There are times when it's clear how close you came to major trouble, like one instance Zach remembers clearly. The crane operator, loading full containers, had just completed a row, three high across the barge. One empty container on the third level on the other side of the barge was needed on the dock. The crane operator couldn't actually see it at all. Zach and another man were on the spreader bar. "I was gonna give direction to get the bar on the box—all I wanted was for him to track forward a little, drop the bar on the box, and then I could finish it up. So he's going forward and he didn't realize he had his boom lever down. I don't know how that happened." The spreader bar went lower and lower, closer to the container, and Zach only noticed when they got out of view of the crane. "It lays down on the box, all the way on the outside, half on the box, half hanging out, three containers high. The wire goes slack, and the bar's teeter-tottering with the two of us, ready to go over. I make a leap of life onto the box and run across to where he can see me. The other guy is frozen." Zach screamed at the crane guy, who realized what was happening and hauled up the bar again. "When the spreader bar hit the first time, if it had fallen off the containers, it would have dropped five or ten feet and then come up against the wire. Either the wire would have broken or at least it would have knocked the two of us off the bar, and down we would have gone."

Zach never saw anyone get seriously hurt. "You're so aware of your surroundings all the time, you're on the lookout. That's what kept you safe." And the job is getting safer, he adds. "Just like on the Intracoastal Waterway, regulations are creeping in everywhere, to make things better, safer, less exciting." Increased regulations and requirements concerning safety and pollution, while no doubt valuable, are taking the fun out of the business. "What guys find exciting is being pulled away."

In addition to the fun, Zach appreciates the fact that in Alaskan waters he got to run a tug as captain years earlier than he would have anywhere else. "Hundred-and-twenty-foot, 5,000 horsepower tugs—but nobody else wanted to do it." And you never would forget what a serious business you were in. "The fishermen, of course, have an even more tenuous hold on their world. Every winter, at least a couple of times, you'd hear chatter on the radio: 'Where's Johnny?' or 'Has anyone seen such-and-such a boat?'" and another man would have gone overboard or another boat would have gone down.

Zach is now in Portland, Oregon, working for a stevedore company. "Where I am now, with the union, you don't blow your nose unless you have the right kind of tissue paper. Up there, we did things that would make people here faint. We'd jump from container to container, four feet apart and thirty feet off the deck, all the time. And yet there are many more accidents here than we ever had in Alaska. When you're in a situation where you know your life is in your hands and those of the people around you, your sense of awareness is incredibly heightened, and you're on the lookout for things that are gonna cause you harm.

"In the States, there are rules upon rules, turned into one-, two-, three-step repetition; you become complacent. The sun will rise and the sun will set—this is how it is. Then one little thing goes wrong, and no one pays attention—it worked the last 3,126 times. And then a pin lets go, but no one's paying attention. Or you do silly things like trip on a lashing on the deck, or take a misstep and twist your ankle on a gangway.

"That kind of thing never would have happened in Alaska. It was much more dangerous, but much more safe, too. If things went wrong there, they'd go horribly wrong." There were no Coast Guard stations anywhere near—they weren't nearby to help you in a crisis. "OSHA wasn't hanging out on the dock, either. It was up to us to police ourselves, not to do things going to get us hurt—and we didn't." They consciously took risks. Looking back, Zach admits some of them were foolhardy but, other than bumps and bruises, no one was ever hurt on his boat.

Convoy to Prudhoe Bay

At an average of about one knot, it took a long time to get a convoy through the ice-filled waters to Prudhoe Bay, and there was only a short window each summer to make the trip. Head-to-tail, a convoy of Crowley tugs and barges would make annual treks for the Alyeska Company to Prudhoe Bay, north of the 70th parallel and some two hundred miles beyond Point Barrow, the northernmost tip of Alaska. Prudhoe Bay is the land base for the North Slope oilfields; from there the Alaska pipeline runs eight hundred miles south to Valdez. The bay is frozen in for all but a couple of months each summer.

For several years, Captain Bob Glover sailed aboard Crowley's salvage tug *Arctic Salvor*, first as second mate and then as chief mate. The big tug went along on the trip as an insurance policy, "to babysit the convoy in case a barge started to sink or a tug got in trouble," Bob says.

The *Arctic Salvor*, now known as *American Salvor*, is a 213-foot-long salvage vessel. She carries divers and a decompression chamber, a machine shop, pumps capable of pumping 12,500 gallons per minute, and a 35-ton crane. With 300,000-pound line pull, she has more bollard pull than any other salvage vessel in the United States. She also has a lighted helicopter deck, and several times during Bob's tour welders or other specialized workers, and sometimes executives, came aboard via helicopter. "She sleeps twenty-four, and has good accommodations," Bob adds.

On the Prudhoe Bay trips, she carried power packs for the other tugs, cylinders for their main engines, fuel, and anything any member of the convoy might need. The other tugs were all Crowley's Invader-class boats and all had the same engines: EMD

American Salvor, formerly *Arctic Salvor.* COURTESY OF CROWLEY MARINE SERVICES.

diesels, which more commonly run electric propulsion systems in freight locomotives. The ones the *Arctic Salvor* carried were all standard diesels, though, running through reduction gears to the shafts. If a tug should blow a piston or cylinder wall, it could come alongside, and her crew and the *Arctic Salvor*'s could take it right out and replace it with a spare.

A dozen men sailed on the *Arctic Salvor*. Like the other tugs on the convoy, she was on a three-watch system, with captain, chief mate, second mate, engineer, cook, and three deckhands. In addition, she had a salvage master, a second engineer and two divers. For several years a retired head chef from a San Francisco four-star restaurant served as cook. "He got bored with retirement," Bob explains, and somehow ended up on the *Arctic Salvor*. "He could debone a game hen in seventeen seconds," says Bob incredulously. "He was a phenomenal chef." Offshore, a good chef makes a huge difference in a crew's morale.

The years that Bob sailed to Prudhoe Bay, in the 1980s, between eight and twenty-three tugs made the trip, making the largest non-military convoy in the world. Each boat towed a pair of 400-foot-long barges, 100 feet wide, loaded to ten or twelve feet deep, carrying equipment for the Alyeska Company. The oilfield was newly developed, and the town and facility were growing. The barges brought entire buildings up from the lower forty-eight, prefabricated and completely finished inside. Some were as much as twelve stories tall.

For best control, each barge was on its own $2^1/4$-inch-diameter tow wire, each wire controlled by a separate drum on the tow winch. Surge gear, a 90-foot length of 3-inch-diameter Dialock chain between the tow wire and the towing bridle rigged from the corners of the barge, gave a spring effect, reducing the surge-stress from swells in the open ocean. The barges had skegs aft, which were not parallel with the water flow but instead angled out twelve or fifteen degrees, opposing each other, to keep the barge towing straight.

The convoy took off from Seattle and Portland and made their first stop at Port Clarence, just before the Bering Strait, on the southern side of the Seward Peninsula. There they'd wait until the ice opened up enough to let them through the strait. "That's a nice, protected, shallow bay," Bob explains. This was also where the tugs changed out their towing gear from the ocean-going rig to the ice-towing arrangement they'd use for the rest of the journey. In the ocean-going configuration, the tows were out on 2,200 to 2,600 feet of towing wire, depending on sea conditions. The barges were spaced approximately five hundred feet apart, or two layers of towing wire on the tugs' tow winch drums.

When they continued on their way from Port Clarence, an icebreaker led the

The convoy of Invader-class tugs and barges headed for Prudhoe Bay.
COURTESY OF CAPT. ROBERT C. GLOVER III.

procession. The tows were pulled right in tight from then on. Each tug's first barge looked to be right on top of her stern, and the second, on a wire that passed underneath the first, just behind that. Each vessel followed as close as sixty or eighty feet behind the one in front, in order to keep ice from getting between them. They moved at one knot or less, just enough to keep headway, clutching into gear and clutching out. It's hard on clutches. The *Arctic Salvor* followed the rest of the fleet, sixty feet behind the last barge.

Then they'd wait at anchor at Wainwright, just west of Point Barrow, until they got the go-ahead from the ice scout who, regularly flying from Point Barrow to Prudhoe Bay, watched for the breakup. "The same guy was doing this for twenty-five years," Bob says. It would be the second or third week in July before they could get around Point Barrow and head east to Prudhoe Bay.

It's shallow water up there, only thirty feet in most places. Their cables dragged on the bottom all the way. There's little sea, and no swell—the ice keeps it down—but wind can cause some headaches. "When it gets snotty, it gets nasty," Bob says. "Forty-five or fifty knots. But even if it gets windy, you just get a short chop." That wouldn't bother vessels of this size. "It was a long, protracted march," says Bob. "And it's light twenty-four hours a day—that's weird, too."

Once they started on the last leg, they'd just keep going. "It took a day or more to run all the way across," Bob says. "Navigation was all by radar." The land is flat

The small push tug used to grab barges from the Invaders and put them onto the beach. It only draws five feet. COURTESY OF CAPT. ROBERT C. GLOVER III.

The inside passage, Canada's Grenville Channel. It's a natural fjord, forty-two miles long, twelve hundred feet deep, but narrow. "You gotta be careful," says Bob Glover, "because you get around a corner, and there's a rock." COURTESY OF CAPT. ROBERT C. GLOVER III.

tundra. "When you get a mile or a mile and a half offshore, you can't see land," Bob says. At strategic places there were racons, electronic devices that send back a Morse code signal. "It shows up on your radar screens. You can get the distance from it and triangulate from three or four at the same time." Of course now it's all cross-checkable with GPS.

The divers kept busy with maintenance duties, like everyone else, until they were needed. Naturally, it was everyone's hope that they would never be called upon to actually dive. Bob remembers one particularly bad job for the divers. "They had to pull a walrus out of the wheel of a tug," he says. When the tug hit the animal, one engine was jammed to a stop. (Walruses are huge, sometimes reaching almost two tons.) By using the other engine, they managed to get to where they could anchor, and then the *Arctic Salvor* and her divers came to help. The walrus had gotten pinned between the bottom of the tug and the propeller. They had to attach wires to it and use the crane and leverage to free it. "It was under there two days and was bloated. It was the most godawful smell I've ever smelled," Bob says. "It was putrid."

When they reached Prudhoe Bay, the *Arctic Salvor* stood by until the barges were unloaded. In late August, the ice would have run a ways offshore but by the end of September it would be back, and it was time to be gone. Some of the tugs went home earlier on their own once they'd unloaded their barges.

Small push-tugs took the barges ashore, pushing them in, stern to the flush face of the dock, where the sand had been graded, leaving only a foot and a half or two feet of water beneath the barge. (The tidal range is just a matter of inches in these waters.) They'd take the hatch covers off and pump water aboard to sink the barge onto the bottom, in effect making it a solid extension of the pier. With cutting torches, they'd cut the buildings loose from the barges. Then huge, low-profile Caterpillar tractors, something like those used to move the Space Shuttle, would pick up the buildings and take them wherever they needed to go, as much as ten or fifteen miles inland. "Bolt a few pipes together, and turn it on! Then they'd dewater the barge, put the manhole covers back on, and send the barge on its way," Bob explains. For the *Arctic Salvor,* the round trip took seventy to ninety days. She made some stops along the Inside Passage on her way home, but the bulk of the summer was taken up with the one job.

Servicing the Oil Rigs

Throughout the world, companies exploring for oil and gas in marine environments provide challenges to the huge tugboats that service their oil rigs, but nowhere more than in northern seas. There are several categories of vessels working in the oil fields, including tugs. Among tugs, there are the ones that haul big barges and equipment. These look like regular tugs only much bigger. The anchor-handling/supply tugs are also traditional-looking but have huge winches and long after-decks. Finally, there are the smaller supply vessels.

For a decade, starting in 1978, Steve Santos, professional AB, worked in the oil and gas business on offshore vessels on both sides of North America. He worked on supply boats and on the huge anchor-handling tugs for the oil rigs in the Bering Sea and Shelikof Strait, and later he towed icebergs in Davis Strait and off Frobisher Bay.

There are always offshore jobs available, he says. Wages are low, and it's hard, hard work. Why would anyone do it? "Because they don't know any better." The crews are often on a thirty-day rotation, working thirty days, and off for thirty, or sometimes forty days on and twenty off. They get paid on a per-day basis regardless of whether they work five hours or eighteen, and sometimes it's longer than that.

Offshore, they work three watches, four hours on and eight hours off, which sounds wonderful compared to the normal coastal routine of six-hour watches that never allow a full complement of sleep at one time. "But when they needed a lot of men on deck, you'd work whatever it took."

Discharging cargo was time-consuming, hard labor. Some of the most dangerous work was loading and discharging pipe, both drill pipe and casing. The pipe was sixty feet long, a foot or two feet in diameter, and it had to be moved around on deck and chained together for the rig's crane to grab onto. There were containers of food to unload too. Fuel and water and cement and the "mud" and other liquids needed for the drilling operation would be run out through hoses.

Add weather to all this, and you've got a project. The Bering Sea is only 250 feet deep, which makes it inviting for drilling, but its shallowness makes for harsh seas. "You can be out in the middle of the Pacific," says Steve, who's been just about everywhere, "and a thirty-foot sea's not so bad because you have big swells. But it's nasty in shallow water. It's steep and quick."

Sometimes they'd get to the oil rig and have to wait on the weather. They'd pick up a mooring buoy if they could, but when the seas got over fifteen feet, they'd have to drop off the mooring and jog back and forth. They'd run twelve miles into the weather and turn back again. "You've gotta turn real quick—when the ship is broadside to the waves, everything's flying around, including people," says Steve. Then they'd run back twenty-four miles before the weather, going as slowly as they could because it was the only time anyone could get any sleep. Another quick turn, back twelve miles to the rig, see how things were looking, and then jog to weather again if need be.

They might have to make the deliveries in spite of the conditions. In thirty- or forty-foot seas, the supply boat would come as close as it could to the rig—fifty or maybe a hundred feet off—and pass slowly by while the people on the rig would send the crane out with a hook to snatch a container. "Sometimes we might have to make five attempts to take one box off," Steve says. When they couldn't tie up, they might have to work for six to eight hours at a time passing cargo across. And sometimes, when the sea was relatively calm, they'd tie on and have five hoses out delivering water and fuel and cement and materials for the drilling operation, and weather would come up and break the hoses. Making a supply delivery could take one day or three, and the crew would be working straight through with no rest to speak of. "You might lay out on deck with your work suit on and sleep for ten minutes," Steve says.

A floating oil rig is moored in place with eight or more anchors weighing up to 40,000 pounds apiece, and Steve worked on one of the vessels that moves these anchors about, sets them and retrieves them again later. Serious work that takes very large and strong tugs.

Finally, Steve spent two years chasing stray icebergs on the *Freedom Service,* a 220-foot-long supply boat, 42 feet wide and 20 feet deep. They worked out of St. John's, Newfoundland. The field was seven days' run north, and *Freedom Service* might be at sea for a couple of months. She could fuel up and get everything she needed from a big supply boat that came out regularly. Crew change was accomplished by helicopter, which usually landed on the drill ship or an oil rig, though once it landed on pack ice alongside the *Freedom Service* and the men walked out to it from the boat.

Ice is a serious threat to the oil-drilling rigs. Whenever an iceberg came within a dozen miles of a test rig, the *Freedom Service* would be dispatched out to deflect it one way or the other. At all times, they'd keep as far from the iceberg as they could. "If you hit one," Steve says, "it's like hitting steel. We just nudged a growler [little iceberg] once, and put two huge dents in the boat." Using a 5,000-foot floating poly line, they would encircle the iceberg, shackle the two ends together, and tow the ice away from the rig. Occasionally it would tow them—Steve remembers one pulling them backward at two knots. Bergs could tip over and tangle the line, and it would take six or eight hours to unsnarl it. Some bergs would be too big for one vessel to handle—they'd weigh as much as eleven million tons—and two boats would pass the rope around it. "They'd be so big that the temperature would drop twenty or thirty degrees when you got close," Steve says.

There's a lot of talk about how hard fishing is, and he won't belittle that, but off-shore supply at least rivals offshore fishing for treacherousness. A lot of guys get hurt. Steve says he never had any major injuries, but some of the "minor" ones still bother him fifteen years later. He sloughs it off. "We all have those. It's a younger man's sport." He loved the deep-sea work when he was doing it. He could still do off-shore work, he says, and probably better than he used to. "We're slower as we get older, but we're so much wiser. We know where to be, how to work." He admits he's happy to be in the harbor now. Yes, it's tame, "but that's why I'm doing it." He likes being home with his kids. "And the money's right there, too.

"Offshore supply is one of the toughest marine businesses there is," says Steve. "The people in supply boats don't get credit for what they do."

8
Freshwater

In October 2001, the *Mount McKay* came to Duluth, the largest port on the Great Lakes. Built in Buffalo in 1908 of riveted iron, she was modernized in 1948 with a Kahlenberg oil engine, a popular engine of its day on the Lakes, although years back, Kahlenbergs were banned from commercial use because they were such extraordinary polluters. (It's not an issue anymore. There are very few left, and this is the only one of its size still running.)

The boat had been laid up in Michigan City, Indiana, since 1989, and when a man from Duluth bought her, he hired Captain Franz VonRiedel of Zenith Tugboat Company to bring her home. There was no reason to think her huge, archaic engine wouldn't be happy to go back to work—the sellers had assured him that everything aboard was just fine and that she was well equipped with everything she could need. He'd allowed two days in Indiana to figure out how the engine worked and make it do so—how much time could it take?—and then they would head out.

Four men went down for the trip: Franz, engineer Brian Elfving, and two men as deckhands. Franz and Brian had seen the old Kahlenberg engines before, but never run them—which was true of the sellers, too. The thing stands eight feet tall; it's only four feet wide but eighteen feet long, and it has a flywheel four feet in diameter. It's air-start, explains Franz, but if one or more cylinders won't take off, you have to heat the huge glow plug with a blowtorch until she lights up. "A good engineer, which Elfving surely is, can just tell by listening which cylinders are going and which aren't. You get to know the old gals better than your wife. You can tell what they need by their sounds, smells and temperatures. They talk to you, if you're willing to listen." Franz feels the Kahlenbergs are the best engines ever made.

It's a six-cylinder engine, each cylinder producing 65 horsepower. The cylinders are exposed and wrapped in small quarter-inch or less pipes and the copper lines that make up the oiling system. It has to be oiled by hand—every half hour, thirty or forty little drip cups have to be adjusted to drip the right amount onto each bearing and part. (After the engine uses the oil, it just throws it out and into the bilge. No wonder the things were banned!) It's a beautiful engine that would run forever with no heat buildup once it was adjusted right. (It took them a little time to get everything just so, with a half turn on one valve and a quarter turn on another, until the cooling water was coming at the right rate.) There is no reduction gear; the propeller turns at the same rate as the engine. "They say it'll burn anything," Franz says. "Pour Pepsi in it, and it'll turn over."

Franz and his gang spent a day figuring it out and another day in sea trials learning how to actually run it. Since it's a direct-reversing rig—you stop the engine and fire it up again in reverse to back down—they found the first trip off the dock to be a little scary. You don't know for sure that you'll make that reverse on the first go, · but you have no chance to learn how—you just have to do it. They got it right.

Despite the sellers' assurances that everything worked, nothing did. They had no lights, no radar, nothing whatever. Nonetheless, they headed out on the third day, leaving early in the morning so they'd have all day to tinker. By dark, there were decapitated extension cords connecting things, and duct tape everywhere. They did have GPS, because they'd brought it with them, but there still was no radar, nor even a compass. "But the engine ended up running great," Franz says, "and in the daytime we didn't run the generator because we didn't need any electricity. The engine makes a wonderful *pblump-pblump-pblump* sound—you'd feel it rather than hear it—and it burns practically no fuel at all."

All there is in the pilothouse is a steering wheel, a bell pull, and, on the ceiling, a little electric buzzer to the engine room. The *Mount McKay*'s a bell boat to this day, dependent upon the engineer to run the engine. There are remnants of an attempt made to install a chain system so the helmsman could control the engine from the wheelhouse, but that never worked. Probably wouldn't have been a good idea anyway. If the engine were shut down but the shaft was still turning—which you couldn't tell from the wheelhouse—the engine would start back up again in the same direction it had been going. "And if you want to be in reverse," Franz says, "chances are very good you don't want to be going forward again!"

At the top of Lake Michigan, they realized they were going through oil like crazy and were going to run out by midday the next day. They went in to Frankfort, Michigan, tied up, and pumped the oil out of the bilge into the reservoir tanks, hundreds of gallons of it. To reclaim it, they filtered it with flannel shirts, or whatever they could find lying around, and went on their way again.

It was getting dark as they approached Gray's Reef, a treacherous area of Lake Michigan. With no radar or compass, they didn't want to go through at night, but they figured out a safe way to keep going. The *Salty Dog No. 1*, a big calcium chloride barge, was coming up behind them. They ran over to the edge of the channel, shut down, and called him on the radio. "We're having engine problems. Go on by," they told the barge. As he passed by, they fired back up again and followed his stern lights closely until the danger was past.

By morning they'd gotten through the Straits of Mackinaw and the Soo locks. "I went back to take a little nap—I hadn't slept in a couple of days. The deckhand was wheeling," Franz says. "He ran us aground on Martin's Reef." Martin's Reef is marked by a light set atop some cribwork, but the *McKay* went too close and bounced right off the rocks. "He didn't get us stuck, but he hit hard—knocked me right out of bed. We had to take sledgehammers to the hatches—they hadn't been opened in a while—to get down into the ballast tanks and make sure everything was OK."

They took off across Lake Superior on a course for the Keweenaw Peninsula, where a canal cuts across the peninsula and saves a lot of mileage on the lake. Again, Franz headed below for a nap. In three hours, the engineer was pounding on his door. They were on a collision course with three ships, all calling on the radio,

Franz VonRiedel was hugging the quarter bitts to catch this storm picture.
COURTESY OF ZENITH TUGBOAT COMPANY.

and the lights on the *Mount McKay* weren't working. "Well, I got us out of that and got back on course to the Keweenaw. Of course, we always get to these places just as it's getting dark." By the little town of Houghton, partway through the cut, the fog came in. "GPS is one thing, but on a river in fog, with no radar and no spotlight, it's not much help. It was one of the scariest moments I've seen," Franz says. "What an eerie feeling, having your river literally disappear." He rang for slow ahead, and they peered out the windows in amazement, wondering where the river could have gone.

"The guys had been cooking chili on the engine heads because the stove in the galley didn't work. They were all so excited about eating their damn chili—and in the pilothouse too. Don't ask me why. The fog was getting so bad, I finally had to say, 'Get that crap out of here and shut the lights off. I can't see a thing out here!'"

They hung out the doors, idling along, listening for sounds and blowing the whistle to listen for echoes, just like the old steamer captains did. The *McKay*'s whistle works on compressed air, like a steam whistle. The fog finally cleared up a little overhead, but it was still thick down on the water, and they couldn't see any buoys or the canal banks. "We could see the tree lines, and all of a sudden there was no more river. We were dead-ended, trees all around us—it looked like we were in the woods."

The *Mount McKay* in Duluth in October 2001, just after her arrival.
COURTESY OF ZENITH TUGBOAT COMPANY.

Franz checked the charts and determined that there was no way they could have taken a wrong turn—the channel had to be out there. "It seemed like forever—it was probably fifteen minutes—and then we could see that the river took a turn to the right there." The cul-de-sac had been an optical illusion.

They reached the north end of the cut at midnight or two in the morning. One of the deckhands said he'd heard a weather forecast: the wind would be on their tail, ten miles an hour, three- to five-foot seas. "I should have verified that myself," Franz says in retrospect. Once more, he tried for a little sleep. This time he woke up to things crashing off the table. "The boat was rocking good. The seas were building. It was raining and miserable out there. It's a twenty-four-hour run from the cut to Duluth, and we're several hours into it and it's getting rougher. We never thought to turn around, and we couldn't even get off our course now, it was building so." The wind was on their nose. If they'd tried to go across it, they might easily have capsized.

The Coast Guard was calling them, but the radio was so bad that they couldn't communicate. They were the only ones left on the lake—all the ships had gone in somewhere to hide. The seas had grown to twenty feet. They would push the tug right out of the water, and then she'd crash down in the trough, throwing green water over the pilothouse. "The whole boat was trashed. The galley was turned upside-down. It was raining down the hull plating that makes up the engine room walls, and the old riveted hull plating was shaking loose. The pumps were going like crazy, and we all had our survival suits out—we thought we were all done."

But they made it, and in Duluth the tug was cleaned up and put to work doing a little icebreaking and towing—though not much, because of the inconvenience of her direct-reversing engine. The plating went back into shape on its own. She can break two feet of ice easily, so she was used to keep the docks open in the fall and loosen them up again in the spring. "She's a museum piece, completely original. Her navigation equipment is all original too," Franz says, "because there is none."

She blows big smoke rings three feet across and sends fireballs out the stack if her timing's not adjusted properly. "Two times, the Coast Guard has come out to see if we were on fire. And of course you can't run the bilge pumps, or you have a slick of oil behind you." Instead, they pump the used oil into a truck. "Back in the good old days, no one cared." Franz would like to rig up a pan to catch and reuse it.

When the owner of the boat died in 2003, the boat was laid up. At nearly a hundred years old, the *Mount McKay* may have finally retired. But Franz still believes in her. He bought her to seed a little maritime museum for the area. He has already made some hull repairs and intends to get her going again. She will live on.

Duluth

Duluth is the largest port in the Great Lakes, sixteenth in the country, with 1,100 vessels handling about two billion dollars' worth of cargo a year. Iron ore and coal account for by far the greatest share of the shipping; these cargoes come in by rail and go out by ship. Grain is the next largest product going out of Duluth, and lumber, stone, and lime come in by ship. Ever since 1899, the port was served by a single docking company, Great Lakes Towing. It's the largest American-flagged tug company in the Great Lakes, operating thirty-eight towboats on the five lakes and the St. Lawrence Seaway. They have three boats based in Duluth: the *Kentucky,* built in 1929, the *North Dakota* (1910), and the *Minnesota* (1911). All have 1,000-horsepower 12-278A Cleveland diesels.

While there are also a couple of marine contracting companies with towing services, in 2000 Franz VonRiedel saw an opportunity to get into ship-assist work along with the miscellaneous towing jobs he had been doing. While all docking in Duluth is done on a long-term contract basis by Great Lakes Towing, he managed to obtain a few contracts for his Zenith Tugboat Company and was encouraged about his docking prospects in years to come. Zenith and its affiliate, Acme Marine Services, own or lease five tugs and a few other vessels. Until recently, they still used the old *Mount McKay* occasionally, too. The most modern of their tugs is the *Jodi Elizabeth,* built in 1956. Their primary docking tug is the diesel-electric *Seneca,* a 1939 former navy tug,

Approaching the Duluth Ship Canal is the 1927 tug *Kansas* towing a dead ship in winter conditions.
COURTESY OF ZENITH TUGBOAT COMPANY.

later, for a time, called the *Mary L. McAllister*. They're all single-screw boats, and all but the *Seneca* are clutch boats.

The old boats work well on the Lakes, Franz says. "It's cold up here. There's a lot of ice in our work." The trick to Great Lakes icebreaking is speed and a narrow beam. The sharp bows of the older boats break ice well, and speed gets a pretty good wake rolling.

Towboats get paid well for their services on the lakes, even though they are often small and elderly vessels compared to those on the coasts. Zenith pays crew members by the hour, with an eight-hour guarantee and time and a half after that.

In New York's Erie Canal, the little tug *Benjamin Elliott* pushes a load of piers destined for the New Jersey Turnpike. This lock is much smaller than those on the Mississippi River system. Courtesy of Don Sutherland.

They can go home when the work's done—usually that's less than eight hours' work, but sometimes it's twelve, perhaps even for weeks at a time. "We're glad to give them a break the rest of the time," says Franz's wife Jodi, Zenith's treasurer.

They always run crews of three, though they are all day boats. When Franz visited Maine, he was very surprised to find just two men on the Fournier tugs. "It's unheard-of out here." And Franz is particular about who he hires. When people ask to apply for a deckhand position, he says he has no use for deckhands. "I hire engineers only, and you better know how to throw a line. These aren't steam tugs—if the engineer is going to be hiding below when we're about to make up to a tow, he'll be on the street." He wants everyone to be an engineer because he loves the old engines and therefore wants everyone else to appreciate them too. "I say that sarcastically, but in reality, if you've got the mechanics of a tug down, chances are you'll be a better captain. Everyone benefits from having minimal wear on the machinery."

Icebreaking on the River

The incoming tide drove ice quickly upriver past the *Thunder Bay*, a Coast Guard icebreaking tug out of Rockland, Maine. "But at least it's in little pieces," said Lieutenant Jim Andrews, the commanding officer, as they readied for a second trip from Bath up the Kennebec River. The goal was Gardiner, about twenty miles north. At the request of the State of Maine, the Coast Guard was opening the river to minimize spring flooding. The day before, March 7, 2001, accompanied by the smaller Coast Guard icebreaker *Shackle* from Portland, the *Thunder Bay* had reached the Richmond bridge. It was the first time in a dozen years that an icebreaker had gone that far up the river.

Chief Bos'n's Mate Paul Dupuis had the controls when the *Thunder Bay* left the Stinson sardine canning factory on the Bath side of the river. "You're too awesome!" said executive officer (XO) Steve Ramassini to the chief as *Thunder Bay* walked smoothly sideways from the ship she had been tied to. "He's using only the wind and the current, with just a little bit of rear," he explained, meaning that Paul was relying on the engine only a little bit, in reverse at slow speed. No rudder, no switching gears forward and back or messing with the throttle.

Normally, the job of handling the wheel goes to one of the lower-ranked men aboard, but Lieutenant Junior Grade Ramassini likes to take the wheel once in a while. "It's good to go back, remember how it feels." Before you get after an inexperienced seaman who is having trouble keeping his course in a current, it's good to be reminded of how hard it is.

Captain Andrews believes that putting the most junior people on the helm is the best experience he can give them—a responsibility and learning opportunity that they might not be given on a larger ship. "We thrust them into it right off. We work toward having them not just stand there parroting orders but to think about it and use their noggin, be part of the ship's operation. He's got the best view—he's right in the center—and he can see the stick on the bow and see which way the boat is going."

If an order doesn't make sense to the helmsman, left when he'd expect right, for instance, he simply asks, "Command, sir?" and if there's a mistake, the conning officer will catch himself.

There are no women on the *Thunder Bay*. She has just two berthing spaces for enlisted crew, so there would have to be six or seven women if there were any. The best place for a woman would be as commanding officer, Jim says, because the CO has a private cabin. There have been female COs on *Thunder Bay*'s sister icebreakers on the Great Lakes.

Thunder Bay has a single propeller, described by her captain as "about as tall as me." The single screw is suited for her job, as it is well protected amidships. She runs on the direct-current diesel-electric propulsion system, with engines to run generators to run electric motors that provide 2,500 horsepower to turn the propeller. She has no thrusters to help her maneuver, just ship handling. Her hull is reinforced with thick plating to withstand the pressures of ice, and her bow profile, with a knuckle at the waterline, allows her to climb up onto an ice pan and crush it. Her windows are heated, and polarized shields can be lowered over them when the glare off the ice is too great. She is 140 feet long, draws 12 1/2 feet, and her beam is nearly 38 feet. All winter, she is on a three-week rotation with two other cutters, working the Penobscot River and local harbors. This Kennebec trip was out of the ordinary.

Soon, the icebreaker reached a section of refrozen brash where a track had been broken the day before. A crewmember stood on the bow ready to drop the anchor in a trice should there be trouble. *Thunder Bay* ground on through, *Shackle* behind her and a little to starboard, widening the open channel.

At the Richmond swing bridge, some ten miles from Bath, cranes were on hand to raise the power lines to make room for *Thunder Bay*. The bridge swung open. It's a narrow span, sixty-three feet. "You gonna squeeze through there?" someone asked.

"Get some grease," suggested the XO.

The original plan was that the sixty-five-foot *Shackle* would go through the bridge first, breaking a path for the *Thunder Bay*. But the little vessel, backing and bashing forward, climbing onto the ice, breaking it under her weight and backing off again, could barely progress a half of her own length with each attack. At that rate, the pair had no chance of reaching Gardiner by nightfall. *Thunder Bay* took the lead.

The *Thunder Bay* can slide right through up to thirty inches of ice, but snow makes for harder going. The six inches of snow on top of a foot and a half or more of ice at the bridge brought her to a stop. Twice, she had to stop, back, and ram forward before she cleared the bridge. It was tight—it didn't look like twelve feet on each side—but at least there was a good frozen cushion between hull and bridge abutment.

And beyond was virgin ice, smooth and snow-covered, complete with snowmobile tracks. It seemed like driving a boat across an open field. It was very loud, with the boat rumbling and growling and vibrating in a slower, crunchier rhythm than in open water. Navigation in fast ice is easy, said Steve. (Fast ice is held solidly on both banks.) "If something's wrong, you pull the throttle back, and you stop."

"I get paid for this," said Texan Jonathan Cripe incredulously as he stood on the afterdeck. He is on the engineering team, ranked MK3, machinery technician third class. "MK means Machine Killer," he said. "It's a Coast Guard joke." He has been on the boat longer than most of the others, and he loves his job. He had hoped to work on helicopters, but even though he'd never been on boats before joining the Coast Guard, he says he wouldn't want to leave the water now.

He'd prefer to be somewhere a little less cold, but on this trip, in the lee of the superstructure where he was standing, the sun was wonderfully warm. And to think, some folks pay money to go on cruises in the Caribbean.

The Coast Guard icebreaker *Thunder Bay* heads across a meadow of ice touched only by snowmobiles.
AUTHOR PHOTO.

Just before the final corner of the planned trip, the ice and snow became too much for *Thunder Bay* to just keep chugging through. She had to stop and back and crash forward a couple of times before continuing the rest of the way, and then, still at full throttle, she moved at less than three knots instead of the nearly four she'd made earlier. But she got to Gardiner, which had been the captain's hope if not his totally confident expectation. They were being met there by a crewmember in the boat's van. "How will I find you?" he had asked the captain. "We'll be the 140-foot icebreaker tied up there," Jim told him.

Docking wasn't easy. "When the water's solid, it's really hard to go sideways," remarked Captain Andrews, watching his junior officer struggling with the task. Chief Dupuis also watched every aspect of it carefully.

Was it hard for him not to have the conn? One might have thought he was glad it wasn't his problem this time, but no. "I always want to be driving," he said. "When I first came aboard, they used to ask me, 'Chief, do you want to drive?' I told 'em, 'It's always yes—just tell me when I can.'"

Even when he's not in charge of the movement of the ship, he continued, "I always like to consider how would I handle each situation—there's always more than one way to do something."

Even though the job wasn't done gracefully, neither the chief nor the captain was critical of the younger officer, and they allowed him to finish the docking. There was no danger, and he was learning.

During the time it took to dock the *Thunder Bay*, the sun lowered in the sky and the breeze picked up. The air lost its Caribbean feel. *Shackle* broke ice along the pier and helped nudge the *Thunder Bay* into place. She finally settled into her berth under the eyes of the many spectators who'd come out to admire the strange sight of two icebreakers in town.

River Work Runs in the Blood

The towboats of the American river systems don't look much like saltwater tugboats but they share common characteristics and a common purpose: they are extremely powerful vessels whose function is simply to move barges. That they do it in inland waterways that don't have ocean weather makes their job no less difficult, and they move tremendous amounts of cargo along the nation's inland waterways. The Mississippi River System—some fifteen thousand miles of the main river and its sixteen navigable tributaries—spans the country from Pittsburgh to Sioux City and from Minneapolis/St. Paul to the Gulf of Mexico, below New Orleans. Nearly 70 percent of

Coal barges on the Ohio River, 1953. AUTHOR'S COLLECTION, PHOTOGRAPHER UNKNOWN.

the grain grown in the Midwest is barged down the river system, and agricultural production from the interior Northwest travels similarly down the Snake, Columbia, and Willamette Rivers. Coal and petroleum transport are also big business on the river systems. On just the Ohio River, where Captain Jim Cheatham has spent most of his working life, annual commercial traffic averages more than 150 million tons, most of it consisting of bulk forms of energy: coal, crude oil, and petroleum products. Other major commodities transported include sand, gravel, iron and steel, chemicals, and grain.

Jim Cheatham's first job on the river doesn't exist anymore; he rafted logs down the Ohio with his stepfather. When he started his river career in 1962, he "didn't know a ratchet from a tow knee." By 1969 he was in the wheelhouse, and there he is still, working forty to sixty days at a crack. "Most go thirty, but with wages not keeping up with inflation, I have to work longer to live like my family is accustomed to. Typical guy is thirty on, fifteen off, now."

It's been a while since the log rafts came down the river. But Jim remembers when mules dragged the sawlogs to the riverbank. "One of the boys fed my lunch to a mule once," he says.

"One of my jobs was to take a cant hook—a big, long wooden-handle thing with a metal hook on the end of it—and roll the logs down to the river." They'd roll the logs into the river, bind them together with chain dogs, and create a big flotilla of them "fixed so two boats could control them and get inside locks with them." They didn't want to have to tear the whole thing apart to get through a lock.

They'd make the rafts six hundred feet long, each consisting of a couple of thousand logs, with a boat on each end. By today's standards, the boats were very small—sixty or seventy feet at most, with two or three hundred horsepower. They had living quarters on them, and cooking facilities, but just one deck with a little pilothouse standing by itself. The engine room was built down into the boat. "One boat would pull, the other one would be on the back end, holding it all straight so it didn't go all over the place, and both boats would work together getting into locks.

"You had to walk the rafts every day, which was very dangerous, but you had to keep the dogs tight or you'd lose the logs. My dad wouldn't let me do that—said if anything happened to me, my mother would never forgive him." There was just a captain and a man on each boat. "We lived on those boats, ate on those boats—gone thirty days, forty, fifty days, to make up these rafts and get 'em down. We'd stop for the night, tie off to the bank, trees, or whatever we could find. Those guys been working the rivers so long, they knew where to go, depending what they wanted to do—like, if they wanted to go to town, they'd know where to tie up.

"The old sawmills is about gone," Jim says. All the timber nowadays goes by truck, and there's not many men left who would know how to bring a raft of logs down the river.

He loves the history the rivers represent. The Ohio, he says, "is history just by itself." He describes the first vessel to come down it: "a beat-out canoe, made from a log by Indians." Then the river became a major highway for settlers headed west. "Pittsburgh was the starting point for the way west from New York and Pennsylvania, where people came in on boats from Ireland, and so on. This is where people drawing their family tree go back to, Cumberland Gap and the Ohio River."

He describes the two kinds of river-users in the decades before and after 1800: "Settlers going west built a flat-bottomed boat, put everything they could get on it—chickens and cows and everything—and floated to Cairo, Illinois." From there they went overland north to St. Louis, the gateway to the west.

The second batch of river-boaters loaded up a keelboat with anything they could sell and went to New Orleans. It was a rough way to go, he says. There were treacherous rapids along the way, such as the ones at Louisville, which the boats could only negotiate at certain times. Now there are bypasses and locks, of course. When they got to New Orleans, "no way were they gonna get these things back upriver—they'd sell their cargo, dismantle the boat, and sell the lumber. Lumber was almost worth its weight in gold in New Orleans. They'd come back by the Natchez Trace. That was a dangerous stretch—a lot of people were robbed and killed."

Today, Jim says, "The Ohio River is nine hundred miles of harbor. Dock after dock after dock—gasoline docks, refineries, grain docks, chemical docks, rock docks—you name it, it's there. The closer you get to Pittsburgh, the closer all that is together. The river traffic hauls more commodities for less money than any other way." And he himself has pushed some of it all, at one time or another: "Coal, gasoline, flight fuel. When they started the Space Shuttle, we brought it down the Tennessee River. (You talk about security—*that* was security!) Alcohol, high potency—the taxes alone on one bargeful are a million bucks. Sometimes salt, cottonseed, or seed, or most anything, going up. Or empty barges to go to the grain elevators to be filled. One time, I picked up a grain barge in St. Paul and took it to St. Louis, and I took that same barge of grain back to St. Paul. It had been sold four or five times in the meantime. Somebody made some money on it, and we got paid for pushing it.

"You never know what you're carrying till the office tells you, 'Pick up barge so-and-so at this place.' Everything has at one time or another been shipped on the river."

And Jim is awed by the world of the rivers. "Even today, I pass by a big bluff, and I look up and wonder if an Indian were up there today, what he would think. They were the first Americans."

On the rivers, the boats are called towboats. Jim admits the name is backward because towboats always *push* their barges. But that's what they're called, nonetheless. Inland, a tug is a smaller boat that is called on to assist when picking up and dropping barges or sometimes when going through bridges.

As on coastwise tugs, the boats carry two watches, with a captain and a pilot each heading up a watch. Jim sometimes sails as captain, sometimes as pilot; the only difference—not an insignificant one—is that the captain is ultimately responsible for the boat. (On the rivers, the term *pilot* refers both to the equivalent of the bluewater *mate* and, more generically, to a person running a towboat.) Watches work six hours on, six hours off. As on blue water, the captain has what they call the forward watches, from six to twelve, and the pilot has the after watches, the twelve-to-sixes (only for some reason the watches actually start a half-hour before those hours). The crew varies, but is likely to be the two officers, a mate (who on the rivers runs the deck), an engineer, and two deckhands. Used to be a cook, too, but, as on the East

The towboat *Charles F. Detmar* running light. COURTESY OF JIM CHEATHAM.

Coast tugs, the companies found that scrapping the cook's position was an easy way to save money.

Jim describes the midnight watch. "We get called at eleven to go on at eleven-thirty. I'm one of the quick ones. I get up and wash my face and brush my teeth—I take a shower before I go to bed—and in ten or fifteen minutes I'm ready.

"First thing is, the deckhand checks all the barges for water—they have hatches on the side of them—in case they bumped a bridge too hard, or a rock." (If a barge is found to be taking on water, the first step is to take pumps out from the boat and try to get enough water out of the barge to see where it's coming in. They carry shingles and oakum and other materials for making emergency patches. If they can't patch it well enough, they may have to take the barge to a shipyard to be repaired—if there's a yard handy. Or they may have to get someone with a crane to offload to another barge.) "Then the deckhand checks all the rigging, steel cables, ratchets, what have you. Then he starts cleaning—sweep, mop, dust.

"The pilot's on deck—all he does is drive the boat. If it's a real clear night, and you don't have a lot of obstructions in this particular stretch of river, your mind wanders. You think about a lot of things: you make yourself a millionaire—you think

The pilothouse controls of a river towboat: two controls with a pair of levers each are for steering—bottom for forward, top for backing. The three levers in between are throttles for the three engines on this triple-screw vessel. COURTESY OF JIM CHEATHAM.

View from the pilothouse. COURTESY OF JIM CHEATHAM.

about how you miss your folks—you think about what you got to do when you get home. You been on the river year after year, you do your steering by looking automatically. You don't even think—you see, you go, it's just as quick as that.

"The midnight-to-six is a lonely watch. You got your music radio, and we have three VHF radios—it's regulation that you monitor 13 and 16, and the other's the walkie-talkie for when the guy walks out on the tow—but it's a whole different world by yourself. You're in two separate worlds, really, your own dream world and the work world.

"Things is not as fast out there on the river as on land. Your top speed, running with the current, is ten or twelve mile an hour. Northbound, two-and-a-half to seven. You get out there, you get thinking what am I doing here?

"But once you're home a day or two, you start getting restless and you're ready to go again."

While the image one has is of the towboat pushing its huge flotilla of barges along, a goodly amount of a watch is spent dropping barges, picking up barges, and negotiating locks and bridges. Without a delay, above St. Louis there'll be at least one lock per watch, Jim says. Maybe there won't be a bridge on every watch, but they're a challenge, too.

Most of the towboat companies own their own barges, but the company that Jim works for pushes for other people. "We're trampin'," he says. "Take whatever we can get."

There are several types of barges, to carry different cargoes and to make up different parts of a tow. The main cargo barges are either open hopper barges or cover tops, whose covers can be removed and stacked on each end. There are two other sizes, but the most common barge is 195 feet long and 35 feet wide with a 13-foot hold. It draws nine feet of water when fully loaded. On the upper rivers, it would most likely be loaded only to 1,400 tons, whereas on the lower river it would carry 1,600 tons because the water is deeper. Petroleum barges are wider.

Every type of barge comes in two hull configurations: box and rake. The body of a box barge is square throughout, while a rake barge has a bevel on one end to go through the water more easily. A bevel barge is much faster than a square one, especially against the current. Also, when just in front of the towboat, it gives the wheelwash a place to go when the towboat backs down. Stopping a tow is slower with a square barge-end butted up to the towboat.

A captain tries to pick up tows in units of four or five barges apiece, with a rake on both ends and two or three boxes in the middle. "Lots of times it doesn't work that way, though." A typical tow on the Upper Mississippi is fifteen to seventeen barges, three strings of five apiece, and perhaps an empty barge on one or both sides of the towboat. "Loaded barges are too hard to steer on the hip." Sometimes there's one more barge, known as a spike barge, all by itself on the head of the tow. That puts a 35-foot wide, 195-foot long open place on either side, making bridges and locks that much harder to manage. The whole tow is likely to be very nearly 1,200 feet long, the length of a long lock. "I always said that if I died and came back as a barge, I didn't want to come back as a spike or a hip barge—boy, do they get a lot of cussing!"

On the Ohio and the upper rivers, a tow of hopper or cover tops can have thirty barges, while on the Lower Mississippi, where there are no locks, the standard tow is thirty-five barges and the record is over seventy.

Towboats vary in size and horsepower. "When I first started working out there," Jim says, "a 3,200- to an 1,800-horsepower was a big boat. Nowadays, they got 10,500 horsepower. Twelve-hundred is nothing—just a harbor tug anymore." The big boats are up to two hundred feet long, forty-five feet high, with three or four decks. The quarters for the men are palatial—though on an older boat, says Jim, "the shine leaves it." They're between twenty-eight and fifty-four feet wide, and typically have a triple-screw configuration to deal with the shallow waters of the rivers.

The barges get picked up and dropped off at "fleets" or "parking lots." These are simply places on the river where there's something on shore to tie off to. Often a tug comes out to help. "You might spend twelve or fourteen hours dropping and picking up barges. An hour a barge, you figure, though sometimes you can drop one in ten minutes."

Locks are another time-consumer. "Every day, you have locks to make. You have to go through in one locking, if you can—there's so much traffic." Between St. Louis and St. Paul there are only three 1,200-foot locks, and the rest—some two dozen of them—are only 600 feet long. On the Ohio, it's the other way around. All but three of the twenty locks are 1,200 feet long. Throughout the river system, they're 110 feet in width; a tow is usually 105 or 108 feet wide.

"That don't give you but two feet to play with to get in there. It's a challenge every time you try to do that." When the water's high, it gets even more difficult, particularly going downstream. When the flow gets so fast, sometimes they open the dam up wide, putting a tremendous outdraft on the wall at the approach to the lock, which usually sets along one shore beside the dam. The outdraft is like a funnel, pulling the boat and tow out into the river, away from the lock and toward the dam. If there's no helper tug, it can be very difficult to get the tow against the wall to approach the lock. "You've got a man out on the front of the tow and he's got a check-line, and both of us together are trying to hold you against the wall. But it's a six-hundred-foot wall, and you've got a thousand-foot tow. Sometimes the outdraft is so bad, the current gets you broadside onto that dam. That's when you sink barges, or turn 'em over, or hang 'em up on the dam." And what happens to the towboat? "If you're fast enough and have a good enough crew, you can knock the boat away from the tow, get your boat in the clear. Save your crew first."

"There has been some sunk." Jim says he's never had it happen to him, thank God, but he's seen it. Three or four boats get in this trouble every year.

You might have to wait six to twelve hours for your turn in a lock. If it's a short lock, six hundred feet, you'll have to break up the tow, send through nine barges first, and follow through with the boat and the rest of the barges. On the Ohio, if you have thirty barges, the tow will be broken down so a helper tug can take half the barges through. It's to everyone's advantage to make locks as quickly as possible.

In planning for a break, the tow is put together with a different rigging between the barges where the break will be so as to simplify the process later.

"You push nine barges in, tie them off—say, on the left hand side—then back out." The lock keepers lock the first set of barges down, and then use a machine cable to pull those nine out of the lock and tie them off outside. "Then you shove the rest in, go through, couple back up, and go." It takes an hour and a half to do it. That's when a line of boats waiting to pass the lock might form. In a twelve-hundred-foot lock, the tow needn't be broken up. A single locking only takes fifteen or twenty minutes.

Tank barges are up to 297 feet long and 54 feet wide. They also can be either boxes or rakes, and a unit tow is from a thousand to eleven hundred feet long. "We haul everything in them—gasoline, fuel oil, diesel, even manure."

Maneuvering the short locks is, of course, different with the wider petroleum barges. Jim describes going upriver: "A six-hundred-foot lock, you get part of the tow in, tie it off on the left, say, then scoot over to the right of those barges and make up to them. You're 108 feet wide, then. They close the lock gates, lock you up, open the upper gates. You turn the first bunch loose, shove the whole mess out, tie off on the upper wall, turn loose, back down, and hitch on behind again. That's called a set-over."

Wind is always a threat with light barges, which stand up high out of the water and want to sail. "To this day, the wind is my Achilles heel," says Jim. "I hate that wind. You haven't got too much control. You try to get the tow pointed into the wind, but you gotta go up the river sideways sometimes." When it gets too bad, pilots let the wind blow them under a hill, where they hang out until it eases. Making locks with light barges also is affected by the wind. Unless he has an assist tug, Jim won't even try to make the lock with a wind of twenty or twenty-five miles an hour blowing off the wall. "Parking time for me," he says.

The wind is rarely a problem with loaded barges. "I've only had to stop two times," Jim says. In the right wind conditions, Lake Pippin, below St. Paul, gets big waves, rollers. "Barges start coming up and down, and rigging breaks. Then you have to stop."

The locks might seem to be the most difficult part of towing, but actually the river itself is trickier. The channel is supposed to be nine feet deep; of course it's not always. There are always places that silt in, and the height of the river varies both seasonally and day to day. The Coast Guard publishes the river stages every day, and sometimes makes official notification that a certain part of the river has only eight or eight-and-a-half feet of water. The Corps of Engineers dredges from time to time or contracts to have dredging done. Good, experienced pilots know where most of the shallow places are, and of course the towboats have depth sounders, one of them set out on the front of the leading barge. "We're supposed to have nine feet, and when it says eight, we're praying the sounder head is down in the water a foot."

The channel doesn't necessarily stay on one side of the river, but instead meanders back and forth across it. "Every so far, there's a light on the bank," Jim explains. "In old steamboat days, they were kerosene lights, and the government paid farmers to go up and down the river—they might have two or three lights, and they'd fill 'em with kerosene every night. That's what got us started on navigation lights." Later, the lights ran on batteries, but now most of them are solar-powered.

Each light is known by a name and has a mile marker on it. They're green on the right descending bank, and blink just once. The lights on the left, as you go down the river, are red and blink twice. They all have day-markers on them, too, fluorescent-colored boards shaped according to their meaning. If the channel continues straight on through, the markers are square; if the channel changes sides, the board is a diamond shape. There are only lights on the side where the channel is.

Ice creates another challenge for pilots on the northern stretches. "By Thanksgiving, they try to get everything out of St. Paul," says Jim. By December fifteenth, the river is usually shut down. Until it opens back up again in March, there's no barge traffic up there.

They used to try to work the Illinois River when the ice was forming up, Jim recalls, "but it'd be so bad, you couldn't move a half a mile in twelve hours. We used to do what we call mule-training—put one barge in front of you, string the rest behind you, and use the one in front to break the ice. Sometimes you'd have to stop, drop that barge in front of you and drop the line behind you. Then you'd take the boat out in front and break the ice, and try to move again." But the Illinois only has three or four weeks of ice, so a lot of people just tie up till it goes out.

High water brings big changes to the river. With high water come stronger currents that whirl around corners and under bridges, but bridges are a challenge at any time.

The bridges along the upper Mississippi are very narrow and often get hit. "With the water running, you try to get a thousand feet of tow lined up—it's hard. Each one of those barges holds fourteen or fifteen hundred tons, and fifteen of them in front of you is a lot of weight coming down on the Louisiana bridge, say, or the railroad bridges. You gotta put a man in each corner of that tow, talking to you: 'You're six hundred feet above the starboard pier, four or five feet in the dark,' or 'in the bad'— that lets me know I gotta steer to my port side a little bit or we'll hit. Those men are your eyes out there."

There are several bridges that get torn up every year—the town of Louisiana in Missouri has one, Burlington, Iowa, another. More and more often now, a captain will hire a tug to handle the head end of the tow going through while the towboat handles the stern. "Insurance is so high, and your license is in jeopardy."

Some of the bridges have blind approaches. The drawbridges and swing bridges all have radios and can let a towboat know if trains are coming, or let trains know there's a tow coming. "Coming down from Quincy, Illinois, headed on to Hannibal, Missouri, I can't see the bridge. I'll call him from a mile or two out, let him know I'm in the vicinity, and he'll say 'OK, I've got no trains.' Or if he's expecting one, we say a few cuss words to ourselves, because if we have to stop, we get out of shape too much to line up with the bridge.

"But ninety percent of the bridge people are nice, decent people, and they'll hold up a train if they've got time. They have panel boards that light up, I think, and so many miles out they know a train's coming. They have radios, and they'll let him know to start slowing down."

Jim's wife, Rose, used to ride with him on the river occasionally. It was not to her liking. One trip was particularly adventurous, starting with hitting the bridge at Burlington, Iowa. The barges scattered. "We had to gather 'em all up. It happened in slow motion—it seemed to take forever," she says. "I cried when it was all over." And then, later on, the boat caught on fire. "It was some piled-up oil filters or something back aft. He was fixin' to go through a drawbridge, and the bridge tender called and asked if we knew we were on fire. First I thought, 'They must be talking about someone else,' and then I wondered, 'What the hell am I doing here?'"

Towboat *G.R. Packet* with tow. Courtesy of Jim Cheatham.

Pleasure boaters are another reason towboaters make occasional rude remarks under their breath. "Hemorrhoids, that's what I call them," Jim says. "A pain in the butt. They have no idea of the rules and regulations, they don't know anything about safety—they'll drop a water skier right in front of you. Even when you have a wide river, they've got to be right in front of you." He admits that, once in a while, one will radio him and ask the best course to keep out of his way, but it's unusual.

Meeting traffic also offers its challenges. There are places on the rivers where there isn't room for one tow to pass another, and there are blind corners. Downbound traffic has the right of way; ascending has to get clear. A descending pilot will make security calls on channel 13, the bridge-to-bridge channel on the river as on the ocean, to alert others that he's coming. Anyone headed his way will answer. "As southbound, you just take his word that he's gonna be where you tell him to be."

An experienced pilot will be tracking a boat mentally once he's heard a call, five or ten miles ahead. "We can always tell a green pilot—he's telling his position every mile post. He's either scared to death, or he wants everyone to know he's a pilot."

A pilot takes immeasurable pride in what he is. He knows it's taken him a long time to get where he is; it takes time to learn about the river. A person who would like to become a pilot comes aboard as a steersman, working under a pilot as an apprentice. "A steersman comes on, you don't teach him—there's no such word on the river—you got to learn him the river."

Jim's son Jimbo is a pilot too. He's been riding riverboats most of his life. "My first trip I can barely remember—I was a little-bitty guy." But he can tell you the name of the boat, the *Chicago Trader,* and he knows she was 1,400 or 1,600 horsepower, very small by today's standards. The summer before first grade, he rode with his father from St. Louis to St. Paul, a trip of ten days to two weeks. His teacher didn't believe his "what I did on my summer vacation" story about steering a riverboat. "She thought I lied. I swelled up and cried," says Jimbo. His dad straightened her out the next time he was home, and she apologized to them both. "I was raised with the river. It was nothing new to me, but I always looked forward to going on the boat," says Jimbo.

He considered a number of professions and tried a few, but kept coming back to the river. "I always got bored with everything else I've done. On the river, I've never got bored." He went steersman with his dad for a year and was thrown loose, as the rivermen call being pronounced ready to go it alone. His license permits him to run any vessel on the Western river system, the Mississippi and all its tributaries. He's upgrading his license now, and would like eventually to get an unlimited master's license with international endorsement. Presently, he runs the *Mary Lynn,* a small towboat, from St. Louis to St. Paul, a 667-mile stretch of the upper Mississippi River, but he'd like to run the big boats that take as many as fifty-six barges to New Orleans. "I've seen a lot of guys who say they wouldn't do that again, but I'd like to do it." Or he might like to get onto cruise ships. There are so many possibilities.

In the meantime, he's not leaving the river. He likes the money and the time off—working thirty days and getting fifteen off is certainly appealing for a fellow who wants to see the world—but there's a lot more to it. "Out there it's my connection—to myself, to my spiritual guides." For Jimbo, the river has always been a place of healing. "I've been pretty much broken, and the river brings me back."

"There's so much to learn, it can overtake you sometimes—but God gave me the gift to learn it. Without my faith, I don't know if I would have it. I don't say, I'm gonna make this bridge—I take the assist from God's hand. I kinda flow with him." And Jimbo likes learning. "There's a lot of rivers for me to learn."

The best learning, says Jim the elder, is on-the-job training: "Be there, do it. You gotta know your river." And Jim says that each river is actually five or six different ones, depending on conditions, and a pilot has to know what to do in each one of those rivers. "You take a nice day with conditions normal, that's one, and then at night the river changes completely, and you gotta depend on your radar and your knowledge, what you see in your head, to know where you're at." Rain creates another river—when it's too heavy, the radar shuts out. High water is another issue. So is fog: "Nothing looks the same. Ninety-nine percent of pilots will stop in fog. You hole up. Or at times, if you can't get to the banks, you hold out in the river where you're at. There are rock dikes to keep the river flowing, fingers out into the river, keeps it moving, scouring out the channel—if you get caught in a place like that, it really makes you sweat. And when you got empties, they're just like sailboats. If you got no place to stop, you're really in trouble."

Each lock has different characteristics, and each bridge, and each turn in the river. "You don't just get on a boat and drive it around a bend." Some of those turns the river makes are so severe that you can't simply steer a thousand-foot tow around them. "You gotta do what we call 'flanking' those bends. You work with the current, let the current help you. You get your boat in a certain position and let the current shove you around. You go real slow till you get to a certain point—and you gotta know where this point is, because you gotta start coming ahead with everything that boat's got and shove out of that flank, or it'll take you right into the bend or a sandbar. It's not like getting in an eighteen-wheeler and driving down the street."

"Dad's been at it so long now, it's just like putting on his shoes," says Jimbo.

But it takes more than dedication to the muddy waters to earn respect as river pilot. Jim tells of an old captain he knew when he first came into the pilothouse himself; we'll call him Charlie. Charlie always called himself a company man, but the things that he tried in order to save time or money cost the company more in the long run. Charlie couldn't do things the common way. "He had to try and do it different."

One time, coming down the upper Mississippi, he saw a company barge at a grain dock and decided—wrongly, as it turned out—that the barge was ready to go to St. Louis. Without any orders from the office, he picked it up. The office was not happy when they heard, and by then he was some way down river. He had to tie his tow off and take the barge back. He didn't save any time with that escapade.

Once, on the Ohio, "Charlie took a shortcut that wasn't." When the captain came on watch to relieve him, Charlie was on top of the pilothouse trying to find out where he was. All he could see was willow trees.

It wasn't unusual for Charlie to be out of the wheelhouse anyway. "One day I came upstairs on the outside of the boat at noon to relieve him," says Jim. "No one was in the wheelhouse, and the boat had a dead bead for the bank! I grabbed the wheel and straightened it up. I looked down the steps on the inside of the wheelhouse and there he was, wiping down the wall at the foot of the steps. You could come to the pilothouse about any time, and Charlie might be on top of it or outside doing something, and no one would be at the controls!"

He would not stop in fog either. "If you stopped, he would stand your watch and want you to work part or all of his when the fog cleared," Jim says. "We told him that if he came and took the controls on our watch, then he had them until we would come on watch again. Sometimes the old man worked eighteen hours before he would get relieved."

Charlie was always in a hurry. He couldn't bear waiting for a lock turn if he could help it, and more than once pushed ahead of another tow. When meeting other boats, too, he had to keep going, getting in the way of other vessels and passing too close. "I still meet boats out there that want to know what happened to that captain who always got in the way."

On the Illinois River, Charlie often built his tow backward. He probably thought it would be easier to break it down again. When he got into the Mississippi, he would turn the tow around and get on the other end. This didn't work so well for him one time in high water. He came out of the Illinois without backing the tow down or slowing at all, and told the deck crew to knock the boat out. "Well, they got the boat loose from the tow, but the tow was moving so fast that he couldn't get to the other end fast enough. The tow topped around and hit the rock bank just below Grafton, Illinois." It didn't do much good to the barges that hit first.

This was hardly Charlie's only accident. "I know that one time, coming out of the Illinois River, Charlie ran aground six times in two watches.

"But Charlie thought more of that old boat than he did of his family. If they had let him, he would have lived on it. When it was time to make a crew change, he would stand on the river bank and say, 'There she is, the grand old gal.' Charlie lived and breathed towboating. There was not anything else in the world for him.

"As any riverman will tell you, he will curse and quit the river many times throughout his career, but he will always come back and ask the old river for forgiveness. Just like a good love for a woman, a riverman loves the river."

9
Tugs and
Friends Respond to 9/11

Fireboat people certainly don't think of their vessels as tugboats, and tug people are adamant that tugs aren't fireboats, but the fact is that the distinction can be a bit hazy. Tugs often carry serious firefighting equipment, and many tugs have been turned into fireboats or have at least been used to fight fires. Some fireboats have been turned into tugs, too, including a couple from New York that went to New Orleans in the 1990s. New fireboats are very similar to big tractor tugs—Los Angeles has recently had such a new fireboat built—and, as the fireboat *John J. Harvey's* Huntley Gill says, "they're all of a family."

At one time, New York had ten fireboats in service, and they were working all the time. The peak of the port's traffic came during World War II, when 80 percent of all the war materiel headed to Europe went through New York. On one day in March of 1943, there were 540-odd vessels at anchor. With hundreds and hundreds of piers around the harbor, there's no saying how many vessels were docked at that same time. There were fires all the time, says Huntley, who has learned more about fireboats in the last few years than he ever suspected he'd have reason to do. All the cargo was break-bulk—uncontainerized—meaning that cases of highly flammable naphtha might be sitting on a pier right next to cotton bales, as in one example that Huntley cites. And the piers themselves were built with creosoted pilings and timbers—easy burning. There were three big fireboats on the North River alone, going out every day. One of these was the *John J. Harvey,* the nation's first modern fireboat.

In 1999, the *John J. Harvey* went on the auction block, and Huntley and several of his friends bought her. Why? "It was just a mistake," he says, but clearly he feels no such thing.

The 130-foot riveted-steel *Harvey* was commissioned in 1931, the first fireboat with internal combustion engines, which gave her more power for propulsion while pumping than her steam-powered predecessors had. Designed by the well-known firm of Henry Gielow, she was faster through the water than her contemporaries, too, although her steering system took some getting used to. She had two propellers with a single rudder between them, which makes her difficult to handle, particularly in close quarters.

She was converted to diesel-electric in 1957, when she was fitted out with five 600-horse Fairbanks Morse opposed-piston engines. Each of these runs a pump on one end and a generator on the other, and her propellers are actually driven by electricity. She could travel at twenty knots and she could pump 18,000 gallons per minute—that's eighty tons of water a minute, the equivalent of twenty fire engines today—and she had an unlimited supply of water, since she just pulled it from her surroundings. She had eight monitors—water cannons—the largest of which could shoot 3,000 gallons a minute, and she also had reels with 4,500 feet of hose in varying sizes and twenty-four connections for external hoses.

The *Harvey* was called on to pump water at all kinds of disasters. Perhaps her most famous fight was at the 1942 fire that destroyed the huge and supremely luxurious ocean liner *Normandie,* but she was involved with hundreds of other situations, including many pier fires in the 1960s and '70s. (In many of these, arson was suspected but never proven. The piers today are home to multimillion-dollar condominiums, and it was very convenient that so many of the old structures burned just as the conversions were to be started.) In any case, the fireboats had a busy decade or two. Since then, however, life has become more peaceful in the harbor, fire-wise. There are few piers remaining, and none that handle break-bulk, the most hazardous cargo.

The *Harvey* was taken from regular duty in 1995, over the seriously expressed displeasure of Bob Lenney, her pilot for sixteen years. When the Fire Department of New York retired the boat, he retired too. On February 11, 1999, she was sold at auction, sixty-nine years to the day from the death of the firefighter for whom she was named. John J. Harvey, pilot of the fireboat *Thomas Willett,* had been killed in an explosion while fighting a fire on the German ship *Muenchen.*

Huntley Gill's friend John Krevey owns Pier 63, where he keeps his historic lightship *Frying Pan;* he was the one who learned of the upcoming sale of the *Harvey.* "He talked us into buying her," says Huntley. "She was just too cool a boat not to buy. By the time we realized what we'd gotten into, it was too late." Huntley and his cohorts saved the old boat from the wreckers, outbidding the scrappers at the auction and buying her for $28,010. They found her in surprisingly good condition after so many years, and with some yard time but primarily with many man-hours of work, they brought her back to fully operational shape. They were really lucky to find Chief Engineer Tim Ivory. His instantaneous understanding of the complex machinery aboard the boat is a gift from God, Huntley says, and Tim would rather fix an old piece of equipment than replace it. Tim began as an employee, but the owners "gave him a hunk of the boat." Huntley describes him as a *Harvey* addict now, though he is still paid for the work he does.

The engine room, with its seven engines, six main generators, four main fire pumps, all sorts of other equipment, and innumerable controls—all several decades older than Tim—is "like a factory floor, intense, not elegant," in Tim's words. Thanks to Tim, the *Harvey* is operational today. When he saw that she was complete, not scavenged as many older vessels are, he knew she could come back to life. "It's not so much that anything needed replacing," Tim remembers. "It just needed to be gone over carefully to be certain there was no pending damage, no surprises when we started it up." In case the machinery had been allowed to freeze, he looked carefully for cracking and, engine by engine, made certain that everything turned freely. First they'd take a big wrench and turn things over by hand, make sure oil was getting to all the bearings. Only then did they apply power. "At first we were very cautious—the first engine gave the answers to a lot of questions as to how the rest were. It took a couple of days for the first one and the second, but we did the last three in a day."

Electrical equipment that sits too long absorbs moisture, so the first job with the generators was to be sure everything was dry. Then they checked the wiring visually, and finally put the power on. "There it was. It worked pretty good."

The propellers were in tough shape. While she'd been working for the city, she must have run over sunken objects, for there were chunks of bronze missing from the 5½-foot propellers. There was a lot of vibration the first season, and the boat smoked a bit and spat oil from the exhaust pipes. In 2000, she spent time in the shipyard, where the propellers were repaired, the bottom was cleaned up, and some holes were taken care of. Tim rebuilt one engine, tuned up the others, and worked on the generators. "By the end of the season, we were making pretty good speed times," Tim says. When she was built, the *Harvey* was the fastest in the fleet, but she didn't keep her title long; *Fire Fighter* took it over when she came along in 1938 and has held her own even against the newer boats. But she's aging now, and the *Harvey* can keep up with her or maybe even outrun her. "We're drag racing everyone we can."

The old pilot Bob Lenney withheld his enthusiasm for this miscellaneous group of unknowns who had his boat until he saw her in drydock at the Caddell yard, which Huntley describes as the best—and most expensive—in New York Harbor. Bob knew then that the boat was going to be well cared for. "He taught us how to steer her, how to land," says Huntley. And at least once a week now, Bob's down at the boat.

"We bought a boat and it turned into a whole volunteer-based thing none of us expected." The *Harvey* participated in Op Sail 2000, spraying water and giving rides, and her owners frequently give free rides to the public. (Without Coast Guard inspection and all the changes that would require, they can't take paying passengers. They do, however, sometimes come by paying work in commercials.) There've been some odd friendships made on the *Harvey*, says Huntley, people who in the ordinary course of things might never have crossed paths at all. Old Irish, dot-commers, lesbians and gays, colorful New Yorkers of many descriptions have come together on the boat.

Today there are only three full-time boats in the Fire Department of New York: the diesel-electric *Fire Fighter*, the *John D. McKean* (still a bell boat!), and the smaller *Kevin C. Kane*. It's unusual nowadays for them to be called out to fight ship fires—Tom Guldner, of Marine Firefighting Institute, says that in his nine years with the city fireboats, he only went to three ship fires—but the boats are essential when such an event does take place. They have other missions: fighting shoreside fires and pumping water for land-based engines. They handle rescue, too—bridge-jumpers, for example. During Tom's career, fireboats also assisted at a helicopter crash and pulled ashore a seaplane that was unable to take off. And, of course, everyone loves the fireboats' skyscraper-tall, brightly colored streams of water at festive occasions. (The dye used nowadays is ecologically blessed and vastly expensive, at $500 for a five-gallon bucket.)

The two big New York fireboats were called to work on September 11, 2001. The *McKean* actually got to the scene before the World Trade Center towers fell. She took frightened evacuees across the river to New Jersey and then returned to the Battery, where firefighters were standing helplessly, watching high-rise buildings burn. No water was available west of the disaster site because main waterlines were broken and rubble had buried hydrants. So the *McKean* started pumping from the river and didn't stop for several days. As soon as the *Fire Fighter* could get to the site, she too started pumping water from the North River into the maze of hoses on the ground.

And the owners and crew of the *John J. Harvey* scrambled to their boat from all directions and brought her down to see how they could help. A hundred and fifty people jumped aboard the boat from the seawall when they first got to the Battery, but as they were taking those people north to safety, the Fire Department radioed them. Would they put their passengers ashore as soon as they could and come back to help the city boats pump? Of course they would.

They got back to the Battery about eleven, to extraordinary quiet. Normally, there's a single-tone roar to the city, Tim says—cars and airplanes making a constant white noise—but that day there were no cars, no horns, no planes flying overhead. "You never realize how much noise there is till it's not there." The only traffic was on the river, but from shore, even tugboats are quiet as they go by. Tim couldn't leave the boat until three in the afternoon, when he walked inland. "Once in a while you'd hear a bird—it was out of place." He describes groups of people standing, not talking, looking toward the site of the World Trade Center, waiting for something to happen. "There was no definition to anything, it was all dust. It was like a black and white dream, with an inch of dust everywhere. The wind would kick up once in a while, and it would be like a fog had come in, but you couldn't breathe. There was no color, just black and white and gray—except that people's eyes would show, bloodshot from the dust."

Everything had stopped in its tracks. All the firefighting equipment that had pulled in during the first hour after the attack—many millions of dollars' worth of fire trucks and ladders and engines—had been abandoned. Either the firefighters were gone—dead—or the equipment was destroyed, flattened by the falling buildings. Hoses were still attached, but they were dry. One truck the fireboats were feeding was a ladder truck with a basket on the end of the tower, partially raised. "It didn't run, but we were forcing water through it."

Buildings were burning. So were cars. Seeing fire trucks with running hoses but no one using them, passersby grabbed the hoses off the trucks and started putting out the car fires. No one needed to give orders, in fact, people were hardly talking. They just pitched in where they thought they could help.

The fireboat *John J. Harvey* puts on a show. COURTESY OF DAVE BOONE.

In the quiet, all that day and into the next, papers kept coming out of the sky, says Tim, papers blowing from building tops like big flakes of snow. "Where we were, there was an even layer of dust and paper."

On Wednesday, the *Harvey*'s retired pilot, Bob Lenney, hitched a ride across the river to do what he'd done all his life. Huntley Gill says the hardest part for Bob was that people kept stopping by to tell him of one firefighter or another that was dead, all people Bob knew, or sons of people he knew. Bob didn't say much, but his face showed how intensely personal it all was for him. "He was glad he was there, though," Huntley says. "He'd fought for the boat, and this was his redemption. It was kind of a 'Screw you, guys. I was right and you were wrong—you needed this old boat. But I'm glad we could be here when you needed us.'" Tim asked Bob what came into his mind first when he heard that the *Harvey* was back working. "He said he just had to get there, be with the boat."

Tying up wasn't simple. At the Battery there are big seawalls to accommodate a six- or seven-foot tide, but nothing to tie to. Captain Pamela Hepburn, evacuated from her own home, came aboard to handle the lines. "I was grateful to go aboard the boat as a mariner and do something productive for a while." They tied to trees.

Tim describes a moment when they saw what seemed like thousands of people running toward them. Forty or fifty people came aboard the boat. Was something big happening? Or was it panic for no particular reason? Should they cut loose? But who would they leave hanging if they did that? They looked to Bob, who quietly said, "We'll wait."

It turned out that a surveyor had noticed a bit of a lean in a building at Liberty Plaza, across from the World Trade Center, and he was afraid it too was going to topple. But the building always had that angle, and later the word came through that everything was all right, so the crowd left again.

After that, the boat crews attached the boats to the trees using toggles, pipes running through eyes in the lines, so they'd be able to yank the pipes out and free themselves quickly and take off if need be.

For thirty-six hours, the *Harvey* pumped. After thirty hours, Assistant Engineer Jessica DuLong managed to get across the river to the boat, relieving Tim for the first time. He strung a hammock on deck, between the wheelhouse and a forward deck monitor. "If anyone needs anything, wake me up," he told people. "Fifteen minutes of sleep is about as good as it got—I was constantly worrying what was happening in the engine room. We did repack a pump and change out a fuel injector, but we were able to change the engines around, so it was no problem." The worst part was being tied to the wall, banging against it. Tugs were coming in and out and nudging the *Harvey*, which is not covered in tires like a tugboat, so she had no protection. There wasn't really any damage, Tim says, but he was nervous about it.

The *Harvey* is technically a pleasure boat today. Nobody ever thought she'd have to do this work again. But she—and her people—were ready when they were needed. And the *Harvey* wasn't the only vessel that responded. Among the dozens, maybe hundreds of pilot boats, ferries, tour boats, yachts, commuter boats, and tugs that tied up at the Battery or waited their turn in the river was the *Adriatic Sea*. She was halfway back through the Kills after getting fuel when someone hollered that the World Trade Center was on fire. Captain Vernon Elburn watched the second plane hit. We're under intentional attack, he assumed, and ran the boat for the company dock on Staten Island. The harbor was shut down immediately, no traffic in or out, but when the first tower collapsed, the Coast Guard asked all available boats to go to the lower Manhattan seawall to help with the evacuation. "We grabbed guys from the office and all the extra life jackets we could find. At ten-forty-five the second tower fell, and at twelve-thirty we were on the scene," Vernon said. "We couldn't get in to the Battery for all the boats, three-deep, waiting to get in. A spare pilot boat anchored off the Battery took over as the local traffic controller. Everyone accepted them as dispatcher and worked with them."

Most people went to the ferries, though every kind of boat showed up all around the island to help. The Coast Guard announced over the air that the capacity rule was suspended, each boat should load up as many people as it could. From the East River side, they took people to the Brooklyn piers, and from the North River and Hudson, they went to an old pier on the Jersey side. New Jersey ambulance people tore down a fence to get onto the pier and to let people out. "It was the most organized unor-ganized evacuation ever known," said Vernon. "Everyone worked together."

The *Adriatic Sea* was so close to the Trade Center that they didn't get many peo-ple evacuating. They made two trips from the Battery to New Jersey, carrying twenty people the first time and fifteen the second. Captain John O'Reilly had jumped on at the yard. "The *Adriatic Sea* was going between North Cove and South Cove on the west wall of the Battery, picking up survivors and bringing extra firemen and EMTs back across all afternoon." He remembers an Asian tourist couple in particular. "They were in matching black nylon sports suits—everything on them was the highest price, and they had big cameras. But those people were so lost." The couple didn't know what had happened, didn't know where they were going—all they knew was that they were being pushed aboard this tug. "Nothing was right in the world," says

John. "I took them aside and tried to explain it to them: 'The Red Cross is across the other side. They'll take care of you, and if your hotel isn't too close to the World Trade Center, they'll get you back there.'"

Firemen and police officers came aboard to wash their faces and eyes, and the *Adriatic* handed out ice. On the second trip to New Jersey she loaded up with sandwiches for the workers. "Everything had to be wrapped in Saran wrap—the boat was covered in dust." The *Adriatic* stayed until ten or eleven that night, when the evacuation was over. They returned to the yard, and everyone had a few hours' sleep before going back to Manhattan the next day.

Tied along the Battery wall in subsequent days, the *Adriatic* and other K-Sea boats provided fuel to the fireboats, and a great long fuel line made of hoses hooked together ran up the street to fuel the fire trucks. "We didn't actually do much," Vernon says, "but we laid in there in case something happened. We'd have been fire equipment if there was a fire by the water. On shore they had men but no equipment."

Before the attack, the *Adriatic* had been all set to take gasoline to Albany. After a couple of days, she was given clearance to go because by then Albany was running out of gas. The Coast Guard escorted them past the devastation, and when the *Adriatic* passed by the nuclear power plant at Indian Point they came aboard with sidearms and rifles. "They meant business," said Vernon. They checked every compartment of boat and barge. "The whole crew had to get up while they checked the forepeak and everyone's closets and everywhere." For nearly a month, going up past the plant and coming back, they were boarded. After that, though passing boats were no longer boarded and inspected, a police boat and a Coast Guard boat were tied up at the bulkhead at the power plant, watching. "You had to check in with them and run to the far side of the river."

It's a tradition on the water that if anyone's in trouble, whoever's around comes to help. When Manhattan was in trouble on September 11, the men and women on the water showed up in force, on old fireboats and new, on working tugs and on hundreds of other vessels.

10
Old-Time Tugboating and Old-Time Boats

There are people around who can still tell of working on steam tugs, and more who can speak of bell boats, those tugs whose captains rang bells to tell the engineers what they wanted, relying on the engineers to pass the commands on to the engine. These older storytellers say the men they learned from were of a different character than we find today. Even in this new century, there are other eras coming to an end. In this chapter we watch two traditional ship-launchings at Bath Iron Works, with ships sliding down the rails and splashing—but those days too are over.

It seems ages since coal-burning steam tugs worked the harbors, but people remember. Captain George Kraemer worked in New York Harbor starting in the 1940s on 200-horsepower tugs that burned a ton of coal an hour, hooked up. Those were considered medium-sized tugs at the time. Nowadays a smallish tug might have 3,000 horsepower. "When I think of the work we did with 400 horsepower, boy, it'd scare you." A big steam tug would load on twenty-five or thirty tons of coal, one side at a time. "It'd lay way over on one side," George describes, "and they'd very carefully back down on the head line and spin her around and load the other side."

Penobscot River pilot Bill Abbott tells about working with coal-burning steam tugs like the *Walter Ross* on the Penobscot River. Bill would be on the tanker's bridge, which in those days was well forward, and as they went up around the point by Fort Knox he'd have the *Walter Ross* on the port bow. "You'd be up there in a northwest wind—they'd throw those black diamonds to her, and the black smoke would come up and take your breath right away. Sometimes you couldn't even see."

Some of the older men who worked on tugs in the 1950s and '60s enjoy remembering the captains they sailed under. Captain John Doak, who hasn't been in the towboat business for decades now, feels he came into it at the best time—during the transition from steam to diesel, and at the tail end of an era. "I had the privilege of working with some of those men of the old school," he says. "They had different values, different standards. They had experience. They came up with no electronics, no radar or satellite navigation—they were clock-and-compass men."

Captain Jack Colomara, still running tugboats himself after forty-five years, describes the old-timers' navigation skills. "They'd steer in thick fog by their own sense. They'd have a book in their back pocket or in their shirt, and they knew the barge they were towing and the boat, and they'd have a stopwatch, and they'd look in the book. There was no way of measuring speed except by rpms and time—gotta run five minutes on this course, then change to that course four minutes. They'd have their head out the window, and they had a sense—a second sense—and might change course a little early or a little late. Of course, some didn't make it, either. But in daylight hours they'd practice, with the stopwatch and the rpms. You do that fifty times and maybe you'd have it down."

Jack speaks of the formalities of the earlier age. "Unless the captain left orders otherwise, saying he'd be late, nobody sat down at the galley table until he sat. Everyone would just walk around in circles until he sat. He got the first plate." And there were no cigarettes on the bridge at night. "God forbid you ever go on the bridge and light a match. He'd accuse you of ruining his night vision and chew you out, and you'd be out the door."

Back in the days when Jack was a deckhand, there were no autopilots, and someone always had to be on the wheel. "You'd steer, they'd give you the courses and all. You weren't allowed to smoke, nor to talk. You'd spend a whole watch up there and never say a word."

Pennsylvania Railroad steam tugs *Trenton* and *Canton* awaiting the scrapper's torch at Fieldsboro, New Jersey, March 1960. There's a submarine next to them.
FROM THE COLLECTION OF DAVE BOONE.

Most of the old guys smoked pipes, Jack says. "They'd have a whole array of pipes in a rack, and they'd come up in the wheelhouse with their rack and start with pipe #1. They'd ream it out and clean it and fuss with it for a half an hour, and finally light it and puff on it two or three minutes, and then the bowl would get too hot, or something would be wrong, and they'd go on to the next. They had all kinds of tools to dig it out with, and pipe cleaners—they'd spend hours on it, and I don't think they'd ever smoke. That's what they'd do when they were on watch, sit in the chair with all that stuff and dig."

Captain Doak says the old-timers were good men to work with and knew their business. "You could depend on what they told you, and if they told you something, you'd better be listening."

One of these men was Captain Jeddy Hallowell, who came from Dennysville, down east. "He was a little, short fellow. Wrinkled his nose like a rabbit." John never saw the old guy get rattled. He tells of a ship docking when he was deckhand on the *Seguin*. "One day, it was rougher'n a cob out there. We had a line made up on the stem head. She come up on a sea, slapped down, broke that stem head right off." John was deckhand at the time. He says he was half-petrified. But the captain stuck his head out the window and quietly said, "When you got time again, why don't you make that line up on the bitt?"

And unlike some of the older masters, Captain Hallowell was happy to share his knowledge. "You'd be around a ship, and he'd say, 'You pay attention. I'm going to show you a little trick.'"

Many of today's older captains—the Jack Colomaras, the Vernon Elburns, with more than four decades in the wheelhouse—are looked upon by the younger men as mentors, the best of boat handlers and true gentlemen. It's a field where there's a great deal to learn, and technology changes fast. Younger men of each generation can't imagine working with the tools available to the older men when they started and—for good reason—feel great respect for the older men still in the business.

Master of the Old *Clyde B.*

John Doak was the last master of the last working coastal steam tug in the United States, the *Clyde B. Holmes,* of Belfast, Maine. He had run her for a decade when she finally was retired from service in the end of 1975. And although he continued on with Eastern Maine Towage another few years, as long as the company was in business, he didn't feel the same way about the diesel tugs that he had about the old

The *John Wanamaker* on the Delaware River in 1925. FROM THE COLLECTION OF DAVE BOONE.

Clyde B. When she was turned into a restaurant, someone asked him if he'd been down to Camden to see her. It's not even twenty miles away. No, he said, and he still hasn't visited her. "That's just one notch better than going to the boneyard." He wants to remember her as the working tug she was.

The tug was built in 1925 for the city of Philadelphia and was originally known as the *John Wanamaker,* after the Philadelphia businessman and philanthropist. She was given a big engine for that day, 1,000 horsepower, and was supposed to be an icebreaker and a barge handling boat, but they also put in a mahogany-paneled cabin aft, with a bar and settees—"so the mayor and his friends could go out for a ride on the Delaware River," says Jim Sharp, who converted the boat to a restaurant. "She was built without regard for expense."

In John Doak's living room there's a portrait of the *Clyde B.,* painted by his daughter Sharon. "I don't talk to many people about towboats anymore," he says, but the smile on his face as he tells one story or another shows that the *Clyde B.* and the days he spent working her are still right with him.

When he was thirty-three Doak got his master's and pilot's licenses. For nine days, he was taking tests, five for the master's and four for pilotage. The rules and regulations aspect of piloting are covered in the master's testing. For the pilot's ticket, he had to draw charts from memory of each harbor for which he was getting licensed: Rockland to Bangor, including Castine, Searsport, and the whole Penobscot River. "It was a happy day when I walked out of Portland with that baby in my hand."

The new Captain Doak's first command was as relief on the old steam tug *Seguin*, which by then was a backup boat. His full-time job was as mate aboard the *Clyde B. Holmes*. It was several years before Captain Harold Spurling's retirement gave John the opportunity to run the *Clyde B.* himself, but once he took her over, he was with her up to the end. "I enjoyed her and was proud of her, and hated to see her go."

Certainly, there were times when running her—or any other tug—didn't seem like the best occupation. "In the wintertime, it's colder'n blazes, and ice and vapor is out there on the bay, and you wonder why, *why* would a man ever want to make a living on one of those things? You sit in the galley and you sip your coffee and you watch the clock, and you just have to drive yourself into the wheelhouse," John was recorded saying at the time. "And the same with your deckhands. They'll hang around and hang around—they won't want to take in the light cord or let a line go or single up." (Singling up is letting all the lines go but one, preparatory to sailing.) But he wouldn't say anything to them, and when he got into the pilothouse, "out on deck they go, and they do their job, and I'm doin' mine, and the engine room's doin' theirs, and we go. That's all there is to it."

Clyde B. Holmes. PHOTO BY STEVE LANG FROM THE COLLECTION OF BILL ABBOTT.

The *Clyde B.* was a comfortable boat. "I've seen that old girl coming up from Portland when it was nasty. She was an easy boat, that old girl. She'd dive deep and come up slow and go again. You didn't worry about whether she'd be under you when you looked around—she was there."

He admits she did have a bad feature or two. "If you were tied up beside a ship, she didn't like to be towed. She'd crawl up the side of a ship." Inch by inch, she'd roll, the side against the ship rising, the outboard side dropping. "I've had her beside a ship, her rail right down in the water.

"But she'd handle like a dream. No man who ever handled her didn't say that." He corrects himself. One of her masters hated her. "But that was a love affair with his previous boat." No boat would have matched up to that one, no matter how good.

"When you had steam on, you could go full ahead to full astern—if you have a good man on the throttle in there and plenty of steam, the only thing near steam is diesel-electric. You could back and fill her almost in her own tracks."

In Searsport, if there was a ship at each of the two docks, the 117-foot-long *Clyde B. Holmes* couldn't go in between them and turn around. Not a problem for Captain Doak. He'd back her in. It's not always an easy trick to steer a single-screw boat going backward. "She was a sweetheart that way," he says.

It took teamwork to run the *Clyde B.*, though. Three men were required in the engine room: engineer, fireman, and oiler. "It's a fairly complicated system. The boiler room had three furnaces. You could run one, two, or three, hard or not so hard, hot or cold. You had to gauge that steam. And you had to preheat the Bunker C oil—there's a critical temperature range for it to burn—so they're tending fuel pumps and preheaters as well as the burners." Running light, they could get it get worked out for a steady speed. "Then the fireman can go set on his haunches." But working a ship is another matter. "You might need all the steam you can get, and then the next minute ring for stop engine." It was the job of the engine room crew to keep pressure regulated. "They were trying to keep you with steam enough to work, without going over. You don't want to go blowing off the safety valve and have to wait till it settles down and lose time. The engineer knows that if he hasn't got steam enough, the captain gets ugly."

There was a morning that they were tied up in Bangor at the foot of Dutton Street and awoke to find six inches of blue ice around them. The Penobscot River is tidal at Bangor, but the fresh water coming down the river is lighter than the salt water. It flows on top and freezes more quickly. "It was twenty below zero, and you know how it goes those kinda days—nobody's ever early," says Doak. "The fireman's late and the engineman's late. We're supposed to undock a ship in Brewer, and I know what's going on in the engine room—the engineer's wild, working the boiler, trying as hard as he can, but in a half an hour, he didn't have a half a head of steam."

Doak heard from the pilot on the radio. "Where are you? We need you to break the ice in front of the ship."

The chief engineer called up the speaking tube, telling the skipper to go ahead and try her.

"We're crashing around, breaking up the ice," John describes, "and we've used up all the steam. We're just limping along, with barely enough steam to turn the wheel over." The pilot's raging on the radio. "Just relax," John said to the men in the engine room. "When you guys get her ready to work, you let me know." Captain Doak chuckles, thinking about the old and fitting expression "haven't got enough steam up to cook a hot dog."

He describes what he heard from the pilothouse. "They're banging around, and the little old furnaces are just a-singin', and in about ten minutes I get a call: 'We're ready to work.'"

The *Clyde B.* wasn't a good icebreaker, though. John remembers a year when the bay froze. "The Penobscot River was shut up. There was ice in the bay clear down to Lincolnville," he says. There were two ships and a tug and barge stuck in the river, all trying to get up to Bangor and Brewer, and nothing was moving. Fuel oil supplies were getting short in this part of the state. "They was pumping the bottom of the oil tanks up there, but it never hit the radio, so nobody panicked," he recalls.

Captain Doak had orders to take a load of water to a freighter off Searsport. It's a ten- or fifteen-minute run, normally. "I was two hours pounding ice. You couldn't hurt her—you'd just have to pound and shatter."

The one big advantage the *Clyde B.*'s steam system had over a diesel unit, John says, is that she had a compound engine, with high-pressure and low-pressure cylinders. Steam went into the twenty-inch high-pressure cylinder at 185 pounds, the maximum allowed for its boiler. As the steam was exhausted out of that cylinder, it went into the low-pressure piston, forty-four inches in diameter, to be used again. "In a pinch," John explains, "you can bypass the 185 pounds of pressure into the low-pressure piston, and milk that, maybe twenty-five percent higher horsepower, for just a few minutes. In a squeaker, it can bail you out." This operation is called "the Doctor."

He describes undocking at Bucksport in a heavy tide. "I've watched a ship coming up by the mill, and she'd be slowing down and slowing down in the strength of that tide. Just before she'd stop, I'd holler for the engineer to give her a little work.

They'd put the Doctor to her for just a minute or two, just enough that you'd see the ship start picking back up again, coming back out into that tide. Just enough. Things like that, you never get with diesel. When you got her full ahead on that diesel, that's all there is. There's no reserve."

The summer he was seventeen or eighteen, Corliss Holland's son Glenn filled in a few times as deckhand on the *Clyde B.* He remembers the Doctor. "You'd feel the whole boat jumping—she'd kinda vibrate, like she was almost galloping."

Steam does have one serious shortcoming compared to diesel, and it ultimately led to the end of many steamships in general and the *Clyde B.* in particular. They don't just turn on and off. "When we were working, we kept steam on her. We'd fire her twice a day, and we could be going in a half hour." But if the steam was down, for instance for boiler inspection, it would take two days to come back up to pressure. The boiler had to be fired very slowly or it would warp. The nature of towboating requires that the vessels be ready to go at all times, and that meant burning fuel the clock around, whether or not there was work to be done. The 1970s were quiet on Penobscot Bay and the river, with only a couple of dockings a week. Belfast's two diesel tugs could be shut down and restarted immediately; the *Clyde B.* consumed fuel whether she was working or not. When the cost of fuel escalated from eight dollars to thirty-two dollars a barrel, that was it for the *Clyde B.*

Asked what it was like on a steam tug, the first thing Captain Doak says is, "It was quiet." His wife says she liked to go on the *Clyde B.*, and one gets the impression perhaps that was not the case with the diesels.

Soon after the *Clyde B.* retired, Captain Doak was interviewed by Steve Lang. "I've laid in my bunk a good many nights and I've listened as the firemen got the steam up and the engineer readied the engines for the next job," John described. "The steam engine is so quiet! And it's got almost a rhythm to it. Your valves and your pumps and the—oh, I don't want to say rumble—it's more a kind of bass background noise. And then that high-pitched whistle of steam. Why, you've got a kind of a melody going. I could almost lay half-asleep and know just what was going to happen next. It's like the chicken farmer—when the chickens quit hollering, the sound is deafening!

"I guess it's the little things about her I'm going to miss, and especially that whistle. She's got a ring to her, and a deep sound that goes right through you and would shake the whole of Belfast.

"The only regret I've got," says Captain Doak even today, "is that I never had a tape of her whistle. Somebody came one time with professional recording equipment and taped her whistle, but I never heard it. I'd give my right thumb for a recording of that. It was a shrill old whistle."

An Old Tug Lives On

The next stage of the *Clyde B.*'s life was a different matter altogether.

"Yeah, it was the dead of winter," Captain Jim Sharp starts his tale of the *Clyde B. Holmes* coming to Camden in February 1977. "The ice cakes were flowing all around Camden Harbor." Jim had agreed to buy the old tug if the owner of Eastern Maine Towage, Clyde Holmes, would deliver his namesake to Camden. He'd much rather see her preserved as a restaurant, where the public could enjoy and help support her, than broken up for scrap. "That old tug has a history as long as your arm and an amazing story to tell the world!"

Jim had gone to the town to make sure it would be all right to have a floating structure in place at his wharf. The Camden code-enforcement officer said it was a harbor issue, not in his bailiwick. The harbormaster said it was behind the wharf line and so it wasn't his problem. The Coast Guard said it wasn't in their jurisdiction as long as it was permanently docked and chained to the wharf. It seemed that the only permit needed was a victualer's license from the state. But, one suspects, perhaps Jim didn't make it clear just how large a vessel it was he was bringing in. "After all," he says, "I didn't want to stir up too much fuss ahead of time."

Jim continues, "They were going to tow her in with the tug *Mary Holmes* at the crack of dawn. That night, late, I went down to the slip where the vessel would be lying to push the ice cakes out of the way, dozens of them. Sam Manning came walking by. I couldn't believe it. 'Hey, Jim, what the heck are you doing?' he asked.

"'Oh, I'm playing games with ice cakes,' I said.

"'What on earth for?'

"'Well, couldn't sleep and got nothing better to do, I guess.'"

Jim calls the *Clyde B. Holmes* "a leftover relic." Eastern Maine Towage had tried to sell her but no one wanted her. They tried to donate her to a foundation but couldn't even give her away. "So Clyde decided he was going to scrap her. I couldn't let that happen. I was between marriages, infected with the utter abandon you get after a divorce, and decided to buy her." Jim paid the scrap price.

The old *Clyde* came into Camden and nosed up into the slip at high water early, early in the morning. "I had pushed the ice out of the way, and we shoved the boat and grounded her as far up in the slip as we could."

The crane *Ichabod* lowers the *Clyde B. Holmes*'s stack. PHOTO BY NEAL PARENT, FROM THE COLLECTION OF JIM SHARP.

She had 18,000 gallons of Bunker C fuel in her when she came. "We steamed the fuel so it would pump—it congeals like tar when it's cold—blew the old whistle one last time, and pumped the bunker off into tank trucks. I sold it for thirty-six hundred dollars, bought a 100-ton, 100-foot boom crane, and had six hundred dollars left over." Jim named his crane *Ichabod*. He had never run a crane before so the guy he bought it from showed him which levers did what. He put a chain around a granite block and went at it. "I waited till there were no people, no cars, and no little kids around so I could learn without squashing anything important. Then I picked off that beautiful tall stack and laid it gently on the ground. Next it was boilers, tanks, piping, bulkheads, and a myriad of miscellaneous motors, pumps and gears." Jim left some of the more picturesque parts of the machinery in place. He had plans for that.

Jim kept pushing the tug further into the slip. "We'd draw her up more with every high run of tide, every storm tide, and then, to get her to ground out a few feet higher, I hooked onto her stem with the crane, lifted and dragged her ahead with my station wagon. Took the transmission right out of her with that one!"

They built floors, moved equipment into the kitchen, stocked the wine locker, and opened the restaurant, with the boat once again bearing her original name, *John Wanamaker*.

Having the tug float once in a while made dining not always perfect. "I remember a gale of wind, and the old thing started to rock. The chandelier overhead in the dining room was swinging back and forth. Some diners were starting to turn green from the motion." Finally he got the boat up far enough that she wouldn't float off at all. He supported the entire tug with huge elm tree trunks, the spoils left over from the victims of Dutch elm disease on the town landing.

The chandelier was one of many elegant appointments in the new restaurant. But the most fun was the engine. Jim was determined to get the engine to roll over quietly using an electric motor. "The journals [the bearings of the crankshaft and connecting rods] were so heavy that the electric motor, geared down to 64:1, still wouldn't roll her over." He had to remove the pistons. (Fortunately for Jim's working exhibit, no one would be able to see that they were missing.) The low-pressure piston was big—Jim exaggerates when he says it was probably ten feet across, but it was immense, and it wouldn't let go. They put three chain falls on it, took the nut off the huge bolt that held the piston in, and squirted penetrating oil in it. "Every day as we were scrapping, I told the guys to pull the chain falls and take a sixteen-pound maul and pound on that piston until they were winded, and then go back to work. We all did that. On the eighth day, I was the guy who came down on that thing—I never thought I'd be the one—and *BANG,* she let go and the piston came out." He then polished up the engine, painted the appropriate parts, and encased it in glass.

He finished the interior of the restaurant with thick carpet and painted the surfaces black overhead. He put plaid tablecloths on the tables, dressed the waiters in cummerbunds, and hired a harpist. There were pictures of tugs all around, and tools on the wall. It was truly impressive. "My sister ran the restaurant, and I did the technical stuff like fix the sewage tank when it overflowed."

People were fascinated by the engine. "When the music crew had finished, they'd punch a button, and the thing would start to roll over slowly, and everybody would jump out of their chairs and run over and look at it."

The restaurant sat 125 below, and they served lunch for an additional 75 people on the top deck. Jim rigged the three-tone whistle to a compressor, and at 11:30, opening time, they'd blow a long and two short, which means "drop your lines, we're ready to go." One day a tourist charged into the chamber of commerce at one o'clock, complaining, "That tug blew its whistle, and I waited an hour and a half to see that thing go out, and it never did. And I want to know why not!"

But the restaurant business is not all fun and glamour, even on a tugboat, Jim says. "We had twenty-two employees, and it was an elegant restaurant. We served the finest of steaks and fine wines and all that. But my sister was run ragged. I came back one time, and she dissolved in tears—a waiter had broken his leg, the cook was out sick, and the sewage system had overflowed."

Four years was enough. Jim leased the tug to some people in Boston. She hadn't floated in three years and he'd scrapped out a great deal of weight. To stabilize her for the trip, he had two truckloads of cement dumped into her bowels.

"When they got to Boston, there was a big bilge full of water. They flipped out and called me. I knew she didn't leak, so I told one of the crew to take a big adjustment wrench and look at the stern gland. They tightened her up and she was as tight as a jug."

The Boston restaurant failed, but Jim came out all right. "It's a volatile business. We had a hard time of it too, in the beginning. Just as those guys decided they couldn't pay the rent, I saw an article in the paper about an outfit on the Cape that wanted to convert a wooden tug into a restaurant." He convinced them they'd prefer to have a steel tug ready to go, and sold her to them with a good mortgage rate. After ten years,

In Portsmouth, New Hampshire, 2002. Author photo.

they failed too, but they paid Jim off when they sold her to restaurateurs in Portsmouth, who, after a few more years, lost her to creditors themselves. The word is, she's being refurbished and will again be a restaurant somewhere.

Running the Bell Boats

Jim, always a good storyteller, also remembers bell boats. "In this day and age, no towboat operator will use a bell boat," he says. He explains the system: "All the controls are in the engine room. The only thing in the pilothouse is steering gear and the bell." There was one more communication device, too, either a whistle or another bell with a different ring to it. "You ring bells to signal the engineer—engine on, engine off—and then use whistles for how many rpm." The engineer was in charge of making the actual changes to the engine. Like anyone who's used it, Jim remembers the system well. Actually, the commands are still used—many pilots and tugboat captains still refer to one bell or two, meaning forward or astern, and the tugs' whistled acknowledgments of pilots' commands use the same code.

Captain Clarence Nickerson ran the *Seguin* on bells. "Hopefully you rang it soon enough before you knocked the dock down," he says.

Captain John Doak remembers the bells, too. "The bell was a big gong. You pulled the bell pull, it rang that gong. Then there was a little bell like a cowbell on a rocker. That's the jingler." Some boats, like the ones Jim ran, used a whistle in place of the jingler. The signals for slow ahead, full ahead, stop, slow astern, full astern, all were made with the bell and the jingler. In John's pilothouse, one pull would have a loop on the end, and the other a bar, "so if you reach down in the night, you know which you've got. But you're just as much a part of that pilothouse—it's as if you're reaching for your doorknob at home."

Most of John's work was ship docking. "You'd be steaming across the bay to get to a ship and ring one bell, and you'd hear the galley door slam and the throttle man running down the deck to get to the throttles. So you'd plan in a little time lag. But the throttle man was right on there when you were handling a ship. He knows what you're doing as much as you do. A good throttle man is a good asset."

On the ship, the docking pilot needs the tugboat to respond to his commands as quickly as it can. "The tug has to be on the ready," says Jim Sharp. "You don't think about the number of backs and fills you can use up when you're running an electric boat—on a diesel-electric, it's easy and automatic. On bell boats, it gets a whole lot more complicated, especially on a deep-draft and heavy-displacement tugboat.

"Say you're laying by with a slack hawser and the pilot orders two bells, hooked up." That's full astern. "First you've got to ring the two bells and one whistle to get the boat backing. As the line takes up, you must ring off—the inertia of the tug could stretch the line to the breaking point. If you're still backing too fast, you've got to ring one bell to give her a kick ahead and break that momentum so you don't come up all standing on that one line. Then ring off and ring two bells to finally get backing with, first, one whistle to stretch the line, then finally two, three, and four whistles to get the backing full. But it can be done fairly quickly with a good engineer."

Captain Sharp enjoyed playing with one of his engineers. "Old Leo Mazzerol prided himself on being very attentive," Jim says. Leo kept his eyes fixed on the bell wire that went up to the handle in the wheelhouse. "He'd start a maneuver when he saw the string start to move the bell. He was guessing what was going to come, so every once in a while I'd give him a soft bell. I'd pull the hammer up and cock it and wait—I could almost hear him chafing—and then I'd lower it very slowly so it wouldn't ring. He'd get some ol' mad! We had a speaking tube from pilothouse to engine room, and I would stuff a rag in it so I wouldn't have to listen to the bad language and the wrenches he was throwing around the engine room."

Picking a pilot off even an anchored ship really put the test to the bell system, according to Jim. With any boat, inertia makes it tricky, and on a bell boat, it's even more so. The pilot is climbing down the rope-sided Jacob's ladder; with a light ship, it might be thirty feet down to the tug. No matter if the waters are quiet, it's a long climb, and sometimes the pilots are no longer youthful and agile. Jim says that rather than coming alongside and taking the chance of hitting the ladder and trapping the pilot's legs between the tug and the ship—or worse yet, knocking him into the water—it was better to come in straight on, nose first, and land alongside the ladder. If you bump into the ship gently, it doesn't hurt, but you have to be ready with a bell forward to hold the tug so it doesn't bounce away while the pilot climbs off onto the pudding.

Jim says that for a real kick, a captain should try running a boat that combines a bell system with a direct-reversing engine, on which the engine actually has to be shut down to change direction. The helmsman rings two bells to go astern, and the engineer kills the engine, throws a cam lever, then starts the engine back up in the opposite direction. Arthur Fournier's old *Cape Fear* was a direct-reversing bell boat. "You're heading for the dock with plenty of momentum, and you ring off," Jim describes. "The whole boat is quiet, and you're still making seven or eight knots toward the dock. When you're ready to stop in a hurry, you ring two bells and four whistles, so she's hooked right up—but there's so much inertia, the first turn of the propeller doesn't seem to do anything. Then on the second turn, the froth comes out from underneath her bow on both sides, and you know she's stopping."

Jim loved the challenge of the *Cape Fear*. He describes her: "Rotten as a pear. There were holes in her deck, holes in her tanks, holes back under her quarter, all filled up with Bondo." But she was still a powerful boat, with a 1,700-horsepower, twenty-cylinder, opposed-piston Fairbanks Morse engine. "She was such a powerful thing, and once you got used to her, as Arthur would say, you could pound nails into the wharf with her."

The problems during one of the *Cape Fear*'s jobs in 1977 were caused neither by her bell system nor by her direct-reverse engine. Bath Iron Works was launching the largest ship they'd ever built up to that time, the 722-foot container ship *Maui,* and the *Cape Fear* was the hawser tug, the position of most responsibility.

The gravity launch into the Kennebec had to be done at slack tide, which lasts only about fifteen minutes on the fast-running river. The tug had to be ready to go and had to go fast when the moment came, explains Jim. "When the ship comes down the ways, she'll be making fourteen knots. Of course the water slows her down quickly, but the top speed of the tug is twelve knots. So I have to strike right out at the moment of launch, tight as I can go, to stay ahead of the ship and keep the hawser from fouling either the ship or the tug."

He was out in the stream on a long hawser while the launching ceremonies were going on, and the ebb current was sweeping the tug off. "They had a little yard tug there called the *Kennebec,* and he came alongside me in the middle to push me sideways into the current until it was pretty close to the time of launch. Everyone was worried because a few launchings back, the hawser tug had gotten off to the side, and when the ship roared down the ways, she yanked the hawser tug sideways, which tripped the little tug. She rolled and went down, and men drowned."

Jim was depending on the little *Kennebec* to hold him up in the current, and he didn't dare put strain on the hawser for fear of prematurely launching the ship himself. "It was as delicate as sailing on the edge of a jibe," says the old schoonerman. "The guys in the yard tug must have gotten nervous looking at the enormous stern of the vessel looming high over their heads and just about to cavort into the river at fourteen knots. Probably imagining it chasing their little six-knot boat all over the river, they panicked, and left. So I'm out there trying to hold the tug in what's left of the current while keeping no strain on the hawser." He put the wheel hard to port and gave just the slowest bell to keep the *Fear* in the right attitude while nervously he waited for the voice on the radio to announce the launch.

"Everything had to be right! It's a desperate situation for us if the ship passes me, so I stationed a couple of guys aft with axes to cut the hawser if anything went wrong. But if that towline came up with too much strain and broke, they could be swept off the stern, so they were hiding behind the house on each side."

Jim could hear the countdown on the radio. "Finally they hollered, 'We have a launch! We have a launch!' so I gave one bell for headway and four whistles for hooked up. Right away, the tug jumps ahead, but she feels the wash from her huge propeller almost immediately and swings off to port."

There was a lot of lag time in the electrical steering of the *Fear,* and many turns from lock to lock, so she steered slowly, and of course the recent launch accident was on Jim's mind too. He had to keep in line with the ship as she slid into the river, and the towline had to be snug now. "I'm rolling the wheel over to straighten her rudder—I'm spinning the hell out of the wheel and I went beyond the center, because the adrenaline's running and I'm oversteering. And the ship's catching up with us now—smoke is pouring out the ways. I see the towline going slack back there, and I'm trying to stay ahead of it, and then the towline isn't straight behind us, and I've over-steered again, and she's started to sweep back to the right. The pilots come on the radio, 'You having trouble out there? What's wrong with that tug?' With as calm a voice as I could manage, I say, 'Well, she's steering a little slow, Cap, but she's coming on her now.'

"I finally get her straightened out, and now the towline's starting to take up." The ship slowed up once she hit the water, and her stern and all the dunnage shot up a wave that looked like Niagara Falls. The tug, with her inertia, was still going ahead. Jim rang off and then rang astern as the towline came up tight, stretched out, sprung back, and came up tight again.

"We're in control now, but hell, that wasn't the end of my worries," Jim says. As they took a strain on the ship and turned it around in midstream and the docking tugs made up alongside, the engineer called him on the speaking tube. "The generator just died," he said. "I can't get the damn thing running again. How many more starts and stops do you have?" The generator is necessary to pressurize the air to start and stop the engine.

"Man, I don't know," Jim said. "Gotta finish turning the ship around, then go under the bow and push her alongside the wharf."

"Well, use as few as you can. We have only one tank of air!"

The pilot was giving commands to the various tugs: full ahead, stop, hard this way, hard that way. They got the ship alongside the dock, and Jim's tug was sent under the bow. "I'm pushing the bow on this huge container ship. The pilot up there says to me, 'One bell dead slow, *Cape Fear,*' and I put her one bell dead slow, and he'd say 'Half,' and I'd give her a little more, and then he'd say 'Stop, *Cape Fear,*' and I'd go back to dead slow."

When the pilot said "Two bells, dead slow," Jim would have to stop to go into reverse. "Then he'd say 'Stop, *Cape Fear,*' and I'd give her a long, dead slow in reverse, trying not to give too many bells, because every time the engine stops to start in the other direction, we'd use up air."

As the ship was making up her lines and settling into her berth, the engineer called again. "The pressure is way down. You probably only have one more start." They still had to get back to the pier themselves. Imagine the embarrassment of having to call another company to push them into their dock!

"So we gathered in our head line and let the tug drift until it turned with the current and the stern fetched against the ship. The recoil knocked the bow away from the ship a little and gave me maneuvering room. The engineer hit our last start ahead, dead slow, and we were able to turn under the bow of the ship and head for the dock. I rang off, she bled off her momentum, and we bounced off the piling, but we had a line around it right away, and I don't think anybody noticed. The pilots didn't know it, nobody on the dock knew it, and I don't think that Arthur even knew it. But *we* knew it."

The Last Traditional Launch at Bath Iron Works

Beginning in the mid-1980s, John Worth and Duke Tomlin of Belfast's Maineport Towboats, Inc., ran the hawser tug for the launches at Bath Iron Works while Winslow had the tugboat contract. The job was a cooperative effort, with tugs belonging to Winslow, Maineport Towboats, and the yard itself. The 1913 tug *Verona* (formerly *Bronx,* among other names) was part of the team.

But times change. Bath Iron Works brought a huge drydock into their Kennebec River facility, and there will be no more gravity launches there. It's far less romantic but a great deal easier on a new-built ship to roll her onto the drydock, which is then partially submerged so the ship can float off.

On June 23, 2001, the ways were greased for the last gravity launch down the building ways before BIW changed over to the new roll-on/float-off system. There were six tugs on the river that day when the five-hundred-foot Arleigh Burke–class destroyer USS *Mason* made her backward rush into the water. One tug was on the hawser, one assisted in keeping the hawser tug in place in the river, three were ready to move the ship into her berth, and one picked up the pieces. (There are always pieces. The blocking floats off when the vessel hits the water.)

The hawser tug has the only line onto the ship when she slides into the river. It is that tug's responsibility to pull the ship's stern around, turning her lengthwise in the river for the other tugs to push her in alongside the pier. If things don't go to plan for some reason, it's the hawser tug that must manage the ship once she's in the water. And it is that tug which could conceivably yank the ship down the ways early if her captain allows the hawser to tighten up too soon.

The river pilot, Captain Earl Walker, liked the way the *Verona* could quietly stay in place in the wind and currents on the Kennebec River, keeping an easy tension on the hawser, so Winslow called on the somewhat archaic *Verona* during launches—two a year, on average, before they brought in the drydock. The *Verona* is a diesel-electric, and her rheostat control allows her propeller to turn at any speed, two turns per minute or 150. A regular diesel would have to constantly clutch in, clutch out, and when the clutch is in, her propeller would immediately be making a hundred turns, causing a jerky movement that would certainly be uncomfortable and difficult and potentially very dangerous.

For the launch of the *Mason*, Captain Duke Tomlin was running the *Verona*. (He and John Worth alternated the launch duties at BIW; they both enjoyed them.) BIW's little yard tug *Kennebec* was made up on the *Verona*'s hip to give assistance laterally, but it was the *Verona*'s job to keep the six hundred feet of hawser tensioned just right.

Captain Duke Tomlin of Maineport Towboats is at the outside helm of the tug *Verona,* watching the hawser.
COURTESY OF PHIL ROBERTS, JR.

The *Eliot Winslow* forward on the USS *Mason,* with quarter lines running both aft and to the ship's bow. The tug can act as a bow-thruster on the ship, and if she backs, her stern won't swing. Another tug is on the ship's stern, positioned fore-and-aft to provide propulsion. COURTESY OF PHIL ROBERTS JR.

"You try to find a balance," says John. "You have the wind and the tide working you up the river, normally, so if you keep both boats working ahead to a certain level, you just stay there."

He admits it's a situation that requires a lot of attention. "It's fairly tense," he says of the hour or so they would spend waiting for the moment of slack water chosen for launch. "The pilot gets concerned if you get too far off. And you want to be right there and ready to go at 'Launch! Launch!'"

The launch of the *Mason* went without flaw. The huge destroyer slid into the river, and *Verona* picked up the slack in the hawser and quietly pulled the ship around. The swarm of Winslow tugs surrounded the *Mason* and pushed her into the berth where she would be finished. *Verona* was dismissed and put back into the dock, her job as a launch hawser tug finished forever, at least at BIW.

"We're sad it's the end of an era," says John, "but it's very likely that Maineport will still be involved with the new drydock in some capacity. It's never a good idea to bite your nails over change. Usually changes create new opportunities." *Verona*'s diesel-electric system is good for ship docking, particularly with a light ship, permitting a softer landing than with a clutch boat. There's still plenty of work for the nonagenarian *Verona*.

11
Restorations

Restoring a large vessel is never simple, but there are always a number of restorations underway, and perhaps a disproportionate number are tugs. There are efforts by museums, would-be museums, individuals who would like to offer paying passengers an unusual cruising experience, and others who simply want an interesting live-aboard vessel. Sometimes the stories have happy endings, sometimes not, and sometimes it seems there'll never be an end at all. But it's always someone's dream on the line—or a series of people's dreams—along with a big pile of money, the finding of which is usually the hardest part. Right now, just to mention a few tug projects at random, there are *Luna* in Boston, *Pegasus* and *New York Central 13* in New York Harbor, the huge *Catawissa* in Newburgh, New York, the *Jupiter* in Philadelphia, the *Hercules* in San Francisco, the *Saturn* in Maine, and *James A. Whalen* in Thunder Bay, Ontario. They follow the *Seguin*, who ended her days in Bath, Maine. One hopes that their futures are brighter.

Elise Ann Conners

"The biggest thing I've learned from this is patience, not something I'm blessed with," says Gary Matthews, co-owner of the second oldest tug in North America, the 1881 iron canaler *Elise Ann Conners*, which is now tied up off the Hudson in Rondout Creek. With his partner, Ann Hoeding, he has been working on the restoration of this old girl for a decade and hasn't yet gotten to the part he's perhaps most interested in, her engine. But to him, she represents the history of canal work, a subject he is passionate about.

The *Elise Ann Conners* was built to tow barges that came down the C&D Canal to Baltimore and Washington. Throughout the nineteenth century, canals were a vital system for bringing natural resources and agricultural products from the interior of the country to coastal cities. The canal tugs were built long, lean, and low. As Gary says, "In 1881, coal was expensive and labor to form plate into complex shapes was cheap." The *Elise Ann Conners* has a hollow entry forward, like an ocean liner or

The *Elise Ann Conners* pushing an oil barge on the New York State Barge Canal, 1952.
The helmsman is steering from the doghouse, or "hello-up-there" house.
PHOTO BY D. MCCORMICK, FROM THE COLLECTION OF DAVE MATTHEWS.

Forty years later: in Rondout Creek, June 16, 1993, day two of the salvage efforts.
PHOTO BY G. HENNE.

yacht, certainly unusual in a tug, but undoubtedly efficient. Their low pilothouses, which allowed them to pass under bridges, are the giveaways as to the canalers' origins. Some had a pilothouse that could be raised and lowered, allowing the captain to see over a light barge or long tow. Others had a doghouse that was put in place seasonally. In the case of the *Elise Ann Conners,* she had an open-air steering station on her boat deck, known in the industry as the "hello-up-there" house. As far as her current owners can determine, she is the only tug still around that towed mule-drawn canal barges from their tidewater locks on the Potomac and Delaware Rivers to saltwater ports, and then kept working after the mules were all retired.

For one hundred years, through the mule and non-mule eras on the canals, the *Elise Ann Conners* worked commercially. She then passed through a number of hands until she sank in Rondout Creek, off the Hudson River, two-thirds of the way from New York City to Albany and about a mile from where she's tied up today. Gary had been eyeing her for a number of years but wasn't able to tempt the owner into selling her before she sank. Then suddenly her owner thought she'd be better off without him, or vice versa, and the investment of a dollar brought her to Gary, as is, where is. It was another three or four months before she was raised—something that Gary says is "not a project one wants to do twice in one's life."

The job was accomplished by a 600-ton floating crane. Gary says he had two thoughts when they were picking her up: "First, we're going to break her in half, and second, she's never going to stay up." He had a vision, if worst came to worst and she did die being raised, of sneaking her into a tugboat graveyard in the middle of the night. But sneaking anything anywhere wasn't likely—the crane was the biggest thing ever seen in Rondout Creek, and the excitement drew newspeople from all around.

The old girl stayed together, and she wanted to float. That was just the beginning. She'd had no maintenance for thirty years, and had spent the winter under the water and ice of upstate New York. "I'm a marine engineer. Half the point of getting the boat was the engine," says Gary, referring to her Atlas Imperial diesel. "But in nine years, I've hardly touched the engine. We really have to do structural work before we can consider it.

"I've been learning carpentry so I can do the project—this is the How-to Tugboat Restoration Project." Unfortunately, Gary says, he also has to earn a living, which he does on a tug that works the Hudson and Long Island Sound, one week on, one week off. When he's not on the *Cheyenne,* he's on the *Elise Ann Conners*. He and Ann make their home there. "It's slow progress restoring her, and incredibly taxing." More money would make it easier, no doubt. But part of the fun is tracking down the equipment and parts they need.

The only usable thing in the engine room is the engine itself. The generators and everything else have been destroyed or stripped out over time. Gary expects that the engine will function, but for now, it's just been stabilized, sprayed down with oil. The time will come. "I'm going to do what I have to, to make it run." In the meantime, he's collecting stuff. He found an unused war-surplus generator, dating from 1943. "Brand new," he says. "The paint's still good. It appears that it ought to go." There's adventure in the hunt, Gary says. "It's a big part of the project but nobody but us will ever see it." He's been years making connections, tracking leads, then actually getting the parts home. "Finding stuff of the right era to put back in is a big part of it. We do intend for this to be a fairly accurate restoration." They have chosen to restore her to her World War II–era configuration, as that's when she was converted over to diesel from steam.

Working in the towing industry, Gary has met people who have squirreled a lot of stuff away. He found an appropriate bronze steering wheel, for instance. Most recently, the *Elise Ann Conners* had been steered with a wheel from a 1948 Hyster forklift. This he knows because he talked with the guy who installed it in the 1960s. Her own wheel had ended up in a bar in Albany to pay someone's bill. "It's not unusual," Gary says, "that steering wheels, running lights, and such removable stuff went to pay bar tabs."

It's not practical to live on the boat while you're restoring it, Gary says. "But it's not practical not to, either. With a 120-year old boat, if something goes wrong, it could go very wrong." Ice is one of the occasional hazards in Rondout Creek. There's an oil terminal across the way, and normally the ice gets broken by the Coast Guard. But two icebreakers were broken down during a cold snap three years ago, and eighteen inches of ice built up in ten days. When water freezes, it expands, and the pressure squeezes everything in the creek. The boat doesn't want to be made skinnier. Because the southern side of the creek is in the shade all day, ice builds up on that side and spreads northward, toward where the *Elise Ann Conners* is berthed. When the ice reaches her, it pushes her into the bulkhead. One night, the pilings crushed. She got hung up on spikes in the pilings and leaned over, making a wider footprint in the creek, which increased the ice-stress all the more.

"Of course it all comes to a head at three in the morning, ten below out. You look down the length of the creek and see a crown on the ice, like on a road, from the pressure." Eventually, because it doesn't want to bend, the ice snaps. Gary says it was like being inside a cannon when it went off. "Books fly off the shelves from the vibrations. It's the scariest thing I've ever witnessed. I'm thinking that's it, the boat's breaking." He called friends, other boat owners. "Holy shit," they said, "it must be

Wheelhouse of the *Elise Ann Conners* in 1993, before restoration. Wheel from 1948 Hyster forklift. COURTESY OF JIM MATTHEWS.

serious." Several people, several chain saws, and several hours relieved the pressure. Since then Gary has kept a chain saw handy.

Hercules

The 409-gross-ton steam tug *Hercules* is unusual in that she is a part of the San Francisco Maritime National Historical Park. She was restored using federal money and a tremendous number of volunteer man-hours—forty-four thousand since 1988. One of those volunteers, and their leader for much of this time, was Tom MacFadyen. He served as the engineer aboard the restored *Hercules* whenever she steamed out across San Francisco Bay, as she did twenty-eight times after 1991. But, at this writing, she is forced to stay pierside, her Coast Guard certification once again withheld for want of five thousand dollars' worth of work on her steamplates. She is at risk of losing the volunteer crew known as the "engine gang," to whom the boat is dead if she can't steam again. And, according to MacFadyen, there is no one in the Park Service today who knows how to operate a steam vessel of this sort.

Built in Camden, New Jersey, in 1907, before the opening of the Panama Canal, *Hercules* started her career by towing her sister *Goliath* through the Strait of Magellan to their new home in San Francisco Bay. A true oceangoing tug, she was huge for her day, 150 feet long and carrying a thousand-horse triple-expansion engine. For several decades, she towed schooners, log rafts, and barges along the North American coastline and to and from Hawaii. Toward the latter part of her working life, she worked in San Francisco Harbor for the Western Pacific Railroad Company, pushing bargefuls of railroad cars back and forth across the bay. In 1962 she was laid up, and in 1975, she was taken on by the California State Park Foundation. In 1978 the National Park Service took her over. A decade later, in a dock trial, the boiler was fired up for the first time since her retirement. Smoke again billowed out of *Hercules*'s stack. Someone on shore thought the old boat was afire and called the fire department. A fire truck roared down, all set to rescue the people aboard, and found they didn't need rescuing at all but instead were firing up the refurbished boiler. "The dock trial is to see if you can get things to work at all," explains Tom, "and later on you get it all to work right."

It took another couple of years to get it all right, and in 1991 she made her first sea voyage under her own steam in nearly thirty years, going out to greet the hospital ship *Mercy* when she returned from the first Gulf War. Ted Miles, of the San Francisco Maritime State Historic Park, was aboard her then, and has made other trips since. What he likes best is to watch people's faces—people who are used to hearing big diesel engines—as she pulls away from the pier in near silence.

Hercules at the San Francisco Maritime National Historic Park. Courtesy of Don Sutherland.

Federal ownership of the boat brings interesting aspects to her preservation. She is in good shape today, except for the matter of certifying her steamplates. Her future is in the hands of bureaucrats. Sometimes these people have both the resources and the will to benefit the vessels left in their charge, sometimes they have one but not the other, and sometimes they have neither. Any volunteer organization has to acknowledge the importance of those people. In the case of the *Hercules*, volunteer help is even more important than usual, because only the volunteers have the experience and knowledge to maintain her archaic systems. There are always political issues—funding being the most basic, both how much and how will it be spent—but nearly as important are questions like, how many volunteers and guests can be aboard for a trip, and who says who gets to come. Fortunately, the *Hercules* should steam again before long, but her long-term welfare depends on the balance between the career Park Service personnel and the volunteers.

A Less than Happy Ending: The *Seguin*

Shipwright Dave Short has gone on to far better things since, but his first experience was supposed to be on the old wooden steam tug *Seguin,* as an apprentice at the young museum that today is the splendid Maine Maritime Museum, in Bath. Her story is not as rosy as that of some of the other old vessels who've gone into restoration, including at least one tugboat that Dave has been involved with more recently.

Designed by William Pattee, one of the most prolific designers on the Maine coast in those times, the 88-foot *Seguin* was built in Bath in 1884. Steam-powered throughout her life, she made the switch from the relatively primitive surface-condenser engine to compound, and finished her days with 350 horsepower. She was the first tug east of San Francisco to have an independent air system and circulating pump. The simple matter of having standing headroom in the fire room was unheard-of on the Kennebec River before the launch of the *Seguin*. The men who worked on her must have appreciated that innovation.

The tug worked coastwise and on the Kennebec until after World War II. Noted marine historian and author and former director of the Maine Maritime Museum, Ralph Linwood Snow, describes her career as including assorted fires and collisions and a sinking during high water at Richmond Bridge. Even so, it was an unremarkable life overall, he says—but keep an eye out for the release of his book about her. The *Seguin* towed schooners and barges along the coast of Maine, took ice to Norfolk, assisted ships moving in and out of docks along the Kennebec and at other Maine ports, and worked at launchings.

In the late 1940s, she moved to Belfast and Eastern Maine Towage, where she spent the rest of her working days primarily as a docking tug. Corliss Holland remembers her from the 1960s: "I made a few trips on her. It was kinda fun. She was getting soft, though. You put her onto towing something, she'd lengthen out about three feet. You pushed something, she'd shorten up."

Her last skipper, Clarence "Nick" Nickerson, remembers the *Seguin* vividly "because most of it was nightmare stuff." He didn't take much note of it all at the time,

Seguin.
POSTCARD,
DATE UNKNOWN.

even though the *Seguin* and her stablemate, the *Clyde B. Holmes,* were among the last steam tugs around, because, he says, it was just a job. He ran two wooden boats, the *Seguin* and the *Pauline Holmes.* They both leaked down through the decks and were hard to keep repaired. After the *Seguin* was hauled in Rockland each year for routine maintenance, Nick would want to take her straight home, but he was told to let her lay at the dock for two or three days first, "to go back in shape. They were afraid she'd get out by the breakwater and sink."

Corliss remembers when she nearly did sink. "One winter, January or February, before we towed it to Bath, *Seguin* was just settin' there. We come back from working over the weekend, and one of the guys went down to check the *Seguin,* and she was half-sunk. The sump pumps had failed to pump—it wasn't because of electric failure, just the motors."

She wasn't reliable at work, either. They only used her when they needed three tugs on a ship, Captain Nickerson says, and she was so light and had so little power that she couldn't actually do a great deal. "We didn't use her much, which was a good thing. A few days before we were going to use her, we'd want to be sure most things were somewhat working on her." Most often they weren't, he says. She had no living quarters, no place for the men to stay aboard, so they always brought her home after a job, even if they had to make the trip alone—not a good idea with her. One night, crossing the bay, they discovered that the water tank was empty and they had nothing to put in it. The boiler can't run on salt water. "I thought we'd have to tie up to the bell buoy," says Nick.

John Annis was the engineer. "We'll get her to the dock if we have to blow her up," he told Nick, for whom the men always came first, and the heck with the boat. They did get home, but, Nick says, "she was some hot."

In 1966, Clyde Holmes offered to give the *Seguin* to the young Maine Maritime Museum on her retirement. "How soon and when?" asked Nick when he heard, ready to see her go, but it wasn't until 1969 that the transfer took place. "We had enough problems just trying to keep it afloat—finally Clyde decided it was just too risky to have it around."

They dressed her for a last trip around Belfast Harbor, flying signal flags from stem to stern. "We didn't know what order we put 'em in. Don't know to this day if we spelled naughty words or not," says Nick. She poured out smoke during that jaunt. "That thing would hardly run that day—that's why there was all that black smoke. Some settler unit or pump, something in the cooling wasn't working. All we done was run away from the dock just far enough that we could get back to the dock, hopefully."

A day or two later, she was off to Bath under tow. They towed her almost all the way to Bath, then cut her loose on her home Kennebec River at Doubling Point, and she finished the trip on her own steam. The museum at that time was above the old bridge between Woolwich and Bath. "I couldn't remember the whistle signal for the bridge," Nick says. "I just blew, and they opened it up. They probably knew I was coming, anyway." There was a welcoming ceremony at the museum. "Captain Clarence Nickerson, master of the tug *Seguin*," Nick signed the guest book.

The trustees of the museum were a conservative group, Linwood Snow says, and probably they didn't really know what was entailed in keeping a big, elderly wooden vessel alive. The Boothbay Harbor Schooner Museum took her on for the first few years, but didn't do much more than superficial maintenance. Snow came to the Maine Maritime Museum as executive director in 1972, and it was two or three months before he even learned that the old tug belonged to his museum and was his responsibility. He says he didn't know much about wooden vessels, but he could see that things weren't going well with her.

In November of that year the *Seguin* sank in Boothbay Harbor—through no fault of her own, actually. She caught her guards on a piling and was held down when the tide came in. Could have happened to anyone, and not much harm was done. But a year later she sank again, spilling some oil and causing consternation locally and with the EPA. The Schooner Museum had had it with her. That summer, 1974, she had to leave. She spent a couple of years hanging out at a dock in Bath while preparations were made to haul her at the old Percy & Small yard, which was the new home of the Maine Maritime Museum. A skidway had to be built, and she had to be partially dismantled to lessen her weight. With her water-cooled boiler and compound engine, she was a heavy old thing. There was no money, so the work was all done by volunteers. She was finally hauled in December 1977. They built a pole building around her and got some work done on her.

Terry Geaghan was a trustee of the museum at the time, as he is again, and was one of the primary volunteers. Snow says today, "I would probably have shot myself without him." Geaghan isn't a tugboat enthusiast, but he enjoyed the camaraderie and did a lot of work. His field is marine art, specializing in Down Easters, the big, deep-water sailing vessels from Maine. "A tugboat is perfectly good in the foreground of a painting of big sail," he says, echoing a friend of his who says that horses are only good for holding up Indians in pictures. But he did recognize the value of a hundred-year-old wooden steam tug, the likes of which wasn't to be seen elsewhere.

At age eighteen, Dave Short came to the museum to work as an apprentice on the *Seguin*. He was involved with some of the efforts to stabilize her. John Nugent was working on the *Bowdoin*, which was also to be hauled at the Percy & Small yard, and found himself killing time until a high-enough tide came along to get the deep-keeled schooner out of the water. Under John's tutelage, Dave and another apprentice took the lines off the old tug and lofted them full size in the shipyard's renovated mold loft. But soon all efforts on *Seguin* stopped, and Dave was put to work on the *Bowdoin*. Later the lines in the mold loft were painted over for another building project at the museum, and what documentation had been made of the *Seguin* was thereby lost.

In the fall of 1981, Linwood Snow resigned from the museum and moved to San Diego. By then, for a variety of reasons—"most of them fiscal," according to Snow—the museum had suspended operations on the *Seguin*. It had a lot of other priorities. Although the tug had consumed enormous amounts of time and energy, no one remaining at the museum had any interest in her. "The *Seguin* was always a millstone," recalls Snow.

The museum called together a committee to decide the fate of the old vessel. Some feel that the conclusion the committee would come to had been decided before it met. Sure enough, they recommended to the trustees that the *Seguin* be broken up and, after saving a few parts, disposed of. "The decision alienated some," says Snow. "Most people didn't give a damn."

Among those who did care were Snow and Geaghan. "At best," says Terry Geaghan, "it would have been very difficult to complete the job. A very small cadre brought her as far as she got—money was very hard coming. But I thought that since she was stable, they could have been more patient. We had poured so much energy into her. . . ." He admits that probably letting her go was the practical thing, but then declares, "It wasn't the right thing to do." And he's still upset that, once decided, the disposal took place so fast. "There was literally not time to coalesce any opposition."

Dave Short, today a master shipwright of national renown, still dreams of the *Seguin*, of walking down through the shed to where the saws and other tools were on the other side of her from the *Bowdoin*. "The *Seguin* was just a big, dark presence," Dave says. "We were always walking around her." Knowing what he knows today, he says she *could* have been saved.

Terry Geaghan agrees. "It was not a technical problem to restore her, it was a money problem and a willpower problem." They had neither money nor the institutional will to do it, and the *Seguin* was broken up, and the pieces not saved—most of her—were hauled off to the landfill. Recalls museum Library Director Nathan Lipfert, "We didn't have a funeral pyre or anything."

Luna

Built in 1930, the Boston tug *Luna* only worked for a little over forty years, but as an early diesel-electric tug, she is of historic significance too. (Although it has been said she was the first diesel-electric harbor tug, this honor apparently goes to a New York tug belonging to the Pennsylvania Railroad, which went to work in 1924.) *Luna* has had fanciers trying to restore her for decades. The *Luna* Preservation Society, her current owners, rescued her from the knackers in 1995. During the next few years, they came up with $750,000, much of it in a federal grant, which allowed them to make the most critical repairs and bring her hull back to its proper condition. Still wearing the rubber roofing membrane diaper that had kept her afloat for five and a half years while they raised the money, *Luna* was towed to Samples Shipyard in Boothbay Harbor, Maine, in the fall of 2000. She had been at that same yard in the late 1950s, for what most likely was the last significant work done on her before her restoration.

Once known as the queen of the Boston Towboat Company's fleet, this wooden boat spent her working years on the Boston waterfront. Built in 1930, she was designed by John G. Alden, best known for his sailing yachts. Her hull and deckhouses were constructed at the M. M. Davis Shipbuilding Company in Solomons, Maryland, which had built thirty tugs since 1885 and some Alden-designed sailing yachts too. She was finished at the Bethlehem Steel Shipyard in East Boston. Her then-innovative diesel-electric system was developed by General Electric, which for more than two decades featured her in advertisements. To this day, there are docking masters who prefer diesel-electric for its precision of movement and the gentleness that can come with it.

The *Luna* was finished with more elegance than the average tug, with a white hull and bright houses, inside and out. Structurally, too, she shows more refinement than many commercial vessels. Many deck beams were braced with both vertical and horizontal knees, and her bulkheads were double-diagonally planked with oak.

She still has all her original equipment: her Winton diesels, General Electric generators, and the twenty-ton motor that actually turned the wheel. They're not looking any the better for fifteen months spent under the waters of Boston Harbor during one of the most difficult periods of her retirement. There is hope that several components might be brought back to operating condition, but it was the lack of replacement parts that was the last straw leading to the end of her working career back in 1970.

At Samples, shipwright David Short was the project manager, the owner's representative, as it were. Dave's work has taken him around the country—three years on Long Island, a few in Rhode Island, New York, Pennsylvania, Massachusetts, and occasionally some time at home in Maine. He was pleased that *Luna* gave him reason to come back to Maine. It was good to be home, and the ten to twelve hours a week he was to give to the *Luna* project allowed him to work on his own house in Liberty.

Although his role didn't require hands-on time, it was serious work. Mentally, the project manager has to use all his background and force of will to iron out any troubles that might come along. "I'm the eyes and ears of the owner," Dave says. But there were very few difficulties at Samples, "no substantial instances of misunderstanding or conflict." (This is not always the situation for project managers.) In *Luna*'s case, as in that of any wooden boat work, the scope of work to be done couldn't be known fully before it started but there were no significant aspects of the work that hadn't been at least contemplated. For instance, though it looked at first as if it mightn't have to be done, when they got into the underlying structure, it was clear that the whole stern should be rebuilt—the horn timber and everything behind the sternpost, the whole fantail.

Luna, ready to leave Boothbay Harbor, May 2002. Author photo.

It was up to Dave to say that this plank or timber had to go, or that a less urgent aspect of the planned work should be skipped to provide money for another job that had gotten bigger, and to negotiate the price of any change in the work plan. He had to look over all the bills and "keep the yard honest," though honesty was never a question at Samples. "The yard's in business to make money, and it did, but the boat was well served, with excellent work. They went beyond what was expected. The individuals on the project at every level took a lot of pride in having *Luna* there."

Dave himself got some time in on her. "We were having trouble rounding up caulkers," Dave says. "I said I'd caulk if it wasn't a conflict of interest." The *Luna* Preservation people had to check it out with the Massachusetts Historical Commission, as the vast majority of the money for the work had come through their hands. But they said that under the circumstances, on this unique project, it would be all right if the project manager actually worked on the vessel—as long as he wasn't paid with their money. OK. Red tape. "It was beneficial that I was there all the time," Dave says. He saw each plank as the seams were reefed out.

And today the *Luna*'s hull looks great. "First, we planed down all the boards to see what condition they were in," says Chris Braga, co-owner of the yard. "It looked bad, but those three-inch planks were in good shape." She is nearly brand new from the waterline up, with new horn timber, rim timbers, frames, a lot of deck beams. "Just about everything," says Chris. She has a new two-inch oak shoe and new inner and outer stems, but most of the structure below the waterline was okay.

They did replace a couple of thousand board feet of planking, and they reefed and caulked all the seams. The planks were originally all treenailed and wedged inside and out, and are once again. They found locust for the treenails in a nearby town, and one of the guys at the yard cut it into small blocks, which they took to a pegmaker in New Hampshire.

At re-launch, she was good and tight. The pumps kicked on for only one minute every half hour or so, and soon it was only a minute a day. The boat is now back in Boston and ready to stand by until the rest of the restoration work can be done. No more diapers for the *Luna*!

12
Characters
and Character Tugs

Tugnuts

Some people who work on tugs do their job and go home, while others love their job and the vessels themselves. Then there are the many non-tugboaters who also love the boats. To some of these people, there is nothing more fun than to ride tugs. In fact, on his annual vacation, one British fellow flies across the Atlantic, walks in on some tug dispatcher and asks, "What have you got, going where?" and spends his two weeks on tugs. And another gave himself two days' steady riding in New York Harbor for his sixtieth birthday. All these enthusiasts are known as "tugnuts," and they collect stuff. They collect data about tugs, photographs of tugs, and information about tugs and tug companies and the work they do and have done in the past. They collect stories and artifacts, and they share much of what they learn with one another. It was inevitable they'd get together with some degree of formality, and in fact there are a number of organizations, including the Tugboats Enthusiasts Society of the Americas, the online Yahoo! Tugboats group, and Lekko International Tug Enthusiasts Society, a far larger group based in the Netherlands. On the West Coast of the U.S. is a group of tugnuts most of whom live on or vacation on retired tugs (when they aren't rebuilding them). Each group encompasses the whole range of people interested in the subject, from people born and bred in the business all the way down through people like me, who can't say why, but are captivated by tugs. Is there another field in which lay people—at least, intelligent, thinking, respectful lay people—are so much accepted by the people in the day-to-day grind?

Joe DeMuccio was a tugnut like many others, but also not like any other. A New York City policeman, he used to hang out on Staten Island, where many tug companies make their homes, and watch the tugs come and go and take pictures of them. By 1990, he had retired from the force and had founded the Tugboat Enthusiasts Society (commonly known as TES) for fellow tugnuts.

There are about four hundred TES members, running from presidents of major tug companies to regular people-in-the-street who just like tugs, about half being present and former tugboaters of all stripes. There is usually an annual gathering in some American port where members visit with one another and ride tugboats, thanks to the generosity of and acceptance by local tugboating companies.

The society's journal *Tugbitts* appears in TES members' mailboxes quarterly. It is a labor of true love, put together by the joint efforts of many members spread across the country. It is filled with stories and photographs of tugs, tug companies, and related industries. For example, a couple of years back, "Building Gotham," by editor-in-chief Brent Dibner filled twenty-six pages as it chronicled the sand-and-gravel business in New York City. Subsequent issues included other members' recollections and photographs of the same subject. *TugBitts* always reports launchings, purchases, and tug events of note in many regions around the country, news largely contributed by local members. And for a while, as long as the supply lasted, they would reprint a short piece by the late Carl Wayne, in recognition of his tremendous contribution to the archives of tugboating.

Carl Wayne, like Joe DeMuccio, retired from another field entirely but was always interested in tugboats. He set up an online database of information that included the statistics of some seven thousand tugboats, most of the tugs registered in the United States. There were several sections of the database, showing the registrations during different time periods. It was possible to look up an existing tug and uncover her earlier names and owners, as well as her date of building, length and tonnage, power, and any repowerings she'd had over the years. One could also research a vessel from an earlier period. Carl also started an online discussion group on Yahoo!, where a diverse mix of people, mostly American, British, and Dutch, post messages and photographs or simply lurk and read.

Unfortunately, both Carl and Joe have passed on, but TES continues, and the database site has largely been restored. Meanwhile, with more than three hundred members, the Yahoo! tug group list has gone wild. On any day, there might be a couple of requests for information—perhaps from Captain Franz VonRiedel, who seems to be collecting photos and data about every tugboat ever built, or maybe from another member looking for the history of his own boat, or one that crossed his path recently, or one that simply came to mind after many years. There's always someone posting photographs—one of K-Sea's executives, Bob Mattsson, has posted a great number showing the tugs he sees going by his office on Mariner's Harbor, Staten Island. Others post shots of historic vessels or particular situations.

Some questions come from passersby, such as the woman who wrote to the group in the winter of 2003 after stumbling onto memorabilia from her grandfather, who'd passed on in 1976. He'd been a Champlain Canal pilot for forty years. She had happy memories of riding tugs with him as a youngster and hoped to find photos or to hear from people who might have worked with him. She mentioned that her great-uncle had also been a pilot and tug man.

Bob Mattsson replied, "Yup, I worked with your grandfather and your great-uncle." Bob told of being on the *Eileen McAllister* with both of them when he was a young fellow working as an oiler, the engineer's flunky back when an engineer had such a helper. The brothers loved to play poker and fight, he said. "Cat-and-dog brother fights that were forgotten the next day. We would tie to a tree or two in the Northern Canal and walk up to a local gin mill. After a few drinks and a couple of shuffleboard games, a small war would break out between the two of them, and one would always try to get back to the boat before the other so as to leave him ashore. The chief or assistant were used to this and wouldn't start the engine, so they would try to intimidate *me* into starting 'er up, but I wasn't that dopey. Eventually everyone would make it back, and we would sleep until morning when the 'fog' lifted."

Bob described the *Eileen* as a strange-looking tug with portlights as pilothouse windows. "No one remembers if this was for some esthetic or safety reason or be-cause the portlights were on hand," he said, adding that he would love a photo of her if anyone out there had one. "I think, when we were younger, we took all this for granted and didn't take pictures because the price of film and developing was a pretty hefty percentage of the salary of the day."

Brian Fournier quickly replied that he had plenty of pictures of the old boat in all her color schemes: McAllister's, his father's (Brian was seven years old when Arthur bought her), and her final paint when she belonged to Roger Hale. The *Eileen* was scrapped after she sank in Prospect Harbor, Maine, in 1982 or 1983. Brian posted a couple of photos of the tug.

Another request for information came from a fellow who wanted to build a model of a particular tug. There was some discussion among the group as to whether the boat had been powered by diesel or steam. Ultimately, the clearly definitive answer was produced—steam—and brought this acknowledgement from the modeler: "Again I must say thanks to the responses. I would have been happy with steam or diesel—actually I wanted to build steam, it allows me to have a steam whistle and smoke. . . . Not to be funny, but I start to think that if I asked questions like how wide were the deck planks or the diameter of the quarter bitts, I could get an answer." He's probably right.

The tug group was helpful to me, too, producing information for this book on regulations, particular vessels, Hell Gate, mechanical issues, and all manner of other things. Photographs, too.

Captain Jim Sharp and *Wrestler*

Besides the multitude of tugnuts (professional tugboaters and otherwise), there are individual characters too. One whom we've already met is Captain Jim Sharp, and he likes to talk about Arthur Fournier, most certainly a character himself. Jim worked for Arthur from time to time over a number of years. Some of Jim's stories, while ostensibly about Arthur, are as much about himself.

"Arthur sometimes is a man of few words," says Jim. The day Arthur told him to pick up a tug in New Jersey, across from the Big Apple, and run it down to Philadelphia to pick up a dump scow, he used very few words. He arranged the crew's transportation so they would get to the tug at one-thirty or two in the morning, which didn't please anyone much, but aboard they piled in the dark of night. Jim did notice that the stack was freshly painted—in a strange mixture of chartreuse and green. When the boat was warmed up and ready to leave the dock, Jim called Arthur for final instructions. He also asked about the paint.

"Don't worry about it," Arthur told him. "Just get out before dawn, and don't get your head too far above the pilothouse windows." Oh boy!

They ran down New York Harbor, rounded Sandy Hook, and started down the Jersey coast for Delaware Bay. "We were asking each other about the status of the union work-stoppage in the big city. None of us were up-to-date with the waterfront news."

But it was indeed a union story. Arthur had recently been hired to take a dredge and two dump scows out of New York during a union strike, and pick up a scow in Philadelphia. He used a tug named *Cold Point*. When he had made his security call announcing that he was preparing to get under way, there was a lot of hollering on the radio. The unions didn't want one single tug moving in the harbor. "You can scream all you want," said Arthur, "I'm going under the Verrazano Bridge. Get used to it." Out he went. He delivered the equipment to the desired destination and handed the owner a bill for $50,000.

The boat Jim was in would have attracted much unappreciated attention if, like the *Cold Point*, it had been wearing its original blue diamond stack markings. Safer this way.

The story doesn't end there, though. Jim got to Philadelphia and found the scow he was to pick up, a 200- by 80-foot dump scow with its manholes all open. Kids had gotten aboard and thrown the covers overboard.

"Man, I can't take a dump scow to sea with no manhole covers on it, can I? A half-million-dollar tug and a huge barge?" Jim called Arthur. "There aren't any manhole covers," he said.

"I know it," Arthur said. "Just be careful."

"The weather's supposed to shut in here."

"Well, wait till the weather goes by. Just use your judgment," Arthur said. "Oh, and by the way, Jim, it isn't insured."

Since Jim was committed, they tied up alongside the barge, dropped the mooring, and started out, pulling in somewhere to let the weather go by. When the wind turned around, they lengthened out the chain pennants and, with a long towline, lugged the scow on up through the race by Block Island. Jim shortened up again after Cleveland Ledge Light, going toward the Cape Cod Canal channel, where it's narrow and there was a fierce current. The scow was swinging back and forth, brushing the buoys on one side and then swinging out into the channel, and there approaching was an Army Corps of Engineers tug with a barge.

"Calling tug with barge eastbound," the Corps tug called on the radio. "You gonna corral that thing or are you coming at me that way? We have a barge behind us that's behaving itself."

"Well, I know this one's *not* behaving very well, but I'll swing her the other way when we get up abreast of you."

"Come up to the right place," recalls Jim, "I gave a little hitch, she swung off the other way and swung around him, just as if I know what I'm doing—all the time I'm sweating bullets in there."

They got to Boston and took the scow on the hip. "There I was with a huge scow sticking out ahead of me, wanting to get in and get tied up. We were all tired, on this

The *Wrestler* came into Camden, Maine, on a miserably cold day. COURTESY OF JIM SHARP.

damn mission for four or five days—you know how it is, the last mile. I was making eight knots with this rig, and some fool in a Chris-Craft cabin cruiser thought it would be fun to go underneath the rake of that scow. I lay on the horn, but he kept coming, and he disappeared. I came back into reverse as quick as I could, but you don't stop a rig like that, and we kept on a-coming. He came underneath the rake and finally out the other side, going like hell. If I'd run him over, I'd have been in jail forever."

Jim has been owning and running boats of one sort or another for years. Almost always those boats are traditional in nature (his trimaran *Screech* is a stretch.) For twenty-four years, he sailed a Maine windjammer, the former Gloucester fishing schooner *Adventure*. One fall in the early 1970s, he went off looking for a tug. He describes the *Wrestler* as the cutest thing he ever saw. Only fifty feet long, she was built in Staten Island in 1924 to do little jobs in New York Harbor. Except for some cosmetic details, everything about her was original, including the tremendous old Cooper-Bessemer engine, eight feet high and fourteen feet long, with four huge cylinders. "I saw her when she came into the dock there, *chuggety-chug, chuggety-chug*, blowing smoke rings out the stack. Oh man, it was such a neat boat."

The owners of the tug were planning to repower her. "Please don't change that engine out," he pleaded with them, "because if you do, you'll spoil that tug. Instead, sell me the old girl." They had another tug, a steel one, and he suggested they repower her instead. It would make a better work boat. The *Wrestler* was a museum piece.

"Oh no. Oh no," they said.

"Well, here's my card, here's my number. I'm prepared to pay you cash."

"Oh no. We want that boat. We're gonna keep it."

"Well, OK," said Jim, "but if you change your mind, let me know." And in a couple of months, they called him. He went down and bought her. Their engineer showed him how to run the engine.

"She starts on air," Jim explains. "You get everything ready, pump her fuel up, pump her oil pressure up and all that. You pull this great big lever down, and you hear this great rush of air into the cylinders. You have to spot the flywheel—great big, heavy wheel with a great big iron bar you jump on in order to turn her over until she's at the right spot. After you release all the compression releases, then you close them up, and you grab this bar and pull down.

"And then *whoosh*—with that inertia, the flywheel starts, the whole vessel rocks back and forth in the opposite direction, and these little wavelets come out from under the hull. And *whsh zhg zhg zhg*—and then smoke rings start popping out the stack, and she'll be running. It's a joy to start the thing."

The engine had four cylinders. "I named them all: Harry, Herb, Fred, and Charlie.

They were all individual cylinders, built so you can tear one apart while the others are running. You can take the rockers off the top, and take the cylinder head off and service the valves and do whatever you had to do, and put it all back together—all when you're under way.

"Each cylinder had a pyrometer that told you its heat, and you adjusted the fuel in each cylinder so they were all doing an equal amount of work. So we'd say, 'Hey, Charlie isn't doing his share of the load. Go down and fix Charlie a little bit,' and you'd go down and increase the fuel a little bit, and then you'd have to balance it with the other three. She was just such a character. There's one other engine like it in the country, and that's in the Smithsonian."

He fixed up the *Wrestler* inside, with minimal accommodations forward and a little wood stove in the main cabin. She had a couple of small windows with leaded stained glass—a former owner had set her up as a sort of yacht. "It gave her such character, though of course she had a lot of character anyway."

Jim used her for small commercial jobs and towed the *Adventure* to the shipyard and back. One winter he took the *Wrestler* down the Intracoastal Waterway to Florida. "I was hoping to get a few jobs, and I did a give a tow to a couple of boats along the way, but I did it mostly for fun. (Don't tell the IRS that!) We were looking for work, but you can't break into towing work easily, and I didn't want to stop to do construction work for months at a time anyway."

In her day, the *Wrestler* was top-notch, Jim says. "She had everything first-class on her. Going to Florida, she was just like an old trolley car—she'd jump up and down, jiggety jig, jiggety jig. She had these round pilothouse windows that slid up and down, and every now and then one of them would give way and slide down on you."

She almost sank under him one time. "I guess she'd have to blame it on me." Like many towboats, she had black topsides, and in a dry year the spring sun dried out the topsides and the planking seams opened up. "I had a barge to deliver to Cutler, so I had to go offshore. We got a little roll out there, and that meant the topside seams got underwater, and they'd spurt in. Well, next thing I knew, she had a bilge full of water." There was an automatic pump on the engine, which Jim hated to use because there was always oil in her bilge. "But I had to turn that on, and we pumped and pumped and pumped, and we finally delivered that barge. Then, on the way home, it rolled even more. I guess the pump got fouled up, and the water was up over the floor plates." She was leaking so badly, he turned and ran with the wind, seeking protection behind the northern end of North Haven. "We were quite worried there for awhile. But it was only because she had dried out so much. There was nothing wrong with her."

"She had a five-ton bollard pull, but with her enormous propeller and that old engine, the engine never turned more than 300 rpm, tops. You could throttle her right down until she was firing under 60 a minute, so every second, she'd go *bmmb, bmmb, bmmb.* You could count her cylinders—it was just so musical. So she was a love."

Jim owned her for about five years. "She was a great, great little boat. If there's a boat you want to hug and take home and put under your pillow or on your mantelpiece, it's that one. I'm sorry I ever sold her, but you can't keep 'em all.

"I don't know if she's alive today. I sold her to Boothbay, and he sold her to Portland—she sunk down there—and she went to Baltimore and was working there, and then she was donated to the Philadelphia Marine Museum, and I understand she sunk while they had her. I don't know what's ever happened to the poor old thing."

Captain Eliot Winslow and His Fleet

Then there is Captain Eliot Winslow. "I've seen a lot of water," says Eliot, who is in his nineties, "but as towboating goes, I'm way in the rear. My son David is more active now—he's taking over." Even as a kid, David was running tugboats. "Not legally, but as long as I was along, he could handle it," his father said.

Every year, back in the 1950s and '60s, fifteen or sixteen oil tankers came up the Sheepscot River to the power plant in Wiscasset, and every one of them had to have a tugboat to turn it around. At that time, the nearest tugs were in Portland or Portsmouth. Invariably, it would be a multiday job for the tug, and that would run up the cost. "The crew didn't like the trip," Eliot Winslow says. "They took a licking one way or the other. Most generally, you don't get three or four days' smooth sailing in a row.

"One day, the tug couldn't get here, and the ship sat out there—at $10,000 a day. So they got hold of me, asked what could I do?" Eliot, who piloted ships up the river for the oil companies, was also running tour boats at the time. He tied on to the tanker with his three tour boats and long hawsers. "The longer a line is, the more pull you're getting. Leverage."

That was the beginning of the Winslow towing business. Mrs. Winslow, Marjorie, calls their fleet of small boats the Mosquito Fleet. Eliot used those boats for three or four years. "I never got into trouble, but there was no margin, no safety factor. Five hundred and fifty-, five hundred and eighty-five-foot–long tankers—we were lucky.

"When Texaco came along, they said, 'That's a farmer's rig. We don't want that,'" and that's when Eliot bought the *Alice Winslow*. She was built in 1897, originally steam, but already converted to diesel. "She did well by me—paid for herself in a couple of years. She was old, but she held on. I had just her for twenty years."

He describes the old *Alice* as a typical old-fashioned tug, long and narrow, but fast. "Twelve knots is fast for a tug. The average tug doesn't go much more than ten. It's like a workhorse—he can't run, but he can pull." And he explains why two vessels could have the same motor but perform entirely differently: "The difference is in the reduction gear. Take a thousand-horse motor, direct-drive—the shaft will rotate at the same rate as the engine. But you put it through a reduction gear so the engine turns 1,000 rpm and the shaft turns at 333—that's a 3:1 reduction. And as you increase the reduction gear, you increase the size of the propeller and take the pitch out of it, and you have more want-to-go-ahead, but it hasn't got speed. A big blade coming around slowly, rather than a smaller blade coming fast."

The *Alice Winslow* had a 1,200-horsepower GM, a 12-567. That's 12 cylinders, 567 cubic inches each. "They were a dime a dozen after the war. Everything the navy had, had a 567 in it. You could buy them at the corner drugstore."

David now runs the company. He came up through the hawsepipe, starting younger than most. He never considered any other work. He remembers his first job, when he was eight, carrying Santa Claus from Robinson's Wharf on Southport Island over to Boothbay Harbor, on the old *Alice*. "I was running boats long before I got a license. All the kids that grow up in the business do that. And in the 1970s, they'd just come out with licenses—all the guys who worked for Dad were grandfathered anyway."

When the *Alice Winslow* was getting up toward ninety years old, she was showing her age. "I was afraid she'd sink with me on her," says Eliot. "The superstructure was well rusted. Seeing that, you'd wonder what condition the bottom was in, but it was Swedish iron—lasts a long time. That's what held her up. I sold her to the West Indies. Anything that old doesn't bring much money, and I had her advertised at twenty-five thousand. The engine was good, but she was old."

Marjorie speaks up. "You have to remember, this was his first tug. He'd named her after his mother, and she'd done awfully well by him. She was the love of his life. We took one of the other tugs out to escort her down the river, and when he waved goodbye to her, he was in tears."

"She was a faithful gal. She was wonderful," says Eliot. "But I was thankful she wouldn't sink at the dock."

"We came home feeling kinda dejected," Marjorie continues, and then they heard the radio crackle on. It was the new owner of the *Alice*. "Tug base, tug base, we're taking on water and coming back to the dock." Eliot worried that she was going to sink at his dock after all.

The *Alice* had a wooden deck, and it had lost some of its fastenings. When she got outside, a few planks came off. "A tug is low in the water anyway, of course, and the water comes in one side and goes out the other," Eliot explains. "But it lifted some planks, and water was going down in the engine room. We got some cement and reinforcing wire and cemented over the missing planks. I wanted him to wait a couple of days for the cement to harden, but he was in a hurry to go, so he sailed again."

When the new owner got to Florida, he picked up a job to go from the Atlantic coast to the Gulf coast, which paid for his trip down. "But a year later, I got a call from the Coast Guard, said the *Alice Winslow* had sunk off the West Indies. They thought I still owned her.

"An accident is generally the combination of several things happening at the same time," Eliot says. "They'd gotten into some fairly heavy weather, and when a ship rolls, the fuel gets all mixed up. Diesel has algae, bugs that grow in the water that condenses in the tanks. It plugs the filters, and you have to change them, if you don't put something in to kill the algae. Well, the engine stopped, and she drifted ashore. It wasn't her fault—you could say it was improper maintenance.

"That guy lost his son in the accident, too."

Although much of the Winslow business of late has been in Bath or Portland, any tug company gets into the coastal rescue business from time to time.

About twenty years ago, Eliot says, he was running a passenger boat one night when he heard some unusual radio chatter. "I said to my mate, 'I think someone's in trouble—listen!'" It was the big Nova Scotia ferry *Prince of Fundy* being towed into Portland by the Coast Guard. "So I said, 'Let's get these people off this boat, and take the tug and see what we can do.'

"Out we went in the old *Alice,* and when we approached the scene, the captain said he didn't need help, he had all the help he needed." Eliot informed the captain that if commercial help was available, the Coast Guard didn't have to assist. "And of course the captain of the Coast Guard boat was listening to all this on his radio. He couldn't do anything until Boston approved, though, and he asked me what was my horsepower and so forth."

The master of the *Prince of Fundy* told the Coast Guard he didn't want Winslow's help, that he was happy with what he had, but the Coast Guard told him they were going to drop the tow. "Well, my wife was on the air all through this, " says Eliot. "She has a radio at home, and we'd been talking back and forth.

"The captain asked me, 'What is your fee?' and I said my fee will be commensurate with the services rendered. That tells nothing, of course. 'I want to know how much it will cost. I want to talk to the lady ashore you've been talking with.' 'She's only the night clerk. She has no authority,' I told him."

A friend told him later that this was the best late-night show he'd ever listened to.

"'You're drifting ashore. I think you better do something,' I told the captain. I didn't know it, but he'd had a fire aboard, and he couldn't do anything—he had no electricity. I told him to drop an anchor—I didn't know that if he dropped an anchor, he'd have no way to get it up again.

"Finally, he accepted our tow, and eventually I got a letter from the Fundy line thanking me for my assistance. That captain just felt he could get a tow for nothing. And my wife met me at the door and stood there with her hands on her hips. 'So, I'm only the night clerk, eh?'"

Today, the Winslows have several tugs. "The one named after me is the fastest," asserts Eliot.

"The one named after me is the fattest," says Marjorie.

"She has the biggest stern, that's why," quips Eliot.

"It's elliptical," she says, unperturbed.

"When you get your papers from the Coast Guard," he explains, "you fill out a paper with the description of the vessel—the length, beam, type of bow and stern, push tug, tow boat, or what. When it comes to the stern, it could be round or square or elliptical, and hers is elliptical. That's why I named her for my wife, because *she* has an elliptical stern. (People wonder what kind of a wife I have, to let me say something like that.)"

He goes on to describe the 89-foot *Eliot Winslow*. "She has a big single engine, and a big wheel that, when it starts, makes a big hole—a cavity in the ocean—and she drops her stern in it. And then, when she gets going, the wave behind her is bigger than the freeboard, so you look up at the water." They modernized the pilothouse a few years back. "You never should have your wife be treasurer of the company—when money's going out, she wants a new ensemble or a new living room. She questioned whether we should do the pilothouse over, but it has made the tug. You need good visibility, fore and aft, so we increased the size of the windows and dropped the stack so you can see over it.

"She's got good rudder power—turns sharp in a circle like a dog chasing its tail. It's because of the shape under the water and the size of the rudder." Does she turn sharper one way than the other? "Good question. Most engines turn to the right. If you're in the drydock looking at the stern, the propeller turns to the right. When she backs, she backs the other way—the stern goes to port. When she's going ahead, there's a tendency for the bow to go to port. With twin engines, you have one of each, and the boat can spin in its own length with one ahead, one astern, full rudder."

Captain Melissa Terry's first trip towing was aboard the *Eliot*. She went along just for the ride, and wanted more. Soon she was called to deck on a trip to Massachusetts. It was very cold, the boat iced up, and they had to pound the ice off with a sledgehammer when they got tied up in Boston. "It was only an inch, but it was my first ice," she says. They were weather-bound there for a day and a half. Everyone went ashore but Melissa, who was feeling miserable, sick with bronchitis. The rest of them ended up at a bar in a rough area, and someone pulled a knife on them. "Jeez, I'm so sorry I didn't go with you!" Melissa told them when they returned.

The *Eliot*'s accommodations and galley are pretty sparse, Melissa says. The only place for the hawser in the winter is in the galley, all the way aft. "There's no storage, no lockers, no nothing. All the engine room stuff is in the galley, too, and 1,200 feet of 8-strand hawser stacked four feet high takes up nearly the whole galley. To get from one side to the other, you have to climb over the hawser, and to open the oven door—well, you *can't* really open it all the way. But having the hawser in there keeps it warm and dry and pliable."

She loved the trip. "Partly it was the romance of working on a tug—they're powerful workhorses. It always baffles you, looking at a tug. They look so big, but when you go in there, it's all engine and everything else is small. She's very low in the water. We call her a submarine because she's under water more than she's above, always shipping seas."

The *Eliot* was the start of Melissa's towboating career. She hasn't been on the boat in years but she remembers the *Eliot Winslow* with great fondness. "She's a great-handling boat, powerful, powerful, powerful. They let me run the boat sometimes, and I got an appreciation for her."

That Eliot the man also enjoys the qualities of his namesake—perhaps particularly that she's fastest—shows in the twinkle in his eye when he speaks of her.

Character Tugs

Some of the characters on the tug scene are the boats themselves. *Theodore Too* is one of those. "I saw a lot of camera flashes in the two years I spent on *Theodore Too*," says Captain Bill Stewart of Halifax, Nova Scotia, a retired pilot and tugboat skipper. He says that *Theodore Too* is the most photographed boat in North America, if not the world, and he's probably right. The Theodore Tugboat character first appeared on Canadian Broadcasting Corporation television and was carried on Public Broadcasting in the U.S. for many years. He has proven immensely popular, and his real-life floating replica, *Theodore Too,* is welcomed wherever he goes. During much of his first two years, Bill Stewart was his captain. (Despite being a self-confessed old salt, Bill says it didn't take long to get accustomed to referring to *Theodore* as "he.")

Captain Stewart was a commercial fisherman as a young man and has been in tugboats since 1974. He fell in love with tugs during his stint as captain of the pilot boat in Halifax. He says that when he went to work for Eastern Canada Towing, he was about the happiest man in North America, but it is his work with *Theodore* that has given him the most satisfaction.

Involved with *Theodore Too* since before its launch, Bill and his wife Fran were aboard for fourteen of the first eighteen months *Theodore* was in the water, and covered 15,000 miles, going from Halifax south to Florida and into the Great Lakes as far as Chicago.

In October, six months into the boat's life, the Stewarts and *Theodore* were in Chesapeake Bay, having made a stop in Baltimore. Paul Horsboll, the general manager of Moran Towing's Norfolk office, called Bill to ask if *Theodore* could make an

Theodore Too.
COURTESY OF PAUL BEESLEY.

appearance at the christening of the six new Z-drive tugs Washburn & Doughty had built for the navy contract Moran had won. "I wouldn't miss it for the world," Bill said. He left Baltimore the evening before the event, planning to arrive in Norfolk just in time for the noon festivities. But the wind came from the north at thirty knots and pushed them down the bay a lot faster than they expected. Paul called at nine in the morning, asking where they were. "Old Comfort Point," Bill told him. Right at the entrance to Norfolk.

"Oh, my goodness, you're early. You're going to be in and docked before we're ready."

To Paul's amazement, Bill told him they would stay where they were in the lee until it was time to make their appearance.

"If you're going to do that for me," said Paul, "I'm going to send you out some company." He sent out an older tug, the *Cavalier*, plus two other tugs.

"We had our own fun," Bill says. "Two would line up with us, and the other fellow would take some pictures, and then they'd trade off and another one would take the pictures." When the hour came, the three tugs led *Theodore* into the Norfolk Naval Shipyard for the christening. "We went right up to the chamber and worked *Theodore*'s eyes back and forth, did all the things you do with *Theodore*, and it was a great hit with the kids."

Norfolk's thoughts were on a more tragic event at the time, as it was just eight days after the terrorist attack on the USS *Cole*. The bodies of the dead navy personnel had been brought to Norfolk and injured personnel were hospitalized at the Naval Medical Center in Portsmouth. The commanding officer of the naval base asked if *Theodore* could come up the river to the hospital. "It's one of the most rewarding things I've gotten to do in my career," says Bill. "We did our thing, eyes back and forth, and then we turned broadside and dipped our flag in salute to the boys. There were four Moran tugs with us, two of them fire tugs spraying water.

"Through that little appearance, we were invited to go up to the children's ward in the hospital, and we took *Theodore* posters to the kids. One of the most gratifying things I've gotten to do."

Theodore Too isn't really a tugboat, of course. "He's a very typical sixty-five-foot boat. Same size as the fishing boat I owned in the sixties—I could relate to that size boat. Great-handling boat, single-screw. Responds very good to the right touch on the throttle—I'd like to think I gave him the right touch."

The structure of the boat makes it more difficult to handle than the average fish boat, however. "You don't have the visibility—you're looking through a porthole." Bill says you can't operate safely alone. You have to have at least two people on lookout.

"If there were just three of us aboard, we'd only operate in daylight hours. I told the company that, when we had to operate twenty-four hours, we needed four. Four was the minimum for a passage."

Did Fran have a title? "As far as I'm concerned, she did. She was the admiral. We found out very quickly that *Theodore* was a young boy who very much needed a feminine touch. If you couldn't give that boat a proper, almost motherly touch, create the right atmosphere, you couldn't do that job properly. Children related to that."

But you burn out. "You become Mr. Theodore from the time you open your eyes in the morning until you go to bed at night. It's very strenuous." Always being sure the children coming on board are safe, always smiling. Bill says he doesn't find the smiling troublesome, but he admits that sometimes you don't feel so smiley inside. It's exhausting. And you can't ever just hang out somewhere and pretend you're a normal boat. *Theodore* is too well known, too popular. Bill took a month off a couple of times—perhaps finding that to be the most difficult of all.

"It's sentimental," he admits, "having been on him right from the time he slid in the water. Norfolk, first of November, I had to leave, come home, turn things over to another captain. It was about the same as when you leave your firstborn with a babysitter for the first time. But I had to do it—we couldn't stay on continuously. Get burned out. Take a break, come back fresh."

Bill's off *Theodore* now and doing relief work for Eastern Canada Towing. "It's not work. It's like relaxation to do something you like doing. It's wonderful—there's a satisfaction in being in control—and it's like being a kid again, playing with boats, only these are bigger and much more powerful. The one I was on yesterday was 110 feet, 36 feet wide, 420 tons, 5,000 horsepower. It puts me on a high. I don't need drugs or anything else."

Retirement, Bill says, is particularly good. "Now I've got a choice. I'm there because I want to be there, not because I have to be. I can say 'No, thank you.' But I never say that."

For a while, *Theodore Too* saw some hard times. In 2002, when the television show went bankrupt, the boat was placed in receivership and tied up in Halifax. But the following year, he was bought by Murphy's on the Water, a family-owned tour and restaurant business in Halifax. The company upgraded *Theodore* with safety features and other requirements for Transport Canada marine safety inspection, the equivalent of American Coast Guard inspections, and now he is licensed to carry forty-nine passengers. Company principal Peter Murphy, a merchant mariner himself who occasionally works as a relief captain for Eastern Canada Towing, is very enthusiastic about the program his company has developed in association with the Maritime

Museum of the Atlantic. They offer hour-long tours around Halifax Harbor, with a storyteller on board who talks about *Theodore* and the television show, relating them to what's to be seen in the harbor.

Peter hopes that Bill Stewart will be involved with *Theodore* in the future, too.

Aboard the *Bertha*

"She's a barfmobile," unhesitatingly says Darren Vigilant, the owner of the 1925 logging tug *Bertha*. "She's pretty crappy in seas—constantly back and forth." Darren came across from Newfoundland to Lunenburg on his old tug, picking a weather window with care, and after she'd had some work done by the Lunenburg Foundry, he rode her to New York, where she now lives in a clutch of restored historic vessels. There was only one evening of real fright during that trip, he says. But there's good reason for her terrible handling—she has an absolutely flat bottom. "You could lay her down in a parking lot. Her propellers would be a foot and a half off the ground. No way is she ever gonna hit anything!" She never was meant to go to sea at all. Her only other significant sea voyage she made as a passenger on a freighter, soon after her construction in England. She was built to haul logs on the lakes and rivers of Newfoundland, and designed to be self-portaging—able to haul herself along on rollers on the ground.

While the riveted steel boat is eighty feet long, at eighteen feet she's very narrow, and she draws a mere four and a half feet of water. Four boats of her design came from Newcastle. As the prototype, the *Bertha* was the only one actually put together in England, while the other three came across in kit form to be assembled in Newfoundland. "Like a jigsaw puzzle," says Walter Pennell, who remembers seeing two of the boats, the *Bertha* and the *Joan*, working Deer Lake all the years he was growing up. "They'd have thousands and thousands of cords of wood in the boom, and they'd wait for an easterly wind to help them along." He says it would take them two days to go down the lake, seventeen miles. "They'd go very, very slow." Walter rode on the boat himself once, on his way to Junior Forest Wardens' camp.

Deer Lake is a small place, only about five thousand people today, and when Walter was a young lad, you knew everyone, he says. He remembers Max Humphries, an engineer on the *Bertha*, back when she had her original oil-burning engines. (Gardiner Hot Heads, Walter calls them.) Mr. Humphries used a blowtorch to warm the engines before firing them up.

Bertha never did haul herself any great distance over land, but she beached herself regularly and could pull herself across sandbars using the giant winches in her belly. "All she was, was a winch platform," says Walter's son Wally, who owned her for a few years in the late 1990s. She was repowered in 1951 with a pair of Caterpillar diesels, which are in place today.

For nearly fifty years, she worked for the lumber company. Her name was changed from *Bertha* to *Deer Lake* at the time of confederation of Newfoundland with Canada in 1949. In 1982, she was bought for $7,000 by a construction company, which mounted a crane on the back and used her for building wharves on the ocean. They also used her for play at least once, Wally says. One evening when the weather was rotten, some of the boys got tanked up and went out hunting turs. (Turs, he says, are also known as murres but, because it's illegal to shoot murres, they call them turs.) The birds won't fly in such weather, making them easy targets. They shot seven. Of course it cost them $7,000 to get her pulled off a rock and towed back in. She bent a propeller, and to this day there is a dent in her port side from that evening.

Though unrelated, it wasn't long after that escapade that she was hauled up onto the shore with a giant hole in her side and all her windows broken. She was rescued from the beach and taken to Toronto, where she worked as an excursion vessel.

The tug *Bertha* takes 1,500 cords of pulpwood from the Humber River to Connor Brook, Newfoundland. From the collection of Walter S. Pennell Sr.

Later on, she was set up as a drinking establishment. Bars closed at eleven at night, but people could join a club and drink there as long as they liked, and the *Deer Lake* was such a club.

But her condition got too rough even for that job. Leaks left her settled on the mud in Lake Erie, where, in 1996, Walter Pennell's son Wally found her. Wally had frightened his wife too many times in his sailboat, and she thought a powerboat might be better. Wally had an old picture of his mother aboard the *Bertha* taken years ago in Deer Lake. He'd thought the old boat had been scrapped long since, but there she was. He traded his sailboat for her, relieved her of some 26,000 pounds of inoperative machinery, and put money and time into her, meeting his goal of getting her back to Newfoundland for the 1997 celebration of the five-hundredth anniversary of explorer John Cabot's arrival there. She joined the festivities up and down the coast of Newfoundland. But she demanded a lot of Wally—"We burned ourselves out," he says—and he sold the old tug to her present owner, who gave her back her original name. Wally says he nearly gave the boat away, but he wanted her to be a boat and not a restaurant or some other thing. He is pleased that Darren is caring for her, although he can't bring himself to go visit. "It would hurt too much. She's a grand old boat," he says.

Bertha in Lunenburg for a refit, 1999. AUTHOR PHOTO.

Both Darren and Wally can attest to the expense of maintaining such a vessel. "It eats it up fast," Darren says. "If you're not a welder, you have to stay away." Fortunately, Darren is a metal fabricator, who makes custom metal furniture by day and works on the *Bertha* by night. The next project is the four thousand rivets on the bulwarks, all the way around. But there'll be another project after that, and another yet to follow, forever. That's the deal with old vessels.

Norfolk Rebel

And then there is the *Norfolk Rebel*. Is she a tug? Or maybe she's a schooner? Whatever she is, she's one of a kind.

Built in 1980 in response to the energy crisis, the tug was designed from the start as a sail-assisted working vessel. She hails from Norfolk, and used to be an integral part of a family towing business, doing coastal towing and salvage work. She has also fished, longlining for swordfish and other species along the East Coast and Gulf of Mexico.

Her longest tows were made in the 1980s, bringing the three-masted schooner *Victory Chimes* from Duluth to the Chesapeake, and then to Maine. In 1999 the *Rebel* again brought the *Chimes* back to the Chesapeake for her hundredth birthday and home to Maine in time for the schooner to go back to work.

Perhaps her heaviest work was on a contract for a Chesapeake Bay bridge project. The two-hundred-foot barge she towed carried a hundred tons of concrete pilings at a time. Her salvage work has included working with the Briggses' other tug to get a 120-foot clam boat off a sandbar near the Chincoteague inlet, as well as pulling many other boats off the beach. She carries dive equipment and salvage pumps and welding equipment and used to have scanning sonar to locate wrecks. Once, when a railroad barge capsized, the *Rebel* was hired to locate the cars. They found them all, one of them four or five miles from where the barge capsized.

In 1984, she made a "circumnavigation" of her home state, Virginia. ("We took in a few other states, too," acknowledges Captain Jesse Briggs, Lane's son, who worked her with his father in years past and still sails with him.) They went to the Great Lakes tall ships festivals via Halifax and the St. Lawrence Seaway, then on the Chicago river to the Illinois River and down the Mississippi to New Orleans and the World's Fair, and back up to Norfolk.

The fifty-nine-foot "tugantine" displaces forty-nine tons and carries a schooner rig in order to keep her masts under fifty-five feet, the height of a couple of bridges near Norfolk. To allow her to pass under lower bridges easily, her masts are stepped in tabernacles on deck so they may be lowered and raised without the use of a crane. She has traditional gaff main and foresails, a squaresail, a colorful modern genoa headsail, and a spinnaker. Her Detroit Diesel engine used to rate at 320 horsepower, but they've installed smaller injectors to use less fuel now that they're not towing so much. Her propeller is a 44-inch four-blade with 40-inch pitch. Her bowsprit used to retract back inside the hull to allow her to push. Now that she's a lady of more leisure, this feature hasn't been maintained. "It's taken so many beats and bangs that it doesn't go so well," says Jesse. She once was clocked at nine knots under sail—in a full gale of wind. A racehorse she isn't.

Lane Briggs is a believer in the use of sail on commercial vessels. At the time the *Rebel* was built, he helped found an organization to promote commercial sail and he has used the *Rebel* to document the economics of such a vessel. In the early 1980s there were a few boats on the West Coast using sail for auxiliary power, and a company was building fiberglass fishing boats with sail rigs. But when the price of fuel dropped, commercial interest in sail dropped too. The Briggses have always sailed the *Norfolk Rebel* whenever they could, and her dual-power arrangement has proven

Norfolk Rebel under sail in Penobscot Bay, with three-masted schooner *Victory Chimes* in the background. AUTHOR PHOTO.

financially advantageous. At least once, when the engine broke down while they were fishing offshore, she's gotten herself home when a traditional boat would have had to hire a tow.

Since his retirement, Captain Lane Briggs still gets around with the *Rebel*. He lives aboard, as indeed he has for most of her life, and he and son Jesse enjoy going to the tall ships get-togethers and schooner races on the East Coast and Great Lakes. Often the *Rebel* takes four trainees with her. Jesse feels that she offers a different kind of opportunity than most other sail-training vessels. He can teach boat handling with her. "She handles pretty good, but she's got the heft and weight, so she has the feel of a bigger boat. You put her to reverse, and you're not necessarily going to stop on a dime," he says.

Earlier in her life, the *Norfolk Rebel* was a working tug that carried and benefited from her sail rig; nowadays she's living the life of a sailing vessel that carries an unusual amount of weight and power. She's never going to be ordinary!

The *Fannie J.*

Tugboat musters take place in harbors everywhere and are enjoyed by tugboaters and spectators alike. In addition to races, they often include pushing contests and line-handling contests for deck crew. The most popular tugboat at the Portland, Maine, tugboat muster every year is the tiny *Fannie J.*, built in 1874. "We won the first heat by jumping the gun and running a shortcut too shoal for the four other tugs—1,200 to 7,000-horsepower fire-breathing monster-tugs," says Bill VanVoorhees of the first Portland muster, in 1999. Bill, a serious tugboat enthusiast, is yard foreman in Portland for Cianbro Corporation, the heavy-construction company that owns the old tug. "We were voted best in show, grand marshal, and a few other unprintable titles for our pirating that first heat away from the two local ship-docking tug companies.

"We had to run the remaining heats legally and lost our shirts—and almost the farm, as five- to ten-foot wakes came aboard the ol' *Fannie* and tried to drive her to the bottom!" continues Bill. But everyone gives the *Fannie* a little leeway when it comes to pushing—somehow, she always seems to be able to hold her own against the biggest tug around. In 2003, it was the ninety-six-foot, 5,000-horsepower *Vicki McAllister*. The two were officially declared tied as winners of the pushing contest.

The *Fannie J.* was built as the *Rebecca* in Camden, New Jersey. (Lang and Spectre, in their wonderful book *On the Hawser*, give her launch date as 1884, but Bill, with access to the documentation, says that the correct date is 1874.) Originally powered with coal-fired steam, she worked in Philadelphia for nearly ninety years, and then was purchased by a Portland metals-salvage company. In 1968 when Cianbro got her—she came with the waterfront real estate they bought from the salvage people—she had a pair of 6-71 diesels, one in front of the other. "You could not keep the two engines in tune. One was always running ahead of the other, and we were always ruining reduction gears," Bill says. They installed a V-12 Detroit Diesel in 1979.

She's sixty-eight feet long and only fourteen feet wide. According to Bill, "She's not a friendly boat when it's rough." (She rolls.) She draws seven feet and has a dry weight of forty-three tons. She has a sixty-inch, four-bladed wheel and is exceptionally handy. "The secret of the boat is her big, massive rudder. It goes almost ninety degrees each way."

She has an iron hull and a steel superstructure. "She's built like a wooden boat, with ribs. They laid the plate over them. It's all wrought iron, malleable and forgiving. If she were steel, it'd be all welded and one surface, but this is like lapstreak, over-lapped, and that allows it the give. She's been hit and slammed for years.

"She's been sunk twice since we've owned her," Bill says, "both times in the Portsmouth area. The first time—before my time—the guys had been in the tea a little.

The *Vicki M. McAllister* "loses" her pushing contest with the crowd favorite *Fannie J.* at the 2003 Portland, Maine, Tug Muster. COURTESY OF PHIL ROBERTS JR.

They'd left a barge at the navy yard, and on their way home, running light, they missed a buoy and went on a ledge. She fell off it stern first. She had a big open hatchway aft then, and she just filled up. She was down thirty days that time.

"The second time, they pushed her onto the beach and stuck a wooden pile right up through the bottom. The Coast Guard came from two stations with all their pumps, and we had all our pumps, and we got a tarp under and got her up and towed her back to Portland."

The *Fannie J.* doesn't seem to mind the sinkings. It's all in a day's work, maybe, if you're as old as she is.

"She works every week," Bill says. "She's towed cranes and barges from Eastport to Cape Cod." She worked on the new bridge in Portland, and at Sears Island, and often at the Portsmouth Navy Yard. She worked on the docks for the Islesboro ferry. (There's still a crane somewhere off Seven Hundred Acre Island where a barge went down during that project.)

She spent a year in Bangor while Cianbro worked on a bridge up there. "And when she came out of the water after that, her bottom was as clean as a whistle—fresh water kills the growth," Bill explains. "But it was cold, too!" The *Fannie J.* has a wonderful heating system, with ancient radiators still in place, but it requires that the generator be working. "We left Bangor with two barges once, and twelve hours into the trip, the generator quit. We'd got lured into making the trip, and we kept going. We had duct tape over all the holes in the superstructure, and it was cold!"

And, heating system or no, she ices up. "Icing up is our best thing," Bill says, "because it heals up the holes so the wind doesn't blow through."

They put $100,000 into a rebuild a couple of years ago. "And it cost us eighteen hundred dollars a week to rent a boat to take her place when she was out," Bill says. Obviously the company thinks the old girl is worth holding onto. "She got all new wiring and plumbing, new watertight doors, and new tires."

Not being a serious offshore boat, she doesn't carry a tremendous number of redundant safety systems, but she does have a watertight collision bulkhead forward. "So if you run into something, you won't sink immediately. You'll freeze to death and then sink," says Bill.

She used to have a table in her galley, but according to Bill it was useless: "She rolls so bad, you couldn't keep anything on the table." Now there's just a big storage bin for lifejackets and survival suits and the like. "You can sleep there, if you're tired enough. You can sleep anywhere, if you're that tired."

She's just a day boat now, anyway. Most of the long trips are done by bigger,

Fannie J. dressed up for the muster. AUTHOR PHOTO.

hired tugs nowadays. Speaking of a recent trip with one of the newer boats, Bill says, "It took seven hours to get from Portland to Swans Island—with her, it would have taken forty-two. With a big barge, she'll do two or maybe three knots if the tide's right." And if the tide's wrong, she might have trouble just holding her own.

"We were dredging in the river at Hampton Beach one time, and I was on the barge. We had two spuds and four anchors out, and we were still running in the tide. The old captain of the *Fannie* thought he could save us, but he got side-to in the current and she went way over—I swear to God I could see the whole keel, and water was pouring right in the door.

"She came down the river sideways and hit the clam bucket. It brought her upright, and he made a turn and got away from us. Afterwards, the captain told me the only thing that kept him from being scared was that he could see me on the barge, and I was scared enough for both of us."

The barge ended up grounding out and was all right. "We just weren't where we were supposed to be. We were trying to stay working, but we finally realized there were some tides we couldn't work through."

Without a barge, when the propeller's in good shape and the bottom's clean, the *Fannie* might make ten knots. "The other day, the GPS showed eight-and-a-half wide open, with the tide," Bill says. "There's a little pot warp on the wheel.

"Yeah, we put GPS on her. She shook when we put that on!" Bill chuckles. "And we got a new radar. We used to grab the Portland pilots' radar units when they threw them on the dump, and we'd get another three or four years out of them. Then we bought a brand-new one and burned it up in a week. Wired it wrong, I guess. We're on the second one now."

Although she sits idle at Cianbro's pier some of the time, the *Fannie J.* still has jobs. Her small size can be helpful. Back when Bath Iron Works still had a drydock in Portland, the *Fannie* helped move the huge frigates into the dry dock: "She was small enough to go on the stern and go right into the dry dock with the ship."

Bill's young son goes along with his dad on the *Fannie* whenever he can. "He loves it. He's my deckhand, handles the lines and all. And he steers whenever the skipper lets him. It's not every kid that gets a chance like that."

In the last century and a quarter plus, how many young people have learned about tugs from the *Fannie*? Bill has attempted to track it down, but it seems that much of the *Fannie J.*'s history has been lost. "They tell me she's the oldest working tug in the country, though," he says.

(Just as this book was going to press, news arrived that Greg Hartley, of Hartley Marine Services, Inc., has bought the venerable *Fannie J.* He will be taking her to Rockland, Maine, where she will be used to move equipment in and out of Hartley Marine Service's all-too-shallow dock. "She's practically new. No rust, no Bondo, all highway miles," says Greg. "She's really in good shape. They kept her up nice. Billy hated to see that boat go—he said he's got her in the best condition he's ever had her."

"I'm sick about it," Bill confirms. "You don't want to hear what I think about it. But if she had to go, she went to the best place she could have. Greg knows about old boats. He'll take care of her.")

In Finishing

I was sicced onto Vernon Elburn by a friend who had served as assistant engineer on the *Adriatic Sea* for a year and a half some time back. When I first asked Captain Elburn to tell me of his forty-five years in tugs, he replied, "Well, it's just life. Everyday occurrences, seems like."

But of course it's not. Day after day, the work is repetitive, and the quieter it is the better, but it will never be completely routine or totally safe. The boat-handling skills shown by tugboaters are necessary for the job and aren't learned in books. The potential risks posed to individuals and to the environment by tugs and the vessels they move are immense.

Throughout my conversations with people in the industry I've heard about what is seen as a low level of pay for the degree of responsibility tugboaters bear, and the resulting shortage of new people entering the business. I don't know what the answer is, but there will be one, simply because the work tugs do is essential for the economy—and even for peoples' survival, dependent as we are upon goods from around the planet. There will be tugboats, and they will be manned.

For the most part, tugboaters seem to take seriously both their jobs and—whether they admit it or not—their abilities. You won't find Vernon crowing about his prowess, but when, to a man, everyone on his boat says he's the best—and several of them have been with him for years—you know there's something special about the man. And he's not the only individual of that caliber in the tugboating industry. More than once in the course of writing this book I met someone who said he'd be happy to sail any time, anywhere, under some other man I had met. It's a small world, with some outstanding people, many of them ready to leave the business. If the next generation of tugboaters doesn't develop people like them, it will be a shame for the maritime world and for the people like us who choose to learn more about that world.

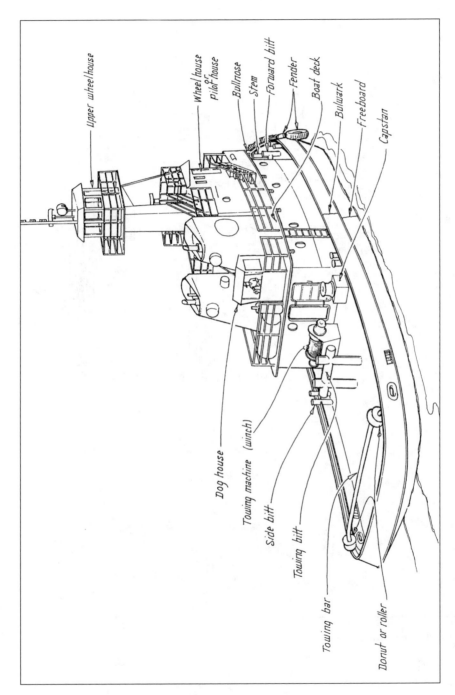

Parts of a tug. Drawing by Sam Manning.

Upper wheelhouse

Wheelhouse or Pilothouse

Bullnose

Stem

Forward bitt

Fender

Boat deck

Bulwark

Freeboard

Capstan

Dog house

Towing machine (winch)

Side bitt

Towing bitt

Towing bar

Donut or roller

365

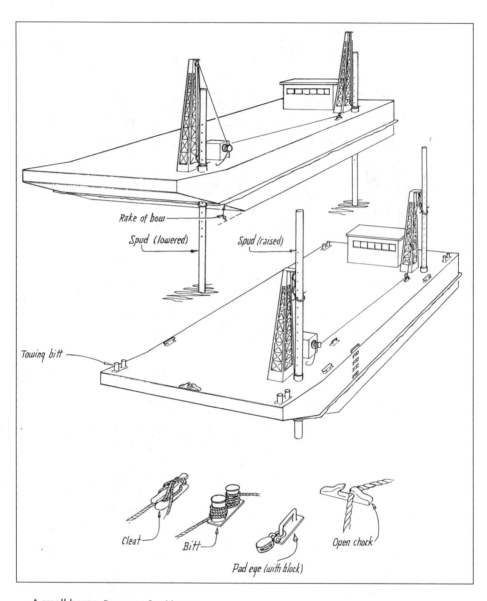

Rake of bow

Spud (lowered)

Spud (raised)

Towing bitt

Cleat

Bitt

Pad eye (with block)

Open chock

A small barge. DRAWING BY SAM MANNING.

Glossary

ABS: American Bureau of Shipping. One of several international classification societies that establish and administer standards, known as "rules," for the design, construction, and operational maintenance of marine vessels and structures, and determine the structural and mechanical fitness of ships and other marine structures for their intended purpose.

AB: Able-bodied seaman, a deckhand who has achieved a certain level of skill and experience.

AE: assistant engineer.

Aft: at, near, or toward the stern (the back of a vessel).

After: the direction toward the stern.

Amidships: the middle of a vessel.

Articulated tug-and-barge unit, ATB: a tug and barge unit connected by pins in the tug that mesh with matching fittings on the barge. Legally identified as a Dual Mode ITB. AT/B is the trademarked term devised by naval architect Bob Hill.

ASD: see Azimuthing Stern Drive.

Athwartships: perpendicular to the keel; across a vessel from side to side.

AWO: The American Waterways Operators, a national advocate for the tug, towing, and barge industry.

Azimuthing drive: a propeller driven through a system of gears that allow the lower unit to be rotated through 360 degrees, thus providing both drive and steering in any direction. Works similarly to an outboard motor. Produced by several manufacturers.

Azimuthing Stern Drive: an azimuthing drive with the drives set near the stern of the vessel. The commonest configuration of azimuthing drives.

Back down: reverse engine(s) in order to stop a vessel.

Bell boat: a boat whose captain communicates with the engine room by bell and gong or whistle; the engineer actually operates the engine and makes changes to speed and switches between forward and reverse.

Bight: a half-turn in a rope; a nasty place to be if tension is suddenly applied to the line.

Bitt (usually plural): a strong short vertical post of wood, steel, or iron to which lines are attached. Bitts are usually fastened to a deck in pairs and often connected by a horizontal bar, forming the so-called H-bitts. May take many forms.

BIW: Bath Iron Works, a leading shipbuilder, most recently of frigates and destroyers for the U.S. Navy.

Black diamonds: a colloquialism for coal.

Blister: a big, fendered protrusion on each shoulder of a tug that protects it and the barge from one another; helps center the tug in the notch and helps it stay in positive contact with the barge.

Blue ice: very dense ice that appears blue because it has no air trapped in it.

Boat deck: the deck where the lifeboat is stored.

Bollard: a single strong post on a pier to which a mooring or hawser line may be attached.

Bollard pull: a measure of the pulling power of a tug.

Bosun's chair: a seat that can be hoisted aloft or lowered into the hold or over the side of a vessel.

Bow thruster: a mechanical device in the forward portion of a vessel to provide thrust, increasing maneuverability. Can be a fixed-blade or controllable-pitch propeller, retractable Z-drive, or jet pump.

Box keel: a skeg formed from two vertical plates, connected like a box.

Brakewheel: a manual device for locking the brake, as on a towing winch.

Break-bulk: cargo that is not containerized, but individually packaged in bags, crates, etc. Also known as "conventional" cargo, as it was the usual method of shipping cargo prior to the development of standard containers and ships to carry them.

Bridle: a Y-shaped rig of wire, chain, or line used to distribute stress on another wire, line or chain to which it is connected, for instance a towing hawser. The bridle is attached to the forward corners of a barge.

Bullnose: a closed chock at, in, or on the stem of a tug.

Bulwarks: the plating or planking that surrounds a vessel's weather deck, in effect an extension of her side.

Bunkering: loading fuel on board a ship from another vessel, often while the ship is either unloading cargo or while she is in the anchorage, waiting her turn at the dock.

Capstan: a vertical drum to provide the power needed to heave a line or cable aboard. In early days, it was operated by capstan bars and muscle, but now the capstan is powered and acts like a winch.

Catenary: the curve a wire rope or chain takes when freely suspended between two supporting points, as in a towing hawser.

Chafe chain: a short length of chain sometimes inserted in the towing line to take the wear where the line crosses the bulwarks of the tug.

Chafe or **chafing gear**: protective sleeving or other means of protecting a line from chafe.

Chine: the meeting of two flat planes in a vessel's hull. In a **hard-chined** vessel, the side and bottom meet in an angle and are not rounded.

Chock: a fitting on the side of a deck that acts as a fairlead for a mooring or towing line.

Clam bucket: the dredging bucket on a barge crane.

Clutch boat: a boat with a clutch-and-gear–driven diesel engine, as opposed to a vessel powered by a diesel-electric or direct-drive engine.

Coastwise: legally, any area within twenty miles of the shoreline; towing routes that stay within that area.

Containers: boxes of uniform size in which cargo today is stowed, transferred, and shipped by sea, rail, or truck.

Controllable-pitch propeller: a propeller in which the angles of the blades can be changed for different speeds or to reverse direction. The engine runs at one speed continuously.

Coon ass: slang with different connotations (negative and positive) to speakers from different parts of the country. Most specifically (and accurately), a coon ass is a person or vessel from South Louisiana.

Creek work: operating in small creeks, rivers, inlets, and the like that are just wide and deep enough to carry barges and small tugs. Usually applied to tug work in the New York City region.

Crosstrees: horizontal pieces crossing the mast athwartships as a platform or to spread rigging.

Cutless bearing: trademarked name for a water-lubricated rubber-lined bearing used to carry the propeller shaft where it extends outside a vessel's hull.

Day tank: fuel tank that feeds directly into the engine. Tugs often have several fuel tanks, and the fuel to be used immediately is drawn from the storage tank(s) into the day tank as required. Using a day tank helps to keep the fuel supply clean.

Deadweight tonnage, DWT: total weight a vessel carries when immersed to her authorized load draft, including cargo, fuel, water, stores, passengers and crew, and their effects. Roughly, a vessel's carrying capacity.

Deck: *v.* to work as a deckhand.

Diesel-electric: a system of propulsion in which a diesel engine turns a generator that creates electricity to drive an electric motor connected to the propeller shaft.

Direct-drive: a propulsion system in which the engine directly drives the propeller, as opposed to other systems using a gearbox. Usually a direct-drive is also a direct-reversing engine.

Direct-reverse: a system of propulsion that requires that the engine be shut down and restarted in the other direction in order to switch between reverse and forward.

Dog: an H-shaped metal fitting with sharpened ends that is hammered into adjacent logs to keep them together.

Doghouse: a small house on the boat deck providing shelter for the helm and towing machine controls and their operator; also protects the operator from a flying line when it snaps.

Donut: a grooved roller that travels back and forth on a tow bar or tow arch to prevent line chafe.

Dragger: a fishing vessel that tows a net astern.

Dump scow: a barge constructed with opening doors in its bottom that are used to dump the contents, usually (nowadays) dredged material.

Dunnage: in a launch situation, wooden blocking and flotation that floats free after the launch; also, wooden packing used in a ship's hold to isolate cargo from the hull and to keep crates, boxes, barrels, etc. jammed in place.

EPIRB, Emergency Position Indicating Radio Beacon: an electronic emergency device that transmits its position to the Coast Guard via satellite.

Facing wires: lines that go from the rear corners of a barge to the stern deck of the tug that is pushing it. Facing wires keep the barge in place and handle the loads imposed when the tug backs. Also known as **pushing wires**.
Fair: curved smoothly and evenly.
Fairlead: a fitting with rounded edges, used to guide or lead a line in a particular direction.
Fair tide: normally, a current going in the same direction as the tug and tow, but sometimes used to mean a beneficial current that is going in the opposite direction, providing steerageway at a slower speed over the bottom.
Fish plate, or flounder plate: the triangular steel plate joining the two chain legs of a barge's bridle.
Fendering: cushioning devices that reduce shock due to contact.
Flake, also sometimes called **fake**: to coil or arrange a rope in long single loops so it will run free of kinks or snarls. Also, to run out free, as a flaked rope can.
Flanking rudders: rudders forward of propellers and on either side of the propeller shafts that provide positive steerage when going astern.
Freeboard: vertical distance from the water to the deck.

Gate lines: lines running from the tug's quarter bitts to the front corner on the same side of a towed barge.
Gravity launch: one traditional method of launching a ship. The vessel is built on sloped ways and is released and coaxed to slide down the ways into the water when finished enough to float.
Gunwale (pronounced "gunnel"): uppermost plank, cap, or rail of a vessel.

Hawsepipe: a fitting in the bow through which the anchor line runs. To "come up through the hawsepipe" means to start at the bottom and rise up through the ranks to a position of seniority and authority, as opposed to coming out of school with an engineer's or deck officer's ticket and going right to work in that position. A **hawsepiper** is a person who has come up through the hawsepipe.
Hawser: a line used for towing astern.
Head: toilet.
Head line: a bow line, the line the tug runs from her bow to a vessel with which she is working.

Heaving line: a light rope attached to a heavier one, such as a hawser, that can be thrown to or from a vessel and used to haul the heavier one across.

Hobble: a short line ending in a shackle that is fastened around a towline to keep it near the center of the tug's stern; also called a **gob strap** and other similar names.

Hooked up: at full power.

Hot-bunking: two crewmembers on opposite watches sharing a bunk.

House: the superstructure on a tug.

Integrated tug and barge, ITB: a tug and barge that operate functionally as one; the tug is not self-sufficient. Officially a **Pushing Mode ITB**.

Jackknifing barges: a technique for pulling a series of linked barges off a dock so they end up in a string.

Jacob's ladder: a rope-sided ladder, often with wooden rungs. A Jacob's ladder is used by a pilot to climb on and off ships from a pilot boat or tug.

Keel: the main structural member of a vessel, its backbone, running lengthwise along the centerline of the bottom.

Kills: channels and creeks in the New York/New Jersey Harbor area, e.g., Kill van Kull (from the Dutch).

Kort nozzle: a cylindrical ring surrounding the propeller that increases power at low speeds by as much as thirty or forty percent by forcing the water into a jet stream as it leaves the propeller. Can be fitted around a fixed propeller with a rudder behind it or integral to it, or on a steering-propulsion unit such as an azimuthing or Z-drive.

Layer (of cable): a convenient way of measuring the amount of cable stored on the drum of the towing machine or the amount of cable that is out.

Lazy line: a quarter line used to hold a tug perpendicular to a ship.

Light: not laden, or in the case of a tug, without a barge.

Lighter: originally, a vessel used to take cargo to or from a larger ship in harbor; now used as a verb, meaning to take cargo off. Common with petroleum-carrying vessels, which are lightered by barges brought to the ship by tugs.

Longlining: fishing using hooks on long lines or trawl lines.

Loran C: a radio-based location-determining system.

Make up: place and secure lines from tug to a vessel to be towed.

Midships: *n.* (short for amidships) the middle of a vessel. *v.* to center the rudder.

Monkey's fist: a ball-like knot on the thrown end of a heaving line, to give it weight.

Messenger: a length of rope tied to a heavier cable or hawser as a means of hauling or heaving it into a desired position, such as onto a dock or aboard.

Norman pin: vertical, round steel pin (often retractable), or similar device used to keep a towing hawser leading over the stern and away from the propeller(s).

Notch: a recess in the stern of a barge shaped to accept the front portion of a pushing tug. May be deep (accepting a large part of tug's length) or shallow (accepting only a few feet of the tug).

Oil Patch: the Gulf of Mexico, where oil rigs grow in great numbers.

Oiler: on diesel-powered vessels, a name given to an engineer's assistant. A carryover term from the era of steam power, when there were usually three men in a tug's engine room: engineer, oiler, and fireman.

On the hip: towing with the towed vessel made up alongside the tug.

Out of shape: when a tug or tow is in an awkward position for the planned maneuver.

Pad-eye: a closed ring, usually welded to a deck or other steel surface, where deck-lashings, rigging, etc. can be attached.

Pendant: a short length of wire or chain, particularly that between the bridle and the towing hawser. Often **pennant**.

Pigeonholes: indentations in the side of a barge that serve as handholds or footholds and act as a ladder in good weather conditions.

PIC: Person In Charge; here a licensed tankerman.

Pilot: a person licensed by local or federal authority to advise the master concerning local knowledge of the area being traversed. On rivers, the person steering the vessel and responsible for the watch. Also, the person in the pilothouse on the opposite watch from the captain, equivalent to a mate on the oceans.

Pin boat: a tug of an articulated tug-and-barge unit that is connected using rams, or pins, that extend from the side of the tug into matching fittings on the barge.

Piston pack: a replacement cylinder fitted with a piston; used to replace a defective cylinder and piston.

Pitch (of a propeller): the distance a propeller would advance in a single revolution if turning in a solid. The design of the propeller, specifically the angle of the blades, primarily, determines its pitch. See **controllable-pitch propellers**.

Pivot point: the point around which a turning vessel turns; usually varies as the tug and/or ship moves.

Poly: shorthand for any of several synthetic materials used to make rope and lines, especially polyethylene or polypropylene. "Poly-pro" is a mixture of polyethylene and polypropylene fibers.

Poop deck: deck over aftermost end of vessel.

Pot warp: the line on lobster traps.

Pudding: the protective fendering on a tug's bow. Once made of old manila rope, now tires or other rubber fendering are the standard.

Pushing wires: see **facing wires**.

Quarter: one of the rear "corners" of a vessel.

Quarter line: a line from the quarter of a tug to a vessel being towed.

Race: an area of strong, erratic currents, often marked by irregular, short seas.

Racks: bunks.

Rake: the inclination from the perpendicular of a portion of a vessel; usually refers to a slanted end of a barge.

Racon: an aid to navigation that transmits a signal that shows up brilliantly on radar, not only marking the racon's location but clearly identifying it by a transmitted Morse-code letter

Recaulking: the process of removing (reefing out) old caulking and inserting fresh caulking, driving it in place with tools such as chisel-like caulking irons and caulking mallets.

Repower: to replace an engine with a different one.

Reverse tractor tug: a tug whose azimuthing or Voith-Schneider drives are aft of the center of the boat.

Scale: to rise up, or lessen, said of fog.

Scow: any barge with raking ends; usually confined to barges carrying sand, gravel, garbage, the spoil from a dredging operation, and similar materials.

Sea buoy: the outermost buoy, marking the entrance to a harbor, channel or port.

SeaLand: a once-American shipping line specializing in the movement of containers.

Ship-assist: the process of tugs helping larger vessels to dock or undock; also called **shipdocking, shipwork**, etc.

Shot: a measurement of anchor chain, 15 fathoms or 90 feet. Often used to describe the length of an anchor line, whether chain or cable.

Shoulder: the forward portions of a vessel's sides.

Single-screw: a vessel with one propeller.

Single sideband radio: a high-frequency radio system that allows communication over much longer distances than VHF.

Single up: let go of all the docklines but one, preparatory to sailing.

Skeg: a keel-like protrusion that provides longitudinal stability; in the case of an escort tug, provides underwater lateral area for use in indirect-mode braking and steering of a large vessel.

Spring line: a line between two vessels or between a vessel and a pier, that runs fore-and-aft from one to the other.

Spuds: sizable poles or tubing that are dropped vertically into the bottom to hold a barge or other work vessel in place. Lowered mechanically through wells in the vessel.

STCW certification: abbreviation for the International Convention on Standards of Training, Certification, and Watchkeeping for Seafarers. The certification shows the holder has demonstrated knowledge of various safety issues.

Steerageway: the minimum rate of a vessel's motion through the water required for maneuverability.

Stem: upright post or bar of the bow; the forging, casting, or rounded plate forming the extreme bow of a vessel.

Stem head: upper part of the stem.

Strap, towing strap: a short spring line between tug and towed vessel, often made up with eyes on each end at the particular length needed for that combination.

Tankerman: a person trained in and capable of performing all duties relating to the handling of liquid cargoes on tank vessels. Licensed by the Coast Guard.

Tensiometer: a meter that measures the strain on a hawser.

Thruster: a small propeller, usually in a tunnel cut laterally through the vessel, that can push the vessel's bow (or stern) one way or the other; may also be a small azimuthing drive unit, retractable or fixed.

Towing machine, towing winch: a powered winch with one or more drums used to retrieve and stow the towing cable and perhaps other wires and lines.

Towing arch, also known as **Texas bar**, **roller bar**, **Dutch bar**: a bar over the stern on which a donut may run to cut down on the chafing of the hawser as it goes over the stern.

Towing staple: a U-shaped bolt or fitting that serves as a fairlead for the towing line.

Tractor or tractor tug: most precisely, a tug whose rotatable propeller system is forward of amidships, as on most Voith-Schneider tugs. In common usage, any tug with Voith-Schneider or azimuthing propulsion systems.

Transverse arrest: a method of slowing a tethered vessel with an azimuthing-drive tug. The tug directs its drives in opposition to one another and thrusts perpendicular to the direction of travel.

Trip: (in reference to a tug) to capsize or be capsized. This usually occurs when a towline pulls at an angle of ninety degrees or more to the centerline of the tug.

Turning basin: a space in a dock system for turning vessels going into or out of their allotted berths.

UTV: Uninspected Towing Vessel. A towing vessel of less than 200 tons operating domestically need not be inspected by the Coast Guard. Licensing of the operator of a UTV is less stringent than for larger or internationally operating tugs.

Voith-Schneider: a propulsion unit using five or six vertical blades that turn in a circle beneath the boat; each blade also rotating on its own axis, thus allowing the helmsman to direct the amount and direction of thrust. (See picture on p. 20.)

Whaleback: the afterdeck of a tugboat.

Weather deck: the deck fully exposed to the elements, as opposed to an interior deck.

Wheelwash: turbulence off the propellers.

Z-card: a form of identification for mariners.

Z-drive: the trademarked name for an azimuthing drive unit built by Rolls Royce Ulstein Maritime Ltd. Commonly but incorrectly used for any azimuthing drive.

Index